D0478228

Childhood Sexual Abuse

Developmental Effects Across the Lifespan

F. Felicia Ferrara
University of Sarasota

BROOKS/COLE

THOMSON LEARNING

Australia • Canada • Mexico • Singapore • Spain • United Kingdom • United States

BROOKS/COLE
THOMSON LEARNING

Acquisitions Editor: *Julie Martinez*
Marketing Team: *Caroline Concilla,*
Megan Hansen
Editorial Assistant: *Cat Broz*
Project Editor: *Kim Svetich-Will*
Production Service: *Buuji, Inc.*
Permissions Editor: *Bob Kauser*

Manuscript Editor: *Linda Ireland/*
Buuji, Inc.
Cover Design: *Roger Knox*
Print Buyer: *Nancy Panziera*
Compositor: *Buuji, Inc.*
Printing and Binding: *Webcom*

COPYRIGHT © 2002 Wadsworth Group. Brooks/Cole is an imprint
of the Wadsworth Group, a division of Thomson Learning, Inc. Thomson Learning™
is a trademark used herein under license.

For more information about this or any other Brooks/Cole product, contact:
BROOKS/COLE
511 Forest Lodge Road
Pacific Grove, CA 93950 USA
www.brookscole.com
1-800-423-0563 (Thomson Learning Academic Resource Center)

All rights reserved. No part of this work covered by the copyright hereon may be
reproduced, or used in any form or by any means—graphic, electronic, or mechanical,
including photocopying, recording, taping, Web distribution, or information storage and
retrieval systems—without the prior written permission of the publisher.

For permission to use material from this work, contact us by
www.thomsonrights.com
fax: 1-800-730-2215
phone: 1-800-730-2214

Printed in Canada
10 9 8 7 6 5 4 3 2 1

Library of Congress Cataloging-in-Publication Data

Ferrara, F. Felicia.
    Childhood sexual abuse: developmental effects across the lifespan/ F. Felicia
Ferrara.
        p. cm.
    Includes bibliographical references and index.
    ISBN 0-534-57645-1
    1. Child sexual abuse—Psychological aspects. 2. Children—Legal status,
laws, etc.—History. 3. Children—Social conditions. 4. Child sexual
abuse—United States.
5. Sexually abused children—Family relationships. 6. Child molesters—
Psychology. I. Title.

    HV6570 .F47 2002
    362.76—dc21

                                                                2001037956

Contents

Preface

This text is a composite of my more than 20 years of experience in dealing with child abuse issues. As a psychologist for the Connecticut State Department of Education, Division of Vocational-Technical Schools, during the early 1980s, numerous cases of child abuse, including sexual abuse, were referred to me for mental health services. As a supervisor of psychological services for 17 high schools and 14,000 students, I sought out appropriate training programs for my staff. However, I encountered a problem that persists today: Formal training programs on the topic of sexual abuse are scarce; conference programs and in-service presentations are the primary arenas in which training is presented.

To address training needs, for both myself and my staff members, I contacted community services that specialized in the area of sexual abuse. Following my own training and certification at the New Haven Sexual Assault Center under Dr. Barbara Moynihan, then director and initiator of the program, I became a certified rape crisis counselor. So, with new training in hand and an obvious need for services, I consulted to the New Haven Sexual Assault Center; I provided individual counseling services, facilitated support groups, and conducted community outreach, including formal training programs for municipal workers such as attorneys, police officers, and other professional youth workers.

Although all mental health educators and child care workers are mandated reporters of child abuse, not all are trained to deal with the overwhelming complexities of sensitive topics that may end up requiring court testimony.

Similarly, not all professionals are comfortable with dealing with mental health issues of a sexual nature; this includes not only sex education, but sexual abuse. Given that all child care workers are required by law to report suspected abuse, it stands to reason that they should be well trained on the dynamics of sexual abuse, as well as the ramifications for family adjustment following social service interventions.

This text, therefore, is intended to shed light on the often deeply hidden, yet powerfully debilitating, experiences of child sexual abuse. Due to the complex dynamics that impact individuals, families, school environments, and society at large, it is imperative that professionals have a thorough understanding of the traumatic, emotional fallout that weighs on an abusee's mind for a lifetime. With that intent in mind, this text presents a compilation of varied issues that may better prepare child care professionals for dealing with the issues at hand.

This book pulls together the multifaceted dimensions surrounding sexual abuse, although no claims are made that it is all-inclusive in regard to every aspect of abuse. Rather, it is designed to present an overall knowledge base of sexual abuse in a textbook format for personnel who work with children and adults as they attempt to resolve issues and develop a manner of coping with residual emotional dilemmas. A historical, judicial, and research perspective is provided, along with a summary of issues that occur at each age group. A wide range of topics related to sexual abuse, appropriate for concerned individuals, is presented. This book is a must-read for professionals, whether the discipline is social science, judicial, or research-based, and of course, for caring parents.

Students will benefit from the convenient, direct-writing format and the two-section format of the book. Part I presents a review of societal trends of child care, the evolution of developmental theories, research databases directly related to child abuse, theoretical perspectives of pedophilia (Finkelhor, 1984), and an in-depth essay on the syndrome of paradoxical states emanating from child sexual abuse. Part II reviews age-specific developmental tasks occurring among age groups ranging from infancy to adulthood, and discusses the adverse impact of sexual abuse and exploitation. A separate chapter is devoted to each age group, and information on the residual effects of the sexual abuse experience unique to the respective age groups is included. References are provided, including on-line references, and discussion questions are purposely intended to fuel an impetus to examine the issues further.

For **instructors,** this book is a 12-chapter book, designed to accommodate a semester of coursework while allowing time for class field trips, films, and other activities as well as a final. Part I, comprised of six chapters, offers a historical-, theoretical-, and research-based perspective to provide students with past and current findings concerning sexual abuse. Part II is also comprised of six chapters, providing specific developmental and symptomatic pathologies across the life span, from infancy to adulthood. Discussion questions that intentionally encourage critical thinking and introspective reflection, as well as applied activities, are provided at the end of each chapter. Small discussion groups can be arranged in class, questions can be assigned to subsets of students to provoke intergroup dialogue, or discussion questions can be assigned as essay examinations.

To narrow the gap between the need for increased services and the scarcity of sexual abuse training programs at the university level, this text and its supplements can easily be adapted to meet curriculum instructional needs in higher education. This book is different from other texts in that it encompasses theoretical, applied, and research matters highly relevant to the topic of sexual abuse, along with a significant number of references to allow readers to extend their knowledge base long after the course is completed. May it serve you well.

Discussion questions in this text not only provoke thought and reflection but also challenge the reader to take further action. The optimal goal is to ignite readers' interests in initiating further research, training, and service delivery, as well as to help them gain an appreciation for the range, depth, and magnitude of the impact of childhood sexual abuse. At the same time, the text will help readers to dispel erroneous stereotypical views of childhood sexual abuse and replace them with an understanding of the healing process. To date, greater emphasis has been placed on the identification and diagnosis of abuse than on examination of the impact that abuse has on an abusee's personality development. This text is intended to increase the available knowledge of the incident rates and impact of sexual abuse.

I have written a supplementary text entitled *Conquered Legacy: A Healing Journey* that is intended to heighten sensitivity about sexual abuse. That text is a dramatic, nonfictional account of the healing process. It was developed to provide a therapeutic distancing technique that would allow clients to view the healing process while minimizing emotional pain. Hence, clients can acquire a sense of hope, strength, and encouragement as they share the main character's progress through the crisis, intermediate, and advanced stages of a healing journey. Several therapists currently use the book as a forum for weekly discussions in support groups to inform clients of the process many abuse survivors undergo once healing is initiated.

As a means of conveying a more positive aspect to the individual who has experienced child sexual abuse, the word *abusee,* rather than *victim,* will be used throughout this book.

ABOUT THE AUTHOR

As a youth worker in Long Lane School, a juvenile detention center in Middletown, Connecticut, in the early 1970s, I quickly realized that the incidence of abuse among residents reached an alarming 95%. Later, as coordinator of psychological services for the Connecticut State Department of Education, where I administered psychological services at high schools, I discovered that the incident rate of disclosed sexual abuse was great. To extend my research skills, I relocated to Tampa, Florida, and began doctoral studies in research and measurement at the University of South Florida. I continued to consult to public schools, however, and within two weeks I encountered my first Florida-based sexual abuse case. Certain people seem to have a calling in life, and mine appears to be the resolution of issues surrounding child sexual abuse.

When I attended the University of South Florida to obtain a doctorate in research and measurement, I specialized in test development and validation, an area that emphasizes statistics, or sadistics as my students say. My dissertation included validation of an attitude scale, the Child Sexual Abuse Attitude Scale (Ferrara, 1996), designed specifically for in-service training programs. The initial response to the topic of my dissertation was, "Oh." My perception that everyone stepped back a few paces when the topic emerged, however, only strengthened my own conviction that information sharing is just a beginning to increasing services for children in need.

As Finkelhor noted in regard to his work, negative reactions are often encountered when the topic of sexual abuse is discussed. Professionals, laypersons, and colleagues wonder why anyone would bother or how anyone could deal with an issue as unpalatable as child abuse. Fortunately, my constitution holds steadfast in the face of adversity, so that I might encourage others to overcome the negative aspects of their pasts that very often diminishes their present well-being. During the 1980s, I treated many individuals and I still remember their names. They all shared very personal and intimate feelings with me as they struggled to overcome the incidents they had endured.

I currently speak to groups and conduct training programs where I encounter adults who are dealing with abuse, often for the first time, with ramifications that alter the personal, social, and career aspects of their lives. It is not unusual to encounter men and women of 60 or 70 years of age who are still immobilized by unprocessed events experienced during childhood, more than 50 or 60 years earlier. For them, a lifetime of unwarranted emotional pain is evident as they continue to struggle with many disabling misperceptions about the abuse experience. All phases of their lives—personal, work, and social—are often undermined by the abuse experience and the insurmountable emotional reactions that ensued.

Regardless of denial or evasion of the topic, if everyone remains silent, the problem will persist. The typical pedophile feeds on silence and secrecy. It is the responsibility of all child care workers to expose the problem and assist the abusee through the healing process. Many researchers continue to examine the issue, hoping to enlighten others in some small way. As research continues and new innovative interventions evolve, service delivery can only improve. Successful intervention means making a difference in at least one person's life, despite the resistance found in those who oppose the cause. As a former "women's libber," phrases such as *it can't be done* and *give it up* do not exist in my vocabulary; I hope they are not in yours either.

ACKNOWLEDGMENTS

An impetus to continue in my field came from reviewing the research completed by so many other driven professionals seeking answers to the issues raised by the unacceptable phenomenon of child abuse. These researchers include David Finkelhor, Debra Tharinger, Judith Herman, Roland Summit, and many others referenced throughout this book.

My local support system ranges from professional colleagues to loyal friends. Although they may not always understand what I do with my time, they believe that what I am doing is something worth doing. While conducting my research, I spent long hours at the Florida Mental Health Institute (FMHI), a research library affiliated with the University of South Florida. Because of the welcome I received from Ardis Hanson, Leslie Chason, and Walter Cone, I always knew I could stop there for expert help with my research or a simple conversation. I thank them for their encouraging words.

Much encouragement came from Diane Smith, director of the Hillsborough Crisis Center in Tampa, Florida. I had the pleasure of meeting this gracious lady several years ago when I conducted a program evaluation at the Crisis Center. Her steadfast encouragement and support are greatly appreciated, as is the dedicated work she does as administrator of a highly effective crisis program in Hillsborough County.

Materials concerning David Finkelhor's work, presented in Chapter 2, were adapted with permission from Simon Schuster, parent press of Free Press Publishers. By far, Finkelhor was a forerunner in exposing elements surrounding the complexities of sexual abuse. His work continues to set precedence and insight into issues relevant to child care workers throughout the world. His systematic view of pedophilic behavior, dysfunctional family dynamics, and interactional behavior analysis is commendable.

Perhaps my greatest good fortune lies in the fact that my children, George and Gemma Cuomo, both highlights of my life, have always encouraged my work. Gemma M. Cuomo is also a therapist specializing in child abuse issues, and she encourages me when I am down, scolds me when I slack, and is forever my most supportive friend. Thank God for her support. Then there is George Cuomo, my oldest child, a grown man now. His abundant creative talents have steered his life's journey toward music, but he also is a pseudo-psychologist, due to his never-ending, innate insight and empathetic nature. I am most grateful for his encouraging words as he supports, compliments, and critiques my indulgence in creative research projects on a regular basis.

I would like to thank the following reviewers for their dedication and excellent recommendations, which were given the utmost consideration: Dr. Teresa Christensen, University of New Orleans; Dr. C. Timothy Dickel, Creighton University; Dr. Peter Emerson, Southern Louisiana University; Dr. Kurt Kraus, Shippensburg University; Martha Sauter, LMSW-ACP L.C.D.C., McLennan Community College; and Dr. Daniel Sonkin, Sonoma State University.

Foremost, I must acknowledge the many children, adolescents, and adults with whom I have worked with throughout the years. All of them have shared private personal thoughts, feelings, and emotions with a virtual stranger, yet were determined to do so to heal. It is the abusees who struggle to overcome negative influences, to conquer painful memories, and to retrieve some semblance of harmony in their lives who must be commended. It takes courage and patience to continue along an often painful and turbulent healing path.

And last, but not least, I acknowledge the many children, adolescents, and adults who have not yet realized the basis of their distress, but need to peel back the many layers of pain hidden beneath a facade of bravery. I hope this book contributes to their healing in some small way, perhaps by stimulating mental health service delivery and professional commitment to help them conquer negative residual effects of childhood sexual abuse.

F. Felicia Ferrara

PART I

A Review of Historical, Theoretical, and Applied Issues

1

Historical Review
of Child Abuse Issues

LEARNING OBJECTIVES

Chapter 1 will address the following learning objectives:

1. A historical review of child-rearing practices in the United States

2. A review of women's rights as mothers in society

3. A review of children's rights or lack of rights

4. A review of child exploitation and work–related injuries

5. A review of the origin of categories of child abuse

6. A review of legislation concerning child neglect and abuse

---

INTRODUCTION

This chapter provides a brief review of child treatment practices in America over the past 400 years. A review of child treatment policies of the past may provide new insights on how to alleviate the abusive treatment of approximately 3 million children that exists today (National Clearinghouse for Child Abuse and Neglect Information (NCCANI, 1997)). A few questions that arise in comparing a typical child's life of yesterday to a child's life today are: What child treatment practices were prevalent in early America? How and when did American courts differentiate, if at all, between excessively harsh punishment and child abuse? When were categories of abuse developed by professionals? What newly sponsored legislative acts were passed to protect children from further neglect, abuse, and exploitation? What legislative movements have addressed these issues across America?

New World America in the 1600s

Influence of English Laws Child development protocol in 16th- and 17th-century New World America reflected English law, as evidenced by court dockets that emphasized ownership of children as properties or assets (Bremner, 1970; Mason, 1998). Children were commonly indentured out, particularly children born to unwed mothers or to slaves; others were abandoned or sold into slavery by their parents. Under the auspices of relieving financial burdens on society, indigent children and orphans were often court-ordered to work in slavery-type apprenticeships that required them to work as much as 60 to 80 hours per week.

Some children in England were sold into servitude and sent to the New World. These children often ranged in age from 14 to 16 years, although some were as young as 6 years of age (Beales, 1985). Work demands in the New World were severe and involved hard labor for 10 to 14 hours per day, 7 days per week. Treatment of children mirrored traditional English child-rearing values, which included the use of corporal punishment if parents deemed it necessary. The demand for labor in New America superseded any concern for nurturing individual children. Children were often kidnapped into servitude for the benefit of society as a whole, as well as for the profit of the kidnappers (DeMause, 1974; Derdeyn, 1976; Fraser, 1976; Speth, 1995). Essentially, children were treated as commodities whose net worth was attributed to their work output.

Paternal Authority In the 1600s, children were considered their fathers' property or assets. Fathers had the right to barter them out as slaves as early as 10 years of age, in return for forgiveness of a family debt or for compensation in disputes of other kinds (Mason, 1994). Worse yet, children were sometimes murdered by a father or a hired hand who wanted to collect insurance benefits (Fraser, 1976). Children also suffered when their fathers died or abandoned the family. Because women had such few rights, children were sometimes taken from the biological mother and awarded to a male guardian, who may or may not have been familiar to them.

After the passage of the English Poor Act of 1601 (DeMause, 1974), fathers were required to support children until they reached a majority age of 21, although they could still apprentice their children. Consequently, fathers maintained a great deal of influence over their children's educational and moral development, work setting, and work conditions. As in ancient Roman patriarchal society, fathers, not mothers, had a right to their children's personhood, as well as to their wages and any other gains they acquired as adults.

For the most part, women had no power over children, and married women could own no property, real or personal (Beales, 1985). Any wealth or material goods women brought into a marriage automatically became their husband's property. When a father died and left young children behind, often the mother was awarded temporary custody, but then the children were boarded out to other families, partly because the mother had no way of supporting them. If the woman remarried quickly, as women often did in order to survive, the new husband and stepfather would then have control over her, her children, and the tangible real estate inherited from the children's father. A formal indenture contract was made for children without estates that would be in effect until boys reached age 21 and girls reached age 18.

Harsh Living Conditions In court recommendations for final dispensation of custody cases, an emphasis on the child's basic survival needs, such as room and board, took precedence over any expressed concern for emotional development or potential abuse (Cohn, 1970; Mason, 1998). Consequently, a child might be removed from his or her family of origin, only to be ordered into servitude to compensate for the costs of room and board. Sometimes these children suffered worse fates and were more exploited than if they had been allowed to remain with their biological mothers.

Living conditions were barren and harsh. Child survival rates have been estimated at one out of four to one out of three children. Many children were expected to die by their 10th birthday, and it was common for 50% of child servants, indentured or actual slave children, to die by 20 years of age. Among the slaves, children, like their parents, were often sold as chattel (Derdeyn, 1976; Speth, 1995). English common law endorsed exclusive paternal rule over family properties, which included wives and children. Decision making and discipline, if needed, were at the father's discretion. This single-handed rule of the father changed only on the father's death. Because children were regarded as a property right, they were often treated as chattel, an arrangement that can be traced back to ancient Roman times when fathers had extensive power over their children, including the right to put them to death if the children were deemed incorrigible (DeMause, 1974; Fraser, 1976).

New America in the 1700s
Severe Discipline Practices In 18th-century New England, indentured servant papers sometimes included clauses regarding educational requirements for male children, based on an underlying belief that moral development depended on a person's educational level. Educational clauses appeared as early as 1705 in the state of Virginia (Mason, 1994). If a father was found neglectful of a child's education, he could be sanctioned by the courts. Since the father had sole responsibility for his children, he had the explicit right to expect obedience and respectful compliance from them. Disobedient children who found themselves before the court for punishment of rebellious behaviors could face a sentence as severe as death, and public whipping of rebellious children appears to have occurred regularly. Conversely, if an 18th-century father was

unduly abusive in his demands and punishment of one of his children, the child could be taken away from him and ordered to work as apprentices under a mentor (Bremner, 1970).

When an illegitimate or bastard child was born to a servant or slave mother, the mother was often publicly whipped as punishment for fornication (Morgan, 1966). The father, even if he were a white man, was often forced to pay maintenance to the town for support for the child, but the father was never beaten. An illegitimate child's future was bleak. A contract of indentureship was drawn against the child, often resulting in a lifetime of hard work and harsh living conditions.

Mothers of illegitimate Caucasian children were usually indentured out as soon as possible after the father's identity was acknowledged. These children were often apprenticed out for a term extending to the age of 25. Unborn bastards who were conceived by a master with a slave mother could be listed as property assets in the master's financial statement; and once they were born, these children could be forced into enslavement for the same length of time as their mother's indenture or longer (Beales, 1985). This contrasts with traditional English law whereby a child takes the identity of the father. Because masters frequently impregnated slave women to maintain the family's assets, they would incur significant loss of assets if all of their children became free from a master's control.

New Republic of the 1800s

By the mid-18th century, kidnapping and imprisonment of children was common; children were frequently held against their will until being shipped out to sea. The spirit trade provoked public outrage as parents searched ships for their missing children. Eventually a registry was established for keeping records of all indentured individuals taken from England (Bremner, 1970).

Child Kidnapping Many children in the late 1800s and early 1900s died at an early age because of harsh living conditions, and then masters requested replacements for them. In London, many children, often as many as 100 at a time, were indentured out and sent across the ocean to the new colony (Beales, 1985; Demos, 1986). New York, then called New Netherlands, was noted for bringing in shipments of children from Amsterdam. Children were often tricked or kidnapped into servitude by *spiriters* who profited from each healthy child they delivered to the colonies.

By the end of the 1800s, slave trade from Africa had ceased, so birthing children became a valuable means of replacing the labor force. As New England politics changed and urban environments arose, slave children were viewed as liabilities, not assets, and were likely to be sold or given away to anyone who would take them off their masters' hands (Beales, 1985; Bremner, 1970). Children who were sold often suffered an even worse fate than those who were slaves; many endured severe hardships, such as working for exploitive employers or living in unhealthy conditions.

Child Exploitation Prohibited In the late 1800s, the U.S. Supplementary Convention (section 1, article 1d; Bremner, 1970), which was concerned with the abolition of slavery, prohibited parents and guardians from hiring out or delivering their children to another person for exploitation. Although it was still common, even obligatory, for children to actively assist the family in maintaining shelter and food, children could no longer be exploited or deprived of an essential education. Child labor laws defined any activity that was too tedious or insurmountable for adults and any activity that was termed exploitative as abuse. Bear in mind that children were still perceived as little adults at that time, so activities that would be considered harsh today were simply viewed as normal expectations at that time in history.

Industrial Era of the 1900s

In the 1900s, children were still being abused and exploited. Such children, particularly those between the ages of 12 and 15, were often physically and mentally stunted. They were denied an education, and they were often injured while working; numerous cases of work-related injuries to children at that time have been cited. Some children lost their eyesight in industrial work settings. Some worked long hours down dark and airless mine shafts, in fields contaminated with insecticides, or in sweat shops with unhealthy slave-type working conditions. Shepherd boys often worked 15-hour days without food or protection from the elements (Jernegan, 1960).

Other, less direct injuries were suffered by children as well. For example, two children froze to death while being transported over 400 miles in an open truck to help harvest crops (Bremner, 1970). Many child laborers were denied basic needs such as room and board and other necessary supplies, which contributed to their suffering, and sometimes to their demise. Dietary provisions, often consisting of meager portions of potatoes or soup, lacked protein. Often boys and girls were forced to reside in large overcrowded rooms, huddled together in unhealthy surroundings with poor toilet facilities, if any were provided at all. Serious illnesses plagued many children, including chronic colds and congestion, as well as skin sores from dense and dirty work environments.

Industrial Injuries In the early 1900s, injuries to children were common in many industries. The shoe manufacturing industry in Spain and Italy provides a major example of child exploitation. The toxic glues used in the manufacturing process caused polyneuritis in children who worked in the factories and inhaled the fumes for 10 to 14 hours per day. Skin problems, eye infections, and paralysis of legs and arms were commonly diagnosed among 12- to 14-year-old girls working in this industry. In fact, injuries occurred so frequently in this industry that allegedly compensation was secretly granted to as many as 6,000 children over 15 years.

Other injuries suffered by children working in the leather industries included heart, lung, and spine problems, as well as neurological impairment of the brain and eyes. Injuries to children were also common in the mining industry. Children working in the mines were often lowered deep into mine shafts without safety precautions, and then forced to work 14 hours per day without ventilation.

Child Prostitution Prostitution was yet another area in which unprotected indentured children were exploited. While the minimum age requirement established by the Anti-Slavery Society in early 1800s somewhat restricted the use of children for labor in industry, the exploitation of children for prostitution was rampant throughout the 19th and early 20th centuries (DeMause, 1974; Pendergast, 1996; Radbill, 1980). Parental pimping occurred when parents indentured out their daughters to agents, who in return loaned money to the parents (Burgess, Groth, & McCausland, 1981; Burgess, Harman, McCausland, & Powers, 1984; Kempe & Kempe, 1984). This was the case with one 16-year-old who was mortgaged out to a brothel via an agent, who then remortgaged her at her father's request (Rabkin, 1980). Virtually all of her allocated portion of earnings, approximately one fourth of what she earned for the pimp, were sent home.

Testimonies from the 1800s and early 1900s attest that enslavement, rapes, and torture were all used to instill fear into the girls who were forced into prostitution, thus intimidating them further into servitude. If girls became pregnant, pimps threatened to harm the newborn babies and thereby ensured further enslavement of the frightened mothers. Hence, as is the case today, young girls had little chance of escaping once they were enslaved into the prostitution ring.

MOTHER'S ROLE AS CHILD PROTECTOR

The State of Motherhood in the 1800s

The state of motherhood during the 1800s carried little esteem, as a poor white woman's child could be taken from her due to poverty, divorce, widowhood, or illegitimacy. A slave mother's child could be taken from her at any moment and the child subjected to abusive treatment at the hands of another master. Whether born to slaves or indigent white women, children taken from their mothers served as laborers as soon as they were physically big enough to work at some job within the household. Beginning with the Industrial Revolution era, as society developed, civilized norms were enhanced, and aesthetic qualities of life became more valued, children began to be looked upon more favorably. They were now viewed as having emotional and nurturance needs, with an emphasis being placed on the *best interest of the child* (Mason, 1994).

Tender Years Doctrine In 1842, a New York Supreme Court case, *Mercein v. People* (1842), defied common law and delivered custody of the children to the mother, based on the "Laws of Nature" and the mother's ability to care for a sickly 3-year-old. However, two years later, the same court recovered the decision and granted custody to the father (Mason, 1994). Dissension was reignited among court officials concerning the custody of children. At this point, the "tender years doctrine" emerged, partly because of society's decision to advocate the need for maternal nurturance for the child in the "best interest of the child" (see *People ex rel. Sinclair v. Sinclair,* 1905). Infants were awarded to mothers more frequently than older children, particularly females, who were often awarded to the same-sex parent.

The second half of the 19th century witnessed the evolution of the women's movement. Fights emerged to ensure women's property rights, the control of their own wages and inheritance, and their right to equal control of custody and indenture of their children. In 1848, Ernestine Rose petitioned for signatures endorsing the Married Woman's Property Act, starting the first attempts to improve women's rights in New York. She appeared with Elizabeth Cady Stanton and Pauline Wright before the New York, 1846 Constitutional Convention to lobby for the act (Dubois, 1981). Community property laws emerged in several states, and courts sided with mothers for custody rights following divorce, superseding the rights of all men (Beales, 1985; Bremner, 1970; Greene, 1902). Consequently, the number of incidents in which mothers and children were harshly separated following a divorce diminished, although economic hardships were surely endured by single mothers and their children.

Best Interest of the Child In 1865, Maria Babour, indentured out at age 9, was returned to her mother based on the judge's interpretation that Maria's mother felt great affection for her child. As a result, 19th-century perspectives on child care changed for many people. But because wealthy private citizens initiated the changes, partly for their own benefit, the poor, orphaned, disadvantaged, and slave children continued to endure the absence of relief in the courts. Court decisions in cases involving disadvantaged children focused on relief of public debt rather than "the best interest of the child" (Bremner, 1970; Mason, 1994).

Once public opinion swayed in favor of motherhood and the position of mother was held in high esteem, another stringent measure of morality was applied to women. The ability of women to work outside the home in any task other than child rearing was curtailed. Women who did so were considered immoral, thus providing grounds for the removal of their children from the home (Beales, 1985). This staunch reversed view of the role of motherhood was verified in an opinion rendered by the American Bar Association, denying the admission of women into the Bar: "The harmony, not to say identity . . . of the family institution is repugnant to the ideas of women adopting a distinct and individual career from that of her husband. The paramount destiny of the mission of a woman is to fulfill the noble and benign offices of wife and mother. This is the law of the Creator" (*Bradwell v. Illinois,* 1873).

Motherhood Revered At the other end of the spectrum, altruistic views of motherhood rose to accommodate perceptions of humanistic, naturalistic, and spiritualistic points of view. Mothers, in some instances, were viewed as having the best ability to nurture and guide a child through life. So for the most part, the role of motherhood became a coveted and revered position. Nonetheless, given this elevated view of motherhood, women remained powerless in society at large, outside of their role as nurturers.

Women's status, however, did slowly improve during the 19th century, and at the beginning of the 20th century, publications and magazines about motherhood were abundant. Similarly, courts perceived motherhood as the prime venue by which to enhance child care practices (Mason, 1998). Because industrialized vocations required specialized work settings, shops, or factory locations, many fathers had to work away from home, leaving the mothers as the primary caretakers. Mothers became the daily decision makers, guiding their children's spiritual and moral upbringing.

Birth Rates Birth rates dropped over 50% between 1800 and 1900 as urban lifestyles rendered children less valuable than they were for the farm dwellers during the 18th century (Mason, 1994). Eighty percent of the U.S. population still lived in rural areas in 1850, and children still contributed greatly to their families' economic welfare, but less emphasis was placed on children as assets or chattels. Instead, the emphasis was on the importance to children of nurturance from mother-child relationships, and mothers gained responsibility for the moral development of their children. Courts across the nation endorsed the welfare of children as well as the mother's essential role in developing the morality of the nation (Beales, 1985; Bremner, 1970).

The State of Motherhood in the 1900s

A double-edged sword emerged as the mother's role grew in importance. On one hand, children were awarded to their mothers in cases in which maternal fitness was shown; however, in cases involving women of ill repute, that is, women who had transgressed according to the moral judgment of the time, mothers were harshly punished. Their children were often taken from them and custody granted to the fathers; fathers who committed adulterous acts were not considered immoral when custody awards were granted. Hence, custody of a child might be awarded to the father, regardless of his ability to educate the child in moral behavior and principles.

The changing trend toward reverence of motherhood was illustrated in a 1907 dispute over a mother's moral fitness to raise her three children. Although the children were initially placed in an orphanage via court order, the decision was reversed and the children returned to their mother upon appeal. The following excerpt is from the court's final decision in the case:

> The deepest, the tenderest, the most unswerving and unfaltering thing on earth is the love of a mother for her child. The love of a mother is the holiest thing this side of heaven. Natural ties of motherhood are not to be destroyed or discarded, save for some sound reason. Even a sinning and erring woman still clings to the child of her shame, and though battering her own misfortune, will rarely fail to fight for that of her daughter. (*Moore v. Dozier*, 1907, LEXIS at 5)

Intervention for Abuse   During the Progressive Era (1890-1920), the concept of the child's best interest that had appeared in court-related custody issues was extended to poor children (Beales, 1985). Child welfare groups emerged that placed new emphasis on what would be in the best interest of the child. Family systems were examined more than ever before. *Childsavers,* as they were called, consisted of well-meaning, socially conscious volunteers from women's clubs, professionals, and laypersons who advocated the improvement of child-rearing conditions and who admonished those who mistreated poor and abused children (Mason, 1994; Melton, Petrila, Poythress, & Slobogin, 1997; Sagatun & Edwards, 1995). Before long, social work professionals emerged; these people had a special interest in child treatment within the family and in family welfare practices.

A second wave of feminism emerged during this era with a focus that extended beyond women's property rights to family issues (Mason, 1994; Wortman & Stein, 1985). In the early 20th century, the women's movement centered on family welfare more than on the individual woman's rights. A new commitment of the movement involved delivering intervention services to needy families so that the families could remain intact. Socially conscious citizens advocated preserving the family unit rather than removing the children from the home and placing them in orphanages or foster homes. In 1874, the New York Society for the Prevention of Cruelty to Children (SPCC) emerged as a model, innovative administrative agency and was subsequently replicated in many states. Although volunteer citizens started the agency, professional social workers soon took it over.

As courts became more involved in child care issues, the association between child maltreatment and disruptive behavior of children became more evident. Child neglect or abuse was identified as a precipitating cause for juvenile delinquency that generated a further decline of societal moral standards. By 1899, court proceedings concerning neglect and abuse of children under age 16 fell under the auspices of the juvenile court rather than the family court alone.

Federal Aid for Dependent Children   In 1909, President Theodore Roosevelt initiated the first White House conference on the issue of dependent children to explore ways to assist needy families without removing the children from their home. The Child Bureau, created by President Howard Taft in 1912, was headed by Julia H. Lathrop, who had also helped found the Chicago Juvenile Court in 1899, a model program for child welfare (Mason, 1994). The question of how to support the poverty-stricken family was a pressing issue. State aid funds were second as compared to funds donated by private agencies. Oppositional groups expressed concern about fostering societal dependency on public aid, a controversy that continues today, approximately a century later. Nonetheless, in 1911, the Illinois legislature passed a bill to fund worthy families. By 1919, some 39 states offered funds for dependent children (Mason, 1994).

By 1931, widows were allowed to handle property, and they headed 82% of families receiving aid. Child care was again placed in the hands of the mother, but prejudiced views were still prevalent. Most states believed that unmarried couples with illegitimate children were not worthy to receive funds. Similarly, women who were abandoned by their partners were expected to fend for themselves and their children, even though they had few options for financial support. Rather punitive standards and rigid moral judgment prompted officials to categorize the needs of these parents differently.

Moral Dilemmas and Contradictions Single mothers in the early 1900s faced still further dilemmas. Although mothers were awarded custody, financial allowances were often sparse. Any attempt to sustain the family by working outside of the home was construed as negligent and as cause for removal of the children from the home (Cohn, 1970; Mason, 1998). Although women now had rights to child custody, society shunned mothers who worked outside of the house. Family abandonment by fathers created a score of women who faced such dilemmas. Thus, single mothers were, once again, forced to place their children in orphanages in order to feed them. Procedures for enforcing financial support from deserting fathers were rare and often remiss.

Reformers actively petitioned for legislation that would hold parents who abandoned their children accountable, and 46 states passed separate laws to punish deserting parents who failed to support their children. Of the participating states, 14 states established abandonment as a felony, punishable by a one-year prison term (Mason, 1994). Punishment could be offset if the deserter proclaimed a plan for support. Single mothers were still, however, subject to the removal of their children from the home, particularly those mothers whose character was considered questionable. Mothers were held to high standards of sexual morality; watchful eyes focused on maternal behavior and judged how it might impact the support and nurturance of the children. Similar attitudes prevail today, as children's behaviors are viewed as demonstrations of the values and moral judgments learned from adult family members (Fox, 1999).

As technology changed in early 1900s, particularly with the invention of the quick picture, escapades of political figures were documented. Although evidence of such immoral acts as sexual affairs and other unmoral behaviors emerged publicly, it was quickly suppressed. In spite of the publicity, higher-status citizens such as politicians were not exposed to harsh moralistic sanctions for their adulterous behavior. For males, adultery and fornication were rarely grounds for prosecution.

As child abuse laws evolved during the early 1900s, the number of socially conscious citizens grew, and parental abuse of children began to be more closely monitored. Theories concerning appropriate styles of parenting and child rearing emerged. At the same time, legal rulings pertaining to parent-child disputes set precedents for new levels of socially acceptable practices in parenting (Beales, 1985; Bremner, 1970; Demos, 1986; Mason, 1998). Whereas in the past, parenting styles had been left to the sole discretion of the head of the household, now parent training programs began to emerge across the United States. Throughout the 20th century, federal and state policies changed, and government agencies were given the power to intervene in cases of child maltreatment, even to remove a child from the home when social work investigators considered that action to be warranted.

Children Removed from Home Government agencies that were given the power to remove children from the home often favored removal of the children over leaving them in a cold, immoral family setting, even though orphanages were often less nurturing than the children's private homes. Agencies could remove children from homes automatically, without written documentation of abuse, by means of an indentureship that involved stringent contract clauses and, finally, adoption (Beales, 1985; Bremner, 1970; Demos, 1986). Agencies tended to prefer rural settings over urban ones and often thrusted children who were removed from their homes into settings that were foreign to them, thus heightening the children's stress. Children forced into farm labor often ran away as soon as they were of age. In an effort to thwart this additional exploitation of children, agencies began to seek foster homes that could offer nurturance and a simulated family life.

To enhance the inventory of families willing to serve as foster homes, payment for foster parenting was advocated. However, foster homes were used primarily for a select population; older, less attractive, "wrong gender" (i.e., female), or physically or emotionally impaired children were often left in an asylum setting. In 1923, the U.S. Census Bureau reported that 64.3% of neglected children removed from their families were institutionalized; only 23.4% were placed in homes, and 10.2% were placed in homes where foster parents were compensated (Bremner, 1970). Abusive acts toward institutionalized children, although known to exist, were seldom reported at that time. Many concerned citizens attempted to intervene in the mistreatment of orphans, although most renowned was Charles Loring Brace (1826-1890), who initiated the "orphan trains" movement. Brace organized the Children's Aid Society (CAS), devised programs to help disadvantaged children with housing and education, and finally formed the "orphan trains" (O'Conner, 2001).

CATEGORIES OF ABUSE IDENTIFIED

Abuse or Discipline?

At the beginning of the 20th century, categories of abuse and neglect emerged in the U.S. States rallied for the establishment of such categories to help in the determination of what actions warranted punishment by removal of the child from the home. The distinctions that were made between negligence, abuse, and abandonment were vague, and the difficulties with defining the difference between acts of abuse and regular parental disciplinary acts continued to obscure final case adjudication. Family privacy was coveted, and legal officials were often reticent to intervene by removing children from their homes

(Mason, 1994; Melton et al., 1997; Sagatun & Edwards, 1995), regardless of the type of abuse that was suspected.

During the Progressive Era, children had the right to sue for realty, or the acquisition of property, but they could not bring suit against their parents for neglect and lack of care. This situation was evidenced by the court cases at that time. In *Hewlett v. George* (1891), a Mississippi court declared that a mother was held harmless for wrongfully causing her nonemancipated minor daughter to be confined to an insane asylum. The court's refusal to sanction the mother was based on the concept of reciprocal rights and duties; the court interpreted the mother's decision to place her child in the asylum as part of the expected parental role, and the child was required to obey.

Courts were reluctant to become involved in familial matters involving actions that were, at that time, considered to be normal disciplinary actions used in the process of parenting. This reluctance was further illustrated in a 1903 Tennessee court case, *McKelvey v. McKelvey.* In this case, the court refused to take action against a father and a stepmother who beat a minor daughter excessively. The court found that, although the father's treatment of a daughter was harsh, the minor child had no remedy in civil action for the inflicted injury.

Another case, however, demonstrates that the courts did punish parents for acts that were considered abusive at the time. In *Roller v. Roller* (1905), a Washington court entertained an action in which a daughter accused her biological father of raping her. The father was convicted and sent to the penitentiary. In a subsequent appeal to the U.S. Supreme Court, that Court upheld the Washington conviction on behalf of the daughter and denounced the father's behavior, stating that family relations were already destroyed by the father's heinous act, so the child would not be returned to the father's custody.

Physical Abuse   Physical abuse was not clearly identified in the 19th and early 20th centuries, partly because corporal punishment was readily accepted in the name of child discipline. Because parents were still viewed as the sole authority within the home, a reticence to interfere with methods of discipline was predominant among citizens, as well as in the courts. Discipline was deemed to be a parent's prerogative and part of sound and moralistic child-raising practices. Grounds for petitions of child abuse against a parent depended on two conditions, *permanent injury* and *acts of pure malice.* Judicial procedures used to deal with the physical abuse of a child were not as effective as those used in cases involving accusations of the neglect of a child.

By mid-20th century, only five states (California, Minnesota, North Dakota, Oklahoma, and South Dakota) had created legislation citing excessive abuse as grounds for the removal of children from the home (Mason, 1994). Eighteen states defended parents' right to invoke discipline (which could include actions such as using knives to chastise a wayward child), and nine states even excused murder if the death occurred while a parent was lawfully correcting his or her child. Excessive physical punishment of children was still tolerated by a majority of states across America.

Negligence As discussed earlier, the Society for the Prevention of Cruelty to Children (SPCC) was formed in 1874, and many other societies soon followed. Most of these organizations were originally run by volunteers but, after the turn of the century, were administered by professional social workers. These organizations worked to develop methods by which to identify and protect neglected and abused children. In 1917, the Massachusetts Society for the Prevention of Cruelty to Children (MSPCC) cited overwork and absenteeism from schools as sufficient cause to charge parents with abuse. Using children to peddle on the streets was also deemed abusive and was considered child neglect by the early 1900s. The New York Child Neglect Law prohibited the use of children to peddle, sing, or play instruments in a wandering occupation (18 NYCRR Part 431; see Grossberg, 1985).

The definition of negligence involved two concepts, incompetence and unfitness (Beales, 1985; Bremner, 1970). Incompetent parents were those who were unable to provide essentials for their offspring, whereas unfit parents were those who were accused of immoral behavior. Single mothers bore the brunt of these definitions of negligence, since they often relied on their older children to help with survival and financial needs, keeping them out of school to help with younger children or to work in the marketplace.

Morality Temporary custodial cases were common during the 19th century as mothers attempted to acquire gainful employment in order to support their children (Beales, 1985; Fineman, 1988). Lack of moral fitness, however, was considered more serious than pandering, often resulting in the children not being returned to their birth mothers. Immorality on the part of the mother provoked the most stringent criminal punishment; behaviors of fathers, such as drunkenness or abandonment of the family, were perceived as being less offensive. Unwed mothers were always morally suspect. These women were often categorized as prostitutes, since any sexual activity outside of marriage was defined as prostitution. This standard of abuse has now been lifted; moral judgment against parents is no longer considered to be grounds for the removal of children from the home, as long as the behavior does not endanger minor children.

Harm and Endangerment The Third National Incidence Study of Child Abuse and Neglect (NIS-3) refers to two standards of evaluating potential harm to a child when assessing parental accountability (Sedlak & Broadhurst, 1996). The "harm standard" is quite stringent in that the child must have suffered "demonstrable harm as a result of maltreatment" (Sedlak & Broadhurst, 1996, p. 10). The "endangerment standard" requirements broaden the definition of child abuse and neglect to include children who are endangered, that is, who have not yet been harmed by the maltreatment but who are at risk of harm based on Child Protective Services (CPS) reports. The child's maltreatment has to be substantiated, however. Perpetrator criteria focus on adult caretakers who permit sexual abuse of a child, who allow other adults to neglect a child through lack of proper food and nutrition, and who endanger a child's physical and personal safety. The NIS-3 identifies six forms of abuse: physical, emotional, and sexual abuse, as well as physical, emotional, and educational neglect.

Severe Abuse Incidents

Infanticide In the latter part of the 20th century, the rate at which children were being seriously injured by neglect or abuse increased by 400% in less than a decade, from 141,700 in 1986 to 565,000 in 1993. Berger (1994) found that infants, from birth through 1 year of age, were at the greatest risk for death at the hands of a primary caretaker. In fact, the problem of infanticide or homicide of an infant at the hands of a caretaker represented 20% of infant mortality incidents.

This problem is not isolated to the United States. In the early 20th century, Britain enacted the Infanticide Act of 1938, which assumed diminished capacity on the part of a mother who kills her own offspring (Marks & Kumar, 1993). Since 1938, more than 60 mothers have been found guilty of infanticide. Because a mental illness is assumed under the law, offenders in England are often treated in mental health institutions rather than being sentenced to imprisonment. In the United States, however, infanticide or homicide of a child is most often processed as a murder, without automatic categorization of a preexisting mental illness. Therefore, in the United States, offending parties who are found guilty are often sent to prison (Lester, 1992).

Sexual Abuse *Sexual abuse* is described in the NIS-3 in three forms: intrusion, molestation with genital contact, and other unknown sexual abuse (Sedlak & Broadhurst, 1996, pp. 2-14). *Intrusion* is ascribed when evidence of "oral, anal or genital penile penetration or anal or genital digital or other penetration" is found on the child. *Molestation* involves some form of actual contact with genital areas, but with no specific intrusion being evident. The category of *unknown sexual abuse* covers allegations of inappropriate supervision of a child's sexual activities, including those in which a child might actively participate, such as preteen sexual involvement. The *endangerment* standard includes cases of abuse where the caretaker might be an adolescent or nonadult.

Ritualistic Abuse Although some children have been kidnapped by cults for purposes of torture, abuse, and other ritualistic activities, others have fallen victim to such cult activities at the hands of their own parents. If an infant's or child's family participates in cult-related rituals, that infant or child may be subjected to any number of abusive acts, either directly or as a witness to another child's abuse experience. Researchers note that cult-related or ritualistic child abuse is often enacted upon the same child repeatedly with multiple perpetrators. Ritualistic abuse often incorporates a form of brainwashing of the child victim, particularly if primary caretakers participate or encourage ritualistic practices (Jones, 1991).

A child who internalizes cult doctrines and belief systems may develop a robotic acceptance and propensity to submit to abusive acts, as though they are expected of all children. If a child is threatened to the point of being immobilized by fear of retribution from the perpetrator, the abuse can continue indefinitely. Long-term learned behavior patterns, such as those developed under the brainwashing of cults, must be broken down and replaced with new patterns of behavior, and the child's belief system must be replaced by a more positive belief system about self and others (Hill & Goodwin, 1993). These are not easy tasks. Meanwhile, subtle or soft signs of abuse may or may not be evident, rendering the child vulnerable for further abuse.

U.S. Incident Rates   The National Clearinghouse on Child Abuse and Neglect Information (NCCANI, 1997) reported that CPS investigated approximately 3 million alleged cases of abuse during 1996. At least one million children, approximately 13.9 children per 1,000 under age 18, were victims of *substantiated* child abuse and neglect. However, these figures may vary based on which data report is used. For instance, the NIS-3 study, the most recent aggregated report of child abuse in the United States, estimated that 42 children per 1,000 experienced some form of maltreatment or endangerment during 1997; this number included both substantiated and unsubstantiated cases. An increase of 67% was indicated between the 1986 (NIS-2) and the 1993 (NIS-3) reports (Sedlak & Broadhurst, 1996).

ACCUSATIONS OF ABUSE
IN CUSTODY CASES

Child Custody Battles

The "tender years doctrine" was the predominant premise that swayed custodial decisions in the early and mid-1900s (Kaff, 1982). By 1936, 42 states had accepted mothers' rights to custody of their children, while 4 states (Georgia, Hawaii, Oklahoma, and Texas) still adhered to the view that fathers had the rights to custody (Vermier, 1970). In the late 1900s, however, a new premise emerged: the best interest of the child. The courts now took the stance that each parent has equal ability to care for a child, and each case must be assessed on an individual basis. Mothers and fathers now had approximately equal chances of gaining custody, barring any adverse impact on the child (Goldstein, Freud, Solnit, & Goldstein, 1986). Professionals and legal specialists alike began to search for meaningful alternatives to child custody arrangements in the best interest of the child.

Some of the custody arrangements created in the late 1900s were complex. They included split custody, partial custody, rotating custody, and many types of alternative visitation schedules. Children who experienced a breakdown of the family unit were often torn by their parents' painful struggles over custody. Providing a nonabusive environment that would offer nurturance and guidance to the child became the primary goal and overshadowed considerations of which parent had greater financial means to support the child (Mason, 1999). Out of fear of losing a child, parents sometimes exhibited abusive behaviors and made allegations of abuse against the opposing parent in an attempt to discredit one another as a potential custodial parent. However, courts strongly denounced such practices; thus, false allegations, demeaning comments, and willful destruction of a parent-child relationship could be considered forms of abuse in and of themselves. Often these behaviors were viewed as a form of parental alienation (Gardner, 1992).

Family Act of 1969 In 1969, California passed a law known as the Family Act of 1969 (Mason, 1994), which set precedence for a no-fault divorce policy. Under this policy, immoral accusations did not need to be made against either marital partner in an action to dissolve a marriage or family unit. In addition to the passage of this law, the feminist movement in the late 1960s and early 1970s was seeking equal rights for women in their work, personal, and social roles in society—a movement that is, perhaps, best reflected in the organizational concerns of the National Organization for Women (NOW) (Kraditor, 1970). Once the equal rights movement supported women's right to work outside of the home, working mothers were no longer viewed as immoral, and new financial freedoms allowed women to support their own children with or without a male partner.

The Pregnancy Discrimination Act of 1978 In 1978, another act of legislation was passed to assist single mothers. The Pregnancy Discrimination Act of 1978 mandated that pregnancy be considered a disability. Consequently, pregnancy acquired equal status with other disabilities, particularly in regard to economic protection from job loss and discrimination based on pregnancy. As attitudes toward pregnant women became more open-minded, more women with children felt free to enter the work setting than ever before. In 1970, only 27% of women with children under 3 years of age worked, but this number increased by 1985, at which time more than 50% of mothers of young children were employed outside the home (Mason, 1994, p. 126). Although strides were being made toward equal rights, a backlash in maternal custody rights prevailed. Equality in the workplace came with a price.

In the past, a mother's time at home outweighed a father's ability to provide time and attention for the children, but by the 1980s, this was no longer the case. Divorce proceedings involving custody now considered the fact that mothers who worked outside the home just as fathers did could not possibly provide more time and attention to the minor children than the father could. Once more, attributes of caregiver qualities were equalized. More custody awards were allocated to fathers in the late 1900s than was the case in the early 1900s. An overriding consideration was the fact that if mothers could use day care or baby-sitters for child rearing, fathers could certainly do the same.

Equal Custody Rights Pose New Types of Abuse During the late 1990s, maternal custody was no longer viewed as an automatic given, but rather as a factor for consideration in family court (Weithron & Grisso, 1987). Each parent could be considered equally qualified to provide nurturance and support to his or her offspring. Consequently, parents who were fearful of losing custody of their children began to strive for the position of primary caretaker. Accusations of child abuse or negligent care from competing parents became all too common in family court disputes. Often, cruel and degrading comments were made to children by one parent about the other in an attempt to discredit the other parent in the eyes of the children. This divorce phenomenon received significant attention from social scientists. Richard A. Gardner (1992) proposed the concept of parental alienation syndrome (PAS), which viewed depriving children of their mothers or fathers as a form of child abuse, and set out a list of behavioral criteria that represent PAS, such as continual degrading of the other parent, minimizing their worth in front of the children, denying the children any contact with extraneous family members and any other behaviors or comments intended to estrange a child-parent relationship.

Typically, family court judges responded to false accusations of abuse with a punitive stand toward the offending parent (Gardner, 1992). Florida passed legislation making false accusations of child abuse that are purposely fabricated to attain custody, a violation of state statutes punishable by the courts (FL ch. 415, sec. 513.19).

Another form of abuse or exploitation of children that increased during the late 1900s was the practice of parents' kidnapping of their children after losing a custody battle (see *Muniz v. State,* 2000). Children who were kidnapped by irate or irrational parents were at times thought to be at high risk for personal injury, if not outright death, at the hands of the kidnapping parents. In an addendum to the Hague Convention of 1980, the International Parental Child Abduction Act was enacted (Pub. L. No. 103-107).

LEGISLATIVE ADVANCEMENTS
REGARDING CHILD ABUSE

Child Abuse Prevention and Treatment Act (CAPTA)

In the late 1900s, child protective agencies increased their efforts to intervene in family child care disputes. In 1974, the federal Child Abuse Prevention and Treatment Act (CAPTA, Pub. L. No. 93-247) authorized mandated reporting. This act provided mental health workers with support from a legislative body in their efforts to report suspected child abuse. The act also opened up funding sources for the education and training of professionals on how to address issues of suspected physical abuse, sexual abuse, exploitation, physical neglect, and emotional maltreatment.

The National Clearinghouse on Child Abuse and Neglect Information (NCCANI) was formed in 1974, as an outgrowth of CAPTA, to aggregate information on incidents of abuse into statistical databases that would provide a basis for further program development and intervention services. The 1996 amendments to CAPTA (Pub. L. No. 104-235), placed NCCANI under the administration of the U.S. Department of Children, Youth, and Families Bureau. The 1996 legislation amended Title 1, "replaced the Title II Community Based Family Resource Centers program with a new Community-Based Family Resource and Support Program and Repealed Title III, Certain Preventive Services Regarding Children of Homeless Families or Families at Risk of Homelessness" (CAPTA, p. 2). Research and evaluation programs were also emphasized under section 104 of CAPTA (42 U.S.C. § 5105) in areas of "(a) the nature and score of child abuse and neglect, (b) causes, prevention assessment, identification, treatment, and cultural and socioeconomic distinctions, and the consequences of child abuse and neglect, (c) appropriate, effective and culturally sensitive investigation, administrative, and judicial procedures with respect to cases of child abuse, (d) research on the national incidence of abuse" (CAPTA, p. 9).

Mandated Reporting Professionals who fail to report suspected child abuse in compliance with the CAPTA mandate for reporting may be subject to both civil and criminal penalties (National Center for the Prosecution of Child Abuse, NCPCA, 2000a). The CAPTA mandate stipulates that mental health workers, schoolteachers, and child care workers or advocates who suspect child abuse of any kind must submit an abuse report, either written or verbal, to state regulatory offices and may be subject to charges for failing to report it. In fact, all citizens are now mandated reporters if child abuse is suspected or witnessed.

Reports of child abuse figures in 1997 cited that 967 children in 41 states had died as a result of abuse or neglect (NCCANI, 2000a). Incident rates of alleged abuse vary across states, however, partly because of the variation in methods of reporting that exist from agency to agency and state to state (a topic that is covered more thoroughly in Chapter 3). Obviously, a standardized reporting system that could be used by all agencies in all states would greatly increase the accuracy of collecting data on reported child abuse incidents.

State Legislative Mandates The CAPTA set minimum standards and identified a baseline for acts or behaviors that characterize maltreatment. The CAPTA standards of what constitutes physical abuse, neglect, and sexual abuse provide a foundation for state standards, although states have had the option of extending or modifying the CAPTA definitions. The American Prosecutor's Research Institute (APRI) publishes a summary list of statutes that provides descriptions of state-mandated definitions (available from NCCANI, 2000c). For example, Alabama law uses the term *harm or threatened harm,* whereas Connecticut law refers to *inflicted injuries by nonaccidental means.* Both terms are somewhat vague in regard to the descriptive acts that would be included under that category. Both Indiana and Iowa statutes use the phrase *acts or omissions,* which again leaves much room for interpretation (NCCANI, 2000c). Consequently, aggregated statistics may be obscured because of the nonstandardized definitions of abuse across the United States.

Interpretation of State Law and Definitions Interpreting the meaning of the law regarding abuse presents a dilemma for legal professionals (Mason, 1992). Adding to the complication of the variations between state interpretations of abuse is the fact that several states hold religious or corporal punishment exemptions (NCCANI, 2000c). (Such exemptions have recently come under scrutiny.) Hence, if an act occurs in a state that holds religious exemptions, the perpetrator or parent might not be adjudicated to the same degree as he or she would be in another state that does not allow religious exemptions.

Another factor that contributes to discrepancies in reporting practices across the United States is that several abuses can occur in the same case but only the most severe form of abuse may be reported to authorities. Therefore, if a child was badly beaten and sexually abused, only the beating or physical abuse may be reported, resulting in an underreporting of sexual abuse. Most authorities agree that child sexual abuse (CSA) is underreported (Eckenrode, Laird, & Doris, 1993; Finkelhor, 1984; Finkelman, 1995a & b; Classen & Yalom, 1995; Hewitt, 1999; Hunter, 1991; Jumper, 1995; Kelly, 1989; Sgroi, 1982; Vevier & Tharinger, 1986; Waterman & Ben-Meir, 1993).

Perpetrator Registry The CAPTA initiatives allocated funds to establish a central registry for the reporting of abuse. As of 2000, 39 states and the District of Columbia had statutes establishing a statewide registry, and 21 of these states allowed for the expungement (i.e., removal) of old records in order to keep the registry up-to-date (NCCANI, 2000e). Timelines for discarding an unsubstantiated report ranged from immediately to five years after determination, depending on the governing state regulations and the final case outcome. Five terms have been frequently used to classify cases: *unsubstantiated* or *unconfirmed, founded, indicated, suspected,* and *substantiated.* Substantiated reports are held the longest; expungement of those records might occur five to ten years after case dispensation or when the victim reaches majority. In some cases, where good cause has been shown, the victim of the crime has to be notified of the expungement of the initial crime report.

Federal law [(42 U.S.C. § 14071) (1994)] requires states to maintain sex offender registration. Failure to do so can result in denial of support from federal funding sources. All states must include the demographic information of the perpetrator, such as his or her address, current residence, and notice of any impending residential move. Perpetrators are required to update their personal information annually. However, the length of time for which they are required to report their location to authorities varies across states from 10 years to life (NCCANI, 2000f). Most states maintain files of the offender's name, address, place of employment, date of birth, other sex offense convictions, aliases, driver's license number, fingerprints, and photographs. Some states, such as Idaho, require offenders to report their information to the registry for 10 years following their discharge from jail or parole, while other states allow perpetrators to petition the court for release from the reporting requirement if no further violations of abuse have occurred for 15 years or more (NCCANI, 2000f). Michigan has a 25-year registration period for first-time offenders and a lifetime registration requirement for those who have committed second offenses.

Enforcement officials have the right to notify the public when a sexual predator is to be released, and the public at large may request access to sex offender registries (NCCANI, 2000g). Additionally, as of 1997, any offender convicted of the crime of sexual abuse is required to take an AIDS or HIV test. Idaho, Nevada, and Tennessee have the most stringent regulations; those states require HIV testing upon arrest, not conviction (NCCANI, 2000g). Results of the test may be released to the perpetrator, spouses, victims, and approved professionals. Testing perpetrators for AIDS and HIV is another practice that varies across states based on state law.

Public Notifications: Megan's Law Public notification of registered sex offenders may be released to involved parties or posted on public access Web sites by law enforcement agencies (NCCANI, 2000g). Public registration of perpetrators was prompted by an actual case of abuse and murder of a child. In 1994, Megan Kanka, a 7-year-old New Jersey girl, was raped and killed by a neighbor who was a twice-convicted sex offender. Authorities and family members believed that, had Megan's family been apprised of the predator's location, greater protective safeguards could have been taken to avoid the incident. Legislative regulations related to those findings are referred to as Megan's Law (Pub. L. No. 104-148), whereby notification of a predator's location is now available to the public.

Once a perpetrator is convicted of abuse, the prosecutor's office calculates the risk of repeat offenses and classifies the offender as low-, moderate-, or high-risk. If an offender is classified as low-risk, only law officials and police personnel are notified. A classification of moderate-risk may mean that community agencies such as churches or schools will be notified. If an offender is rated as high-risk, any public citizen may obtain the offender's information. The intent of the required registration laws is to forewarn potential victims of the possibility of harm to children; the intent is to prevent a repeat of the tragedy that occurred in Megan Kanka's case in 1994.

Professional Court Testimony Throughout time, religious structures imposed standards for acceptable behaviors. During the Progressive Era, courts often influenced family and child-rearing concepts via the rulings of their judicial officers (Mason, 1994/1998). As social science developed in the 20th century, however, courts began to look to social science professionals to ascertain whether acts inflicted upon children were harmful. In the late 20th century, professionals provided exhaustive theoretical and applied perspectives concerning appropriate child-rearing practices, including what behaviors constitute child abuse (Kotelchuck, 1984; Wallerstein & Blakeslee, 1989). Social scientists and judicial leaders alike have searched for ways to process abuse cases as effectively as possible while minimizing any additional emotional or psychological harm to the child victim during court testimony (Sagatun & Edwards, 1995; Walker, 1990). Because of the complexity of this issue, it is addressed in Section 2 of this book in greater detail.

Judicial Proceedings on Child Sexual Abuse In the 1980s, child sexual abuse was under identified as a category of abuse. The topic of sexual abuse in general was slow to gain public attention, as it is a topic that often provokes extensive controversy, heated discussions, and adverse reactions. Dissension arose concerning the burden of proof in child sexual abuse cases (Ceci & Bruck, 1996), particularly in the absence of physical evidence (and often in cases of sexual molestation there is no such evidence). Accusations of sexual abuse now result in harsh sanctions for the accused. Criminal charges are placed against child sexual predators, regardless of whether the abuser is a stranger or a family member such as a parent (Goodman & Clarke-Stewart, 1991; Ney, 1995).

Establishing child sexual abuse beyond a reasonable doubt in a court of law, however, is not an easy task. In a California case known as *In re Amber B.,* a petition of alleged abuse was brought against a father, stating that he had sexually molested his 3-year-old daughter and that she was at risk for further sexual abuse (*In re Amber B.,* 1987). The expert who testified in this case stated that the child's actions during evaluation were consistent with those of a child who had been abused. He based his decision on two factors: the child's behaviors with an anatomically correct doll (she had inserted her finger in the vaginal opening and pushed and twisted it vigorously), and her statements of testimony that he deemed valid. Initially, the trial court found for the child and restricted her father to supervised visitations. However, upon appeal, the initial court findings were overturned (*In re Amber B.,* 1987, at 65). The appeals court cited that the use of dolls was not a scientifically reliable manner of assessment in the scientific community, an evaluation often referred to as the Frye test (Melton et al., 1997).

SPECIAL TOPICS ON CHILD ABUSE

Child Pornography

The incident rates of child pornography increased during the last half of the 1900s at such a rapid rate that new legislation was needed to process the large number of court cases. In 1978, Congress responded to a committee study that cited child pornography as a highly organized, multimillion-dollar nationwide industry by enacting the Protection of Children Against Sexual Exploitation Act of 1977 (Pub. L. No. 95-225). Subsequent legislation included the Child Abuse Victims' Rights Act of 1986 (Pub. L. No. 99-504, amended by Pub. L. No. 98-292), which received a quorum vote in the Senate on September 24, 1986. The purpose of that act, as introduced by Senator Charles Grassley (R-Iowa), was to fill in the gaps that remained in federal and state law regarding the sexual exploitation of children. The act strengthened both civil and judicial sanctions for the exploitation of children, particularly for crimes of sexual exploitation that fall under the auspices of the Racketeer Influenced and Corrupt Organizations (RICO) rulings. A 1990 amendment to the act (42 U.S.C. sec. 132.1) encouraged a multidisciplinary approach to treating victims of abuse.

Civil Remedies Under the Child Abuse Victims' Rights Act of 1986, civil remedies against pornographers or child abusers included a fine of not more than $100,000, imprisonment of not more than 10 years, or both. Repeat offenders could be sanctioned by a fine of not more than $200,000, imprisoned for not less than 5 years nor more than 15 years, or both. In addition, alternative strategies were explored to lessen the amount of trauma incurred by child witnesses in court hearings; section 11 of the act required the Department of Justice (DOJ) to study and recommend a model format for child witness testimony and court procedures according to RICO mandates.

Child Testimony

In response to the need to lessen the trauma for children giving testimony in court, theoretical models of expert testimonies, intervention, and mediation began to surface. Investigative inquiries were made regarding children's personality development and the impact of abuse allegations, of custodial decisions, prosecutory procedures, and court testimony on children's physical, emotional, and psychological development. Emphasis was placed on finding appropriate recommendations for treatment and testimony *beyond the best interest of the child*.

During the 1980s, litigation of child sexual abuse cases continued to increase. To accommodate prosecution needs, barriers to child testimony were dissolved and new state statutes were passed in an attempt to reform procedural and evidentiary rules concerning child testimony. Prior to that time, many children were prohibited from testifying in court because of the concern that they would be retraumatized or revictimized while testifying. Now, however, new accommodations were made to allow children to testify confidentially via (a) closed-circuit television in private, closed courtrooms, (b) closed interviews within judges' chambers, and (c) use of guardian ad litem testimonies (Melton et al., 1997; Sagatun & Edwards, 1995). Some people have questioned whether the implementation of such procedures has denied those who are accused of their right to confront their accusers (Ceci & Bruck, 1995).

Confrontation with the Perpetrator Controversy over the procedural changes in regard to child witnesses became common in forensic circles and in many family and juvenile courts. Innovative court procedures were developed based on amicus briefs filed by the American Medical Association (AMA), which emphasized that the need for special procedures must be determined on a case-by-case basis. Such accommodations would only be made to protect the welfare of the child when the child might be traumatized by the emotional impact of confronting a perpetrator, an event that could prove emotionally harmful for the child (Melton et al., 1997). The Supreme Court stressed that court proceedings must be held without subjecting the child to direct confrontation with the perpetrator; rather, less intimidating surroundings should be used. Evaluation also must be made of the need for the child's testimony, weighing that against any detrimental impact the testimony might have on the child's psychological welfare. Estimating the emotional impact that testifying in court has on a child is a complex task for social service experts. Needless to say, allowing one's child to testify is also a frightening prospect for anxious parents or caregivers.

Child Prostitution

As noted earlier, although the Anti-Slavery Society founded in 1833 established a minimal age requirement for using children for labor, the exploitation of children for prostitution was rampant in the 19th and early 20th centuries (DeMause, 1974; Pendergast, 1996; Radbill, 1980), and parental pimping also occurred when parents indentured out their daughters to agents in return for loans (Burgess, Harman, McCausland, & Powers, 1984; Burgess, Groth, & McCausland, 1981; Kempe & Kempe, 1984). The exploitation of young girls continues today through organized prostitution rings in many foreign underworld networks. For example, underworld links are said to forcibly kidnap and transport Thai girls into German military establishments where brothels are legal. German males often feign proposals to naive Thai girls who hope for a better life but later discover they have been transported to a foreign country to be subjected to control and brutality of nightmarish proportions. Advertisements for hostesses and dancers also attract young girls in pursuit of perceived opportunities with monetary rewards. Interpol has traced the trafficking of young girls into prostitution in England, West Germany, Italy, Nigeria, and Lisbon.

Female Circumcision

Perhaps one of the most heinous methods of child abuse is the practice of female genital mutilation (FGM), or circumcision, believed by some to be a religious ritual inherent in cultural beliefs. Female genital mutilation, as it is conducted on African female children, often involves severe mutilation of the genital organs. This practice has only recently been prohibited by concerned governments. An estimated 30 to 74 million females have received one of three forms of circumcision, consisting of minor, moderate, or severe mutilation

(Bryk, 1974; Foster, 1994; Simons, 1993; Toubia, 1994). As a result, many females have been subjected to a lifetime of repercussions such as painful menstruation, intercourse, and childbirth.

Prepuce or foreskin cutting is considered a minor form of FGM, whereas more extensive surgical procedures may cause the loss of the labia minora. In extreme cases, girls have lost infibulation and have been crippled for life. All of these procedures have been performed on female children between ages of 7 and 12 under unclean conditions and have involved excruciating pain. Rationalization for the surgery is said to be twofold: for husbands to blindly extend their own pleasure, and for men to guarantee that their wives will be virgins. The female child has no rights, even though this barbaric mutilation often leaves the female mutilated with irreversible damage.

In 1977, the congressional subcommittee on the Status of Women organized the Special Committee on Human Rights, which established a Working Group on Female Genital Mutilation Practices. The World Health Organization held a conference in February 1979 in Khartourn, Sudan, and unanimously condemned the mutilations. In the United States, Republican Pat Schroeder drafted the federal bill entitled Prohibition of Female Genital Mutilation Act of 1993 (Pub. L. No. 104-208), which prohibits FGM (Schroeder, 1994). Many countries have passed legislation forbidding such practices; recently, Africa outlawed clitoridectomy (Harris & Landis, 1997). Many elders staunchly adhere to such practices as religious rituals, but oppositionists insist that there is no mention of female mutilation in the Koran or any other religious document. Organized groups against FGM are actively educating followers to the futility of this act, as well as the long-term medical implications for females who are subjected to FGM. Contemporary males who are married to circumcised women and who love their wives are distressed by the amount of suffering they witness from them each month.

Internet Seductions

A recent article in *U.S. News & World Report* (Mannix, 2000) noted that cyberspace communication offers pornographers and pedophiles an open forum for child seduction in the new millennium. Mannix reported that the FBI opened 1,500 on-line child sexual abuse cases in 1999, an increase of 700 from 1998. The crimes range from stalking to outright enticement for sexual exploitation, and, in some instances, the murder of victims contacted through the Internet is increasing at an alarming rate.

Child solicitation is easily achieved in cyberspace by perpetrators who feign a peer relationship with their victims. The FBI has reported that in many cases, simplistic ploys have been used to entice the children into contact with the perpetrators. Because children often have more free time than their parents to spend on-line, and because they are exposed to computer communication systems at an early age and can often out-compute their parents by the time they are 8 or 10 years old, many parents are oblivious to the potential dangers lurking within cyberspace.

Most vulnerable to Internet seduction are preteens and teens, as they are more mobile than younger children. To illustrate, 13-year-old Katie was solicited over the Internet by a pedophile who pretended to be her soul mate. After a six-month Internet relationship, she agreed to meet him, only to find out he was a 24-year-old man. Katie has since turned 18 and written her experience in a book entitled *Katie.com* (Thomas, 2000). Socially withdrawn children who spend most of their time hacking away in computer chat rooms or bulletin boards are also a particularly vulnerable population.

In June 2000, a Massachusetts grand jury indicted a Pennsylvania man for selling pornographic materials to teenage girls via the Internet. In another case, a man of the clergy was arrested by FBI agents for crossing state lines to meet a person he expected to be a 14-year-old boy but who actually turned out to be an undercover FBI officer. The clergyman later admitted to a "sickness" that had propelled him to solicit young boys over a period of many years (McCoy, 2000).

Parental monitoring of children's Internet connections may not uncover a pedophile at work. Parents who monitor their children's e-mail may be fooled by the easy ability with which perpetrators can role-play the part of a same-age child. Web page and e-mail filters can be installed in children's computers, but a perpetrator's cyberspace handle must be identified before these filters can be applied.

Although the FBI and most local police departments have special task forces to identify perpetrators before they strike, increasing numbers of reports of child solicitation and exploitation via cyberspace indicate the severity of the problem. Obviously, the dark side of the Internet can mask the identity of a perpetrator quite easily. Locy (2000) notes that leaving a child on the Internet for an extended period of time is like "dropping a child in the worst part of town."

SUMMARY

Child maltreatment and abuse has been documented throughout history. Within the last half of the 20th century, concerned agencies, groups, and individuals expressed determination to identify and intervene in all abuse cases: physical, emotional, and sexual. At the same time, news releases emerge on a daily basis reporting severe abuse and long-standing acts of sexual abuse to children of all ages. Yet, even with this public acknowledgment that abuse occurs rampantly across society and that it has long-term residual effects on a child's emotional well-being throughout life, serious deficits exist in social service program delivery.

Child abuse is an international problem of significant proportions regardless of cultural mores or ethnic beliefs. For most people, the concept of sexually violating, abusing, and harming a vulnerable child is repulsive. Nonetheless, increased incident rates of sexual crimes against children speak to the gravity of the situation. The complex residual emotional impact of a sexually abusive experience on a child warrants an in-depth examination of the problem. Long-standing unresolved issues can negatively impact the psychological functioning of a child throughout his or her life. Mishandling of alleged abuse cases can, and often does, retraumatize the child, such as when a child is removed from his or her home, familiar surroundings, and significant family members. Emotional fears, extreme distress, and psychological reactions experienced at the time of abuse and during case dispensation can adversely affect a child's future development.

Statistics indicate that the most prevalent perpetrator for all forms of child abuse is the primary caretaker, be it father, mother, aunt, uncle, grandparent, or other trusted family member (NCCANI, 2000a). Treatment interventions require expert knowledge and sensitivity of the painful and often contradictory emotional reactions of survivors of abuse, particularly when the violator is a the child's parent, which occurs in 70–90% of all abuse cases (Greenfield, 1996). Because a vulnerable child often relies on an adult abuser or primary caretaker for basic survival needs yet comes to hate the abusive act of the adult, a paradoxical emotional state often arises that, in turn, is a source of emotional distress in and of itself.

Additionally, court proceedings often provoke stressful thoughts, fears, and even nightmares for a child, including an awareness of hardships placed on other family members as a result of the child's disclosure of the abuse. Fear of the legal system, loss of relationships with loved ones, and loss of presumed friends or other persons adversely involved in the case often causes ambivalent, confusing, and intense emotional reactions within the abusee. Financial hardships may be imposed on the family, which can even result in loss of housing and shelter.

Therefore, a multidisciplinary approach is necessary. Often, basic shelter and survival needs must be arranged, particularly if the perpetrator was the head of household who now has been taken away, imprisoned, or placed out of the home based on a court injunction. Shelter may be needed for the remaining family members or for the child alone if the nonoffending parent has abandoned the child. Community agencies must work cohesively to activate effective case management. Those who work in professional, judicial, and therapeutic milieus must act together to effectively resolve a child sexual abuse case, in the best interest of the child.

DISCUSSION QUESTIONS

1. During the 16th and 17th centuries, children were deemed their father's property. Does this problem still exist today in certain family systems? If so, describe how this belief may impact family dynamics.

2. Why was child punishment so harsh in past centuries? Compare historical methods of discipline with modern-day methods. Are the results improved?

3. Indentured children were commonly abused and exploited. What examples of indentured child workers exist today, if any? What can be done about this situation?

4. Abortion has always been a topic of debate. Have societal views of abortion changed, or are they the same now as they were in the past? What is your opinion on abortion?

5. Why were labor laws initiated? If they had never been implemented, would children still be exploited today? Or do you think children still are exploited in the workplace today? What do you think about the child labor laws in your state?

6. Child custody laws have changed over the years. What is your opinion of the current court procedures for deciding the custody of children? What factors should be considered when making a child custody decision?

7. Picture yourself as a parent in the 17th century. How would your role differ from that of a parent in the new millennium? What cultural influences are involved?

8. Are current child abuse laws effective? If so, why? If not, what can be done to improve them? Explain your position.

2

Perspectives of
Pedophilic Behaviors

LEARNING OBJECTIVES

Chapter 2 will address the following learning objectives:

1. A historical review of pedophilic behavior

2. A review of federal legislation regarding pedophilic offenses

3. A review of the criteria in the *Diagnostic and Statistical Manual of Mental Disorders (DSM-IV)* for diagnosis of pedophilia

4. A review of the pedophile's motivation to sexually abuse a child

5. A review of Finkelhor's theoretical models concerning child sexual abuse

6. A discussion of other theories of childhood sexual abuse

INTRODUCTION

All social service persons involved in intervention programs concerning child sexual abuse (CSA) need to have an in-depth and broad understanding of all issues related to the problem. Whether a mental health worker, probation officer, or judicial officer is dealing with the abusee or the perpetrator, treatment delivery can be enhanced when the treatment specialist has a working knowl-

edge of theoretical perspectives of pedophilic behavior. .
ment of the healing process, the abusee may benefit grea
ter understanding of underlying dynamics that fueleɑ
behavior. Perhaps this knowledge can dissipate any sense ot
or reduced self-esteem as an abusee learns that factors within
alone enabled the offense to occur. Likewise, if offenders are co.
theoretical perspectives, medical paradigms, and contemporary peι
motivation and treatment programs, their own self-discipline to
abusive tendencies can be enhanced. Consequently, this chapter will   ‚ on
various perspectives of pedophilic behavior, including motivational, theoretical, and remedial perspectives.

HISTORICAL BELIEFS

Motivation to Abuse

Traditional views of childhood sexual abuse held that perpetrators were motivated by sexual urges to abuse children (Finkelhor, 1984; Hollin & Howells,
1991; Ryan, 1997). Because sexual abuse was viewed as a sexually driven
crime, little if any concern was expressed for young children's safety from sexual assault crimes until a child reached puberty (Finkelhor, 1984; Mason,
1994). However, based on current statistics citing abductions and assaults of
children below the age of puberty, parents and society as a whole are willing
to discuss, identify, and guard against the typical pedophile. Recent accounts
of children abducted below puberty age serve as evidence that erotic sex drives
known to normal people are not the driving force for child abductions.
Rather, abductions appear to stem from an aberrant attraction for children as
vulnerable objects upon which to vent confused power issues that may also
include a sexual eroticism toward children.

Female Versus Male Incident Rate Similarly, many individuals believed,
and perhaps some still believe, that sexual abuse or violations occur predomi-
nately to girls (Hunter, 1991; Kuehnle, 1996; Oates, 1996). In the past, abused
males were silenced to a greater degree than abused girls because of their fear,
embarrassment and belief that boys should always enjoy sex. Current statistics
note that boys are also in jeopardy of victimization for sex crimes, but many
still remain reticent to disclose their abuse (Hunter, 1991; Prendergast, 1993).
Males who have come forward at an increased rate with admissions of sexual
abuse from perpetrators have subsequently been found to have violated several
other male children over the span of many years. Perhaps recently increased
disclosure of male child abuse is a factor in the increased willingness of the
public to discuss the issue of child abuse in general. However, although males
may be equally victimized for sexually abusive acts, it is females who are
entrapped into pornographic and prostitution rings at significantly alarming
rates within the United States, as well as abroad.

REVIEW OF HISTORICAL, THEORETICAL, AND APPLIED ISSUES

ntal Health of the Perpetrator Another historical misperception is that CSA is perpetrated by emotionally sick or disturbed individuals or by violent offenders who repeatedly stalk a victim to inflict harm. However, based on a review of court documents in litigated cases, it is now known that seemingly normal individuals also may be actively involved in child seduction activities and sexual exploitation tactics. Often, neighbors, family members, and coworkers are shocked to hear that their associate has committed such heinous acts on children. Prior to actual arrests, others within the perpetrator's social milieu often do not recognize overt cues. All of this attests to how well manipulative, controlling, secretive, and determined perpetrators can mask their actions, using behaviors that falsely portray a "good guy" image (Finkelhor, 1984; Oates, 1996).

Masked Behaviors The pretentious mask, so easily adorned by habitual molesters, serves to disguise their identity, so much so that the heinous act continues, often amidst totally unsuspecting friends, neighbors, and relatives. Because the pedophile hides beneath a disguise of charm, friendliness, and playful activities, the pedophile's prey easily succumbs to this misinterpreted "dance of seduction." Even adults who meet the perpetrator do not recognize the mask for what it is, which is why they experience such disbelief when they learn that a pedophile has lived among them. They cannot believe that such a charming and giving man could have committed such crimes. Yet, the determined pedophile uses this type of manipulation regularly.

Countless case histories reveal instances of treachery, describing how children were assaulted or violated within minutes of being out of their mothers' sight by trusted family members, friends, or associates. If unsuspecting adults are so taken in by the pedophile's charming façade, how can anyone expect children to identify and thwart such manipulation? Case history review further reveals that determined pedophiles can strike within seconds and minutes of having a child alone, as when a child is coerced into a bathroom, bedroom, or other secluded room. Once the act is completed, pedophiles can easily recompose themselves and reappear in the public setting as if nothing has occurred. Not a glimmer of guilt or remorse will be evident; once more, the pedophile will adorn the good guy façade. Pedophiles feign friendship to children and families simply as a means of setting the groundwork; they reduce others' inhibitions, build trust, and finally, when sufficient trust is gained, move in and conduct the abusive act.

Invasion of Boundaries Often the trusted adult, be it the child's relative, friend, or acquaintance, invades the child's boundaries, completes the abusive acts, and then minimizes the malintent of the acts (Finkelhor, 1984; Fleming, Mullen, & Bammer, 1997; Giardino, Finkel, Giardino, Seidl, & Ludwig, 1992). When this occurs, the child's perception of appropriate and inappropriate boundaries between self and others becomes blurred. Was the behavior a violation of the relationship, or was the child expected to comply with adult commands? When a child expects enjoyable, rewarding, or reinforcing behavior from a perpetrator but receives harmful unexpected behavior, a chain effect of adverse reactions is set into motion, as reflected in the following case.

> Johnny was 8 years old when his family held a backyard barbecue to celebrate the homecoming of an uncle who had just relocated from another state. Johnny had listened to his father's stories about Uncle Tony, how great he was and what a devoted brother he had been as they were growing up. It was evident that Johnny's mother and father both cared greatly for this man whom Johnny had not seen for two years. During the barbecue, Uncle Tony played with the children continually, and family members watched as he did so.
>
> After Uncle Tony and the children had played for several hours and Johnny was feeling delighted by all the attention he was getting, Uncle Tony guided Johnny into the pool house as they chased a wayward pool ball. Once inside, Uncle Tony's voice became raspy; he picked up Johnny, held him close to his face, and, while whispering into Johnny's ear how much he loved him, rubbed Johnny's genital area with one hand. Johnny struggled to break free, but Uncle Tony molested Johnny for several minutes. Finally Johnny broke free and ran out of the clubhouse with Uncle Tony right behind him. All of the family members playfully cheered at their success in retrieving the ball, and Uncle Tony graciously acknowledged everyone's cheers. No one noticed Johnny's teary-eyed expression.
>
> How could Johnny tell anyone what had happened, given everyone's obvious adoration of Uncle Tony? Could such a good man really have done anything bad, or did Johnny just imagine it? The discomfort of the experience and Johnny's embarrassment made it impossible for him to reveal the truth. Instead he withdrew to his room and closed the door, incapable of dealing with such a complex dilemma.

Even when parents would, in reality, immediately believe their child's disclosure of abuse and come to his or her aid, the child's *perception* of the parents' expected response may inhibit the disclosure. If a child perceives that his or her claims of abuse will be denied or dismissed, there will be no disclosure. On the other hand, if a child perceives that the recipient of the disclosure will believe and protect him or her, the child will be more likely to disclose the abuse. It is essential for children to understand that they are in a safe setting with a trustworthy and caring adult before they will disclose abuse (Gomes-Schwartz, Horowitz, & Cardarelli, 1990; Kuehnle, 1996; Nagel, Putname, Noll, & Trickett, 1997; Swan, 1984; Waterman & Ben-Meir, 1993; Waterman, Kelly, Oliveri, & McCord, 1993).

When children expect positive interactions but adverse incidents, such as molestation, physical pain, or emotional put-downs, occur, they develop confusion concerning how to interpret social cues, how to distinguish between good and bad touches, and their ability to protect self from others. Their self-doubt in all social situations heightens significantly, perhaps resulting in withdrawal from social situations or heightened vigilance and sensitivity in social settings. Eventually, these cognitive patterns become embedded in the children's personalities and dominate all their interactions. Essentially, these children cannot decipher which actions are truly appropriate, sincere, or well-intended, so they become suspicious of all interactions. Their expectations of acceptable adult behavior become vague and ambiguous. They may not develop a clear sense of self-boundaries for physical, emotional, and even sexual touches and behaviors, particularly if their abuse was experienced for an extended duration (Zivney, Nash, & Hulsey, 1988).

Violated children may not have the cognitive or coping skills to rationalize or harmonize feelings of discomfort at the hands of the perpetrators. Yet, at the same time, these children may not (and most do not) have the strength to defy an adult, especially if that adult represents a significant authority figure. Rather, the typical abused child may initially submit to the pedophile's continual manipulation. The perpetrator can force the child into silence through bribery, coercion, embarrassment, or a sense of vulnerability. In more aggressive situations, the abuser intimidates the child by using threats, force, other frightening actions, or any combination of these tactics (Roth, Newman, Polcovitz, Van der Kolk, & Mandel, 1997; Vevier & Tharinger, 1986). Thus, such children remain defenseless in regard to identifying and defending self-boundaries, be they physical, emotional, or sexual.

FEDERAL LEGISLATION

Harm or Risk to Children

The 1996 amendments to the Child Abuse Prevention and Treatment Act (CAPTA; as amended by Pub. L. No. 104-235) define child abuse as "any recent act or failure to act resulting in imminent risk of serious harm, death, serious physical or emotional harm, sexual abuse, or exploitation of a child (minor age as described by state statutes) by a parent or caretaker (including out-of-home care providers) who are responsible for the child's welfare" (p. 29). Thus, harm of any kind that is inflicted on a child by an adult falls within the enforcing guidelines of this legislation. This definition of abuse is broad and generalized, so establishing the occurrence of abusive acts in a court of law is another issue altogether. Interpretations of child abuse laws and criminal law, as well as judicial proceedings, all impact the final dispensation of criminal charges for the sexual abuse of a minor.

Sexual Abuse The 1996 CAPTA amendments (Pub. L. No. 104-235) define sexual abuse as "employment, use, persuasion, inducement, enticement or coercion of any child to engage in, or assist any other person to engage in, any sexually explicit conduct or any simulation of such conduct for the purpose of producing any visual depiction of such conduct; or rape, and in cases of caretaker or inter-familial relationship, statutory rape, molestation, prostitution, or other form of sexual exploitation of children or incest with children" (p. 29).

PEDOPHILIA

Given the broad-based legal definitions of what constitutes child abuse and sexual abuse across legislative bodies, it is not surprising that similar disparities exist among social scientists' definitions of a pedophile. Traditionally, a pedophile was viewed as a mentally disturbed stranger who aggressively sought out children and coerced them into inappropriate sexual behaviors. However, more recent research has shown that primary caretakers, mainly fathers or step-fathers, account for 90% of the cases of CSA through incestual relations (Greenfield, 1996; Trepper, Niedner, Mika, & Barrett, 1996; Weinberg, 1955). However, stranger abductions, which usually consist of more violent acts and threats of harm to the victim, are on the rise (NCCANI, 1997).

Judicial Definitions

As noted earlier, the definitions or terms relevant to CSA case management are problematic for numerous reasons, as standardization across states does not exist. Various criteria are used to define the details of the abuse in all aspects of a case, from the victim's perspective to the perpetrator's adjudication. From the victim's perspective, statutes of limitation, feasible treatment programs, and community support programs may differ considerably from state to state. From the perpetrator's perspective, judicial processing for offenses may vary widely from state to state. Consequently, while one perpetrator may receive stringent sentencing for offenses in one state, a perpetrator of a similar crime in a more lenient state may receive fewer sanctions or even case dismissal. When the perpetrator is the child's caretaker, drastic implications for the child's healing may be involved. Therefore, for the sake of all involved in CSA cases, the treating mental health professionals need to be well versed on leg-islative mandates within the jurisdiction of practice. Case outcomes may be seriously impacted merely by the judicial definition of pedophilia itself. The following section will address several of the issues involved in the processing of CSA cases.

Contrasts with Medical Definitions Pedophilic behavior has been described differently by medical, psychological, and judicial bodies. Forensic bodies involved in the prosecution of pedophiles have debated the appropri-ateness of applied definitions. Martin and Esplin (1997) note that one study defined pedophilic behavior as adults having "had physical sexual contact with a girl under fourteen when they were at least five years older than the victim or with a boy under sixteen when at least five years older" (LEXIS, p. 1, Summary Section). Clearly, this definition is limited and excludes that of the *Diagnostic and Statistical Manual of Mental Disorders, 4th edition (DSM-IV-TR™)*

(APA, 2000), which identifies types of pedophilia involving prepubescent children 13 years or under and differentiates between sexual attraction for females, males, or both. In contrast to common belief, sexual molesters may not seek out solely children for sexual activities, but rather may be simultaneously involved with adult persons of either sex; in other words, individuals diagnosed as pedophiles may have either an exclusive or a nonexclusive attraction to children.

Emotional Propensity Differences also arise in child abuse cases in regard to the testimony that will be allowed in court about the kinds of behavior that constitute pedophilic behavior. Usually, testimony on prior criminal behavior used to discredit the defendant's character is not allowed; however, prior acts of sexual abuse committed against children indicate an *emotional propensity* toward pedophilic behavior and, therefore, have been admitted into testimony. In a court case tried in Kansas (*State v. Bisagno*, 1926), a third-party testimony of "lustful disposition" was used against the defendant based on past incidents. Similarly, the Arizona Supreme Court approved a lower court's instruction to use a testimony of emotional propensity as evidence to uphold a conviction of pedophilia (*State v. Finley*, 1959), stating that "if you find and believe that such crime was committed by the defendant, testimony is admissible for the sole purpose of showing a system, a plan, scheme of the defendant and to prove his lustful and lascivious disposition" (LEXIS at 6). Subsequent cases, such as *State v. Parker* (1970), have contained similar findings.

In 1969, a court upheld a decision to admit testimony on an emotional propensity theory where the defendant had been convicted of a separate act of fellatio on a different minor child where the accused was also charged with molesting two younger girls (*State v. Phillips*, 1969). In the Arizona Supreme Court case of *State v. McFarlin* (1973), the court emphasized the secretive nature of the crime, concluding that this caused severe problems of proof for the state and therefore admissibility of emotional propensity as evidence was imperative. The *McFarlin* case cited other cases that had admitted evidence on emotional propensity, including references to aberrant behaviors like French-kissing young girls, molesting children, sodomy, and lewd and lascivious conduct.

Arguments against the use of testimony on prior incidents also have been made. In *State v. McFarlin* (1973), for example, the argument against the use of emotional propensity testimony was based on a reference to the proximity of the time of the event and proposed that a three-year timeline be applied to the admission of testimony of prior offenses.

To resolve the arguments about the use of evidence based on emotional propensity in court, greater collaboration is needed between the legal and the behavioral sciences fields. Professionals in both areas need to work together to establish solid grounds upon which substantial evidence of prior incidents may be admitted into testimony (Melton, Petrila, Poythress, & Slobogin, 1997; Sagatun & Edwards, 1995).

Repeat Offenses The rate of recidivism (i.e., repeat offenses) is high among pedophiles, as reflected in many court cases. In *State v. Weatherbee* (1988), in which the defendant was charged with sexual abuse of his 12- and 16-year-old daughters, evidence of prior acts of sexual abuse performed on stepchildren from a previous marriage was allowed into testimony. Medical experts testified that the defendant was a "fixed pedophile" with an ongoing propensity to offend. In *State v. Salazar* (1994), a case involving a minor child molestation charge, allegations of rape committed by the perpetrator 21 years and 3 years previously were allowed into evidence. Likewise, in *State v. Hopkins* (1993), testimony on the defendant's former abuse of his adult daughters was allowed to establish his guilt of sexual abuse against his 13-year-old daughter. The court in *State v. Weatherbee* (1988) noted that "exact similarity between acts is not required" (pp. 470–471).

When expert testimony is used to establish emotional propensity, the *Frye* test may be applied (Melton, et al., 1997). Essentially, the *Frye* test emphasizes that evidence must be excluded if it is not grounded in a principle that has attained acceptance in the expert witness's field of expertise. Another consideration is whether the person supplying the expert opinion is qualified as an expert. In *United States v. Amaral* (1973), four criteria were cited for determining admissibility: (1) a qualified expert, (2) proper subject matter, (3) conformity to a generally accepted theory, and (4) probative value compared to prejudicial effect. The Federal Rules of Evidence note that relevancy of the testimony must be evident. As noted earlier, not only do legal definitions of pedophilia vary across states, but the procedural events that lead to final court dispensation in cases involving the criminal sexual abuse of a minor also differ on a case-by-case basis.

PSYCHIATRIC DIAGNOSIS

DSM-IV-TR™ Diagnosis

Psychiatric assessment of pedophilia is described in the *Diagnostic and Statistical Manual of Mental Disorders, 4th edition (DSM-IV-TR*™*)* (APA, 2000). The *DSM-IV-TR*™ is a diagnostic tool to be used by well-trained clinicians who apply a decision-making process in making a final diagnosis based on a holistic evaluation of the party. According to the *DSM-IV-TR*™, a pedophile is an individual who, "[o]ver a period of at least 6 months, [experiences] recurrent, intense sexually arousing fantasies, sexual urges, or behaviors involving sexual activity with a prepubescent child or children (generally age 13 years or younger). The person has acted on these sexual urges, or the sexual urges or fantasies cause marked distress or interpersonal difficulty. The person is at least age 16 years and at least 5 years older than the child . . ." (p. 572).

The legal definitions proposed by CAPTA and subsequent legislation such as the Racketeer-Influenced and Corrupt Organizations (RICO) bill cover a much wider range of behavior than that which is defined as child molestation and exploitation in the *DSM-IV-TR*™ manual. Both the child pornographer and the incestuous father may fall within the definition of a pedophile by law; however, a diagnosis based on the *DSM-IV-TR™* description may not apply to both forms of deviant behavior. While a pedophile may experience sexual arousal or preoccupation toward minor children, a pornographer may deal with children as a means of monetary gain, rather than to sustain a personal sexual contact with them, exploiting them nonetheless, but with motivating factors that are different from those of the pedophile.

Complex Dynamics The fact that various types of child abuse exist has implications for treatment issues. In many instances, a perpetrator who exploits children purely for the sake of monetary gains would warrant a different mode of treatment than that proposed for a pedophile who is driven by a sexual propensity to commit sexual acts upon children (Bradford & Kaye, 1999; Hollin & Howells, 1991). Controversy exists about whether treatment of sexual deviants is ever effective. Treatments used in the past have included aversive shock treatment, chemical pharmacology (Bradford & Kaye, 1999), surgical castration (Greenfield, 1996), and the rebuilding of cognitive distortions (Abel & Rouleau, 1990; Wright & Schneider, 1999). Only surgical castration has been reported to result in a lower recidivism rate, 5% as compared to 80% among noncastrated pedophiles (Greenfield, 1996). Researchers have noted that the rate of recidivism is consistently significant for perpetrators; and an even more frightening revelation is that one pedophile can violate as many as 200 victims during his or her lifetime (Thomas & Jamison, 1995). The levels of manipulation, deviousness and lack of remorse necessary to violate so many victims in one person's lifetime are staggering for a nonabusing individual to comprehend. One can imagine the shock value of these elements to a loving spouse or relative who has never suspected any abuse but discovers that repeated, frequent, and harsh abuse has transpired. Families are destroyed; emotional devastation is evident in both victims and family members. Thus, social scientists must continue to examine, diagnose, and treat sexual abuse of children and the devastation it creates.

Pharmacological Interventions Mental health specialists who work with pedophiles agree that recovery from pedophilic tendencies is a complex process involving both psychological and pharmacological interventions, neither of which has been shown to be successful in conclusively "curing" pedophiles. Based on the premise that the behaviors of sexual predators stem from a sexually driven need, drugs that intervene in physiological responses to sexual urges are often prescribed. The optimal goal of treatment is to suppress the pedophile's deviant sexual urges directed toward children while retaining his or her ability to sustain normal adult relationships.

A recent development in the pharmacological treatment of pedophiles is the use of specific serotonin re-uptake inhibitors (SSRI). Bradford and Kaye (1999) noted that considerable success has been achieved by treating pedophiles with SSRI interventions using penile tumescence testing and peripheral neurobiological markers of serotonin metabolism. This form of treatment is said to contain fewer side effects than previous forms of treatment using antiandrogen and hormonal injections. Although various drug interventions are being used in treatment centers (Rosler & Witztum, 1998; Stein, Hollander, Anthony, Schneider, Fallon, & Liebowitz, 1992), SSRI is reported as the most promising to date by Bradford and Kaye (1999), who have recommended a combination of cognitive and pharmacological interventions for most effective results. Empirical studies based on long-term follow-up of SSRI interventions are not yet available.

Extenuating circumstances that contribute to pedophilic behavior, such as substance abuse, comorbidity, and other psychiatric conditions, are not accounted for in this chapter. Although many pedophiles admit to committing sexual abuse while under the influence of a substance, others report not being under the influence while committing abuse. Treating compound features of abuse is difficult for many reasons. If a pharmacological approach is used to treat sexual offenders, then adherence to the drug regime is a concern upon the perpetrator's release from incarceration. If serious psychiatric difficulty exists or financial hardships prohibit purchase of medication, it is highly doubtful that the parolee will adhere to prescribed medicines. Random urine screenings are recommended for most released perpetrators.

Identifying motivational factors for committing child sexual abuse or exploitation is essential if effective intervention is to occur. Monetary gain is perceived as an external motivator that may or may not be easier than other movitations to treat with behavioral sanctions or behavioral modifications. A pedophile who is motivated out of lust or desire to sexually abuse a child is thought to do so based on some internal motivating factor, possibly unknown to even the perpetrator. External sanctions are less effective in this instance, as may be apparent by the high rate of recidivism among sexual predators (Greenfield, 1996).

ETIOLOGY OF PEDOPHILIA

Deviant sexual or abusive behaviors are often attributed to learned behaviors (as in transgenerational abuse), to inappropriate boundary setting (as in interfamilial settings), or to sociopathic tendencies (severe cases). *Transgenerational abuse* is a term that applies to abuse that is passed down generation after generation, therefore becoming a modeled behavior. Child victims learn that it is acceptable to treat others in similarly abusive manners, so they become perpetrators.

Intrafamilial abuse, on the other hand, refers more directly to relational systems within a nuclear family within which family members cross boundaries of socially accepted behaviors. It may entail sibling abuse, parental abuse, grandparent abuse, or abuse from uncles, mothers, fathers, and so on. Implications for both transgenerational and interfamilial abuse are significant and complex, as it is the nuclear family from which most individuals draw a self-identity or positive self-image. If circumstances within the family unit prohibit the development of a healthy self-image, a person's life adjustment can be, and usually is, impacted throughout his or her life. Finkhelor (1994) notes that 90% of abuse offenses are initiated from a trusted family member who is able to manipulate others in the environment to satisfy his or her need to carry out sexually abusive acts toward others.

Sociopathic tendencies to abuse is not a mutually exclusive classification of any one type of abuser. Similar sociopathic qualities are found in abusers of strangers as well as abusers of vulnerable family members. This category, however, is usually applied to the abusers who commit severe, assaultive, and exploitive acts of child abuse and who frequently and purposefully stalk child victims. These perpetrators are usually strangers who conduct physical, sexual, and, by secondary nature, emotional abuse of children in a harsh and shocking manner, such as those who kidnap children, use them in ritualistic cult-related activities, and exhibit harmful or torturous behaviors in the process of sexually abusing them. Perhaps most detrimental to children is the situation in which their own family members are devout cult members and the children are repeatedly abused or used as sacrificial objects throughout their childhood. Rape, physical beatings, pornographic activities, and ritualistic abuse are all examples of harsh activities by abusers who fall into this category. These types of abuse are more blatant and easily identified than transgenerational and inter-familial sexual abuse, in which secrecy about family activities, loyalty to family members who are perpetrators, and the societal fear of intruding upon family privacy perpetuate the abuse.

The following section will address theories concerning CSA from the perpetrator's perspective, that is, theories about the perpetrator's propensity to commit child sexual abuse. Several theories will be reviewed, and brief descriptions of each theoretical model and its implications will be provided. Although attempts have been made to understand the motivational thought patterns underlying pedophilic behavior, much work needs to be done in this area of research. Other theories about the pedophile's underlying motivation to sexually abuse children will be examined later in this chapter.

MOTIVATION TO COMMIT
CHILD SEXUAL ABUSE

If motivation to commit child sexual abuse could be easily deciphered, then perhaps a more effective treatment process could be developed to deter pedophiles from repeating the act on another child. Although theorists have proposed numerous theories in an attempt to understand the problem, none of the theories have been proven to be universal when applied to all pedophiles. It appears that the motivations to abuse are as vastly divergent as the offending parties themselves. Theorists have examined the pedophile's ability to establish intimate relations on an adult level, experiences with abuse as child victims, substance abuse, physiological imbalance, sociopathic propensity, and an overall need for power and control. These are but a few perspectives that have been investigated in an effort to understand and, hopefully, treat pedophiles with greater success. Several theories of pedophilic behavior are discussed here, along with the historical background from which these theories emerged.

Motivational Needs

Early propositions about CSA conceptualized that the sexual abuse was a sexually driven behavior or sexually motivated. However, subsequent theories readily unraveled a variety of underlying motivators to conduct sexually abusive behaviors directed toward children. Groth (1979) was one researcher who initially proposed power and control issues as motivators that stimulate the behaviors found among pedophiles. Groth described pedophilic behaviors as sexually deviant, representing a "pseudosexual" act rather than a sexual act as defined in the traditional view of male-female sexual behaviors. Finkelhor (1984) emphasized the fact that all sexual behavior is need driven, be it need for affiliation, affection, approval, or, in extreme cases, aggression. If this is so, then identifying pedophiles' inherent driven needs may help in identifying what motivates them to sexually abuse children.

Groth (1979) also emphasized the erotic sentiments expressed through sexual behaviors such as touch, cuddling, and caressing. Thus, a sexual component is readily identifiable in the pedophile's behavior, as well as the underlying need motivators. In addition to the need factors identified by Finkelhor, sexual contact is an inherent reward for pedophiles who assault children. This compound explanation of motivating factors only serves to emphasize the difficult task that exists for treatment specialists who work with pedophiles.

Alternate explanations proposed by Groth, Hobson, and Gary (1982) suggested that pedophiles experience arrested development, whereas other theorists proposed that pedophiles act out of an internalized sense of inadequacy (Hammer & Gluek, 1957; Panton, 1978; Stricker, 1967). Conversely, the sense of power and control that is realized by pedophiles when they force themselves onto children was said to be the driving force that propels them to sexually abuse children (Loss & Clancy, 1983). A more sympathetic perspective posed by Stoller (1975) offers that pedophiles are attempting to symbolically overcome traumas experienced during their own childhood. More extreme explanations state that pedophiles are blocked with a narcissistic love of self as children that is then projected onto child victims who subsequently become love objects for the pedophiles.

Some molesters report the abusive act as "a compelling sexual encounter," indicating that the abuse is sexually driven, while others report "a traumatic victimization as a child," a more aggressive motivating event that propels them to molest children (Gebhard, Gagnon, Pomeroy, & Christenson, 1965). The intensity of the experience drives the perpetrators further into longstanding, extreme emotional reactions such as intense pleasure with intense repulsion. Social learning models have concluded that in some instances, simply having observed a sibling or friend being sexually molested by an adult has caused long-standing negative emotional reactions in perpetrators (Howells, 1981).

Physiological or biological theories about sexual arousal propose a predisposition to desiring a child as a sexual object and note an emotional or mental instability of the pedophile, or perhaps a deviant manner of arousal (Money, 1961). However, if Gebhard et al.'s (1965) theory of transgenerational abuse holds true, a predisposition toward abusing children may have been instigated by the perpetrator's own exposure to abuse during childhood. The abused victim, in turn, becomes the perpetrator as a result of the abuse. Although this certainly does not happen with all children who experience abuse, it does occur in some cases. In some instances, it may be viewed simply as a reenactment of the abuser's own abuse.

Learned Behaviors In the United States particularly, sexual abuse of children is viewed as a deviant behavior that is synonymous with pathological symptoms, perhaps in part because sexual abuse can be carried over from learned behaviors experienced by the perpetrators as children (Gebhard et al., 1965). Criticism of this simplified, unidirectional perspective of pedophiles notes that the offenders who are studied are usually those who have been caught and convicted; therefore, they may be the most frequent offenders and the most severely disturbed individuals. The countless number of other pedophiles who go on undetected might yield quite different motivational patterns for their behavior if they, too, were examined, and perhaps found void of the same identifiable pathological symptoms found among sentenced inmates.

Cultural Influences Cultural influences further impact the diagnosis and prognosis of sexual attraction to children. Some cultures believe that sexual behaviors with children are necessary for the successful maturation of the child (Malamuth, 1984). Within the United States, Elliott and Briere (1995) found that Hispanic children are less likely to make definite, conclusive reports of abuse, while black children are more likely to never report abuse. Caucasian children were found to be more likely to recant their accusations of abuse. Assessment of culturally diverse children concerning sexual abuse requires an understanding of the cultural beliefs of the family of origin (Paniagua, 1998).

European and Asian countries are known to severely exploit children, at times with parental consent in exchange for some financial barter, be it money or material object. Perhaps most alarming is the number of preadolescents and adolescents who are sold into captivity for purposes of organized prostitution on an international basis, along with the escalation of child kidnapping into prostitution that has occurred in recent years. The escalation of these activities has led to increased efforts on the part of Interpol to curtail them (see RICO).

High Rates of Recidivism Rates of recidivism are reported to be increasing, particularly with older abusers (Greenfield, 1996). Legislation in many states allows for the public posting of sexual predators' names and addresses via television and movie theater bulletins, as well as a lifetime listing on a police log. In other instances, pedophiles are required by law to register their living arrangements so that neighbors and surrounding parents can be forewarned of their existence. Yet, attempts at public sanctions have not deterred repeated incidents. It appears that the deviant propensity to sexually abuse a child is deeply embedded in the pedophile's psyche. Even extreme consequences such as prison, public registries, and, in some cases, electroshock therapy or pharmacological interventions are not enough to deter repeated episodes (Greenfield, 1996).

METHODS OF CHILD SOLICITATION

Intrafamilial Abuse

Prison statistics note that 80–90% of inmates arrested for sexual assault report committing the crime on their own children (Greenfield, 1996). Familial abuse accounts for 90% of sexual abuse incidents according to Finkelhor (1984) and Greenfield (1996). Unsuspecting family members fall easy prey to a pedophile's preestablished façade of friendship. Once a child discloses that an adult who was previously welcomed into the home took advantage of a familiar child within the home, the child's caretakers experience considerable stress. If the nonabusing adults do not seek help, they may not be able to assist the child through the ordeal. Professionals agree that parental support upon disclosure is highly instrumental to a child's recovery following disclosure (Deblinger & Heflin, 1996).

Often children rely on adults for survival needs and openly trust them, particularly if the perpetrator is also the parent. Therefore, children might simply not realize when a loving adult-child relationship transposes into an invasive assault with inappropriate behaviors. These invasive behaviors often begin with minor touches to which the child does not adversely respond. Once a child tolerates relatively minor brushes or uncomfortable touches, more aggressive acts occur. Thus, a gradual breakdown of the children's defense abilities transpires. More acceptable, even loving, behaviors mask the intermittent negative behaviors toward the victimized child, and thus the child is gradually conditioned to accept even offensive behaviors from the, otherwise, loved adult.

Case histories reveal that as many as seven or eight siblings in a family have been abused for years while the abuse was kept silent and secret, with even the victimized siblings unaware of each other's abuse. Obviously, the abuser's techniques are extremely manipulative, deceitful, and self-serving to leave other family members so unsuspecting of such culpable behavior. In some instances, nonoffending adults remain in denial for any number of reasons; they evade, deny, and reject obvious clues that a perpetrator exists within their own household. Sometimes they become so consumed with their own anguish that their defense mechanisms prohibit public denouncement of the perpetrator's actions.

Acquaintances

Approximately 12% of prison inmates arrested for sexually abusing a child admitted they knew the child through relatives or friends (Greenfield, 1996). Other abusers come from outside the circle of family and friends, such as entrusted caretakers who abuse children in their care, including members of the clergy, day care workers, baby-sitters and neighbors (Finkhelhor, 1994; Sedlak & Broadhurst, 1996). Because the perpetrator hides behind a false persona of goodness and what appears to be genuine interest, both the parents and the child succumb to the perpetrator's intended actions. Perhaps deception is relatively easy for the pedophile because for most individuals, the concept of willfully or painfully harming a child is counter to their past learning and internal value systems; therefore, they do not suspect it.

In contrast to the emphasis on intrafamilial abuse, Russell and Bolen (2000) reviewed many recent studies and concluded that the percentages of familial abuse among their subjects were lower than those indicated by other researchers. In Russell's 1978 study involving 930 women (*see* Russell, 1983), the prevalence rate for incestuous abuse was 16% of her sample, while 13% of the reported abuse cases were attributed to extrafamilial abuse offenses. A 38% incident rate was found for extrafamilial and intrafamilial sexual abuse reports. A reviewer of such research studies should assess the method of subject selection and the types of questions asked during the interviews. Obviously, differing conclusions are drawn relative to the participants in the study, the method of questioning, and the type of analysis.

Day Care and Foster Care

A 1998 report from the National Committee to Prevent Child Abuse noted that reports of abuse in day care and foster homes represented approximately 3% of all confirmed cases in 1997 (Wang & Daro, 1996). When abuse, particularly sexual abuse, does occur in these settings, publicity is extensive and may present an exaggerated view of the actual incident rate. Finkelhor, Williams, and Burns (1988) explored these factors more thoroughly in a book entitled *Nursery Crimes: Sexual Abuse in Day Care*. Perhaps the most publicized case was the McMartin Day Care story (Eberle & Eberle, 1993; Waterman, Kelly, Oliveri, & McCord, 1993), which will be discussed in Section 2 of this book in the material concerning preschools and sexual abuse of children.

Internet Seductions

In the late 1990s, technological advancements led to an inordinate increase in the number of sexually abusive encounters between adults and children. Children are now solicited via Internet chat rooms and e-mail by perpetrators who establish pretentious friendly relationships with the children. Often the potential victim-child believes that the perpetrator is a same-age peer who is simply a welcomed new friend. The pedophile appeals to the child's or adolescent's interests, then builds a trusting relationship with the child that is sufficient to induce the child into a face-to-face meeting. Perpetrators' intentions for seducing the child via the Internet are as varied as the motivational factors to abuse a child, but statistics show that often state lines are crossed in perpetrators' attempts to meet with the potential victim (Locey, 2000). The perpetrator will travel across state lines to meet the child in person, using a false modus operandi (MO) that is unknown to the vulnerable trusting child. Fortunately, the FBI and state authorities are continually developing methods of tracking perpetrators. Investigative agencies such as the FBI, state district attorneys offices, and local community police departments have hired specially trained detectives with enough computer expertise to track pedophiles through Internet communication tactics.

Adolescents between the ages of 14 and 17 are the most vulnerable population for seduction by on-line perpetrators in actual face-to-face meetings, since they are more mobile than younger children. Meetings are staged in such places as shopping centers, recreational parks, and so on. Younger children are more subject to invasive sexually activated questions in chat rooms, such as "Do you wear a bra?" or "What color are your panties?" In either case, statistics show that children are now more vulnerable to seduction from on-line recruiters than to direct, chance meetings with perpetrators on the street. Parents who believe their children are safe at home doing homework in their room may be surprised to learn that their children may be in danger of conversing with a pedophile on-line in their own home.

THEORETICAL MODELS OF PEDOPHILIC BEHAVIOR

This section presents current theories concerning CSA, focusing on perpetrator motivation and preconditions that enable the abuse to occur. Several models addressing the perpetrator's motivation to abuse will be briefly reviewed, including (a) Finkelhor's (1984) four-factor preconditions model and family systems model, (b) Ney and Peters's (1995) model of intergenerational abuse, and (c) McIntryre's (1981) family systems model. While no overriding consensus exists concerning the etiology of the pedophile's behavior, Finkelhor's work is perhaps the most well-known and his theories the most revisited. Finkelhor's initial work addressed findings in case histories using a comprehensive sample base of subjects.

Finkelhor's Multifactor Model

Finkelhor (1984) proposed a theoretical model for understanding the etiology of sexually abusive acts with children, emphasizing preexisting conditions that enable a perpetrator to actually commit the abuse. Finkelhor proposed a four-factor theory in which four factors contribute to the perpetrator's propensity to abuse a child. These four factors are: (1) emotional congruence, (2) sexual arousal, (3) blockage, and (4) disinhibition (see Table 2.1). All of these factors must be present in some varying degree for the pedophile to complete a sexual act with a child. Secondary factors act as mechanisms that trigger the primary factors, perhaps operating at different speeds antagonistically or synergistically based on the pedophile's unique personality and environmental influences (Finkelhor, 1984).

Factor One: Emotional Congruence Emotional congruence, according to Finkelhor (1984), refers to the *emotional fit* between the adult's needs and the child's characteristics of accessibility. Emotional congruence must exist for the abuser to build a trusting relationship with the child. If necessary, a pedophile will work hard to achieve this sense of congruency with the child by coaxing or enticing him or her into pleasurable or gamelike activities that build a false sense of friendship and trust between the adult and child.

Factor Two: Sexual Arousal Sexual arousal toward children is defined as a physiological arousal in the presence of children or photographs of children. Although theorists have equated sexual arousal with emotional congruence, others attest to differences between the two concepts. Researchers such as Masters and Johnson (1979) have noted that individuals can and do have sexual preferences that are at odds with emotional congruence and that, therefore, occur independently of emotional fulfillment. Perhaps a more straightforward explanation is offered by Howells's (1979) social learning theory, which states that sexual arousal is a response that is evoked or conditioned, based on environmental conditions.

Factor Three: Blockage Blockage, in Finkelhor's (1984) multifactor theory, denotes the individual pedophile's fixation at a particular developmental stage that leaves the individual incapable of progressing to a mutually satisfying adult relationship. While Finkelhor does not offer an explanation about why the individual is blocked, Freud (1909/1936) attributed the inability to fulfill adult intimacy needs to an individual's unsuccessful resolution of the Oedipus or Electra complex. In the case of males, this results in castration anxiety, rendering the pedophile incapable of completing a sexually satisfying and intimate relationship with another adult. Another theory about blockage suggests that the blocked male simply has not achieved the skills required to approach adult females and therefore, out of his fear of women, resorts to children, using them as substitutes for women (Gebhard et al., 1965; Meiselman, 1978). Regressive behaviors are often exhibited by the pedophile; and rather than seeking satisfying adult intimate relationships, the pedophile turns toward children for satisfaction.

Sometimes incestual behavior forced upon the pedophile's own child is rationalized away as healthier behavior than seeking adult relationships out-

Table 2.1 Four-Factor Preconditions of Sexual Abuse and Implied Symptomatic Behaviors

Factor	Personality Attribute	Symptomatic Behaviors
One	Emotional Congruence	Fit between the adult's emotional needs and the child's characteristics (Finkelhor & Hotaling, 1983); and narcissistic identification with the child as the adult's self (Howells, 1981)
Two	Sexual Arousal for Children	Physiological arousal by child stimuli (Abel et al., 1987; Atwood & Howell, 1971); sexual proclivity for children even at odds with emotional needs (Langevin, 1983); an inability to progress through the normal stage of child-adult attractions, leading to regression (Freud, 1925/1953); fixated fantasies that are repeated mentally to the point of becoming an operand in conditioning toward relating sexual pleasure with children (McGuire, Carlisle, & Young, 1965); social learning or modeling from previous abuse (Wenet, Clark, & Hunner, 1981); and physiological precursors due to hormonal or biological factors (Berlin, 1982)
Three	Blockage	Fixations with conflicts of castration anxiety prohibiting adult female interaction (Fenichel, 1945; Gillepsie, 1964); timid, unassertive, inadequate social skill development (Frisbie, 1969; Langevin, 1983); family systems that foster inadequate sexual or emotional gratification with adult partners (De Young, 1982; Meiselman, 1978); and repressed or distorted morals prohibiting extramarital affairs but rationalizing incestual relations as an acceptable sublimation (Goldstein, Kant, & Hartman, 1973)
Four	Disinhibition	Poor impulse control (Gebhard et al., 1965; Groth, Hobson, & Gary, 1982; Knopp, 1982); senility (Karpman, 1954); alcohol and substance abuse (Anderson & Shafer, 1979; Morgan, 1982; Rada, 1976); and social mores that encourage or condone children as sexual objects (Densen-Gerber, 1983)

Adapted with the permission of The Free Press, a Division of Simon & Schuster, Inc. From *Child Sexual Abuse: New Theory and Research* by David Finkelhor. Copyright © 1984 by David Finkelhor.

side of a sexually unrewarding marriage (Goldstein, Kant, & Hartman, 1973). Other pedophiles rationalize their incestual behaviors under the auspices of holding the family together, particularly when the marital spouse is physically unavailable because he or she has abandoned the family or is physically incapable of participating in a satisfying sexual relationship. Pedophiles might also rationalize their behavior when the marital partner is emotionally withdrawn from the family and interacts with family members in a distant and detached manner. Such forms of rationalization are most effectively treated through cognitive restructuring interventions (Wright & Schneider, 1999).

Factor Four: Disinhibition Disinhibition refers to the pedophile's ability to be free of inhibiting motivators, which renders the pedophile incapable of inhibitory behaviors and results in arousal and subsequent child abuse. Numerous personality factors are said to facilitate a pedophile's intent to abuse, such as lack of impulse control (Groth, Hobson, & Gary, 1982; Knopp, 1982), substance abuse (Anderson & Shafer, 1979; Rada, 1976; Virkkunen, 1974), and mental deterioration, or psychosis (Mayhall & Norgard, 1983). Alcoholism is the most frequently reported precipitating factor among pedophiles (Greenfield, 1996). Multiple stressors within the perpetrator's life, such as loss of employment, loss of loved ones, or other highly stressful life events, are also said to reduce the pedophile's ability to resist impulse control. Essentially, theorists view any disinhibiting event as a precursor to the sexual abuse of a child, particularly if the adult is predispositioned to commit such abuse (Hermin, 1981).

Generalizations Although advancements in understanding pedophilic behavior have been made through research, the true etiology of pedophilia remains an unsolved mystery. Finkelhor's (1984) multifactor model of the abuser's personality attributes was a seminal approach toward understanding a behavior that is viewed by American cultural and social norms as aberrant and criminal. The proposed four-factor model is a multiple-factor theory that was developed at a time when little, if any, knowledge of pedophilic behaviors was available.

Although the four-factor model provides a range of personality characteristics that may exist in varying degrees to enable the perpetrator to sexually abuse a child, more investigative work is needed. Any one of the elements proposed in this theory could be examined and developed to further enhance Finkelhor's propositions. Perhaps a more important area of focus for research would be toward identifying the reasons why an adult would be sexually attracted to, or aroused by, the thought of sex with a child. In addition, theorists could look at gender preferences among pedophiles, questioning what underlying factors propel a perpetrator to prefer either male or female children.

Howells (1979) draws a distinction between mediated sexual behaviors, or behaviors that occur because of an ongoing sexual preference for children, and situational abuse, which occurs within the context of a given situation. An individual with a mediated orientation toward children will participate in more pervasive modes of seeking out child victims, such as searching shopping malls, bus stops, and school yards. Findings (Finkelhor, 1994) related to this type of abuse focus on the exclusivity of using children as sexual partners, the intensity of the abuse, and the frequency of occurrence. Current researchers concur that, given the variety in the case history files, more than one predispositional condition exists among pedophiles who sexually abuse children (Gold & Reimer, 1972; Greenfield, 1996; Kempf, 1990; Kluft, 1990; Wright &

Schneider, 1999). A multifactor theme is apparent, but the underlying elements leading to this behavior require a much more intensive examination than they have been given at this point. Future research needs to address the variety of pedophilic behaviors as well as the preexisting predisposition that leads pedophiles to desire children as sexual objects.

A Precondition Model of Sexual Abuse:
A Process Model

Finkelhor (1984) proposed a second model of abuse in addition to the multifactor model discussed earlier. This model emphasizes four preexisting conditions that must be present if the perpetrator is going to outwardly act upon the drive to sexually assault or molest a child (see Table 2.2). Finkelhor based the model on factors cited in previous research on child abuse (Lukianowicz, 1972; Lystad, 1982; Tierney & Corwin, 1983), victims and families (Finkelhor, 1979; Russell, 1983), offender characteristics (Frude, 1982; Groth, 1979; Sgroi, 1982a & b), societal influences (Baker, 1983; Cohen, 1978; Gelles, 1973; McQuire, Carlisle, & Young, 1965; Wenet, Clark, & Hunner, 1981), biophysical hormonal imbalance (Berlin & Meinecke, 1981), and pornographic media (Densen-Gerber, 1983; Dworkin, 1983). This model differs from the earlier proposed multifactor model (MFM) in that the MFM describes attributes inherent within the pedophile him- or herself, while the preconditions model encompasses a wider environmental (or contextual) framework. The preconditions model incorporates (1) internal attributes (motivation to abuse), (2) self-regulating factors (internal inhibitors), (3) environmental influences (external inhibitors), and (4) interactional transactions (overcoming the child's resistance). Thus, the preconditions model is by far, a broader conceptualization of processes required to commit sexual abuse of a child.

The four preconditions of the preconditions model provide a process-oriented conceptualization, proposing specific circumstances that are often present to increase the potential for an abusive act to occur. For example, the abuser must be motivated to sexually abuse, and must be capable of overcoming internal inhibitors, external inhibitors, and the resistance of the child (see Table 2.2). Understanding these preconditions requires examining several underlying components of each.

Precondition One: Motivation to Sexually Abuse Sensual arousal must occur if the perpetrator is to seek out and act upon a child victim. Any number of confounding elements may contribute to the final development of a perpetrator's mindset. Finkelhor (1984) noted that perhaps pedophilic behavior is possible because of early childhood conditioning, internalized reenactment of modeled behaviors, misattribution of sexual arousal due to biological abnormalities, or simply a need to degrade and overpower another. Although a variety of conditions and a range of observed behaviors may be present in any particular pedophile, some consistency in these behaviors is apparent across pedophilic case histories based on social histories.

Table 2.2 Preconditions Model of Sexual Abuse and Potential Actions

Condition	Motivation to Sexually Abuse	Actions
One	Emotional Congruence	Perpetrator has arrested emotional development, issues of power and control, childhood training, narcissism, sexual arousal, blockage, and marital problems
Two	Overcoming Internal Inhibitors	Perpetrator may suffer from alcohol and substance abuse, impulse discord, or psychoses and lives with family dynamics that render potentially abused children vulnerable
Three	Overcoming External Inhibitors	External inhibitors for perpetrator include ineffective or absent mothers, a child who sleeps alone, and a fear of being alone
Four	Overcoming Child's Resistance	Perpetrator will seek and coerce children who are emotionally insecure, deprived, and powerless

Adapted with the permission of The Free Press, a Division of Simon & Schuster, Inc. From *Child Sexual Abuse: New Theory and Research* by David Finkelhor. Copyright © 1984 by David Finkelhor.

Precondition Two: Overcoming Internal Inhibitors Overcoming internal inhibitors refers to the pedophile's ability to set aside a previously internalized ability to restrict undesirable behaviors or impulses. Substance abuse, especially alcohol, has been noted as a preexisting condition in many reported incidents. Another preexisting condition is a mental condition that is induced either externally with substances or internally (e.g., senility or psychosis).

Precondition Three: Overcoming External Inhibitors External inhibitors are those imposed upon the pedophile from environmental sources such as a lack of potential victims. Opportunity to be alone with a child, access to private facilities, or simple inattentive supervision from others is enough to provide the pedophile with an opportunity to abuse. Disinhibition allows the pedophile to unleash advances toward the child and, based on Finkelhor's 1984 model, is a necessary condition for the abuse to take place.

Precondition Four: Overcoming Child's Resistance Although children are often the object of a pedophile's sexual arousal, to act upon that arousal requires opportunity and the child's vulnerable sense of trust toward the adult. A potential abuser is said to be able to pick out victims based on their approachability, capacity to keep a secret, and inability to resist, which occurs even within familial incest cases. One sibling might be singled out over another sibling because of the abuser's sense of emotional congruence with that child. Early researchers (Broadhurst, 1986; Burton, 1968; DeFrancis, 1969; Vevier & Tharinger, 1986), noted that anything that might render the child emotionally insecure, needy, or unsupported could work in favor of the pedophile.

In accordance with the four-factor model, all four preconditions must be fulfilled for the abuse to occur. Finkelhor suggested that this broad-based model serve as a basis for understanding all types of sexual abuse toward children, be it intrafamilial or extrafamilial sexual abuse. A subsystem of the four-factor model that applies the principles of the preconditions model is the family systems model, a model that focuses on father-daughter incest.

Family Systems Model

Within the family systems model proposed by Finkelhor (1984), the four preconditions focus more specifically on family dynamics than on generalized behaviors relating to sex abuse. If sufficient conditions arise in a given household, then sexual abuse may occur. However, this model is a theoretical conception of how abuse may take place in the home; it is not based on empirical data per se, but rather on an accumulation of findings and perceptions from Finkelhor's early work. The following descriptions show how this model would work in a father-daughter incest situation.

Precondition One The father is attracted toward his daughter who is an easy target because she grants him unconditional admiration and is easily manipulated by his commands. Subsequently, he manipulates his daughter to fulfill his sexual and emotional needs.

Precondition Two The father applies a moralistic rationalization that his incestual advances toward his daughter are better than participating in an extramarital affair. Thus, the perpetrator reduces internal inhibitors (Finkelhor, 1984). Cultural or religious influences that accept or even promote intrafamily relations further perpetuate this way of thinking.

Precondition Three External inhibitors are easily negated when the mother is an ineffective parent, the father has instigated competitive relations between the mother and daughter, or the mother is physically removed from the family.

Precondition Four Finally, the daughter's resistance is easily overcome because of her inherent trust in the father figure and her need for attention, affection, and favored status (Finkelhor, 1984). According to Finkelhor's theoretical presentations, motivation to abuse must exist, internal inhibitions need to be reduced, and only when external inhibitors are overcome can the abusive act occur, and then only if the child's resistance is overcome.

The process is represented as a linear flow of events, which may or may not accurately represent the process involved in intrafamily sexual abuse. For instance, although an overt desire to sexually abuse a child may not be foremost in an adult's mind, continued exposure to that child or continued opportunity to be alone with that child may encourage inappropriate actions toward that child over time; yet others who are erotically attracted to children may be capable of enough self-control to divert such advances.

Perhaps one of the most prominent means of assessing pedophilic tendencies is the use of the penile plethysmography (Miner, West, & Day, 1995), a laboratory device used to measure a penile circumference following sexual stimuli in the form of pictures of children. As the penis increases in circumference during erection, a computer records the increased circumference of the penis. This method of evaluation is used on convicted child abusers who (a) are required to take this evaluation by the courts, (b) deny the abusive offense but then are confronted with the results, (c) require an assessment of risk of recidivism, and (d) require monitoring of treatment effectiveness. However, controversy exists on mandating the use of penile plethysmography for individuals accused but not convicted of abuse and for screening job applicants when the job involves work with children (Ney, 1995).

Transgenerational Theories

Researchers note that the abuse of small children often occurs across several generations of the same family. Reasons for this are not fully understood; however, several theories with similar or common themes have surfaced. Certainly, it may be suggested that family dynamics are askew and that individual boundaries are frequently blurred, more so than in nonabusing families. Identification of the causal factors that increase someone's propensity to abuse a younger family member is essential in order to develop adequate treatment programs. Because the type of abuse, the motivation to abuse, and the opportunity to abuse vary significantly across pedophiles, an overall consensual set of factors might not apply to all cases at hand, resulting in the need to assess each case of sexual abuse on an individual basis.

Cyclical Patterns   Ney and Peters (1995) developed a theory addressing intergenerational sexual abuse, wherein they developed a triangular model depicting the interrelations between a perpetrator, an observer, and a victim of abuse. Transgenerational abuse, as defined by Ney and Peters, refers to the cyclical abuse behaviors that occur in families across generations, thereby perpetuating the victimization of all children born into the family. Several overriding behavior patterns were identified in family members as they progressed into adulthood and appeared to reenact roles observed earlier in other adults. The researchers described the three roles played by family members as (a) observer, usually an ineffective family member, (b) victim, and (c) perpetrator.

During first-generation abuse, the adults abuse the children, and the children become preconditioned to sexual abuse. As adults, these children then go on to abuse their own children; thus the victims now become the perpetrators. Underlying the victim role is a passiveness that accepts the behavior as normal, assimilation of the behavior into learned schemas, and finally accommodation of the abusive conditions. In many instances, this syndrome may be viewed as a form of brainwashing, in that the victims are required to accommodate for survival purposes. Accommodation tactics that interplay in intrafamilial abuse are comparative to those enacted within cult abuse, wherein the parents passively observe their children experiencing abuse but, rather than intervening, accommodate the situation by reacting complacently.

McIntrye's Family Systems Model

Early Tendency to Assign Blame Early family systems models such as that of McIntrye (1981) placed the blame of faulty family dynamics on the mother rather than on the perpetrator. McIntrye's own theoretical propositions suggested that the motivation to sexually abuse is always driven by unmet sexual needs. The more complex motivational factors, such as power or control, were not necessarily examined within the family systems model. Apparently, the psychological dynamics that interplay in a child's vulnerability to a trusted parent were not considered to be foremost in understanding the problem. If one applies Groth, Hobson, and Gary's (1982) concept of power as the motivating force in abusing children, then the abuse would take place regardless of the sexual eroticism of the perpetrator. Also, as a simplified theory of abuse, the family systems models do not consider that not all forms of sexual abuse are completed acts of sex; rather, some forms consist of molestation or exploitative acts that allow the perpetrator to dominate the child.

SUMMARY

Chapter 2 provided an overview of theories pertaining to the pedophile's propensity to commit child sexual abuse. Theorists have described perpetrator behavior as being based on either mediated or nonmediated motivators. Nonmediated behaviors suggest adults who engage in an abusive act with a minor individual on a one-time basis, such as a baby-sitter who claims he or she could not resist a young child. Higher-risk factors are associated with premeditated acts of CSA, and perpetrators who premeditate about the act will more aggressively search out victims to satisfy their need. In extreme cases, this type of abuse is much more dangerous to the child, who may be assaulted or kidnapped for purposes of sexual exploitation.

Treatment approaches have received mixed reviews from concerned professionals. Rates of recidivism are high for sex offenders, particularly for offenders who are incarcerated for their crimes (Greenfield, 1996). Perhaps more frightening than the overall sexual abuse incident rates is that family members are the highest contributors to CSA, as reports indicate that 80–90% of all sexual abuse cases involve incestual abuse (Finkelhor, 1984; Greenfield, 1996).

Regardless of the procedure used to overcome a child's resistance to sexual exploitation, seduction, or aggression, the end result is the same. The child is manipulated into inappropriate interactions with an adult. Because these adults are older and expected to be responsible, they are guilty of purposely violating children and leaving them with psychological scars that will last a lifetime.

Dedicated pedophiles are highly secretive and often mask their criminal behavior with a cloak of normalcy. They adopt a righteous façade within the social community by attending church on a regular basis, presenting an overly friendly persona, or simply hiding behind a prominent social position. In many cases, one pedophile can assault hundreds of children in a lifetime if never detected.

Whether social service workers involved in CSA cases are working with the victims or the perpetrators, they must acquire a broad base of knowledge to enhance the efficacy of their treatment planning. Although the optimal goals are to protect children from abusive treatment and resolve any adverse impact of such treatment, the quality of services and therapeutic interventions can be improved greatly when the far-ranging complexities of the issues are understood. Therefore, this chapter provided a brief introduction to and historical overview of theoretical perspectives on pedophilia. Because new and innovative treatment programs continually arise, any caseworker involved in CSA issues must remain current in regard to trends, programs, and interventions that may benefit potential clients. Issues of risk assessment through actuarial tables (Hanson & Bussiere, 1998; Quinsey, Rice, & Harris, 1995), and cognitive-behavioral therapies are currently receiving much attention amongst professionals (Wright & Schneider, 1999). Similarly, judicial statutes and evidentiary proceedings are subject to change on a regular basis, so social service workers should also maintain an affiliation with professional organizations that focus directly on perpetrator treatment programs, such as the Center for Sex Offender Management and the Association for the Treatment of Sexual Abusers.

DISCUSSION QUESTIONS

1. How might exploitation by pornographers impact a child's psychological development? Explain your answer.

2. Researchers note that a parent or primary caretaker precipitates over 90% of sexual abuse cases. How might children's emotional reactions be different if a parent versus a stranger exposes them to abuse? What impact would that have on treatment?

3. Controversy exists between the need to report child abuse and the reluctance to interfere in familial concerns. Discuss the factors involved on both sides of the issue.

4. Based on the views of accommodation theorists, how do victims react following abusive incidents? Use additional resources to construct your response.

5. The psychiatric symptoms of pedophilia set out in the *DSM-IV-TR*™ do not address the topic of child pornography. How would you address the

classification of an individual who participates in pornographic activities that exploit children?

6. Theories concerning the etiology of pedophilia are vague. Identify and discuss factors that make this etiology so complex and difficult to understand.

7. If a child experiences sexual abuse and later, as an adolescent, sexually assaults a younger child, what treatment plans should be considered, if any? What prosecutory steps should be implemented, if any? Research your local statutes or community agencies and assimilate the information you gather into your answer.

8. Given the high incident rates for Internet solicitation of children and adolescents, what recommendations would you make to thwart predators' future attempts to entrap children in this manner? How can communities assist authorities with the tracking and monitoring of potentially harmful Web sites through which perpetrators may kidnap, assault, or solicit children for illegal activities?

3

Documentation, Research, and Relevant Issues

LEARNING OBJECTIVES

Chapter 3 will address the following learning objectives:

1. An overview of early documentation of sexual abuse reports

2. A discussion on initial legislative advances dealing with child sexual abuse issues

3. A discussion of issues relevant to methods of data collection

4. A discussion of issues relevant to mandated documentation of child sexual abuse

5. A review of national crime report databases and their accessibility

6. A discussion of evaluation and test issues related to child sexual abuse

INTRODUCTION

Chapter 3 provides a review of research-based databases that are essential resources for any professional concerned with the problem of child sex abuse (CSA). This chapter will review national databases such as the National Clearinghouse on Child Abuse and Neglect Information (NCCANI) that provide statistics, legislative mandates, and professional regulations concerning child abuse. Associations that participate in the aggregation of national, state, and county statistics will be discussed, as well as on-line Web site resources. Because of the criminal nature of CSA, this chapter reviews national crime databases, such as the National Crime Survey (NCS) and Victim Crime Statistics (VCS), that deal with the criminal prosecution of perpetrators and victim-based statistics. The data collection techniques and the classification of crimes can affect the facts and figures cited in each database and the conclusions drawn from them. Therefore, investigative studies related to child sexual abuse issues should be pursued with an understanding of the criteria and methods used to construct the databases under review.

EARLY DOCUMENTATION OF ABUSE

Abuse of children was addressed as early as 900 A.D. in a publication entitled *Practica Peurorum,* written by a Persian pediatrician. The pediatrician, in discussing *hernia of children,* noted that such injuries might have been intentionally inflicted. A leading Greek medical doctor wrote a publication called *Gynecological Theses,* which contained an entire section on the injury of infants. Additional documents by medical professionals and devoted caregivers appeared occasionally throughout the 16th and 17th centuries (as noted in Mason, 1994).

Similar instances of child abuse were recorded during the 18th and 19th centuries in Europe. In 1860, Ambrois Tardieu, a French professor of legal medicine, published a paper concerning the ill treatment of children by caretakers. His recommendations included removing the children from harmful environments. In 1895, the London-based Society for the Prevention of Cruelty to Children summarized many of the ways London children were battered or abused. Evidence of battering by means of boots, crockery, pans, shovels, straps, ropes, thongs, pokers, ice, and boiling water were documented by medical doctors. Symptomatic behaviors that were noted included vermin-infested living conditions; shivering; being ragged and naked; being pale, puny, limp, feeble, faint, dizzy, and famished; and dying from malnutrition or other contracted diseases. Children were enslaved into employment including peddling and demonstrating monstrosities to the public at traveling shows or circuses, they were often assaulted by drunks or vagrants, and little girls were subjected to sexual abuse (Helfer, Kempe, & Krugman, 1997).

In 1835, a grandmother published a book entitled *Grandmother's Advice to Young Mothers* that was intended to provide child care tips for new mothers. In this book, the author acknowledged the following: "Blows on the head from harsh instruction have been suspected to produce water on the brain, and the mode in which some people gratify their anger toward children by shaking them violently might also lead to serious consequences" (Anonymous, p. 5).

Range of Abuse

The types of abuse reported in early accounts ranged from observable bone fractures to extreme neglect, desertions, cruel exposure, and even death. Concern was expressed regarding issues of suffocation, exposure to extreme temperatures and harsh environmental elements (e.g., on farms), improper infant feedings, and misdiagnosis of deaths in babies. Societal concerns were brazenly exposed in a 1984 publication edited by Reverend Benjamin Waugh, entitled *The Children's Guardian* (Waugh, 1984). Waugh provided advice to the courts and discussed the clinging baby assessment, claiming that if a child clung to his or her mother, that constituted proof that the mother treated that child with love and nurturance. As noted in previous chapters, however, incidents of harsh treatment and abuse of children by their parents were common in the 17th through the 19th centuries, and usually involved no retribution or sanctioning from the courts.

Objective Evidence

Early documentation of abuse emphasized objective symptoms of physical abuse and contained few or no references to sexual abuse or sexual exploitation. From the beginning, it was recommended that objective facts be presented; therefore, collateral information consisted of documented broken bones, physical bruises, the child's emotional response, and extensive interviews with involved guardians or caretakers. Because mothers had few rights in the early 1700s and 1800s, they seldom voiced their testimonies against husbands who abused their children, which enforced the secretive nature of abuse in general, and particularly of sexual abuse of children in the home.

For the most part, the impetus to remove children from the home was reserved for the most extreme and obvious cases (Beales, 1985; Bremner, 1970). Interference with family matters was an area in which many professionals feared to tread, as both religious and governmental bodies of society viewed the family as a unit sanctioned in privacy. Many cultures adhere to this belief today, thus magnifying the fact that abuse investigators often meet with resistance and denial when conducting family investigations.

MANDATED REPORTING: A HISTORICAL VIEW

Although incidents of arrest for child abuse or neglect, including sexual abuse, are documented in early American life throughout the 1600–1800s (Beales, 1985; Hefler, Kempe & Krugman, 1997; Noblitt & Perskin, 2000), child abuse reporting appeared publicly in only the most obvious cases, for example, where a child had overt bruises or died from the abuse. When abuse, even in such drastic cases, was spoken of publicly, public reactions ranged from disbelief to viewing the children's injuries as a secondary effect of punishment for their misbehavior. Clashes occurred between those concerned about abuse and governmental regulations that upheld rights of family privacy, as well as religious sanctions that dictated that children must honor their fathers and mothers. Any attempt to develop a clear procedure for reporting and processing claims of abuse was a source of much dissension across political and religious entities in early America.

Reluctance to Invade Family Privacy

Child abuse is, as it was in the past, an area of child protective needs in which professionals hesitate to become involved (Beales, 1985; Kempe & Kempe, 1984; Russell & Bolen, 2000; Tharinger, Russian, & Robinson, 1989). The sanctity of privacy in regard to family life and the home, which dates back to early Roman patriarchal societies, remains a revered component of a citizen's right to privacy under the Constitution of the United States. However, the line between dutiful parental discipline and harmful abusive acts inflicted on children by parents is a gray area, one that often results in extensive court litigation when abuse charges are levied against family members. Consequently, dire consequences may ensue for such a family; a report of abuse can result in financial hardship, loss of relationships with loved ones, and intense emotional trauma for all involved. Because of these possibilities, much of society, prior to the 1900s, shunned pervasive questioning of family members and aggressive investigative techniques to identify suspected abuse. It was not until the 20th century that child sexual abuse, *the silent enemy,* was more aggressively confronted by concerned citizens who initiated legislative and administrative reform.

Legislative Enforcement

An article entitled *The Battered Child Syndrome* (Kempe, Silverman, Steele, Droegemueller, & Silver, 1962) helped to fuel governmental attention on the issue of child abuse during the second half of the 20th century. This infamous article described physical and emotional symptoms and disorders that are often found in abused children. Although doctors wrote about abuse-related injuries in children throughout history, Kempe et al.'s article appeared at a time of new social awareness in society. Social service agencies and citizens alike banned together to draft legislative statutes that provided funding for new and innovative programs to address the issue of child abuse and neglect.

Confusion on How to Proceed

Prior to the 1960s, little, if any, documented research existed on the subject of identifying effective prevention and intervention programs for children with psychological implications of abuse. Child-based research was relatively difficult to produce for numerous reasons. First, the privacy issue presented a dilemma for professionals who investigated interfamilial practices during the first half of the 20th century. Second, complex dynamics, such as an infant's or child's inability to verbalize details about the abuse, constrained investigations of suspected child abuse. Third, definitions of abuse, reporting procedures, and criminal codes for sexually abusive behaviors varied significantly across states, thereby undermining efforts to collect aggregate reports of child abuse offenses.

Finally, courtroom dynamics concerned judicial members, as courts were inexperienced in dealing with the child witness. Experts were concerned about the traumatizing effects of a child testifying about sexually explicit materials. Many parents feared the prospect of retraumatizing their children in court and wanted to safeguard them from negative publicity; therefore, they often refused to file charges against perpetrators. Court systems usually required hard evidence that could be obtained only with invasive physical examinations that revictimized the children during the prosecution process. As documented in Kempe et al.'s (1985) article, however, emotional trauma resulting from abuse also needed to be considered by evaluators in identifying child abuse:

> The syndrome [battered child syndrome] should be considered in any child exhibiting evidence of fracture of any bone, subdural hematoma, failure to thrive, soft tissue swelling or skin bruising, in any child who dies suddenly, or where the degree and type of injury is at variance with the history given the occurrence of the trauma. Psychiatric factors are probably of prime importance in the pathogenesis of the disorder, but knowledge of these factors is limited. (p. 1)

LEGISLATIVE ADVANCES

During the years from 1600 through 1900, a unified approach on how to handle mistreatment of children was not yet organized at the national level. During the early 1900s, however, there was an increase in the incidents of child abuse, in emerging psychological theories of development, and in social awareness that children have special needs and are not just "smaller versions of adults." Following the New Deal of the 1930s, federal and state agencies were created at a rapid rate. Legislatures began to take on new social causes, in part to reinforce the welfare of the American society as a whole.

It was at this time that a new federal department was formed—the Department of Health, Education, and Welfare: Office of Human Development/Office of Child Development (OCD). Under the auspices of the OCD, and funded by means of CAPTA (Pub. L. 93-247), the National Center on Child Abuse and Neglect was charged with the mission of developing programs related to the prevention, identification, and treatment of child abuse and neglect (U.S. Department of Health, Education, and Welfare, 1975).

National Data Gathering

Once federal funding became available through the enactment of the Child Abuse Protection and Treatment Act (CAPTA) in 1974 (Pub. L. No. 93-247), efforts were made to establish a national registry for the reporting of child abuse. Various sources of data collection were proposed: (a) a research clearinghouse, (b) a registry to track reportedly abusing parents, and (c) a combination of elements necessary for research and tracking. Although initiatives sought to develop an innovative record-keeping plan, carrying out the plan was difficult because of inconsistencies in the record keeping of social service agencies, problems with processing information from multiple sources providing child abuse referrals, and the increasing numbers of unreported cases.

Data Input During early attempts at data collection, only minimal information pertaining to each case (e.g., name, address, and age of child; name of primary caretaker; and nature and extent of injury) was collected. Some state registries cited the number of siblings involved, while others did not. Physicians who suspected child abuse were expected to access the central registry to ascertain if previous incidents were reported; therefore, the registration of nonadjudicated cases was required. This practice raised the question of how to safeguard against false accusations of abuse, for example, by perhaps requiring facts of credible evidence prior to including a perpetrator's or alleged perpetrator's name in the national registry.

Central Registry Many people remained concerned about establishing a central registry containing information that infringed on the privacy rights of families. Although the concern for protecting innocent children outweighed the societal perception of infringement of privacy rights, the unauthorized disclosure of information in the register still posed a concern to policymakers who were fully aware that erroneously accusing an innocent individual of committing the heinous crime of child sexual abuse could have devastating effects in the lives of that individual and his or her family members.

At the beginning of the 21st century, all states are required to report abuse incidents to the federal registry. Most state law enforcement agencies also post names of known sex offenders on a local Internet Web site. By signing onto the Web site and typing in a zip code, name, or town, anyone can search for information about the location in neighborhoods of sex offenders. A comprehensive list of links to national and state law enforcement agency Web sites is available at http://hrlef.exis.net/leresearch.htm.

Developed Language for Reporting In 1963, the Children's Bureau of the U.S. Department of Health, Education, and Welfare (HEW) developed a model for nationwide reporting of child abuse. The principles and suggested language used in this model were established to assist professionals who are in the position of reporting such abuse. Many modifications of this model were made over the years to assist in training child protection services workers. Perhaps the most comprehensive document now available is the manual from NCCANI entitled *Supervising Child Protective Services Caseworkers* (Morton & Salus, 1994), the development of which was funded by the U.S. Department of Health and Human Services (DHHS). The advancements in reporting procedures, language, and descriptors over time culminated in a reauthorization of CAPTA in 1996 (Pub. L. No. 104-235). Punishment for failure to report may range from no punishment to monetary fines or even imprisonment. Individual states have discretion on what punitive stand, if any, will be taken when a mandated reporter fails to report.

Protective Custody Requirements

Investigation of abuse requires the maintenance of records of evidence, including records from the medical examination of the child (such as X rays), color photographs of the injury, a verbatim notation of the child's statements, and any other supporting documents or statements made in explanation of the injuries. In cases where the child may be in danger of further abuse, he or she must be placed in protective custody. The General Assembly of Georgia enacted a protective custody bill after the January 1998 death of a 5-year-old child from extensive child abuse. Although eight abuse reports had been submitted to the protective services in Fulton County, the child was allowed to remain with his grandmother, aunt, and the aunt's boyfriend, who were later charged with his death. The Terrell Peterson Bill, named after the child who died, gives doctors the right to hold a child for 24 hours, for assessment and treatment, when abuse is suspected. Prior to the passage of this bill, only police officers could make a mandatory hold on a child. Iowa and Illinois currently have similar laws.

ISSUES SURROUNDING DOCUMENTATION

A collaborative effort is required to gather evidence for any criminal case to form an objective evaluation of alleged claims. Thorough evidence collection techniques are imperative, partly because of the young ages of the victims in child sexual abuse cases. In-depth, multidata sources include videotaped interviews, observations, play-therapy, inter-rater assessments, collaborative interviews, journaling, self-report measures, supervised visitations, and results of numerous other counseling and assessment techniques that can lead to a comprehensive and thorough investigation of the suspected abuse (Hewitt, 1999; Kuehnle, 1996). Specific regulations and methods for collecting assessment data should be strictly followed. Actual evidence has often been discounted in criminal trials because of evaluator contamination or bias. The court may order the child to be returned to the perpetrator for lack of conviction when errors are made in this essential component of evaluation for sexual abuse. Mental health professionals who may be involved in CSA legal proceedings must ally with professional organizations and acquire forensic training.

Professional Reporting Procedures

As mandated reporters, many child care workers, teachers, and counselors are placed at odds with legal mandates. Although they are under legal mandate to report, they have not always been sufficiently trained to deal with such sensitive matters in forensic settings. While all professionals are accountable for learning legal regulations pertinent to their profession, superficial familiarity with the law does not prepare professionals for involvement in child sexual abuse cases; extended training is essential.

The NRCCSA (1996) reported that nearly half of all abused or neglected children are 6 years of age or younger, indicating that most likely children are enrolled in a school setting at the time abuse is revealed or disclosed. Consequently, suspected child abuse is most often reported via the school counselor, school nurse, or other trusted staff member. In light of this fact, it would behoove school systems to provide the staff with regularly scheduled training sessions and standardized policy manuals on how to proceed when a student discloses abuse. The National Committee to Prevent Child Abuse (1995) has prepared a training program for educators to assist them with developing prevention, intervention, and child abuse reporting programs. Others have evaluated parent education and support programs for families that are at risk of child abuse (Broadhurst, 1986; Soukup, Wickner, & Corbett, 1984; Whipple & Wilson, 1996).

Complex Ramifications Abuse assessments are complex, and final decisions hold grave ramifications for all parties involved. Families may be disrupted, siblings separated, children placed in foster homes, and excessive financial strains or outright losses may ensue. Berlinger and Wheeler (1987) note that "[d]etermining whether a child has been sexually abused is a matter of great importance. If the judgment is wrong a child's physical and mental health may be permanently jeopardized, additional children needlessly abused and their families and communities traumatized" (p. 418).

The ramifications of abuse reports, however, should not deter a professional from making a mandated report if it is deemed warranted. A therapist who has a solid understanding of the potential consequences of such a report for the abusee may better prepare the client, prior to making the report, for what is likely to happen once the report is made. Although by law a report must be made if the child is at risk of further harm or abuse from the perpetrator, or if another child is at risk of harm or abuse, age-appropriate recommendations can be made to help the child or adolescent cope with the after-effects of the report. A multidisciplinary-teams approach can be used to corroborate findings and to support the child emotionally through the reporting process and any resulting litigation (Finkelman, 1995a).

Unique Experiences Further complications in child abuse assessment result from the fact that each child experiences sexual abuse in a unique way. Sexual abuse is a highly subjective experience, uniquely internalized by each victim. This makes evidence gathering more difficult, particularly in light of the emotional impact the process can have on the child. Many parents are reluctant to permit their children to come forward in court proceedings, and children require different levels of intervention following the identification of abuse.

A child's recovery is affected by his or her personality attributes, the circumstances surrounding the abuse, and whether supportive environments are available following disclosure. Healing periods can range across a lifetime, as evidenced by the words of a 57-year-old woman who was molested by her father when she was 10–14 years old: "But why couldn't my father just love me . . . like all other fathers?" More than 40 years after the abuse occurred, this woman was still plagued by lost nurturance from her father. Other clients, however, readily separate themselves from the negative feelings prompted by the abuse. Jane, a married woman who was first dealing with her abuse at the age of 35, stated: "I don't care what happens to my parents at this stage of the game. I am doing just fine without them." And in fact, she was. Her career and personal life were harmonious, and Jane had made peace with life's circumstances following disclosure.

Even though researchers have noted commonalties among abusees—such as underlying insecurities, reduced self-confidence and self-esteem, and feelings of shame, guilt, and unworthiness (Classon & Yalom, 1995; Davies, 1995; Harris & Landis, 1997; Russell & Bollen, 2000), not all individuals experience the same effects. Perhaps it is best to look at the syndrome of CSA as a continuum of symptoms that range widely in severity, intensity, and duration across all abusees. Attempting to fit all abusees into finite behavior patterns not only represents a disservice to individuals, but also risks the erroneous diagnosis of stereotypical behaviors in anyone who has experienced abuse. Rather than making global inferences about all abusees, it is essential that each case be assessed at a finer point of discrimination, identifying the attributes that are unique to each client, including the circumstances surrounding the abusive experience. This is particularly imperative when a case ends up in litigation, as the fine points of a discriminatory diagnosis can lead to grave consequences in the final case dispensation.

Evidentiary Interview Procedures

Traditionally, every area of sexual behavior has been viewed as a private matter. This belief in privacy multiplies tenfold when familial incest issues are addressed (Gelles, 1978; Lasch, 1977). Investigations of family relations, particularly those involving sexual misconduct and domestic violence or spousal abuse, are extremely sensitive. The mandated investigatory procedures and evidence collection methods must be followed accurately because of the gravity of the secondary effects on the family and victim (Mason, 1992; Melton, Petrila, Poythress, & Slobogin, 1997; Oberlander, 1995; Regehr & Glancy, 1997), and state statutes must be adhered to.

Interview Questions The first line of questioning with a child who discloses sexual abuse is relevant not only to the child's recovery, but also in a court of law. Failure to follow specific guidelines for interviewing and maintaining data as evidence can seriously impair the final adjudication of a case. Appropriate interviewing procedures include the use of nonleading questions, nondirective interviewing, and the child's own language. Those who are responsible for reporting suspected child abuse must have detailed information about the judicial requirements for conducting interviews that will be allowed into court testimony (Faller, 1998; Kuehnle, 1996; Sattler, 1998). Training programs that specialize in sexual abuse issues and forensic applications are available through various professional organizations and through federally sponsored programs such as the National Resource Center on Child Sexual Abuse (1994) in Huntington, Alabama.

Association Guidelines All professional organizations, such as the American Psychological Association (APA), the American Counselor's Association (ACA), and the National Association of School Psychologists (NASP), set forth guidelines for mandated reporting of child sexual abuse. These guidelines should be referred to whenever any doubt about the proper procedure for reporting exists. When a disclosure of abuse is made within a school system, the school district's policy on dealing with emergencies and its abuse reporting practices should be followed. The final responsibility for reporting child abuse rests with the first professional to witness or suspect it. Mandatory reporters should follow their state and professional guidelines for reporting abuse and should send written follow-up reports if required at the state level.

Minimal Physical Evidence Difficulties occur in collecting data based on physical evidence of abuse. Although medical examinations are required in cases where children have been raped or sexually assaulted, physical scars are found in only 2% of abuse victims. Most examinations call for advanced methods such as colposcopy, radiographic imaging, and sonographic imaging (Jenny, Taylor, & Cooper, 1996). Regardless of the technique, however, sexual abuse is usually not revealed upon physical examination (Giardino, Finkel, Giardino, Seidl, & Ludwig, 1992). Lengthy time lapses between the time of abuse and visits to the doctor also interfere with physical evidence collection (Finkel, 1988). In addition, the medical examination itself may create further trauma for the abused child (Steward, Schmitz, Steward, Joye, & Reinhart, 1995).

Child Maltreatment Log Reporting practices vary across local municipalities and social service agencies within each state. Furthermore, researchers may operationally define terms used in their studies differently, thus adding further confusion if multiple studies are aggregated. In an effort to offset these problems, the DHHS allocated funds to conduct empirical studies on a common interview tool called the Child Maltreatment Log, an instrument developed by a research subcommittee of the Interagency Work Group on Child Abuse and Neglect to standardize reporting methods. Data on core variables are collected at the agency level for aggregation into a national database that future researchers will analyze. In the meantime, however, when compiling reviews of child abuse, crime, or other related variables, literature reviewers must be cognizant of the context in which the variables were identified, collected, and interpreted (Warner & Hansen, 1994).

Perpetrator Reports The Victim Crime Reports (VCR) and the National Crime Statistics (NCS) are the most frequently used databases for gathering statistics or incident rates about abuse-related crimes. Both databases offer aggregated frequency counts of major crimes and subsets of crimes, with similar data collection inconsistencies occurring across crime-reporting agencies. Consequently, individual data are often masked within the summary tables, dependent upon the initial data reporting methods implemented by the source agency (Callie, 2000). Similarly, the index of crime rates and abusive acts may differ from that found in specific state or county databases. Unless terms of abuse and all other variables related to the abuse (i.e., age, type of abuse, perpetrator demographics, criminal charges) are standardized and defined, misrepresentation of data is possible. Perhaps most discouraging is that some researchers note the incident rate has risen to epidemic proportions (Russell & Bolen, 2000), yet it may still be misdocumented.

RESEARCH TOOLS AND RESOURCES

Conducting a thorough investigation of any research problem always involves accessing numerous databases relevant to the topic. To study any aspect of child abuse, be it physical, emotional, or sexual, the researcher must access the most current legislative mandates that govern all progressive movement of the problem across the United States. This section of text focuses on available databases, both government-sponsored sites related to legislation as well as the national clearinghouse for information specifically on child abuse. The ardent researcher can glean comprehensive information from these connections in an efficient manner as noted below.

Legislative Advances On-Line

In the new millennium, legislative advances can be accessed via Internet searches and online databases. Government agencies that provide the most current account of federal mandates are easily accessed via a Gopher site (gopher://gopher.house.gov) or via the Internet (www.house.gov). The Library of Congress provides references to government databases that are essential for those who wish to do a thorough review of current literature on any topic (www.lcweb.loc.gov). Government reports can also be accessed at www.fedworld.gov/. At this site, thousands of files are available for file transfer. The House of Representatives (www.house.gov) and the Senate (www.senate.gov) are also accessible through the Internet and Gopher services: gopher://gopher.house.gov and gopher://gopher.senate.gov.

Organizational Databases

Several highly relevant databases are available to current researcher in child abuse and neglect as well as issues of sexual abuse. First, CAPTA (1996; 42 U.S.C. sec. 5104) legislation provided for the establishment of a national clearinghouse, NCCANI, to aggregate data specific to child abuse and related child protection issues. The Buros Mental Measurements Institute provides publications and data on test instruments for evaluations of any kind, not just those exclusively related to abuse. Buros also provides critiques of each test instrument that inform potential consumers of test-specific qualities and allow the reader to judge its appropriateness for use with specific individuals or populations. A third set of databases offers crime-related statistics; these include the Uniform Crime Statistics (UCS) and the National Crime Statistics (NCS), victim-based systems, the Offender-Based Transaction Statistics (OBTS), and the Prosecutor Management Systems (PROMIS). Each of these databases contains specific strengths and weaknesses and is discussed in more detail in the following text.

The National Clearinghouse on Child Abuse and Neglect Information (NCCANI) The National Clearinghouse on Child Abuse and Neglect Information (NCCANI) publishes a computerized database on research articles related to child abuse issues; the database is available in CD-ROM form free of charge (NCCANI, 1998). NCCANI can be reached on-line using the organizational Web site (www.calib.com.nccanch/pubs). Extensive resources are available, including federal and state legislative mandates, instructional and curriculum materials, and current statistics concerning child abuse.

Buros Mental Measurements Buros Mental Measurements Institute is another national database. It can be accessed on-line at www.buros.com. On the Web page, a menu series contains the options "Tests in Print," "ERIC Test Locator," "Test Reviews," and numerous other choices. If a particular test is accessed, a description of test qualities is provided along with publisher information. Reviews of test instruments can also be accessed to provide further insight into the professional critique of test instruments, as well as details related to each test itself, including the purpose of the instrument, reading levels, age appropriateness, and other test artifacts relevant to the test user. This Web site offers a search menu that is user-friendly for even a novice researcher.

Crime Report Data Sources

Crime reports are aggregated regularly in all states across the United States. This section will address the numerous crime statistic publications and the problems or concerns with using data contained in each one.

Although states may vary in their definitions of crime, categories of crime, and punitive sanctions for each type of crime, most states adhere to a standardized reporting format. In addition to the hard copy or printed format books that are described in this section, most states have a crime reporting Web site for the state. For instance, in Florida, current information can be found on child predators as well as other criminals at www.fdle.state.fl.us/index.html. Concerned citizens can also find a search page that will allow them to input their zip code and obtain a posting of all registered offenders in their immediate geographical location. A Web site for a specific state can be found by simply searching for *state crime reports,* but replacing the word *state* with the specific name of the state for which information is sought.

Uniform Crime Reports (UCR) Data sources pertaining to crimes are available at national, state, and local levels of crime record-keeping offices. The Uniform Crime Reports (UCR), started in 1929, are aggregate accounts of crimes conducted across the United States. These reports, which are published annually, are based on monthly police reports filed with the Federal Bureau of Investigation (FBI). Initially, the participation of police departments was voluntary, but now it is mandatory. Data are categorized by type of offense, age of offender, gender, race, city, size, and final clearance of crimes (Uniform Crime Statistics, 1998). Data presented in the UCR are based on nonstandardized reports from state and local police precincts; therefore, irregularities appear in the categories reported, the methods of record keeping, and victims' willingness to report. These irregularities can result in inaccurate crime rate summaries.

Index crimes, which are more serious crimes and occur more frequently than nonvictim crimes or misdemeanors (e.g., burglary, motor vehicle offenses, etc.), include anticipated or completed murder and negligent manslaughter, forcible rape, robbery, aggravated assault, burglary, larceny theft, and motor vehicle theft. Researchers using the indices, however, must interpret them cautiously, with knowledge of the source and the maintenance of respective data sources. When victims fail to report crimes or to follow through with the arrest of the perpetrator, the crimes are not reported in the UCR. Additionally, studies have been conducted to compare data collected across data sources such as the UCR and the National Crime Statistics (NCS) reporting systems (Callie, 2000), and the reports of index offenses were found to differ significantly.

National Crime Survey (NCS) The National Crime Survey (NCS) is a police-based data source that is subject to some of the same criticisms as the UCR because of the variations in crime processing methods, such as police officers' decisions to arrest citizens, methods of filing complaints, increased tolerance of certain crimes, and legal code changes that impact reported statistics (Savitz, 1982, pp. 6–11). Similarly, only one crime can be reported per event, even if multiple crimes were committed. An increased number of reports have been given for crimes involving documentation for insurance groups, such as auto theft and petty larceny, as opposed to victim crimes or more serious crimes. Therefore, an arrest for domestic violence may mask a child abuse incident as a separate case. Similarly, if a homicide occurred, a second report may not be made to document an arrest for child abuse. Internet access provides additional resources through Gopher (gopher:view.ubs.ca) or the Internet (www.view.ubc.ca).

Victim-Based Data Sources Victimization surveys originated from reports of the President's Commission on Law Enforcement and Administration of Justice (Lehnen & Skogan, 1981). The U.S. Census Bureau, based on interagency agreement with the Bureau of Justice Statistics, maintains the NCS, the federal statistics program. Data, based on interviews with approximately 60,000 persons randomly selected in the United States, are compiled on a rotating panel design. Samples are divided into six rotation groups, and the groups are interviewed every 6 months or 3 years for seven interviews per household, with the initial interview used only as a base count of crime rates (U.S. Department of Justice, 1981). This process is designed to avoid duplication in the databases.

The NCS is said to be the second most frequently used source of crime statistics in the United States (Gove, Hughes, & Geerken, 1985, p. 491). It captures the crime experiences of the respondent or victim and other household members. Most researchers are concerned about the discrepancies between the UCR and the NCS with regard to incident rate and trends. One reason for the discrepancies is that NCS collects a smaller sample size than does UCR. Also, the UCR counts all crimes; the NCS counts only crimes against people aged 12 or older and against respondents' households, such as domestic violence and child abuse. Concerned researchers have described these discrepancies between the two studies in detail (Blumstein & Cohen, 1992; Menard, 1988).

Court-Based Defendant/Perpetrator Data Sources

Another source of information that is pertinent in the protection of vulnerable children is the perpetrator and court-based databases that allow a search on someone's background related to criminal activity. While states vary in the level of sophistication of their Web page search formats, many of the state Web sites are quite user-friendly. This form of data search allows a concerned party to search for prior arrests of any given individual. For example, in Hillsborough County, Florida, the following Web site can be used to search for individuals' prior arrest records: www.hcso.tampa.fl.us/pub/. Databases discussed in this section provide other information related to arrest records.

Offender-Based Transaction Statistics (OBTS) Court-based data sources, such as Offender-Based Transaction Statistics (OBTS), include personal and prior records of all people charged with one or more felony offenses. The defendant's personal and prior record is gathered, as well as the type of crime, disposition, and sentencing of the case. As with other crime statistics databases, difficulty arises in the classification and crime-rate reporting methods. For instance, as a defendant-based system, the most serious offense charged to the perpetrator is usually the one reported. Therefore, multiple offenses are not readily recorded in the OBTS. Tracking may only occur if a formal court dispensation is awarded, which may relate only to a less serious offense than that originally cited in OBTS reports, causing apparent ambiguity in initial arrest reports and dispensation. Consequently, tracking begins with formal court filing. Arrests may go unreported until court actions are rendered. If court actions reject or convict on a less serious offense than originally counted, data is distorted once more.

Prosecutor Management Systems (PROMIS) A source of defendant-based data is the Prosecutor Management System (PROMIS), which maintains data on defendants such as any prior arrest, disposition, or sentencing, including evidential factors. Records are maintained on all individuals charged with one or more felony charges. As with OBTS, if one or more charges occurred concurrently, the most serious offense committed is the crime that is recorded. Given the disparity of data collection across court systems, records of the disposition of felonies may differ significantly, depending on the geographical region of the intended crime. Hence, the classification and recording of case dispositions and final crime adjudication may differ greatly across reporting court institutions (Gove, Hughes, & Geerken, 1985).

Inter-University Consortium on Political and Social Research The Inter-University Consortium on Political and Social Research is a multidimensional data source concerning funding resources, programs in progress, historical incarceration data, and jail and inmate statistics. A compilation of prison inmates, probationees, and parolees is included in the database, as well as data concerning domestic violence, spousal abuse, and crime reduction efforts. Crime incident and prevalence rates in regard to specific crimes should be collected and documented with an understanding of the method of data collection used by the data source. Data collection methods and subgroup sampling used may or may not accurately represent specific subsets of criminal populations. Similarly, disposition of cases may be classified by ethnicity, class of crime, disposition of crime, or any other specifically directed classification system. Given the discrepancies across data sources, researchers should be circumspect in drawing inferences and conclusions based on data contained in the databases discussed here.

Self-Report Databases

Self-report surveys are frequently administered with respondents who may, or may not, have had contact with legal agencies. Surveyors ask questions regarding the respondents' participation, or lack of participation, in delinquent or criminal activities within a particular time frame, frequently one year or less. Criticisms of these studies concern issues of sample size, geographic location, and the accuracy of self-report interviews, (Borg, Gall, & Borg, 1997).

National Youth Survey (NYS) One example of a self-report study is the National Youth Survey (NYS), conducted by Elliot and Ageton (1987). The NYS self-report instrument included items about offenses comparable to those found in the UCR; researchers removed overlapping measures of delinquency by providing response options that encompassed various delinquent offenses. NYS data was drawn from a national sample of youth, parents and crime rates experienced by using five surveys administered from 1976–1984. This database provides a historical account of sexual abuse crime rates during the late 1970s and early 1980s, among other crime rates as well.

The NYS data have been used to estimate prevalence rates of delinquency and crime, as well as to examine patterns of delinquency. Elliott and Ageton

(1978) examined social class as related to delinquency, whereas Huizinga and Elliott (1984) examined relationships between self-reported involvement in delinquency, criminality, and incarceration rates.

TESTS AS RESEARCH TOOLS

Individual tests that are developed to assess or examine issues related to child care are quite diverse, so a test administrator needs to be familiar with each test instrument's properties prior to administering the test with individuals or groups. Directories of tests are available in such data sources as: ERIC, BUROS Institute of Mental Measurements, Tests in Print, and Tests for Assessment in Counseling, along with many others. The test administrator must select and review the appropriate test or instrument to use with each client, especially when high-stake testing is conducted, that is, when the results could alter people's lives. If a test administrator is using an unpublished test, he or she must make every effort possible to contact the author or copyright holder to secure permission before using the test (see the APA website, www.apa.org/science, for further information related to test use and administration).

Test Artifacts

Although measures of abuse and parenting qualities are available through various resources, the uniqueness of each abuse case requires that a flexible, individualized assessment battery be used. The professional test user must be familiar with standards employed in developing selected instruments, as recommended in the Standards for Educational and Psychological Testing (American Educational Research Association, 1996). All social science professionals— licensed, certified, or otherwise—are accountable for using the most up-to-date, empirically validated instrument that is appropriate for the problem at hand. The standards require each test developer to supply elaborate information on the instrument, such as purpose, timing, test administration, reading level, and other test artifacts. Test administration should not commence without a proper review of test properties and assurance that the existing test properties are appropriate for use with the specific client.

Test Administration

When child abuse or child sexual abuse studies are conducted, the sensitivity of the topic can easily pose a risk for the emotional welfare of the participant. The interviewers' mannerisms, the contextual setting of the interview, and the wording of items or questions should be examined for bias or invasive content. Similarly, the reading level of the test should be appropriate for the participant's level of intellectual functioning (Anastasia, 1988; Sattler, 1998). Otherwise, the child might acquiesce and respond in a compliant manner to please the researcher, yet not comprehend the content of the test.

Participant Characteristics

When a child does not accurately comprehend a test question or the intent of the question, inaccurate responses result. This possibility is magnified if the child has a learning disability, language or cultural barriers, or is economically disadvantaged (Sattler, 1998). Also, the length of time of the interview procedure or test administration can affect completion time or, even worse, provide a source of frustration for the child. The decision about whether to use power (untimed) tests or speed (timed) tests should be carefully considered, particularly when special needs children are tested, as longer time for completion of the test process may be required when evaluating special needs and culturally diverse children. Inappropriate use of test materials or improper administration of a test protocol can seriously impair a child's propensity to respond. Consequently, final test scores may be reduced due to test artifacts rather than the child's true ability or lack of abilities. For a more in-depth discussion on test artifacts, test construction, and the assessment of special populations, see Anastasia (1988) and Sattler (1998).

DISCUSSION QUESTIONS

1. How would one determine if injuries on a child were accidentally versus intentionally inflicted by an abuser? What resources would you defer to?

2. What types of objective evidence should be collected at the time of a complaint medically, psychologically, or otherwise? What resources are available in your community to assist in the process?

3. What controversy exists concerning family privacy and the right to invade a household for questioning? Do you agree with government guidelines? Please document your response.

4. What forms of data collection methods are available in your community? If you are not sure, arrange an interview with a local child abuse agent, either in a protective agency or in the local police or sheriff's department.

5. If you are called upon to conduct an interview with a small child in your community concerning allegations of abuse, to what professional guidelines would you adhere to assure acceptable procedures are followed?

6. Research local legislation concerning child abuse reporting. What Web sites or library resources might you use to conduct this research? Be prepared to discuss your findings in class and provide a copy of statutes that apply.

7. If you need to conduct research on victim-related topics, what databases would you search? What special considerations must you employ to protect subjects if you conduct direct research with abused individuals?

8. You are asked to conduct a study to assess treatment effectiveness with pedophiles. What personal values or beliefs may come into conflict, if any? How would you proceed?

4

Theoretical Models of Child Sexual Abuse

LEARNING OBJECTIVES

Chapter 4 will address the following learning objectives:

1. A review of emotional consequences of childhood sexual abuse

2. A discussion of impact of sexual abuse from childhood to adolescence

3. A theoretical conception of the syndrome of paradoxical states (SPS)

4. A discussion of paradoxical events common to cases of sexual abuse

5. A theoretical model of paradoxical messages received by adults (PROVIDE)

6. A discussion of the model of emotional congruency (MEC)

INTRODUCTION

This chapter provides a review of the emotional impact of sexual abuse and presents a conceptualization of the emotional dynamics experienced by an abuse survivor. Each section presents issues that are based on a combination of theoretical concepts and applied findings revealed by numerous abusees in individual and group counseling over the past 20 years. The complex emotional reactions commonly found among abuse survivors are presented first, including misperceptions about self and others. Developmental issues as they relate to several dimensions of emotional reactions to abuse are also discussed.

This will be followed by a conceptualization of the syndrome of paradoxical states (SPS), wherein abuse survivors realize many contradictory reactions toward themselves, as well as toward their abusers. A child's needs model known as PROVIDE will be presented, with an emphasis on the impact of paradoxical behaviors inflicted upon children from abusive parents. Finally, a model of emotional congruency (MEC) is proposed as a form of identification of paradoxical emotional reactions that often emerge following exposure to sexual abuse, and which are unique to each abusee.

THE ABUSEE'S PERSPECTIVE:
REACTIONS TO CHILD SEXUAL ABUSE

Any professional working with an abusee must be familiar with the complex dynamics that arise when abuse is experienced. Perhaps one of the most essential tenants of building rapport with any client is to comprehend his or her internal frame of reference. Often, particularly in cases of sexual abuse, this is difficult to do. An abused child is often more confused about issues than what is apparent to those involved. This section examines the aftermath of an abuse experience from the child's view.

Complex Aftereffects

A child exposed to abuse may harbor many emotional concerns arising from the abuse. Misperceptions about the experience, including those about self, the abuser, and the behavior or act that was forced upon the child, linger throughout life and can be debilitating. In many instances, total recovery from the emotional trauma may not occur; rather, the abusee develops coping skills to help him or her through the highly stressful recalled memories or ensuing flashbacks that may occur.

For children abused by an external family associate, distant relative, or stranger, the home environment may be looked upon as a refuge or sanctuary from abuse, even if the immediate primary caretakers are oblivious to the abuse. These children at least know that they may close the door to their room, sit in a corner of the home, or go about their daily activities without feeling the perpetrator could assault them again at any given moment. However, young children who are routinely exposed to contradictory and hurtful behaviors from parents or trusted caretakers may experience a state of perpetual emotional turmoil. These children must always be alert to their environments, looking for clues to an oncoming assault or invasion, either physical, through abuse of their bodies, or emotional, through threats and degrading treatment.

Children who are victims of intrafamilial abuse, that is, children who are abused by members of their family, not only must accomplish normal developmental tasks, but also must attempt to cope with added duress and emotional turmoil. There is no safety net, no moments of peace, no place of solitude in which to hide and rest. If children are threatened, coerced, or harmed, they may continually experience intense emotional reactions without the benefit of protective resources. Left alone to cope or to accommodate the situation without adequate cognitive skills or emotional maturity, young children often experience heightened fear, distress, and distrust. Fears that are real, as well as unrealistic misperceptions formed about the abuse, about self, and about the perpetrator, may jeopardize future development and emotional well-being. This can manifest in self-blame, guilt, reduced self-esteem, and self-doubt.

Negative aftereffects are intensified when a trusted adult responds with disbelief or rebuttal when a disclosure is eventually made. If a child senses a negative reaction from the listener upon disclosure of the abuse, he or she may perceive that reaction as additional rejection, repulsion, or abandonment from a previously trusted adult. The child may withdraw in silence and may not disclose the abuse to another adult for several years or more. Within the child's cognitive schema, feelings of shame, self-doubt, and reduced self-esteem are once more heightened and undermine the child's personality development. If the child's reactions to the abusive experience are severe, deep-seated internalized feelings can curtail emotional wellness and quality of life. In cases of extreme traumatization, emotional distress can lead to severe pathology requiring extended monitoring. Regardless of whether the child's emotional response is internalized (directed at self) or externalized (directed at others), short- and long-term problems may interfere with daily functioning.

Perhaps equally damaging to a child's welfare are the ambiguous, contradictory emotional reactions that evolve within a child toward the abuser. Many children, and older adults as well, report feelings of extreme anger, rage, or hatred. At times, victims of abuse project their feelings onto the abuser; at other times, they project them onto themselves. When the abuser is a friend, relative, or trusted parent, emotional reactions may be more complex, as the child struggles with paradoxical feelings of love versus hate toward a trusted adult. If the child is dependent upon the abuser for basic needs and nurturance, feelings of ambiguity can escalate and become a dominant source of stress, anxiety, and prolonged trauma.

Interference with Normal Development

An abused child struggles to cope with abusive experiences while accomplishing normal developmental tasks common to all children. After the abuse, the child expends a predominant amount of mental energy attempting to cope with the abuse, rather than being free to fulfill developmental tasks, such as acquiring social skills, developing a sense of self, and learning to achieve. Although professionals have noted that a "loss of innocence" occurs when a child is abused (Kohm & Lawrence, 1997; Veach, 1997; Weiner & Kupious, 1995), another loss also occurs, that of lost opportunities. Rather than being free of mind to pursue playful, healthy, ego-strengthening activities, an abused child struggles to survive emotionally, and sometimes physically. In cases where familial abuse occurs repeatedly over many years, an abused child must develop self-reliance (Reyes, 1996; Smith & Carlson, 1997) and inner strength as a means of survival; however, not all children are able to achieve this.

Abused children may or may not fare well under such duress, depending upon their unique situations, including their own predispositions to coping and the availability of environmental support. Detrimental traits, such as help-lessness, passivity, and withdrawal from others, may emerge but be unheeded because of the lack of a caring adult in the child's life. As a child matures from early childhood to adolescence, adaptive coping skills may or may not evolve. When conditions of abuse are extremely harsh, intense emotional reactions and behavioral symptoms may require professional intervention. This is true regardless of whether behavioral reactions are internalized (e.g., self-hurting, cutting, dissociative states) or externalized (e.g., reckless use of drugs, gang membership, running away from home, participating in risky sexual activities).

To say that children exposed to childhood sexual abuse receive mixed mes-sages from an adult abuser is an understatement of the problem. An abused child, whether the experience was a one-time event or occurred repeatedly over time, will come to realize several consequences. In addition to any phys-ical pain or potentially visible scars, the child's *being* is violated, usually leaving an indelible mark on the child's psyche. Although overt physical scars initially documented within a clinical or medical setting may eventually heal, emo-tional scars dwell in the child's mind and subliminally shape the child's per-sonality. Oppressive strategies that are used to silence the child, such as frightening words and threats of harm to self or others, magnify the traumatic effect of the abuse. The abuser's demoralizing and degrading verbal comments further serve to keep the child engulfed in a sense of helplessness. Often, such threats are further internalized and seared deeply into the subconscious, result-ing in cognitive schemas of self-doubt, fearful worries, and an increased sense of helplessness, all of which undermine or sway normal personality development.

Denial of Self

Residual effects of the traumatic event are often tucked deeply within the child's subconscious mind. So subtle are these personality encroachments that they are not observed by others, but they exist nonetheless. Outwardly, the abused child may learn to act *normal,* as if nothing is wrong. Yet, in reality, undercurrents of fearful thoughts permeate the child's conscious thinking, act-ing, and responding to others. Spontaneous behaviors may occur due to painful recall of or generalized associations with elements of the abuse, such as when a young child fearfully jerks at the sight of a stress-provoking image that is reminiscent of the abuser. Another example is a child who experiences waves of nausea upon smelling an aroma that is associated with the abuse, such as a cigarette or cigar, perspiration from the abuser, or an odor like one from the location where the abuse occurred.

Both unconscious and conscious cognitive schemas may also direct an abused child's voluntary behaviors, such as when a child angrily refuses to visit a relative who abused the child or a location where the abuse occurred.

Unsuspecting adults cannot understand why the child is suddenly behaving this way, and the abused child may have suppressed conscious memories of the event to the extent that even he or she is surprised at his or her own display of oppositional behavior. Feelings about the abuse may be so painful to acknowledge that the child buries them deeply into his or her subconscious, rather than express them to loved ones who, the child fears, will reject him or her, either consciously or unconsciously. Rather than risk rejection, denial, or, worse yet, punishment from nonbelieving adults, an abused child may continue to interact with adults in a routine manner, all the while harboring the aftereffects of an experience too horrible to be spoken about out loud.

Heightened Sensitivity

Over time, distorted messages that are internalized from the abuse experience are generalized to other situations. Subtle reminders surface from the child's mind as he or she attempts to process incoming messages from environmental stimuli, causing a form of hypervigilence or hypersensitivity to emerge. Every time a child is ridiculed, criticized, or critiqued, reactions may be triggered that are associated with similar events experienced during abuse. Because his or her perception of self is already demeaned, an abused child may easily misinterpret someone's innocent comment about an outfit, a work product, or a behavior. He or she may misread social cues to the point of intensifying the already internalized behaviors, all due to a heightened sensitivity to environmental cues.

Eventually, a heightened sensitivity develops in anticipation of another abusive incident or painful act. The abused child learns to watch and listen for any cues of harm or danger within the environment. The more prolonged the abusive conditions, the more heightened this state of vigilance becomes. A child may also attempt to avoid unpleasant confrontations by futilely attempting to appease an abuser, such as when a child scrambles around the house cleaning in attempts to circumvent an anticipated angry outburst from an abusive or alcoholic parent. Also, an abused child may beg an adult not to leave the house out of fear of what he or she will encounter if left alone with an abuser. A nonabusing adult may view such behavior as an excessive attempt for attention or simple unruliness, and dismiss these subtle outcries for help.

IMPACT OF CHILD SEXUAL ABUSE:
FROM CHILDHOOD TO ADOLESCENCE

Although relatives, friends, and school personnel may influence a child, it is the primary caretakers who are expected to insulate that child from harmful influences in a protective, nurturing manner. The ideal role of the primary caretaker is to guide and assist child development in a safe, secure setting. It is only within a safe setting that a child can develop a *self-identity* (Erikson, 1968) and become *ego-centered* (Freud, 1962). A child is expected to develop a sense The mother.

of self only when a point of maturation is reached, as should normally occur during adolescence. Once maturation is attained, the child is expected to discriminate, evaluate, and subsequently interpret environmental events using critical judgment. When a child is continually exposed to abusive acts, however, mixed messages obscure the child's filtering systems. The child cannot clearly perceive what behaviors are and are not acceptable; as a result, boundaries become blurred, roles become entangled, and relationships become a source of further confusion.

Diminished Self Worth

Even the most isolated child may be exposed to outside influences such as television, peers, and neighbors, all of which help the child form a sense of socially and culturally acceptable behaviors. However, when earlier learned social norms are contradicted, such as during abusive events, an abused child perceives the event as a source of confusion, bewilderment, or even fear, none of which enhance the development of a solid self-identity. Issues of self-blame, distrust of others, and reduced self-confidence further obscure the child's opportunities to develop a solid self-identity. If severe enough, ambiguities in environmental demands (abusive acts) and adverse environmental experiences (nurturance versus neglect) can seriously impair the abused child's emotional welfare. As the child matures and reaches adolescence, emotional reactions stemming from the abuse may intensify. These more intensified reactions can compel the abusee to aggressively resist the abuser; or conversely, heightened emotional distress can provoke harmful acts on the child's self, such as suicidal behaviors, substance abuse, or reckless driving and other risky behaviors. Such extreme self-hurting behaviors and responses occur among abused adolescents for several reasons, a few of which are unique to the child's development during the adolescent years.

Intensified Reactions of Adolescents

First, adolescence is a time when children are most self-conscious and preoccupied with themselves. Many teens who have been abused feel that they are the only one this has ever happened to; therefore, feelings of isolation, alienation, and depression set in. Children who were unable to successfully defy the abuser often experience feelings of guilt, shame, and embarrassment at being weak, passive, or at fault. Themes repeated by adolescent abusees are "Everyone must know that I am not good" and "I am dirty." As unwarranted as these comments are, adolescent survivors of abuse make similar statements over and over again, which perpetuates their reduced sense of self-esteem.

Second, adolescence is a time when individuals come into their own sexuality. Experimentation with intimate relationships and sexual partners is a normal part of development in preparation for adulthood. While this time of life may be enjoyable and playful for the nonabused child, the abused child may be haunted by past images that detract from an anticipated positive experience of shared intimacy with same-age peers in several ways. Abused children may either exploit themselves by participating in sexually promiscuous behaviors or withdraw from any intimate contact with others. In either extreme, the adolescent is cheated of the normal "right of passage" involved in the maturation process of preparing for intimate adult relations. While it is true that not all survivors of abuse experience ambivalence toward intimacy, impairment in adult relationships and an increased propensity to accept abusive partners in adulthood is well documented in research studies of adult survivors of abuse.

A third reason adolescents experience intensified reactions as a result of abuse is that adolescence is the time when moral and values judgments develop that enable the use of abstract reasoning and decision making in situations involving moral dilemmas. At the same time, physical strength and stature are also maturing. For the first time, an otherwise helpless child has grown sufficiently to possibly take some form of action. Adolescents have new strength, greater internal reasoning and physical skills, as well as increased mobility, which may make it possible for them to escape, defy, or report the abuse. Many adolescent abusees have attested to defying or fighting off an attacker or potential sexual assault based solely on physical strength activated by an internal acknowledgment that this form of behavior is intolerable. But physical strength alone is not sufficient for a child to break free from an abuser; many other elements come into play.

Not all children, however, are able to fight back. Some children who become withdrawn and helpless in response to abuse may be increasingly vulnerable in the hands of an abuser. Although a greater sense of self-identity should develop and physical stature should increase during adolescence, maturation and identity formation are by no means an automatic deterrent to victimization. In light of the oppressive nature of abuse of any kind, children who have endured years of maltreatment, particularly within their own household, may not have the inner strength and ability to seek appropriate help. This may be true for any number of reasons, ranging from a child's feigned bravado persona, to learned helplessness, to severe pathology.

Emotional Reactions

Short- and long-term emotional reactions from abuse impact every realm of a child's life, including all of his or her relationships (Harris & Landis, 1997). Children experience a wide range of reactions during and following abuse. These emotional reactions vary in severity, ranging from mild to extremely severe. For example, some abusees cope with residual issues from the abuse, such as recalled memories, flashbacks, and other symptoms, in a self-sustaining manner, whereas other abusees experience severe, acute, and chronic reactions, such as mental illness resulting in debilitating depression, severe psychosis, or dissociative disorders.

Prior to providing intervention, professionals must identify the issues and challenges that are unique to each abusee, as well as develop individualized therapeutic plans (Harris & Landis 1997; Oates, 1996). Complex dynamics ensue particularly when the abuser is a family member who plays an integral part in the child's development. Because children rely on adult family members for sustenance and nurturance, adverse responses to abusive treatment can be devastating. An abused child may be the recipient of love and hugs one moment but of aggression and coercion the next. Needless to say, a state of confusion sets in as a young child attempts to anticipate what will happen next. In cases of sexual abuse by a parent, a child may seek out normal fatherly or motherly affection, only to have demands placed upon him or her to perform sexually abusive acts under coercion. When this occurs, not only were initial childhood needs left unmet, but the child must also process and attempt to overcome the impact of the abusive treatment. Essentially, the abused child must now confront two obstacles to development, lack of need fulfillment and abusive treatment.

Debilitating Effects   Even though positive developmental experiences may have been exchanged between an abused child and the abusing parent before the abuse occurred, once the child is abused, the abuse obscures or obliterates any previous positive interactions. It may take only one abusive incident to alter a child's overall belief system from that of an innocent trusting child to that of a cynical, frightened, and guarded being. The belief system itself may be thwarted in various ways, depending on the unique personality attributes of the child and the ability of that child to sustain abuse. Eventually, any trusting relationship or positive belief systems that have been developed may be altered or negated, especially when no intervention has occurred.

Equally as debilitating is the impact of inconsistent treatment at the hands of caregivers, who send messages that shift from caring and nurturing to harsh and abusive. Inconsistent messages from caregivers can have a cumulative effect; each harsh or abrasive treatment adds to the insult and pain experienced earlier. As this cycle continues, whereby the child receives positive messages on some days but harmful ones the next day, or even the next hour, the child learns that unpredictable behaviors from the abusing parent may occur at any given time. In a dysfunctional home, both parents may display aberrant behaviors; collusion may be present between the offending parent and the non-offending parent (Deblinger & Heflin, 1996). If such is the case, the child truly has no safety net within that setting.

Ramifications of abuse within households are stifling, particularly when the abusers are significant caregivers who ingratiate themselves with the children as part of the manipulative process, or "dance of seduction," that is common in abuse cases. In this dance of seduction, the abuser purposely directs activities to build a trusting relationship with the child, usually by buying toys, providing gifts, or simply giving the child a lot of one-on-one attention. Once the trust is built and the child innocently acquiesces to the adult's attentions, the child's innocence is violated. The child is engaged in what he or she believes to be an enjoyable or playful interaction with a caring adult, but then an abrupt change in relationship dynamics takes place, and abuse occurs. The adult who was viewed as a caring confidante now takes on the role of a threatening and menacing villain.

Contradictory Interactions Directly following the abusive act, an abused child may experience extremely stressful reactions such as withdrawal, depression, self-doubt, nightmares, and others, only to be left to process these reactions alone in silence. As time passes, the child rationalizes, accommodates, or assimilates the abusive event, and adjusts to the environment with whatever coping skills he or she has available in order to survive the experience. As reported in case histories of extended abusive relationships, particularly between family members, the abuse often occurs for extensive time periods—months, years, or even an entire childhood, whereby the child's confusion continues.

Interactions between an abused child and the abusing adult may appear to be in accordance with a socially acceptable adult-child role or parent-child role. In fact, the abuser may excel at fulfilling the role of a responsible caregiver, projecting a public appearance of socially acceptable behaviors, such as taking the child to church, school, or social events. The child becomes more and more perplexed as a cycle of changing behaviors repeats itself time and again. First, abuse takes place, then the abuser masks the damage by fulfilling other parental duties including acts of nurturance and caring, but then, sooner or later, the abuse occurs again; and so the cycle continues.

Needless to say, the child's emotional state fluctuates as the child attempts to process periods of normal parent-child interactions with the abusing parent that are then spoiled by the abusive acts inflicted by that same parent. Each time the child is abused again by his or her caretaker, the child's ambiguous emotions toward the abuser fluctuate between feelings of hate and love for the adult, confusing and obscuring a formerly trusted relationship. As the child matures and gains a greater sense of self as a separate being entitled to live in a safe and secure setting, emotional confusion escalates. Eventually, outward signs of emotional distress are evident. The child's anger may be directed at self (e.g., bouts of depression, self-hurting behaviors, suicide attempts) or at others through aggressive or acting-out behaviors. In either case, abusive treatment leaves the child or adolescent in a perpetual state of confusion about how to deal with others as well as with the residual emotional turmoil.

Undermined Development Any child who is abused experiences paradoxical notions that undermine his or her peace of mind and emotional stability. Personality traits observed in adulthood are formed, at least in part, by the cumulative effects of early childhood experiences. Therefore, one can easily understand how a multitude of unresolved conflicts initiated during early childhood could plague a person and affect his or her emotional adjustment in adulthood. If the emotional conflicts are the result of abusive treatment by a significant caregiver, these paradoxical messages may contribute to emotional dysfunction or post-traumatic stress symptoms during adulthood.

Regardless of whether the child experiences physical, emotional, or sexual abuse, or a combination of the three, the child's thoughts are consumed with processing the event for some time after the abuse occurs. Erikson (1962) purported that developmental tasks, such as the development of autonomy, initiative, and a sense of accomplishment, are diverted, abandoned, or suppressed in an abused child. An abused young child may not have the peace of mind required for the pursuit of the typical developmental tasks, whereas a nonabused child is free to flourish—to gain a solid sense of self as a respected being, and to participate in skill-building activities in preparation for adulthood.

Therefore, although an abusee in treatment may initially present his or her primary concern as past physical, sexual, or emotional abuse, the abuse itself is not the only focus of concern. Secondary emotional problems, such as symptoms of sleeplessness, agitation, depression, nightmares, flashbacks, and so on, need to be identified, and each symptom needs to be addressed separately as therapy proceeds. As emotional concerns surface during intake or throughout therapy sessions, it may become evident that any number of residual problems are occurring at the same time. Usually, each symptom or emotional concern vacillates along a continuum of paradoxical concerns, such as love/hate or trust/distrust directed toward the offender or as a consequence of the offenders' actons. This is where the syndrome of paradoxical states (SPS) comes into play.

SYNDROME OF PARADOXICAL STATES

Researchers have noted that a significant number of intrafamilial child sexual abuse (CSA) cases exist (Finkelhor, 1994; Greenfield, 1996). This section focuses on the emotional reactions that emanate from the situation in which a child is sexually abused by a trusted adult-caretaker. Contradictory feelings are often expressed in reference to self, toward the abuser, and about the abuse incident itself. For instance, it is not unusual for a child to experience feelings of hate for an abusive parent, as well as feelings of guilt for hating his or her parent, while at the same time expressing love for that parent. Similarly, it is not unusual for a child to experience self-blame while, at the same time, knowing that the blame lies with the abuser.

Consequently, each thread in the complex dynamic of interfamilial sexual abuse is often contradicted by another thread of oppositional, and perhaps unrealistic, conclusions about self, the abuser, and the abuse incident. As these contradictory messages continue to be received over time, paradoxical emotional reactions about elements of the abuse can develop within the individual to such an extent that he or she is plagued by a lifetime of unresolved paradoxical states. Therefore, the author presents the following propositions embedded in what she calls the syndrome of paradoxical states (SPS).

The SPS essentially originates from continual exposure to paradoxical messages from primary caretakers. It is manifested as an ongoing, heightened state of distressful emotional reactions in response to perpetual exposure to inconsistent behaviors from a trusted adult. For the most part, these reactions stem from two critical components present in an abused child's environment: harmful and contradictory messages sent during the abuse event, and ineffective parenting that leaves a child void of essential nurturance and protection. As this type of inadequate fulfillment of needs continues, it exacerbates emotional needs and other adverse consequences for the child.

Sexual Abuse and Neglect

Neglect from caretakers includes such things as the lack of meals, inadequate supervision, and even abandonment. Neglect renders a child vulnerable to distorted cognitive perceptions of self. When a caretaker victimizes his or her own child who is already suffering from neglect, but now experiences physical harm, the impact of that abuse is tenfold, as there is no relief in sight. A neglected, physically abused, and sexually abused child not only has to endure deficits in parenting and possible physical danger, but also must endure physical violations through any number of forms of sexual acts.

In intrafamilial abuse cases, the child is expected to act as if nothing is wrong when other family members are present, an expectation that is usually enforced by some coercive act or threat of harm. Consequently, from the child's perspective, emotional needs must be suppressed, denied, and ignored, which in turn enforces the message that the child is of reduced self-worth, and not to be validated. Sexual abuse within family units may be the least reported, most difficult to validate, and most silenced form of abuse; and it is by far the most detrimental form of all abuse in that physical and psychological invasion transgresses the child's sense of self.

Added to this equation is the fact that an abused and neglected child may endure other forms of harsh treatment that purposely render the child vulnerable to the abuser. If a child receives nothing but scolding, punishment, and harsh treatment on a regular basis, he or she will have difficulty attaining a secure sense of self and others. Such a child may crave attention from an adult (and certainly deserves positive attention), but the sexual abuse may represent his or her only source of attention from an adult, through an experience that is painful, harmful, and detrimental to the child. Since it is quite normal for any child to need attention, to be affectionately held by a parent, to be talked to warmly, and, most of all, to be loved, a sexually abused child suffers repeated betrayal each time he or she seeks nurturance but receives abuse.

Sexual Abuse Without Neglect

Child sexual abuse is not differentiated across socioeconomic status; children in affluent homes may also be sexually abused. Households that superficially appear to be meeting a child's needs may still be harboring a dark secret. In contrast to physical abuse or neglect cases, a sexually abused child may, in fact, be well cared for by the abusing party, aside from the abuse itself. Housing, medical, and clothing needs may all be met, at times even with abundance; yet behind closed doors, sexual abuse is ongoing. Needless to say, this kind of quasi nurturance sends extremely mixed messages to the child. The child may remain loyal to the abuser in light of his or her dependency upon the abuser for survival needs; but once again, the child receives contradictory messages surrounding the sexually abusive experience.

For self-survival, such a child must process the abuse experience and accommodate it in some manner. In doing so, the child may develop highly sporadic emotional reactions that, if endured long enough, eventually become personality traits observed in interactions with peers or other adults. For example, as the abuse continues, the child's stressful and uncontrollable emotional responses can cumulate and become generalized in distrust of others, exhibited by the child distancing or withdrawing from others. Eventually the child may withdraw from social interactions altogether, rather than risk exposure to further harm; thus, the child is deprived of potentially valid relationships with other adults and peers. These personality traits, however, may contrast sharply with other traits within the child, such as a desire to achieve, a competitive drive for success, and the confidence to excel in other aspects of life.

A child who continues to generalize distorted emotional responses eventually responds to all situations from a state of paradoxical reasoning and emotional incongruency. Even if something feels bad, the child may endure it because that incongruent feeling is something with which the child is familiar. Consequently, emotional incongruency increases the child's propensity to develop the SPS. If left untreated, emotional states of incongruency become a routine manner of interaction and remain with the abusee throughout a lifetime.

Trust Betrayed

The SPS and its underlying emotional reactions can be quite stressful and even debilitating for any child, adolescent, or adult who has experienced sexual abuse. As stated earlier, the child's experience of sexual abuse, although harmful and painful for the child, may represent the child's only source of attention from an adult; and because the child's need for attention, affection, warmth, and love is normal, the sexually abused child is sorely betrayed by the abusive interaction. Very young children and highly vulnerable children, such as those with special needs, remain vastly loyal to abusive adults who are attentive to them, partly because of their need for attention and partly because of their naïve ability to trust others and, at times, be easily led.

The literature on child sexual abuse clearly shows that special needs children have a five times greater chance of being abused than other children. When abuse occurs as part of a trusted relationship, a vulnerable child may acquiesce to abuse only because the trust has been formed. A phenomenon that is well documented in the literature is that of loyalty to an abuser and reluctance to disclose the abuse, particularly when the abuser is also the caretaker (Finkelhor, 1986; Kramer & Akhtar, 1991; Kuehnle, 1996; Prendergast, 1993; Vevier & Tharinger, 1986). Therefore, it is not surprising that revelations made during individual and group counseling demonstrate that many survivors of abuse still long for the abusing parent's approval, years after reaching adulthood.

Residual Emotional Concerns

Residual emotional concerns can interfere with all aspects of adult life in personal, social, and work settings. Undesired emotional reactions that deter fulfillment in adulthood can be more effectively treated and overcome if knowledge is acquired about the source of the emotional concerns. By gaining an awareness of the nurturing that they should or could have received as a child, abusees can acknowledge that there is a realistic basis for their distress, a fact that can be comforting to many individuals. Often survivors of child abuse blame themselves for not gaining control over their emotional reactions to the abuse. Rather than placing the blame where it belongs, on the abuser, children who have been abused often assume responsibility for adult behaviors. The following statements are common among abused children: "If only I could have tried harder, he wouldn't have hit me" and "If only I got better grades, he would leave me alone."

Importance of Providing Information to the Child

The sharing of information about the circumstances surrounding child abuse can be therapeutic in itself. When abusees learn about the SPS, childhood needs, and the evolving incongruent emotional reactions that impact abused children, a greater acceptance of self emerges. Once abusees learn about the factors surrounding abuse, they can say, "Hey, I'm okay after all. It truly wasn't my fault" or "You mean, I am not really losing my mind?"

Informational sessions restore a sense of peace by employing two essential components of effective interventions: first, the abusee acquires *knowledge* of the dynamics of the problem, and second, he or she receives *validation* that current emotional reactions are quite normal under the circumstances. Once the information has been shared, the abusee must then, as an important step toward healing, identify the specific emotional needs that are unique to him or her. Aspects of abuse and emotional responses to abuse differ significantly among abuse survivors. Also, since the aftereffects of abuse may last a lifetime, emotional needs may change over time, with different elements of the abuse surfacing and needing attention at different periods in the abusee's life. For many survivors of abuse, coping strategies will be needed for a lifetime.

Emotional Needs

Erikson (1962), a developmental psychologist known for his theory of psychosocial development, noted that developmental tasks may never be accomplished if parental encouragement is lacking. In cases of abuse, effective parenting is replaced with harsh negative parenting that regresses emotional development rather than enhancing it. Consequently, unfulfilled emotional needs can adversely affect a child, making age-appropriate developmental tasks difficult for him or her to attain. In addition to deterring a child's developmental skills, abuse may also interfere with the child's interpersonal skills. Relationship issues (e.g., trust building, role ambiguity, boundary setting, self-doubt, and self-image) emerge in the individual as personality attributes that remain with him or her into maturity. These emotional deficits may significantly impair personality development and quality of life during adulthood.

THEORETICAL MODELS

The following sections illustrate two intervention models that deal with the impact of childhood sexual abuse. Both theoretical and applied components are used to describe elements of the SPS, as illustrated in Figure 4.1. These models were developed by the author based on actual concerns and statements that were revealed to her during a 20-year period in which she provided individual and group services for victims of sexual abuse. The SPS is inherent in most cases of child abuse, regardless of situational variables. In all types of child abuse—physical, emotional, and sexual—contradictory messages are received from and conflicting behaviors are observed in an adult. The contradictory messages evoke incongruent emotional reactions in the abused child, particularly a child who is abused by his or her own caregiver rather than by a stranger. A series of two-dimensional emotional elements that contributes to SPS can be best examined from two perspectives: childhood needs for healthy development, and emotional concerns following sexual abuse.

The first model, a seven-factor model known as PROVIDE, identifies childhood needs that may or may not have been met in the child's environment, yet have highly impacted the child's personality development. By using PROVIDE to review the core needs of children, therapists can identify the deficiencies in the abused child's household and help the abusee identify his or her emotional concerns. Once these concerns are identified, strategies can be developed to help the abusee overcome the emotional aftereffects of abuse, or at least develop coping mechanisms that can be used to make them tolerable. If the abusee is quite young, therapists can use the childhood needs model as a checklist when developing an intervention plan.

Second, a two-dimensional model known as the model of emotional congruency (MEC) is proposed as a means by which to identify underlying emotional concerns that originate from exposure to abuse but leave the abusee in a state of emotional incongruency. Incongruent behaviors can be either internalized or externalized, depending on the abusee's reaction to the abusive experience. Ideally, incongruent emotional reactions, once identified, can be brought into congruency through therapeutic intervention.

The two-dimensional model of emotional congruency (MEC) uses the two dimensions of emotional reactions that often occur among abused children. Both emotional reactions are often expressed toward the abuser or toward self as the abusee processes the experience and the aftermath. Because emotional reactions are often volatile, spontaneous, and unpredictable, particularly at the crisis stage of counseling, it is not unusual for an abusee to experience each contrasting emotional state at varying times throughout any given day, week, or month. The ideal objective of the model is to identify unique emotional concerns, apply intervention techniques, and bring incongruent reactions into emotional congruency for the abusee. Once emotional congruency is achieved, the abusee is well on the way to finding a peaceful resolution to emotional turmoil. The MEC represents a series of emotional opposites that underlie or contribute to the SPS.

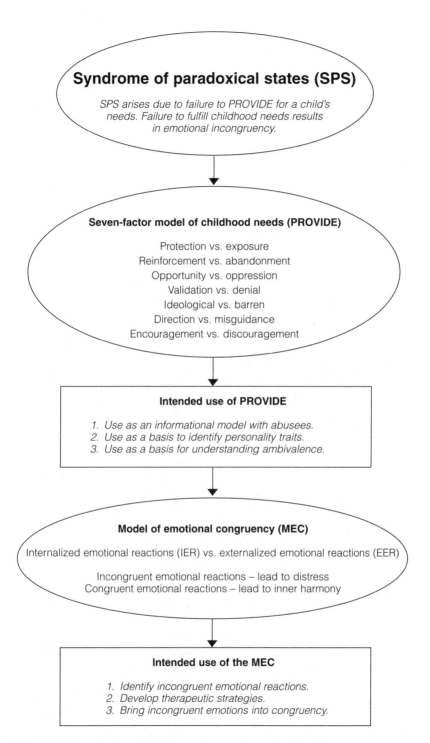

FIGURE 4.1 Theoretical model of the syndrome of paradoxical states, the PROVIDE and MEC models.

Detailed descriptors of the MEC are provided and should help therapists to identify issues that are relevant to each abusee. For each abusee, an accurate focus of treatment must be developed based on an in-depth review of his or her perception of events. Since each child interprets the environment in a unique way, several children exposed to the same event may each interpret it differently. Therefore, a child's individual needs must be clarified in accordance with his or her own internal frame of reference. In reviewing each element in collaboration with the abusee, the therapist can help the child identify the essential elements of emotional incongruency.

Seven-Factor Model of Childhood Needs (PROVIDE)

The seven-factor childhood needs model is represented by the acronym PROVIDE (see Table 4.1). The model consists of opposing elements that impact a child's emotional adjustment: Protection versus exposure; Reinforcement versus abandonment; Opportunity versus oppression; Validation versus denial; Ideological versus barren; Direction versus misguidance; and Encouragement versus discouragement. With potential to assist the treatment process in several ways, PROVIDE represents a structured framework, depicting what caregivers should *provide* to reinforce well-being in the children with whom they work. The model could assist the treatment process in several ways. Although the model has elements similar to Erikson's (1962) proposed stages of psychological development, in that two-dimension parenting objectives are listed together, PROVIDE differs from Erikson's proposals in that it does not list stages in which one element is more prominant than another. Also, consequences arising from ineffective parenting skills are represented as outcomes specific to abused children.

By reviewing the history of abusees, professionals can develop an understanding of what elements of caregiving were missing from the abusees' childhoods. The seven factors of the PROVIDE model represent actions imparted upon the abusee from an outside source, that of a parent, guardian, stepparent, or any other primary caretaker. The two-dimensional factors were developed in part based on Erikson's (1962) concept of parental influences and in part based on actual concepts expressed by abusees in support groups.

Unique Reactions to Abuse Clarification of specific emotional concerns is essential if effective therapeutic intervention is to occur, particularly when dealing with complex intrafamilial dynamics. For instance, in a family of many children, several siblings may have been abused by the same person, but the impact of that abuse may be realized or processed quite differently by the different siblings, as depicted in the following case.

Mary Jane, a 38-year-old woman, was one of three sisters abused by their father. Mary Jane found the realization that her own father was a pedophile repulsive, and she developed tremendous hatred for him, hatred that consumed her to the point of dysfunction. Yet, Joan, her 25-year-old sister who was also abused by the father, was more concerned about gaining acceptance and approval from him and her mother, as both parents had initially rejected

Table 4.1 Seven-Factor Childhood Needs Model (PROVIDE) Illustrating the Syndrome of Paradoxical States

Paradoxical States	Consequential Outcomes
Protection vs. Exposure	While all children are entitled to protection, that protection is violated when they are exposed to abuse experiences. An abusee may have to work through issues related to the lack of protection by trusted caretakers. Mistrust issues are prominent.
Reinforcement vs. Abandonment	Nurtured children receive reinforcement and encouragement from parents that guide them into adulthood, but survivors of abuse, particularly intrafamilial sexual abuse, may develop a sense of abandonment from loved ones. Insecurities may become a fixed part of personality, along with attachment syndromes that enforce distant and unfulfilled relationships.
Opportunity vs. Oppression	In oppressed children, the desire to seek out new opportunities, such as higher education, career advancements, and new life adventures, is restricted. The cost to the child's future quality of life is impacted, not only by the abuse, but also by lost opportunities that are stifled by the aftereffects of the abuse.
Validation vs. Denial	When a child's disclosure of abuse is met with validation and supportive reinforcement to help the child deal with the emotional turmoil resulting from the abuse, the healing process is greatly enhanced. Conversely, when a child's emotional feelings are minimized, disputed, or denied, the child may develop a pattern of self-doubt and self-denial that will continue into adulthood.
Ideological vs. Barren	Ideological value systems are acquired from environmental circumstances, learned behaviors, and family influences. If solid value systems are not internalized, identity crises may emerge and ego-strength is weakened. Having no inner strength to draw from, the child or adult may adopt a chameleon personality type, one that is easily influenced by others and subject to change.
Direction vs. Misguidance	Direction from caretakers can take many forms, such as modeling desired behaviors, advising, or social learning based on family dynamics. A child who is exposed to harmful or abusive experiences may internalize the negative influences, adapt the same beliefs and behaviors as the abusing adult, and lead a similarly problematic lifestyle.
Encouragement vs. Discouragement	Encouragement in the form of emotional support is essential to increase motivation and positive development. If a child is continually criticized, humiliated, and degraded, a sense of discouragement evolves that can inhibit positive goal-setting behaviors essential to future achievement, productivity, and fulfilling of aspirations.

the disclosure and ostracized Joan from further contact with them. Joan found herself crying uncontrollably for months and experienced severe depression over this event, more upset by the ostracization than by the abuse itself. Consequently, Joan's unfulfilled need for parental approval became the focus of therapy, while her sister Mary Jane's treatment centered on the tremendous hatred she felt for her father. Each sister expressed a unique issue that needed to be resolved, yet prior to clarifying the issues during individual therapy, neither sister could identify the source of her immobilizing distress.

Reactions to Paradoxical Messages Normal child development evolves best under conditions of consistent parenting skills, boundary setting, continual nurturance, and supportive guidance and reinforcement from significant adults. However, when messages received from significant others are hurtful and abusive, a child cannot always process the paradoxical messages. Think about how hurtful it is when adult partners who know the boundaries of the relationship argue with one another. Both know the boundaries of the relationship, yet one sentence of hurtful words can undermine the entire relationship and be remembered for the duration of the relationship, only to be brought up time and time again. Now magnify the experience 20 times over for children who have more limited cognitive ability and fewer coping skills than adults. One nasty or harsh sentence can devastate a child; frequent and harsh abusive treatment severely jeopardizes a child's emotional welfare. Since caregivers are the young child's only source for feedback, responsiveness, and self-evaluation, they carry an awesome amount of power and responsibility in shaping that child's personality.

Learning is enhanced under favorable or enjoyable conditions. Conversely, if trauma is experienced, witnessed, or observed, emotionally laden images or messages can obliterate earlier learned lessons, behaviors, or emotions. Traumatic images can remain ingrained in a child's mind for long periods of time. When children experience trauma, not only do they receive paradoxical messages, but previously learned positive messages can be forgotten, obscured, or obliterated. So, even if appropriate caregiving is provided during the early part of a child's life, hurtful and harmful acts can abruptly replace a child's previous sense of security with feelings of fear and uncertainty. A sort of retrograde amnesia can occur if the events are so traumatic for the child that memories associated with them override preexisting knowledge, memories, or beliefs. Thus, the child must now process paradoxical messages that threaten earlier previously healthy personality development.

A child's parent or guardian should provide the child with sufficient nurturance to enable the child to achieve a positive self-image and sense of achievement in preparation for adulthood. Understanding paradoxical interactions is essential for providing abusees with effective treatment. Abusees need to understand that their ambivalent and mixed feelings toward the abuser are not unusual, particularly when the abuser was a significant person in the abusee's life. The ambivalence is clearly evident in women's support groups where women may openly admit that they want to kill those who abused them, but at the same time ask, "Why couldn't he (she) have loved me like a normal parent?"

The seven factors in the PROVIDE model represent essential childhood needs, along with their polar opposites, that must be met if a child is to develop a well-rounded sense of self and a secure self-identity. Developmental stages do not differentiate when these needs emerge; the needs are ongoing throughout life, although perhaps they are most essential during childhood. Each two-dimensional behavioral pair is examined in the following text, which will help to clarify the impact of contradictory behavioral patterns on the formation of paradoxical states among abused children. The following list and outcomes are not all-inclusive, as the range of needs and responses when those needs are not met are significant.

1. Protection Versus Exposure All children are entitled to protection, but protection is nonexistent at the time a child is exposed to abuse. Regardless of whether the abuser is a primary caretaker or a stranger, the effect on the child is the same. Vulnerability is increased, feelings of isolation are heightened, and other emotional and behavioral reactions emerge. An abused child may experience emotional problems anywhere along a continuum of behaviors, ranging from extreme withdrawal to severe acting out. Exposure to harm or violence, then, especially at the hands of caregivers, can be extremely traumatic for children. Not only must such children endure the abuse, but they also have no supportive adult to whom they can turn for protection. Children who are betrayed by trusted adults have more complex reactions, including issues of trusting others.

2. Reinforcement Versus Abandonment In circumstances of familial abuse, children are not given the natural reinforcement that would be expected if healthy parenting behaviors were present and a child made a disclosure of abuse. When a nuclear family member is the abuser, double jeopardy may occur upon disclosure. The children not only are denied much-needed emotional support, but sanctions are also placed on them for making the disclosure. In this situation, there is a greater risk of long-term residual effects. When the disclosure is met with detrimental actions, the children are set back in terms of confidence-building skills, self-acceptance, and absence of guilt.

For example, in one case, a 13-year-old girl, who was poorly groomed and physically underdeveloped, disclosed sexual abuse. When authorities were called, the caseworker who responded did not validate the claim of abuse in the initial interview with the child and left the child in her home. The girl was not physically harmed, but she was emotionally ostracized from the family, made to eat alone and remanded to her room from which all furniture except the bed had been removed. The child never spoke of the abuse again, but family members continued to isolate her from the family activities, and she became estranged from her sisters. The entire experience drastically undermined the girl's development of a sense of self-worth and acceptance.

3. Opportunity Versus Oppression Abuse of any kind is oppressive to the individual who receives it. For abused children, whether the abuse is physical, emotional, or sexual, oppression may overshadow emotional development. Diminished self-identity oppresses these children further, as they may internalize negative self-concepts from the abuse experience, and perhaps from all future experiences. Aspirations, dreams, and goals that may readily emerge among nonabused children are stifled in abused children, as these children are consumed with the need for psychological and emotional survival. Rather than focusing on homework, dreams of acceptance into college, or a position of high status in life, abused children are riddled with self-doubt, withdraw from others, and become preoccupied with the constant need to fend off their abusers. The home front is not a safe haven, as it is for nonabused children.

Hence, the emotional development of abused children is thwarted by distorted perceptions of self, perceptions that deter emotional fulfillment during childhood, adolescence, and on into adulthood. When such children reach out for assistance but are denied or ignored, they often make no further attempts to get help, as reported by many adult survivors who waited years to disclose their abuse after experiencing a rejection upon disclosure during childhood. Consequently, rather than seeking out new opportunities in life, abused children are likely to succumb to residual effects of the abuse, and perhaps retain oppressive views of life because of a sense of helplessness under oppression.

4. Validation Versus Denial Once disclosure is made, validation of a child's emotional needs is essential if a healthy self-identity is to emerge. If others repeatedly deny the experience, minimize its effects, and basically ignore the child's emotional needs, the child may be forced to adapt by denying his or her own emotional needs. Such a child may remain out of touch with his or her emotional needs throughout life. Numbness, lack of self-acknowledgment, and lack of trust for expressing needs and wants to others are all prerequisites for living unfulfilled adult lives. Many adult survivors who deal with abuse for the first time in their 20s, 30s, or 40s describe scenarios wherein they attempted to disclose their abuse, but were immediately shut down by the listener, and the entire concept of sexual abuse was silenced. Without emotional support from a caring adult who validates abuse issues, and without any acknowledgment that the child was not to blame, abused children often develop cognitive schemas that reiterate similar themes. If no one cares, why should emotional feelings be expressed? Abuse survivors who have carried these schemas into adulthood often suppress their own emotional needs and may not be able to identify their needs even with encouragement from a caring partner. Validation of disclosure of abuse is paramount to letting children know that they are valued, respected, and entitled to expression of their feelings, all of which constitute an essential premise for developing fulfilling adult relationships.

5. Ideological Versus Barren Ideological views represent values, beliefs, and philosophies toward life in general, as well as ideologies of self-existence. These concepts contribute to the development of self-identity. A child who does not internalize a positive belief system has difficulty with establishing a positive self-identity, setting boundaries for self and others, and having the ability to differentiate between acceptable and unacceptable behaviors. Abusive home influences deprive children of a fertile learning environment in which to develop ideological value systems; therefore, these children remain barren of substantive concepts of self.

Without a strongly developed internal belief system, an individual may be prone to react as a chameleon; the person's value-based discriminatory skills are remiss. Thus, without a solid ideological concept of self, children may easily follow a persuasive adult, teens may more easily succumb to peer pressure even when the activities being shared are unhealthy or illegal, and adults may blindly follow anyone who will provide them with sufficient attention. A vivid example of this occurs when a woman who experienced abuse during childhood becomes victimized by adult male partners who abuse, exploit, or harm her; she accepts the situation as part of her ideological view of self worth and inability to set healthy boundaries.

6. Direction Versus Misguidance Healthy environments foster instruction, guidance, and direction for children that will enhance their lives in adulthood, in spite of the negative events, mistakes, and misguided circumstances experienced along the way. Healthy environments contain role models who demonstrate for children what is involved in building healthy intimate relationships with others, acquiring a sense of productivity in the world of work, and maintaining a healthy perspective of self-image and self-worth. For abused children who lack such direction and guidance from concerned others, the detrimental effects of abuse tend to be magnified. When much-needed healing interventions are never realized, the adverse impact of the abuse remains implanted on the child's psyche. On the other hand, when children receive immediate and adequate direction and guidance from concerned others, the adverse impact of the abuse can be addressed early, giving the abused child a chance to rebuild a positive self-image and prepare for adulthood in a more constructive manner.

7. Encouragement Versus Discouragement When children receive positive and encouraging messages throughout childhood, and in particular after a disclosure of abuse, positive self-esteem is fostered (Fraser, Nelson, Rivard, 1997). For children who receive negative comments, treatment, and punishment from significant others on a daily basis in abusive homes, where will their encouragement come from? If encouragement is never encountered, children internalize an underlying sense of discouragement that permeates all other aspects of their lives. Discouraging thoughts do not prepare children to take initiative in pursuit of a fulfilling life, but rather restrain them from seeking out new activities, friends, and experiences. Once again, the abused child is robbed of the opportunity to gain inner strength and self-confidence and to advance in life by successfully completing the developmental stages. If negative responses from others continue, these children develop a sense of discouragement that can persist throughout their adult lives.

PROVIDE and Paradoxical Emotional Reactions The seven-factor childhood needs model (PROVIDE) illustrates the source of underlying residual emotional reactions, reactions that are often paradoxical to personal values or socially acceptable norms. When a child feels love for a parent, yet also hates that parent for abusing him or her, a paradoxical state emerges. When a child seeks positive reinforcement from a caregiver one day, but experiences abandonment by that same caregiver the next day, a paradoxical state emerges. In these situations, ambivalence and confusion persist if no intervention is obtained. However, a review of each element of the PROVIDE model can help an abusee attain a greater understanding of his or her unmet needs. At times simply offering an explanation as to why an abusee reacts to certain triggering stimuli is therapeutic in itself; however, this is only the beginning. The abusee must, as the next step, identify the core emotions that underlie distressful reactions and understand how these emotions stem from inappropriate messages received during childhood, which in turn resulted in ambivalent and incongruent emotional needs.

Two-Dimensional Model
of Emotional Congruency (MEC)

This section will examine another model proposed by the author, the model of emotional congruency (MEC). The MEC is comprised of adjectives often used by abusees in expressing their emotions. Emotional reactions can be classified as either internalized emotional reactions (IER), directed toward self, or externalized emotional reactions (EER), directed outward (see Table 4.2). The objective of using the MEC is to identify abusees' concerns along a continuum of two-dimensional reactions, ranging from congruent to incongruent emotional responses in both the internalized and externalized modes of expression. The idealized goal is to bring an abusee into congruency, or emotional harmony, as another step toward minimizing or illuminating the abusee's stressful reactions.

Internalized Emotional Reactions (IER) Internalized emotional reactions range in severity across a continuum of responses. If these responses negatively impact the individual, the reactions are incongruent with self, whereas reactions that are aligned with internal belief systems are congruent with the abusee's self, resulting in emotional harmony. For example, while sadness is a normal reaction to being violated by someone and needs to be processed appropriately, when the magnitude of that sadness consumes the abusee, that emotional reaction may need to be improved if the abusee is to ever reach a sense of congruency with self. Otherwise, the abusee may be needlessly consumed with nonproductive, harmful, or adverse emotional reactions that only serve to extend residual pain from the abuse. The ideal treatment goal, then, would be to help the abusee to obtain congruent internalized qualities that empower and strengthen him or her, while minimizing incongruent qualities that restrict his or her recovery.

Table 4.2 Model of Emotional Congruency (MEC)

Internalized Directed Toward Self		Externalized Directed Toward Abuser	
INCONGRUENT	*CONGRUENT*	*INCONGRUENT*	*CONGRUENT*
Abandoned . . . . .Wanted		Abusive . . . . .Indifferent	
Alone . . . . .Supported		Aggressive . . . . .Indifferent	
Ashamed . . . . .Self-accepting		Anger . . . . .Dispensation	
Attention-seeking . . . .Self-approving		Approval-seeking . . . .Self-approving	
Bad . . . . .Good		Ashamed . . . . .Indifferent	
Blocked . . . . .Freed		Bewildered . . . . .Understanding	
Condemned . . . . .Acknowledged		Blocked . . . . .Freed	
Confused . . . . .Clarified		Confused . . . . .Clarified	
Disappointment . . . . .Adequacy		Controlled . . . . .Indifferent	
Embarrassed . . . . . . .Self-confident		Defiant . . . . .Accepting	
Evil . . . . .Good		Despising . . . . .Indifferent	
Frightened . . . . .Comforted		Disappointment . . . .Acceptance	
Frozen . . . . .Released		Discarded . . . . .Indifferent	
Frustrated . . . . .At Peace		Disgusted . . . . .Accepting	
Guilt-ridden . . . . .Guilt-free		Distanced . . . . .Effortless	
Helpless . . . . .Empowered		Embarrassed . . . . . . .Disregard	
Incapable . . . . .Capable		Fearful . . . . .Indifferent	
Inferior . . . . .Adequate		Hatred . . . . .Indifference	
Insecure . . . . .Secure		Inaccessible . . . . . . .Accepting	
Needy . . . . .Fulfilled		Love . . . . .Peace	
Overpowered . . . . . . .Empowered		Oppositional . . . . . . .Indifferent	
Overwhelmed . . . . . . .In Control		Overwhelmed . . . . . .Peaceful	
Passive . . . . .Assertive		Pity . . . . .Indifference	
Promiscuous . . . . . . .Discrete		Powerful . . . . .Ineffective	
Self-blaming . . . . . . .Self-accepting		Repulsed . . . . .Indifferent	
Self-doubting . . . . . .Self-confident		Revengeful . . . . .Indifferent	
Self-rejecting . . . . . . .Self-acknowledging		Rigid . . . . .Flexible	
Submissive . . . . .Decisive		Shocked . . . . .Dismayed	
Weak . . . . .Strong		Spiteful . . . . .Indifferent	
Worthless . . . . .Worthy		Vindictive . . . . .Indifferent	

Externalized Emotional Reactions (EER) Externalized emotional reactions are those expressed toward the abuser and other persons. When the abusee's externalized reactions that are incongruent with the abusee's unique needs can be brought into congruency, a more harmonious emotional state results. Perhaps the most frequently expressed emotion in response to past abuse is that of anger directed toward the abuser. While processing this anger may indeed serve as a healing process for some abusees, anger that is of such magnitude that it immobilizes the abusee from moving forward in life should be addressed. Ideally, exercises and discussions aimed at dissipating the anger can lead to emotional congruency for the abusee. Ultimately, psychic energy is freed from stagnating influences and the abusee can move forward in the healing process and, perhaps for the first time since the abuse, achieve personal goals and aspirations. Once a sense of emotional congruency is obtained, quality of life can be improved.

Identification of Congruent and Incongruent Emotions Both congruent and incongruent dimensions of emotional reactions are presented in the MEC. Incongruent emotional reactions are those that cause a sense of disconnectedness, lack of internal harmony, and distress, thereby interfering with daily functioning. Although it is quite normal to experience intense emotional reactions when a traumatic event occurs, abuse survivors may need assistance to bring these emotional reactions into a more congruent state. For example, an individual who is dealing with abuse for the first time and is in crisis often displays spontaneous and intense emotional reactions, such as excessive crying, acute depression, or severe anger states. All of these reactions are draining on the individual and may be in conflict with his or her usual personality traits; therefore, the individual experiences a sense of incongruency with self.

Once incongruent emotional reactions are identified, treatment plans can focus on helping the abusee to process those emotions in a more effective manner. The optimal treatment goal is to have the individual attain a sense of inner peace and congruency. Cognitive energy formerly spent ineffectively processing the event can eventually be directed toward more self-satisfying activities such as academic pursuits, career goals, building healthy relationships, and other success experiences.

Successful events in life can be empowering in and of themselves, and therefore are healing in nature. Not only will emotional states become more regulated and consistent, but erroneous concepts acquired in light of the abuse also can be clarified. Erroneous beliefs such as self-blame, diminished self-esteem, and even self-hatred can be replaced with concepts of self-confidence, self-appreciation, and self-love. In essence, by bringing incongruent emotions into harmony and congruency with self, self-perceptions are improved and self-worth is enhanced.

Contradictory Emotional States If healing is to occur, it is essential to examine core symptoms and emotional reactions contributing to the syndrome of paradoxical states. Careful history taking, interviewing, and evaluations must be conducted. A therapist must be astute enough to discern subtle cues that the abusee reveals in dialogue, particularly during sessions immediately following disclosure and in the crisis stage of counseling.

In familial abuse cases, often the family unit is disrupted and either the abused child or the abusing parent is removed from the home. This abrupt disruption of the family unit causes financial, emotional, and physical hardships. The abusee may experience a tremendous sense of guilt, in that if he or she had never disclosed the abuse, the family would not be enduring such hardships.

Consequently, an abusee must revisit, evaluate, and, if appropriate, reconstruct the series of complex cognitive networks he or she has been harboring. This is no easy task. Years of indoctrination must be torn down and rebuilt. Even where a family unit's dynamics have a detrimental impact on a child's welfare, the child is familiar with that unit and may experience any change or threat to it as very frightening. A sense of loyalty toward all family members often compels an abused child to deny abuse allegations, regardless of how dysfunctional the child's household may be.

Cognitive schemas formed early in life are difficult to break down, modify, or eliminate, since the individual is forced to adorn a new identity that is foreign to him or her. Even though a family member sexually abuses a child, that abuse is only one portion of the relationship between the child and that family member. When the abuse is not taking place, some of the child's needs, such as social interaction, medical and health issues, and clothing, meals, and shelter, probably are being met. So although the child may hate the abusive act performed by the abusing adult, he or she maintains a certain amount of allegiance to that adult. This may change as the child matures, particularly in adolescence when a greater sense of independence evolves and matured cognitive skills allow the child to process the abuse in a more mature manner. As noted earlier, however, it is not unusual to find adult survivors of abuse, well past mid-life, still longing for a positive relationship with their abusing parents.

Reconstructing Psychological Dynamics Reconstructing psychological dynamics, albeit a recommended part of the healing process, poses a new threat to abused individuals. These individuals must attempt to unravel the inner belief systems that form the core of their personal identity. Old habits are hard to change, especially if changing means facing rejection from significant others in life. Fear of disbelief, rejection, and denial from family members comes into play. In addition, even though an individual knows that the abuse was wrong and may hate the abuser for exposing him or her to the abuse (whether physical, emotional, or sexual), he or she may still need some form of love, acceptance, or acknowledgment from his or her abusing parent. To many children, and adults as well, even bad love is better than no love at all.

Hence, many abusees often resist the healing process because of fear—of rejection by all family members, of denial from the abusing parent, and of the unknown. Many survivors of abuse remain silent for years, fearing what might become of them if they do disclose the abuse. Severing ties with the only family one has ever known, as a possible consequence of disclosure, is a scary prospect. A parent figure who was also the abuser and the source of the trauma may also represent the source of personal identity, whether good, bad, or indifferent. Hence, a web of intricate and complex emotional relations is at the core of the therapeutic dilemma. Mental health professionals who are not apprised of such complex dynamics should refer abusees elsewhere as any ill-informed recommendations during therapy can erupt havoc on the very core of an abusees psyche.

It is estimated that for every abusee who receives therapeutic intervention, another abusee never addresses his or her emotional issues, yet remains plagued by unresolved emotional conflicts or turmoil (Harris & Landis, 1997; Prendergast, 1993). Because the abuse event is such a personal experience, each individual can seek help only when, or if, he or she becomes ready for it. Often abusees are reluctant to seek assistance because of (a) a stigma, cultural or otherwise, placed on those who receive psychological services (Pope & Brown, 1996); (b) fear of disrupting a controlled façade with emotionally traumatic events (Classen & Yalom, 1995); (c) fear of losing anonymity and confidentiality (Harris & Landis, 1997); (d) complications from extensive mental illness such as depression or psychosis (Loftus, 1993); and (e) numerous other influences inherent in each individual.

Treatment, including probing, invasive interviews and other interventions, should never be forced on an abusee until he or she is emotionally ready to respond to it. The intensity of feelings and reactions can be frightening for an abusee, and often these feelings and reactions trigger further issues of concern, sort of like opening Pandora's box. Significant partners and primary relatives are often perplexed by the onslaught of acute emotional upheavals and reactions that can erupt at any time once the abusee has acknowledged the abuse (Classen & Yalom, 1995; Harris & Landis, 1997).

Environmental Support   Early childhood interactions with significant caretakers significantly contribute to a child's learned belief systems, attitudes, and behaviors. Messages received during the early years are internalized and thereby shape the child's attitudinal approach toward life in general. As a child matures and struggles to accommodate new learning experiences and to assimilate new concepts into cognitive structures, each accomplishment is tempered with underlying beliefs, values, and lessons learned from the experience.

Adult personality traits are, in large part, a product of childhood influences. Even though all individuals have innate traits and tendencies that are unique to them, no one can dispute the impact of environmental and familial influences. Regardless of whether a child is abused by an immediate family member, distant family member, family associate, or stranger, a significant caretaker's reaction to the child's disclosure of abuse significantly impacts recovery.

Supportive empathy is the most helpful reaction, as long as the abusee is not at risk of suicide, homicide, or abusing others. If severe concerns for the abusee's welfare arise, as often happens during the immediate crisis stage, crisis telephone numbers in the local community should be called for advice on how best to proceed. In dealing with friends, family members, or loved ones who have experienced abuse but are still too devastated to seek help, it is essential to remain supportive, patient, and understanding. Pushing or forcing individuals into confronting the past prematurely can precipitate devastating emotional reactions in them. Every abusee is entitled to privacy, respect, and understanding as he or she comes to terms with the past. It is a uniquely challenging, and often painful, process.

SUMMARY

First, the impact of child sexual abuse was discussed from the abusee's perspective, within the framework of the syndrome of paradoxical states (SPS). The SPS was operationally defined as a state of mind stemming from perpetual incongruency in messages received from primary caretakers. The seven-factor childhood needs model (PROVIDE) was presented to emphasize parenting traits that enhance a child's emotional well-being. The seven factors that are represented by the acronym PROVIDE were defined as: Protection versus exposure; Reinforcement versus abandonment; Opportunity versus oppression; Validation versus denial; Ideological versus barren; Direction versus misguidance; and Encouragement versus discouragement. When these essential nurturing qualities are not provided, or are provided only intermittently, by primary caretakers, the child receives ambiguous messages and develops incongruent emotional reactions that remain with the individual well into adulthood.

To define elements of SPS, particularly as it relates to sexual abuse, the model of emotional congruency (MEC) was proposed, indicating bipolar pairs of emotional reactions that are often identified among sexual abuse survivors. Contradictions and ambiguities in messages received from primary caretakers have serious implications for personality development.

If you have difficulty understanding the impact of paradoxical messages, think of a recent event in your own workplace, when you received contradictory messages from a supervisor or manager. How stressful was it for you to carry out your routine in the workplace? How insecure or anxious did the contradictory messages make you feel? Now magnify that effect tenfold for a child who depends on a primary caretaker and does not have the cognitive skills to understand, cope, or adapt to such paradoxical messages. Sustained exposure to so many emotional contradictions fuels the development of the syndrome of paradoxical states.

DISCUSSION QUESTIONS

1. Does the abusee's relationship with the perpetrator have an impact on his or her healing? Discuss your answer.

2. Many note that recovery is never possible, only that coping skills may be developed. What is your opinion? Explain your answer.

3. Imagine your instructor changing the mood of the class each time you meet. One time there is humor, another time there is tension, and then the next time there is chaos. How would your interactions be affected?

4. Have you known anyone who might have benefited from counseling, for any purpose, yet dreaded going? Explain your answer.

5. If a dear friend came to you and spoke of former abuse, how would you advise him or her to proceed? What would your reaction be if you were told the abuser was her or his parent, a person you also knew and trusted?

6. How do you think that contradictory messages received from parents can impact a child? Why do these messages distort a child's self-image?

7. If a client or friend came to you and told you that he or she was abused in the past and is currently experiencing many turbulent emotional moods, how would you assist him or her?

8. How might paradoxical messages received by children impact the stages of development throughout childhood, adolescence, and adulthood?

5

Theoretical Models
of Diagnosis, Treatment,
and Recovery

LEARNING OBJECTIVES

Chapter 5 will address the following learning objectives:

1. An illustration of how residual emotional and symptomatic reactions cumulate over time

2. A discussion of personal attributes that allow an abusee to initiate therapy

3. A presentation of a five-axis model for diagnostic evaluation (ABCDE) that can assist in the treatment process

4. A discussion of a four-factor initiation of therapy model (ABLE) based on personality attributes

5. An illustration of how a six-factor recovery process model (WAIVES) can identify strengths to aid in recovery

6. A discussion of the practical application of theoretical models

INTRODUCTION

The previous chapter reviewed complex emotional issues relevant to all survivors of sexual abuse. Although a common core of emotional issues appears to impact all abusees, each individual has unique issues stemming from this very private, personal invasion of self. Therapists need to understand each client's unique issues; and the identification of these emotional issues appears to warrant a conceptualization of their key elements.

The *Diagnostic and Statistical Manual of Mental Disorders,* 4th edition–Text Revision (*DSM-IV-TR™*) (APA, 2000) provides essential information for therapists to use in classifying severe pathology, and also contains V codes to designate special problems that may impact Axis I diagnosis, and thus require attention during treatment. For example, child abuse, neglect, and sexual abuse may be differentiated by the use of V codes. While *DSM-IV-TR™* categories assist in making global classifications of mental disorders (Axis I), personality disorders (Axis II), and developmental disorders (Axis III), these classifications do not allow for the identification of core emotional concerns that must be worked through during weekly therapy sessions. Similarly, the classification of psychosocial stressors (Axis IV) and a global assessment of functioning (GAF; Axis V) assist in gaining an overall perspective of an individual's functioning, but these categories are not sufficient to summarize clients' cognitive, emotional, and psychological attributes.

This chapter will propose three conceptual models for diagnosing personal attributes that may expedite therapy or impede its completion. First, a five-axis model, simplistically called ABCDE, is offered for diagnosis. This model differs from that of *DSM-IV-TR™* in that it takes a deeper look at the interpersonal attributes that are unique to each client. The next two models address the ability of sexual abuse survivors to sustain the counseling process, an ability that differs among abusees, as resiliency differs between individuals. As weekly sessions become emotionally draining or upsetting, some clients abandon therapy prematurely, without resolution of their issues. So what makes one individual continue the therapy process, while others do not? What personal attributes allow one individual to recover, while another person remains emotionally distressed throughout life? The two recovery process models offered in this chapter (ABLE and WAIVES) allow therapists to identify qualities that enable (ABLE) abusees to initiate therapy and then, once engulfed in the emotional healing work, sustain the rough ride through the emotional waves (WAIVES).

FIVE-AXIS DIAGNOSTIC EVALUATION MODEL (ABCDE): A MULTIDIMENSIONAL APPROACH

A five-axis diagnostic evaluation model referred to as ABCDE is offered to illustrate a structured means of diagnosing the client's current level of functioning and developing subsequent treatment plans, given the conditions of abuse. Within this model, the five diagnostic axes include Axis I: Attributes; Axis II: Balance; Axis III: Cognition; Axis IV: Diagnosis of Mental Disorders, if any; and Axis V: Environmental Support—hence the acronym ABCDE (see Table 5.1). This model, which is based on the five-axis diagnosis patterns in the *DSM-IV-TR™*, can be instrumental in building a hierarchical treatment plan based on

Table 5.1 Five-Axis Diagnostic Evaluation Model (ABCDE)

Dimension	Description
Axis I: Attributes of Personality	Preexisting individual characteristics of the abusee as evaluated through a standardized mental health examination that includes use of any relevant assessment tools.
Axis II: Balance of Emotions	Reactions from the abuse that may throw emotional balance off-key, which in turn jeopardizes the healing process. A harmonious approach toward problem solving, coping, and everyday adjustment helps the client to maintain balance.
Axis III: Cognitive Awareness	Cognitive awareness of factual data surrounding abuse issues in general, building upon the unique connotations that are relevant on a case-by-case basis.
Axis IV: Diagnosis of Mental Disorders	Diagnosis of any preexisting or coexisting mental disorder (comorbidity, dual diagnosis) that can impair the therapeutic process, such as substance abuse, mental impairment or developmental disorders (e.g., mental retardation), and health-related disorders (e.g., epilepsy).
Axis V: Environmental Support	A supportive environment that enhances recovery. Involvement of supportive family members or friends in the healing process helps to minimize daily stressors.

the level of severity found on each axis. By focusing on the underlying elements in each axis, a therapist can isolate elements and develop strategic treatment approaches for each level of concern. Qualities in a client's profile can be reinforced by the identification of strengths that are also found on each axis.

Axis I: Attributes of Personality

Axis I (Attributes) refers to the unique personality attributes, personality disorders, or personality traits that may impact treatment processes, but are a relatively fixed part of the client's personality, for example, narcissism or histrionic personality disorder—or, conversely, resiliency or adaptive traits. A personality factor identified on Axis I is differentiated from any severe diagnostic concerns identified on Axis IV, concerns that may be situational, chronic, or dominate the focus of treatment due to their urgency. Any steadfast personality traits identified on Axis I must be considered when implementing a treatment plan and deciding on an approach in therapy. A passive-dependent person may encounter greater distress if family members abandon him or her than an antisocial individual, who may have become emotionally detached from others at an early age.

Axis I also corresponds to an individual's preexisting personality attributes or psychological functioning, which needs to be considered during the counseling process. If an individual is predisposed toward negative thinking, then every situation he or she faces is viewed negatively. Treating an individual with long-standing negative views toward life will, most likely, require more in-depth and lengthier intervention services than treating someone with a predisposition toward positive outcomes, who will be more open and receptive to the therapy process. Similarly, a quiet, withdrawn individual may need to progress through counseling at a slower rate than an individual who is more assertive and confrontational about pursuing his or her problems. As with all therapy processes, the therapeutic relationship must be built upon client needs and expectations (Classen &Yalom, 1995; Harris & Landis, 1997; Prendergast, 1993).

Axis II: Balance of Emotions

Axis II (Balance) refers to the client's ability to balance emotional concerns on a daily basis. Anyone with a tendency to find emotional balance, regardless of life's stressors, obviously has a better chance of coping appropriately through the often turbulent healing process. Assessing balance in an individual's life includes noting the individual's attention to self-perceived descriptions of balance and harmony. Professional research studies have found that an increase in the stressors in life can exacerbate or heighten all other concerns in a person's life. Certainly, when an individual builds logical problem-solving skills, adequate coping skills, and an overall ability to adjust under pressure, all other obstacles, hardships, or disruptions in life are handled in a more proficient manner.

Balancing emotions also refers to the manner in which an abusee reacts to the abuse experience. For example, with an individual who experiences severe depression, therapy work will proceed much more slowly, if at all, than it will with an individual who responds in an emotionally balanced manner, that is, in a manner that is not disproportionate to the event. Because all individuals respond to traumatic events in a unique way, treatment plans must be developed on a case-by-case basis. Even though there are common elements among abuse survivors, such as issues of self-esteem, boundary setting, and the development of coping skills, the unique internal frame of reference of each client must also be considered. Individuals who are acutely, emotionally distressed from the abuse require an expedient treatment plan, and hospitalization may be needed in extreme cases. During the initial contact with a client in crisis, professionals should adhere to professional practices such as assessing the individual's intent to harm, implementing environmental support systems, and so on.

Axis III: Cognitive Awareness

Within Axis III (Cognition), cognitive awareness includes awareness of the issues surrounding the abuse experience; this is essential in helping a client build an understanding of the events that occurred. Although a client's cognitive awareness of the issues does not necessarily heal emotional pain, it does provide the client with a basis upon which to build appropriate cognitive perception of the event. Many clients withdraw emotionally because of feelings of alienation, shame, and hopelessness. Once a client understands the facts concerning child sexual abuse (CSA) and the healing methods that are available, a sense of hope and empowerment replaces the client's hopelessness, and therapy can be more effectively completed. With cognitive awareness of the facts surrounding CSA, pending legal issues or procedures, and the process of recovery, any stress that was provoked by uncertainties can be easily alleviated. Axis III assesses the client's knowledge base of the topic of sexual abuse, and subsequent treatment plans can include the dissemination of educational literature about CSA based on the client's level of cognitive awareness.

Cognitive awareness of the abuse requires an ability to interpret, synthesize, and evaluate. If a child is too young to understand, cope, or cognitively process the abuse, a multisensory technique in therapy may be required. Play therapies and creative tools and techniques can reach children on their level of functioning (Landreth, 1991). However, older individuals, such as adolescents and adults, may be capable of intellectually coping and processing relevant issues through dialogue or cognitive and behavioral interventions (Clark & Fairburn, 1997; Dobson & Craig, 1996).

Axis IV: Diagnostic Severity

In Axis IV (Diagnosis of Mental Disorders), diagnostic severity should be assessed and documented. Any comorbidity issues, substance abuse, developmental disorders, and other preexisting issues or issues subsequent to the abuse should be identified. Treatment plans should reflect the same progressive intervention techniques that are standard for any other client. However, with therapy for a survivor of child abuse, any mental illness or coexisting diagnostic issue will require a more complex treatment plan and, perhaps, an extended prognosis for recovery. Additional community resources may be required, particularly if any of the ensuing complications fall outside the therapist's scope of professional preparation or licensing.

Recovery can also be impacted by the length, frequency, and duration of the abuse, as well as the type of abuse (Classen & Yalom, 1995; Finkelhor, 1986). With clients who have experienced abuse over long periods of time, an extended prognosis for recovery may be required. For individuals with minimal overall functioning or long-term difficulties in overall adjustment, treatment planning may require long-term therapy, as well as the implementation of community resources; interventions using pharmacology, medical assistance, and other services may be deemed appropriate. Assessing the overall functioning of an abusee is an inherent part of the diagnosis and evaluation, as emphasized in the *DSM-IV-TR*™.

Axis V: Environmental Support

Axis V (Environmental Support) is essential, as recovery from abuse can be greatly enhanced if family members, significant others, and any other involved parties are supportive of the client's recovery process. Literature in the field readily notes that following disclosure, family members often withdraw, leaving the abused party alone and abandoned as he or she attempts to sort out a new onslaught of emotional conflicts resulting first from the disclosure itself, and then from abandonment by family members. Therefore, environmental support, if available to the abusee, can expedite the healing process significantly. In addition to identifying sources of emotional support, the identification of basic needs such as shelter, financial aid, clothing, and meals is essential in assisting the client through the healing process, especially if the client is in crisis at the time of the initial meeting and has, perhaps, been abandoned by family members.

As with all mental health issues, psychosocial stressors can jeopardize the recovery of sexual abuse survivors, whereas supportive family members or friends can greatly enhance the healing process. Therefore, it is essential in treatment planning to assess not only the client's environmental stressors, but also the client's support network, significant family members and friends, and other influences that offer emotional support for the abusee (APA, 2000). In the absence of concerned family members, support groups are beneficial, often providing cohesiveness and bonding between group members (Harris & Landis, 1977). Once diagnosis is completed on all five axes, a deeper assessment of personal attributes may prove beneficial. The four-factor model (ABLE) is presented to identify core attributes that enable some abusees to seek professional assistance while others may not.

FOUR-FACTOR INITIATION
OF THERAPY MODEL (ABLE)

A four-factor personality attributes model is represented here by the acronym ABLE, which stands for: Attitude, Behavior, Learning, and Environment (see Table 5.2). How abusees function on each dimension of this model significantly impacts the recovery process. Why are some clients able to initiate and complete therapeutic intervention, while others remain immobilized by the abuse experience? All individuals possess unique dimensions of *attitude,* react to stressful events with different *behaviors,* grasp new concepts, good or bad, based upon unique patterns of *learning,* and respond to the need for therapy based on supportive influences within their *environment.* Each element of personality contributes to an individual's overall propensity to initiate the recovery process, and thus forms a base of identifiable skills that render him or her *able* to recover.

Attitude as expressed in the ABLE model refers to an individual's personal convictions and willingness to pursue therapy. Personal values and religious convictions may either propel an individual into recovery or inhibit that person from seeking out a healing process, particularly if personal values deny or prohibit the acquisition of therapy. Resistant attitudes toward obtaining therapy often restrict an individual's daily functioning as well; withdrawal or denial may be used to avoid environmental demands. Such a person may remain in denial and forestall confrontation with the facts of the abuse, only to harbor recriminations of self, internal turmoil, or, worse yet, self-destructive behaviors. On the other hand, an individual with a preexisting positive attitude may

Table 5.2 Four-Factor Initiation of Therapy Model (ABLE)

Element	Operational Definition	Application to the Healing Process
Attitude	Emotional Affect	
	Perspective toward overcoming adverse experiences from childhood. Range of attitude barriers that may enhance or prohibit successful completion of the healing process.	Blocking, resisting, and procrastinating are all attitudes that can act as barriers to healing, whereas being proactive, willing to work on issues, and determined to heal will enhance recovery.
Behavior	Previously Learned or Sublimated Behaviors	
	Actions taken in response to emotional occurrences or upheavals, often based on habit, previous learning, or sublimated behaviors due to a pre-existing belief system. Internalized behaviors such as self-mutilation and externalized actions taken to resolve distress.	Negative internalized behaviors (e.g., self-mutilation) prolong the need for therapy. Positive, proactive behaviors and active efforts to seek assistance shorten recovery time.
Learning	Past and Present Learning	
	Past learning such as concepts of right and wrong and a learned ability to verbally express needs and desires, and present learning and ability to understand information about CSA syndrome.	Recognizing old and learning new concepts allows the individual to understand the elements and dynamics of the abusive event, and to thereby gain a greater awareness of the event's total impact and, perhaps, gain control over aspects of the event.
Environment	Environmental Support	
	Physical and emotional support from significant others in the individual's environment, which is a key element to the speed of the child's or adults recovery.	Regardless of the age of the client, parental support, or the lack of it, affects the speed of recovery. When protective others empathize and acknowledge the child's or adult's abuse experience, self-doubt is minimized. Significant partners can enhance recovery if they are supportive, understanding, and patient with the individual during therapy.

be more receptive to the concept of obtaining help, and therefore overcome negative emotions earlier than those who are resistant.

Although treatment goals must be individualized and will differ among abusees, there are some common underlying threads or patterns of thought in individuals following childhood abuse experiences. These include a sense of oppression, worthlessness, inadequacy, self-doubt, and so on, all of which contribute to feelings of powerlessness. Therefore, initiating the first contact for therapy can be empowering in and of itself. The simple act of making a phone call to schedule an appointment with a therapist can be therapeutic for an abusee; after all, it is the first step toward empowerment.

Once therapy is initiated, abusees face another challenge, that of maintaining therapy throughout the roller coaster ride of emotional reactions that surface during therapy. Often, abusees must deal with painful and emotionally charged memories of experiences and acute, intense emotional reactions that resurface during the treatment process. If the intensity of these reactions becomes too severe or painful for the abusee to endure, therapy may be prematurely terminated. So, what personal factors strengthen an abusee's determination to ride the emotional waves?

SIX-FACTOR RECOVERY PROCESS MODEL (WAIVES)

A six-dimensional therapy model known as WAIVES illustrates the essential elements that allow an individual to adhere to the often painful therapeutic process (see Table 5.3). The acronym WAIVES stands for: Well-being, Aptitude, Intellectual Processing, Validation, Education, and Strength. Individuals often experience varying levels of each personality factor, which is what makes each abusee's experience unique to him or her. This model represents personality factors that may explain why some clients endure the emotional roller coaster of therapy, while others abandon therapy prematurely when it becomes too overwhelming. An abusee may abandon the therapy process because of issues, memories, or dreams that are emotionally frightening, repulsive to view, and often contradict religious or personal value systems. If further help is not sought, the abusee may confine him- or herself to a life of silent suffering or unsatisfying relationships rather than working through therapeutic issues concerning the abuse. The following discussion of the six-factor WAIVES model will lead to a better understanding of the healing process.

Well-Being

In assessing a survivor of abuse, the therapist must first consider the individual's overall emotional well-being. For example, if an individual is predisposed to negative thinking and chronic mood swings, or experiencing a confounding mental illness, each complicating factor will impact his or her decision to follow through with therapy. Any additional stress caused by the treatment process will surely exacerbate any preexisting conditions; therefore, if not monitored, preexisting conditions can force the client to evade the distressful content unraveled during therapy. Professionally trained mental health workers would surely identify these issues at the onset of treatment, but the impact of each factor on the successful completion of therapy must also be considered so that appropriate interventions can be initiated. Methods of identifying these attributes include standardized test instruments (Anastasia, 1988; Sattler, 2001), surveys and rating scales, and informal intake interviews.

Table 5.3 Six-Factor Recovery Process Model (WAIVES)

Element	Operational Definition	Consequences for the Healing Process
Well-Being	Previous predisposition for positive affect.	A preexisting predisposition for positive thought helps the abusee to develop or strengthen a determination to move forward on the healing journey and to confront issues as they arise.
Aptitude	Potential to proceed in light of the emotionally distressing issues that must be dealt with.	The propensity to assimilate all elements of the healing process, partly built on the ability to cope under stress, aids in healing. If coping skills are preexisting for the survivor, then departmentalizing, intellectualizing, and overall understanding of the abuse experience is possible.
Intellectual Processing	Cognitive processes that are necessary to reason, rationalize, and mentally accommodate the actions that have transpired with a minimal sense of confusion or misunderstanding of the circumstances.	An ability to intellectually process and acquire knowledge of the facts concerning self-reactions, perpetrator behaviors, and any intervening events is important. An accurate knowledge base of the dynamics of the CSA syndrome hastens the healing process and allows the abusee to gain a sense of control, to become empowered, and to acquire and implement new coping skills.
Validation	Validation of the event, feelings, and any personalized reactions to the abuse, particularly from significant partners, close friends, and family members.	Because each survivor responds differently and uniquely to an abusive experience, any trauma realized is unique to the individual. Attempts to minimize, deny, or evade acknowledgment of the abuse experience and the survivor's response to it can greatly inhibit the individual from seeking help or processing the event at all, and thus leave the residual negative impact of the abuse unresolved.
Education	Learning facts, details, and coping skills to overcome the abuse experience, which enhances the healing process by minimizing misperceptions that can stigmatize the survivor.	Fact gathering can serve as an empowering event, as the survivor takes control of the situation by actively participating in his or her own healing process. For individuals with a lower level of intellectual functioning, the healing process must be delivered with activities of a more simplistic nature.
Strength	Inner strength and coping skills that are essential if the survivor is to adhere to the therapeutic process until healing is achieved.	Inner strength, defined as a coping style, is what propels the abusee to move forward on his or her healing journey and to ride the waves of the emotional roller coaster, regardless of the conflict, emotional pain, or level of frustration that must be endured to accomplish treatment goals.

Aptitude

The individual's aptitude to heal, or potential to work through the healing process, is another important consideration. Aptitude for coping with numerous emotional concerns on a daily basis may be impaired or absent in sexual abuse survivors, particularly those experiencing post-traumatic stress disorder (PTSD) or other emotional reactions to the event. The roller-coaster effect is common among individuals undergoing therapy; some hours or days are filled with periods of calmness, while other hours or days are riddled with unraveled nerves and high anxiety states. If the abusee cannot find the inner strength or coping mechanisms to remain on the healing path during these stressful times, he or she may prematurely terminate therapy. Therefore, assessing the individual's aptitude to heal is essential for determining whether the individual is likely to complete the therapy process. This can be accomplished by assessing past performance of the client in personal, social, and work-related settings that reflects his or her ability to persist through stressful periods of life. Similarly, assessment instruments that reflect coping skills or mannerisms may provide a structured means of identifying personal factors that may need strengthening through the therapy process.

Intellectual Processing

Another important factor to consider is the individual's overall intellectual processing capability. Flexible intellectual processing will enable an abusee to integrate elements of the abuse experience and the mixed messages he or she has received. Often individuals at all levels of functioning become emotionally blocked or unable to function in all modes of daily life, when they experience trauma. However, abusees who possess lower intellectual ability may not be capable of grasping the concept of what has happened to them; their reactions can range from naïve unawareness of the adverse effects of the abuse to extreme agitation and distress because of the abuse. Researchers have noted that abusees' cognitive or intellectual processing of events directly impacts their emotional reactions to the abuse (Beck & Emery, 1985; Beck & Freeman, 1990). This aspect of a client's functioning is easily assessed through standardized IQ tests, although it is most beneficial if a pre-abuse index of intellectual functioning is available such as past school records or standardized test files.

Validation

Validation, or having others acknowledge the abuse event and the emotional pain attached to it, is also essential to the healing process. Without validation from significant others, individuals may feel abandoned, disbelieved, and even ostracized from meaningful members of their environment. If external pressures are placed on the abusee by disgruntled family members, the abusee may feel compelled to terminate the healing process to please significant others. While it is imperative that the client's feelings about the abuse experience are validated and acknowledged by the therapist, recovery is always enhanced if validation occurs from significant family members. Thus, to strengthen this area of therapy for the client, it may be necessary to work with any number of other family members, helping them to cope with issues related to the abuse. For example, a mother may be in denial that abuse occurred at all, a spouse may become enraged when a loved one discloses for the first time, and other family members may also need intervention services to help them cope with the ramifications of sexual abuse. By helping family members surrounding the client, they, in turn, may prove more supportive of the abusee and thereby provide the validation that can hasten the healing process.

Education

Educational information is essential in propelling an abusee along the healing continuum. By acquiring a knowledge base of facts and perspectives on child sexual abuse, an abusee can cognitively process the event. The educational model of service provisions can be therapeutic in itself, particularly when a client is at the crisis stage of treatment when emotions are raw. By focusing on a less threatening task, such as reading various materials and viewing suggested films, the client can distance him- or herself from the emotional pain that unravels during traditional therapy.

Also, erroneous beliefs and distorted facts can be dispelled, thereby alleviating unwarranted sources of fear and distress for the abusee. For example, the concept of self-blame can be a great source of stress for abusees, but when they are armed with knowledge about their lack of blame and about the incident rates of abuse, this stress can be alleviated. Similarly, knowledge about theories of pedophilic behavior can be healing, in that understanding about the problem may eradicate erroneous myths that can undermine recovery. As noted earlier, educational materials that can be effective include reading materials and discussion of the prevalence rates of child sexual abuse, etiology of pedophilia, and other sources of information on issues to be worked through in treatment sessions. All of these tasks serve to enhance the client's sense of empowerment.

Strength

Finally, and perhaps a summation of all the previous factors, is the element of strength. Strength and inner determination to overcome extreme events is essential if an abusee is to acquire positive outlets for coping with, processing, and overcoming the abuse. Inner strength is perhaps best defined by examining the abusee's tenacity and determination to proceed regardless of how painful the process may be during the early stages of treatment. What coping skills did the abusee bring into the therapy process? Surely, an abusee with a more directive coping style can take a more assertive stance toward healing, whereas someone with an evasive coping style may have to enhance his or her coping abilities to activate any inner strength. Inner strength and coping styles are reciprocal in nature, as one fuels the other. As a client processes new information during therapy, inner strength increases and coping skills strengthen. Similarly, as coping skills are enhanced, new information can be processed.

Attainment of Treatment Goals

Based on the existence of and level of functioning on the six elements of treatment contained in the WAIVES model (well-being, aptitude, intellectual processing, validation, education, and strength), individuals may progress through the treatment process at varying speeds. By understanding the underlying personality elements that are associated with the healing process, the client and therapist may better address each facet of psychological functioning as it impacts the therapeutic process. This model may serve as a framework for understanding why some individuals sustain treatment in spite of the painful distress that surfaces during treatment, while others abandon treatment prematurely, only to endure emotional distress associated with the abuse throughout life.

Extreme Mood Changes During the therapy process, it is not unusual for an abusee to experience disruptive, unexpected, and extreme mood changes as past events are recalled and discussed. Extreme mood changes are provoked through recalled memories, flashbacks, and dreams or nightmares. A memory that occurs spontaneously may be frightening to the individual, often triggering further reactions such as disturbed sleep and lost appetites. Physical reactions to a spontaneous event are common among adult survivors of abuse; thus emotional trauma associated with that memory can be emotionally exhausting as well as physically immobilizing.

It is natural for people to withdraw from an unpleasant experience, just as babies pull away from hot stoves, or nonreaders avoid attending reading classes in school. An abusee's resiliency to withstand the emotional upheavals experienced during therapy is a key element in whether the healing process will be completed. Therapeutic interventions such as systematic relaxation, biofeedback, journaling, physical exercise, spiritual retreats, and many other intervention techniques too numerous to mention here may all serve to help the client withstand the therapy process.

Fear of Remembered Images When flashbacks, or memory recalls, occur spontaneously, abusees are often frightened by the timing, intensity, and content. They may experience feelings of vulnerability at the lack of control over their own thoughts, as well as embarrassment if others witness their reactions. These events can be like waking up from a deep sleep to find oneself shouting because of the fear provoked by a nightmare, only to have a partner cross-examine one about that fearful reaction. Similarly, work tasks may become intolerable and be continually disrupted; and emotional and cognitive processes may be interrupted throughout the day. Abusees often find spontaneous recalls or flashbacks during their daily routines to be invasive, disruptive, and emotionally upsetting. For example, Joan, a 33-year-old woman, was making a sales call when a sales contact greeted her smoking the same brand of cigars that her abuser had smoked. The long-forgotten association with that smell instantaneously invaded her thoughts. She was overcome with tearful memories, complete with the same emotional reactions experienced during the abuse. Of course, there is no ideal time for such an event to occur, but when spontaneous recall is encountered in public, during business meetings, or under the scrutiny of uncaring people, the event becomes even more traumatic and upsetting.

The abusee must develop coping mechanisms to weather the storm, so to speak, of these remembered images. In some instances, reexperiencing an abusive event can be cathartic, as it allows the abusee to release formerly suppressed memories. Many clients have related that vivid recalled memories reaffirmed their own thoughts about the abuse, in that the memory validated formerly identified aspects of abuse. If distress is experienced at the time of the memory or flashback, the abusee needs to realize it is okay to process any emotions associated with it, and that it is a common element of the healing process. It is essential that the therapist reaffirm that the client is progressing in an expected manner and that the reactions are normal. Ochberg (1985) refers to this as normalizing the client, an essential process to alleviate fears and unwarranted self-deprecating statements such as "I am losing my mind" or "I guess I really am crazy."

The following case scenario may demonstrate this concept. A young woman described enjoying a Saturday off from work, completing chores and making a routine visit to the car wash. While driving through the car wash, she experienced a flashback to a childhood event when her father had molested her during a car wash process. She was immediately gripped with fear, physical tension, and tears, as the memory propelled her into a highly distressed state. Before she had entered therapy, she would have reacted with a substantial loss of composure and would have gone directly home. However, during the therapy process, this woman had been emotionally prepared to experience these reactions without the fear of going crazy and without punishing herself with self-directed recriminations. She had developed coping skills that allowed her to take a few minutes to compose herself. By using deep-breathing exercises, she was able to continue with her weekend tasks rather than retreating to her home.

Abandonment of Therapy   If the woman described in the previous section had never gained an understanding of what to expect when memories arose or of her own manner of processing the abuse experience, the result of her flashback in the car wash could have been disastrous. She could have become so distressed that she returned home and continued to condemn herself for "losing it." If that had happened, a major setback in her recovery process would have occurred.

Treatment patterns are often cyclical, not linear. Clients may attend to the healing process only when their emotional stress interferes with their daily functioning and then, once minimal progress has been made, abandon treatment. This cycle can continue: therapy is attended, and then it is not. Perhaps of most concern are the clients who sometimes abandon therapy at the height of distressful flashbacks out of fear of the memories. Ironically, this is the time when a breakthrough may be imminent. Therefore, therapists must inform clients, through educational resources, of expected behaviors throughout the healing process. If individuals understand that the emotional waves are a "normal" part of the healing process, their adherence to the counseling process can be maximized and excessive anxiety minimized.

SUMMARY: APPLICATION
OF THEORETICAL MODELS

Child sexual abuse (CSA) was initially discussed in the previous chapter from the abusee's perspective, under the umbrella of the syndrome of paradoxical states (SPS). The emotional impact of abuse on internalized and externalized emotional distress was examined. Discussions illustrated how contradictions and ambiguous messages received from primary caretakers have serious implications for a child's overall personality development.

This chapter presented three conceptual models for diagnosing personal attributes that affect the treatment process. The five-axis evaluation model known as ABCDE provides a format for the assessment and diagnosis of elements of functioning that are unique to each client (see Table 5.1). The four-factor initiation of therapy model addresses elements of personality that compel an individual to actively seek therapy. This model (ABLE) encompasses attitude, behavior, learning, and environment, all of which are personality factors that can help a therapist to understand a client's level of functioning and expedite the healing process (see Table 5.2). The third model, the six-factor recovery process model known as WAIVES, examines personal attributes that strengthen an abusee's ability to sustain the emotional waves that are common during the healing process (see Table 5.3).

Each of these models is proposed to enlighten mental health workers about elements that impact treatment and the underlying dynamics that impact healing. Table 5.4 summarizes these diagnosis and recovery models by presenting a comprehensive model that illustrates parallels between the elements of the client's profile that may enhance or restrict recovery. As shown in Table 5.4, therapists should start with Step 1 (diagnosis), and proceed to Step 2 (evaluation of personality attributes). Revisit Step 3 as often as necessary if the client does not progress through therapy in a linear fashion. For instance, if an abusee attempts to heal but curtails the treatment process because of distress or discomfort, applying the WAIVES model, shown in the table as Step 3, can help to identify which of the client's personal attributes require reinforcement.

Professionals can also use the comprehensive model as a training tool for clients to help them understand the depth of the emotional intricacies that stem from childhood sexual abuse. When the model is used in conjunction with input from a client, greater gains can be made by helping the client to understand how his or her responses and behaviors fit into the elements of the model. The treatment plan can be revised to readdress issues that arise at different points of the therapy.

Theoretical models presented in this chapter are based on the author's experience over a 20-year period of working with adults, adolescents, and children who experienced sexual abuse. Each model presented in this chapter is based on actual issues brought forward during individual and group therapy settings. Figure 5.1 provides a complete summary of models presented in the previous chapter as well as those presented here for a comprehensive illustration of all models under the context of the Syndrome of Paradoxical States.

Table 5.4 Comprehensive Model for Assessment and Treatment of Childhood Sexual Abuse Survivors

Step 1	Step 2	Step 3
FIVE-AXIS DIAGNOSTIC EVALUATION MODEL (ABCDE)	FOUR-FACTOR INITIATION OF THERAPY MODEL (ABLE)	SIX-FACTOR RECOVERY PROCESS MODEL (WAIVES)
1. Personality Attributes	Attitude	Well-Being
2. Emotional Balance	Behavioral Reactions	Aptitude
3. Intellectual Processing	Learning	Intellectual Processing
4. Diagnosis of Mental Disorders	Environment	Validation
5. Environmental Support		Education (fact finding)
		Strength

The models are intended to serve as a framework from which professionals can examine, diagnose, and treat future clients who struggle to overcome the adverse emotional impact of CSA.

DISCUSSION QUESTIONS

1. How can use of the ABCDE diagnostic evaluation model assist in identifying an abusee's needs during the treatment phase of healing?

2. Can you think of additional means of identifying client needs other than those provided here? If so, please list them and explain each method.

3. Balance in a person's life can be achieved in many ways, in addition to traditional counseling. What other means of intervention can a person use to overcome emotional stress associated with abuse?

4. What activities can be introduced into the counseling process to assist an abusee in gaining more information about the abuse experience? How do these activities help to empower the abusee, if they do?

5. What interventions can help to strengthen emotional support that is remiss from a client's environment? How would you advise an abusee to gain this support?

6. Why is it that some individuals can initiate therapy with no problem, whereas other individuals are reluctant to seek therapy or even immobilized at the thought of going to therapy?

7. If the recovery process is so emotionally distressful for an abusee, why should anyone seek professional intervention? Explain your response.

8. What factors might cause an individual to abandon therapy completely, rather than persisting until all therapeutic goals are obtained? How would you address a client who revealed that he or she would not return, although treatment goals remain unfulfilled?

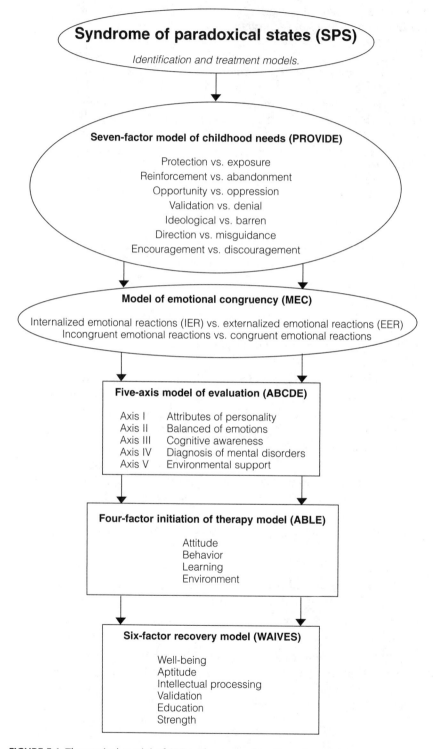

FIGURE 5.1 Theoretical model of SPS and proposed treatment model.

6

Emergence of Child Development Theories

LEARNING OBJECTIVES

Chapter 6 will address the following learning objectives:

1. An introduction to developmental theories in the social sciences

2. A review of Freud's psychoanalytic theory of child development

3. A review of Erikson's theory of psychosocial development

4. A review of Piaget's theory of cognitive development

5. A review of Kohlberg's moral development theory

6. A discussion of contemporary theories of development

INTRODUCTION

By the early 20th century, children were beginning to be viewed as special human beings with unique needs, rather than simply as "little adults." Just as medical science made great strides in gaining insight into physiological development, social scientists investigated the intellectual, psychological, and social aspects of the developmental process. Freud, Piaget, Erikson, and Kohlberg are four prominent scholars who proposed the most far-reaching theories of child development. Each theorist emphasized a series of developmental tasks associated each maturational stage, along with a description of impaired functioning that might arise if opportunities to achieve developmental tasks were deprived due to abuse or neglect.

Impact of Trauma

Social scientists agree that normal child development requires the successful integration of all modes of functioning—physical, psychological, and intellectual. For an abused child, this may not be possible. Traumatic events can render a child incapable of the successful integration of developmental tasks, which later contributes to emotional well-being. In fact, current specialists acknowledge that simply witnessing a traumatic event can trigger psychosocial stressors that can emotionally distress a child. For children exposed to direct physical harm, psychological threat, or sexual assaults, emotional reactions can be severe, emotionally debilitating, and pathological in nature, thus rendering the child incapable of fulfilling age-related tasks essential for adult adjustment.

Although many adults view childhood as a time of play and games, for a child, each newly acquired skill is an accomplishment. For a toddler, the first step taken independently of the parents may be a seemingly large task, but after much determination and preliminary work through standing and wobbling, a child finally walks independent of his or her parents. For a school-aged child, developmental tasks such as learning the alphabet and how to write and learning to socialize all require a conscious effort. For an adolescent, learning to make independent social judgments, acquiring a first job, and learning about sexual intimacy with peers are all stressful tasks that require conscious efforts if success is to be achieved. However, a toddler, child, or adolescent who is preoccupied with surviving, with getting through each day without pain or harm, and with getting a night's sleep without a sexual assault from a family member has little energy left to accomplish these other essential activities. A child who is made to feel worthless, violated, and undeserving may not attempt new activities that could otherwise provide success experiences and strengthen his or her self-confidence toward future goal attainment. An abused child will withdraw or abandon such tasks, thus compounding the debilitating effects of child abuse or assault of any kind.

Developmental Tasks

When a child experiences any traumatic event, whether it is intended or accidental, experienced or observed, physically invasive or psychologically traumatic, normal developmental accomplishments are deterred. For example, children who are sexually abused may regress to bed-wetting, withdraw from social interaction, distrust others, and withdraw from goal achievement due to feelings of inadequacy, fear, or high anxiety as a result of abuse. These reactions undermine a child's normal developmental progress. Although each theorist discussed in this chapter perceives task attainment from a different perspective, whether it be psychoanalytical (Freud, 1920/1977), cognitive (Piaget, 1952), social (Erikson, 1968), or moralistic (Kohlberg, 1981), all of them agree that the effect is cumulative. Early childhood tasks must be accomplished at respective age levels if the child is to progress toward a fulfilling adulthood.

When severe pathology occurs as a result of abuse, family members, spouses, and offspring may also bear the brunt of the abuse. The adult abusee's diminished self-worth may prohibit the individual from pursuing more fulfilling life choices, curtail life perspectives, distort career choices and educational pursuits, and sabotage attempts to succeed. In other words, an adult survivor of abuse may respond to all aspects of environmental demands (personal, social, and work) from an inappropriately developed or underdeveloped sense of self.

The sections in this chapter will provide an overview of four main theories inherent to child development. The theories include (a) Freud's psychosexual stages of development, (b) Erikson's psychosocial theory of development, (c) Piaget's theory of cognitive development, and (d) Kohlberg's theory of moral development. The basis of each theorists' work will serve as a framework within which to elaborate on how sexual abuse may impact development at each stage of life. Key concepts of each theory will be discussed as well as the consequences for altered development following exposure to abuse. Age-specific developmental tasks that are impacted when sexual abuse occurs will be specified for each age group in Section 2 of this text.

FREUD'S PSYCHOANALYTIC THEORY

Psychoanalytic theories are said to have originated with Freud and Breuer's thesis, entitled *Studies in Hysteria* (1895). Although Freud began his professional career as a medical doctor, the inner workings of the human mind soon became the focus of his study. At the time of his initial research, Freud noted that many individuals who behaved in an unusual fashion did so without a clearly identifiable or observable reason. To address his curiosity of this phenomenon, he searched deeper for some rationale, some understanding of the dynamics behind such mysteriously occurring disorders. He later described the underlying structures in the human mind by referring to the *id, ego,* and *superego,* percepts that are initially derived in the child over a series of progressive stages of development. These concepts now serve as the basic tenets of Freud's psychosexual theory of development.

The Id, Ego, and Superego

According to Freud, the underlying structure of the unconscious is comprised of three entities, unique to the human mind, that are governed by the pleasure principle. These three entities include the id, ego, and superego. Freud expands this proposition in a book entitled *The Ego and the Id* (1923/1960). Basically, the pleasure principle is what drives most behavior; humans will seek out activities that are pleasurable. For infants, all behaviors are driven by pleasure because there are no restrictions. Infants simply attempt to fulfill their drive for pleasure or out of needs for physical and psychological sustenance; for example, they may cry for food, a diaper change, or because of a need to satisfy another physical sensory need. Only when children become toddlers do they learn to respond to and deal with restraints, such as a spanking or scolding.

Functions of the Id   The id is said to function on the premise of immediate gratification, such as when a baby seeks food or attention. The id does not understand the concept of waiting or delayed gratification; therefore, an infant will cry or carry on until all needs of the moment are met (Freud, 1928). No entity exists within the infant that may alter or moderate an infant's cries, as infants are driven solely by primal needs.

Ego Development   Freud (1936/1967) noted that the ego develops during the first year of life. An organism's ability to maintain itself is based on how it perceives reality, with a gradually increasing awareness of environmental cues. As infants gain greater insight into their surroundings, the ego becomes responsible for regulating appropriate behaviors required to satisfy needs. For example, a child who is spanked for placing his or her fingers near an electrical outlet associates touching the outlet with an undesirable event. This form of associative learning is more advanced than any associative learning that occurs during infancy.

The Superego   The third element of the unconscious is the superego, which develops at about 5 or 6 years of age, but should mature fully by adolescence (Freud, 1923/1960). The superego is said to monitor behaviors based on a matured internalized value system and moralistic views of right and wrong. As the superego evolves, more complex events in the child's life are interpreted and acted upon with an internal mode of self-discipline. For instance, if the superego evolves appropriately by preadolescence, the adolescent should refuse to steal because it is morally wrong, not just because external sanctions such as jail will occur. Consequently, the superego serves to monitor future behavior, eventually leading to critical thinking as an adult and thereafter monitoring the adult's behaviors (Freud, 1928).

Mental Well-Being

Freud (1923/1936, 1920/1977) stated that a mentally healthy individual maintains harmony among the id, ego, and superego, with each element contributing to daily functioning in a reasonably healthy manner. Mental illness is said to emerge when one of these entities is disproportionately distributed within the individual or when events force a disruption among the natural interchange between the id, ego, and superego. For example, if an individual did not develop further than the id stage, immature and regressive behaviors would be evident. The person would demand instant gratification in all phases of life, without the ability to monitor or sanction behaviors. Similarly, if the ego takes over and dominates an individual's mental functioning, spontaneity, usually occurring from the id, is lost. The individual may lead a dull, reality-oriented life. Finally, in extreme cases when the superego dominates personality, observed behaviors may include obsessive acts of self-righteousness such as praying, judging, or chastising others in a compulsive manner. However, when the id, ego, and superego are in harmony, they serve as a means of balance and maintenance of mental health (Freud, 1923/1960).

Defense Mechanisms

According to Freud and Breuer (1895), defense mechanisms occur unconsciously when an organism is psychologically threatened by an event (see Table 6.1). If the organism is sufficiently threatened, defense mechanisms allow the mind to distort the reality of the situation, resulting in relief from insurmountable stress. In extreme cases, reality may be so severely distorted that psychosis or dissociation sets in. Cases of extreme abuse have resulted in this distortion of reality as illustrated in the late-1960s movies *Sybil* and *Three Faces of Eve,* in which characters portrayed multiple personality or dissociative disorders that arose from their extreme childhood abuse. While it is true that all individuals use defense mechanisms on a daily basis to some degree, if one of the nine defense mechanisms described by Freud dominates a personality, personality disorders or emotional disturbance may arise.

Because defense mechanisms are enacted by the unconscious mind, individuals may not be aware they are using them. For example, an adult may come home from a bad day at the office and kick the dog, rather than telling off the boss at work. The adult is sublimating his or her need to talk to the boss. Similarly, a person who withdraws from confronting problems may be using that withdrawal as a defense mechanism because confrontation is too stressful to bear. It should be noted that not all defense mechanisms are unhealthy, as they can serve to protect the individual from psychological discomfort when situations are too difficult to bear.

Psychosexual Stages

Freud (1940/1949) conceptualized progressive stages of psychosexual development, each one dependent upon the successful integration of previous stages. By age 6 or 7, a child should have successfully transgressed the first three psychosexual stages: the oral, anal, and phallic stages. However, if an individual, as a child, experienced an event or trauma that prohibited successful integration of a psychosexual stage as well as the accomplishment of the prescribed tasks at that stage, the individual's personality might become fixated at that stage of development. If fixation occurs, symptomatic behaviors ranging from minor to severe can emerge. Occasionally, people with such fixated states are humorously referred to as individuals who have issues with oral gratification or anal-retentive personalities (Freud, 1923/1936b). Conversely, successful completion of each psychosexual stage prepares the individual to continue to accomplish more advanced stages of development, thus achieving a healthy state of mind in adulthood. The following sections will clarify the expected accomplishments at each psychosexual stage of development according to Freud (1923/1936b).

Table 6.1 Freud's Defense Mechanisms

Defense	Behavioral Implications
Regression	Displaying behaviors associated with earlier ages when an event is too stressful to deal with. For example, a 3-year-old may regress to thumb sucking when a new infant is brought into the home, or a 9-year-old may regress to earlier childlike behavior after being sexually molested.
Repression	Unconsciously repressing stressful or traumatizing memories to the unconscious mind, perhaps to resurface when the organism is better able to deal with them. *Repression* is a term that is commonly used in sexual abuse cases.
Sublimation	Replacing undesirable behaviors with more socially acceptable behaviors, such as channeling aggressive behaviors into excelling in sports.
Projection	Attributing one's thoughts, feelings, or attitudes to another individual, without consciously realizing the extent of one's own thoughts, feelings, or attitudes. For example, a person might accuse another of lying about an event when it is really the person making the accusation who lied about it.
Reaction Formation	Reacting in an opposite manner from the one desired. For example, a person who wants to be angry with someone might behave warmly toward him or her instead. Perpetrators often publicly attend church or adapt a socially acceptable role in the community, thereby convincing themselves and others that they are good citizens.
Denial	An outright refusal to consciously accept a concept, idea, or event. Denial can occur at the unconscious level of processing.
Rationalization	Making compensatory statements to offset discomfort with a cognitive thought, e.g., "I didn't really want to buy that pretty dress anyway."
Withdrawal	Turning thoughts inward and emotionally removing oneself from the environment when a distressing situation arises. This is often thought of as a passive-aggressive means of dealing with unpleasant issues.
Distancing	Establishing emotional distance from others or events due to an anticipated fear of involvement with the circumstance, person, or event.

Oral Stage: Birth–18 Months Infants initially respond to the environment orally. All objects, contacts, and modes of expression are approached orally, which, according to Freud, also provides a source of sexual pleasure for infants. A lack of fulfillment of oral needs during this stage serves to deny gratification; consequently, distorted behaviors may be observed. People who are deprived of oral needs during infancy may exhibit excessive needs for oral gratification in adulthood through compulsive eating, smoking, and so on. Conversely, if needs are appropriately met during each stage, no disproportionate or excessive needs for oral gratification will occur.

Anal Stage: 18 Months–3 Years Psychosexual needs are achieved anally during the anal stage of development (Freud, 1923/1936b; Freud, 1967). The ultimate task of a toddler is to successfully achieve potty training, which represents a healthy tolerance for pleasures associated with relieving one's self. If the process of potty training is particularly traumatic for the child (e.g., if a caregiver uses excessive punishment for wetting accidents), the child can remain traumatized throughout life. A child who is severely beaten for wetting his or her pants or missing the potty is predicted to develop negative self-concepts more so than a child who is allowed to develop at his or her own pace.

Phallic Stage: 3–6 Years During the phallic stage of psychosexual development, a child must overcome pleasurable sexual attachments toward the opposite-sex parent, as Freud poignantly delineates in the case of Little Hans (1909/1936a). Romantic attachments to the opposite-sex parent often evoke attitudes of rivalry in the child, directed toward the competing, or same-sex, parent. Therefore, a boy's romantic feelings toward his mother may propel him to compete with his father for her affections. If he cannot resolve his feelings for his mother and views his father as the competing force, he may develop a fear of castration and feelings of inadequacy, a process often referred to as the Oedipus complex. Similarly, little girls who cannot properly overcome a sense of competition with their mothers for their fathers' affection may develop an Electra complex. An Electra or Oedipus complex develops when feelings toward the opposite-sex parent remain unresolved and can interfere with the acquisition of fulfilling opposite-sex relationships in adulthood. On the other hand, resolution of these feelings of attraction for the opposite-sex parent prepares the child to fulfill intimate relationships in adulthood.

Latency Stage: 6–12 Years As the name implies, the latency period is a stage wherein developmental tasks subside or remain latent (Freud, 1920/1977). The age range in which this period occurs may be debatable today given the escalated maturational rates among youth. By this stage of psychosexual development, fulfillment of the oral, anal, and phallic stages should have been accomplished, resulting in a strong gender-specific identity. Now, socialization within society should occur with minimal internal unrest as the child progresses toward adolescence.

Genital Stage: Adolescence to Adulthood During the genital stage, the libido is energized and repressed sexual urges emerge, resulting in psychological turbulence as the adolescent acquires a sexual identity. A young adult would be capable of developing satisfying intimate relationships in a healthy, age-appropriate manner if the normal path of psychosocial development has occurred. An acute awareness of opposite-sex peers emerges along with growing sexual desires, all of which represent healthy maturation in preparation for adulthood.

ERIKSON'S PSYCHOSOCIAL THEORY

Erik H. Erikson (1902-1994), a German-born Jew, fled Germany during the Nazi era, settling in the United States in 1933. Given the rich foundation of Freud's teachings, Erikson was able to expand upon Freud's work, focusing on a psychosocial theory of child development. Erikson placed less emphasis on the implications of sexual influences that shape personality and focused on the social interactions that impact adult personality attributes. Of most significance is his work *Childhood and Society* (1950), in which he delineates, in "Eight Stages of Man," a modified version of Freud's work, with more emphasis on social interactions in the environment than on psychosexual development.

Erikson's Experience

Often researchers develop theoretical perspectives based on their unique experiences, and this is the case with Erikson. Upon immigrating to the United States, Erikson experienced an identity crisis due to cultural and ethnic differences. After World War II, Erikson's practice was comprised of white males of all ages who appeared to be experiencing similar ego disintegration. Erikson reflected upon his clients' accounts of childhood experiences; consequently, many of his findings were then integrated into his theory of psychosocial development (Erikson, 1968). Two particular occurrences in Erikson's life appear to have shaped his philosophical approach to the study of children. First, as a former student and believer in the Montessori method of socially educating children, Erikson perceived social influences as prominent in child development (Morris, 1996). Second, Erikson's own search for identity when he immigrated to the United States as a minority fortified his focus on identity issues. Both events fueled the direction of his theoretical propositions including his construct of the eight stages of psychosocial development.

Eight Psychosocial Stages

Erikson (1968) proposed a series of eight stages of life that must be successfully overcome to achieve a fully integrated ego (see Table 6.2). A child must successfully complete tasks related to each of the eight stages with either positive or negative outcomes, either of which shape the child's psychological perspective of the world and self. If the child experiences degrading or unsuccessful events during any respective developmental stage, negative perceptions of self may arise. A child who has been sexually abused often receives contradictory messages about psychosocial aspects of life; consequently, he or she may develop distorted cognitions of self in many aspects of personality development. The following sections summarize Erikson's (1959) definition of the psychosocial stages realized during the life cycle.

Stage I: Trust Versus Mistrust (0–18 Months) Stage I states that children must obtain supportive, nurturing attention from primary caretakers on a consistent basis, in order to develop trusting relationships with adults. Obviously, when maltreatment occurs at the hands of caretakers, children cannot appropriately develop trust of others. They may remain suspicious or hyperalert to environmental cues. Similar qualities of hypersensitivity have been associated with sexual abuse survivors (Hewitt, 1999; Ochberg, 1993). This is not to imply that all persons who are hyperalert have been sexually abused, but a close

Table 6.2 Erickson's Psychosocial Stages of Development

Stage	Developmental Tasks
Stage I	Trust versus Mistrust (0–18 months). External influences impact the development of trust. An infant's sensitivity to abuse or maltreatment can greatly alter personality at this time. Bonding and separability are issues at this age.
Stage II	Autonomy versus Shame and Doubt (18 months–3 years). Independence is accomplished. If this stage is not successfully integrated, doubt and shame may prevail. Severe sanctions can force a child into a fixated sense of doubt and insecurity, whereas nurturance and unconditional acceptance foster a sense of independence.
Stage III	Initiative versus Guilt (3–6 years). Initiative to aspire toward new tasks and achievement should be developed here. If this stage is not successful, the child will develop a sense of failure and guilt.
Stage IV	Industry versus Inferiority (6 years–puberty). New skills—academic, social, and personal—are acquired. If this stage is not properly integrated, a sense of inferiority will arise. School life encourages the acquisition of academic and vocational skills, e.g., through college-prep coursework.
Stage V	Identity versus Confusion (puberty–young adulthood). Development of self-identity is essential to fulfillment in adulthood.
Stage VI	Intimacy versus Isolation (young adulthood). Intimate adult relationships should be developed, including personal commitment to others. Abusees may incur significant difficulty in this area.
Stage VII	Generativity versus Stagnation (middle adulthood). Tasks include nurturing the next generation as a caretaker. The implications of childhood abuse for future parenting vary from no lasting effects to significant difficulties.
Stage VIII	Integrity versus Despair (old age). Elderly citizens must accept their role in life and prepare for the end of life, or despair may set in.

association between children who have been abused and hypervigilence and hypersensitivity is found in the literature (Classen & Yalom, 1995; Finkelhor, 1986; Harris & Landis, 1997).

Stage II: Autonomy Versus Shame and Doubt (18 Months–3 Years) Stage II takes the child through the potty-training stage. Accomplishment of toilet training can either leave the child with a sense of independence, if successful, or doubt and shame, if the task is not accomplished successfully. Often emotional trauma experienced by a child can hinder, delay, or traumatize the potty-training period. If Erikson's theory holds true, a child who is exposed to adverse treatment during this stage of development will experience shame rather than a sense of pride at mastering the difficult task of toilet training.

Stage III: Initiative Versus Guilt (3–6 Years) During Stage III, children begin socialization activities with other children. If successful, they acquire a sense of initiative toward new ventures, a concept needed to advance in life. Conversely, children who are traumatized, rather than encouraged, during this stage of life may abandon new concepts and tasks, rather than confront them enthusiastically. Distressed children may remain underachievers throughout life, which can provoke a sense of failure and guilt in them. Initiatives that could prepare them for a quality life may be constrained and abandoned, thus they are not only robbed of their innocence but are also penalized due to lost opportunities.

Stage IV: Industry Versus Inferiority (6 Years–Puberty) Stage IV is a time when children begin to acquire a sense of self-efficacy versus inferiority. The primary social influence at this stage is the classroom setting. Young children often compare their work to that of their peers, and any child who does not measure up to his or her peers may easily develop a sense of inferiority. Excessive criticism and harsh reprimands for errors, omissions, or failures from caretakers further restrict a child's ability to form an industrious attitude. Rather, a sense of defeat sets in, along with the attitude of "I can't succeed, so why try?" In instances of abuse, a child's sense of inferiority is exacerbated by the actions of cruel and harshly critical caregivers, potentially resulting in a long-standing sense of inferiority.

Stage V: Identity Versus Confusion (Puberty–Young Adulthood) Perhaps the most significant for all individuals is Stage V of development, where a self-identity is formed based upon past experiences and environmental influences. Identity crises can evolve for any number of reasons. If adverse events have impacted a child during earlier stages, the child may develop mistrust, shame, doubt, guilt, and a sense of inferiority, all elements associated with abuse survivors. Once more, the child's life path is restricted by negative experiences, and the child cannot move forward with confidence and a positive identity. Abused children may withdraw from their environments due to a sense of shame, worthlessness, and self-doubt. Therefore, they may not assertively seek out opportunities, as compared to peers who were free of unwanted oppression during childhood. Because the puberty stage of life is also a time for adolescents to come into their own sexuality, sexually abused children may be faced with the very difficult task of overcoming distorted messages about sexuality that were internalized along the years, thus forming a self-identity at this time is a much more difficult task.

Stage VI: Intimacy Versus Isolation (Young Adulthood) During Stage VI of the life span, fulfilling intimate relationships should be achieved and maintained. Long-term commitments and the ability to relate to others in an intimate manner are to be accomplished now. However, residual effects of abuse may continue to play havoc with any sense of fulfillment. Former abuse may have stifled successful completion of the developmental stages that prepare the individual to form intimate adult relationships. Past relationships that should have fostered trust may have actually destroyed the abusee's ability to develop trust in others. In any event, self-identity that is not strongly developed during childhood renders a child more vulnerable to seeking out affirmation of self-worth from external sources. Thus, abusive adult relationships may also persist as a residual effect of former abuse.

Stage VII: Generativity versus Stagnation (Middle Adulthood) and Stage VIII: Integrity versus Despair (Old Age) Stages VII and VIII can represent problems for individuals who experienced negative consequences during earlier developmental stages. According to Erikson, the psychosocial stages of development should be successfully integrated by adulthood. But this may not occur for an adult who experienced abuse as a child, as advanced stages of development are dependent upon cumulative effects of earlier stages. While Erikson proposes this stage of life to be one of inner reflection and introspective analysis of past achievements, adult survivors of abuse may still be attempting to sort out their former harmful experiences and lost opportunities.

PIAGET'S THEORY
OF COGNITIVE PROCESSES

Jean Piaget (1896-1980), a Swiss-born researcher, conducted in-depth, highly detailed studies in Paris, France of children's cognitive functioning, hoping to standardize a test that Alfred Binet developed, currently known as the Stanford-Binet Intelligence Scale (4th ed.). Piaget (1952) proposed a complex theory of cognitive functioning comprised of many schemas, key concepts, and developmental stages. He proposed stages of cognitive development that are associated with specific tasks unique to that stage, although each stage is also cumulative in that earlier task accomplishments must be mastered if more advanced tasks are to be learned.

Piaget observed students within a private school setting daily. Intrigued by the students' methods of answering correctly or incorrectly, Piaget looked for clues to the thought processes involved in the completion of each task he presented to the children. Later, as the director of a Swiss institute, Piaget married one of his students, whereupon they banned together to closely study the daily functioning of children, including their own three children. After years of insightful documentation of children's cognitive functioning, Piaget's findings were synthesized into the world-renowned theory of cognitive functioning.

Cognitive Structure

Piaget identified sequential cognitive processes based on the concept that a child can acquire more advanced concepts only after basic ones are mastered. He prescribed approximate ages for each stage of development in accordance with his meticulous observations of how children think. Each stage is described on the basis of cognitive structures and the thought processes that take place as children are faced with a cognitive task. Once a preliminary task is accomplished, a more advanced cognitive task is attainable; these concepts form the framework of cognitive development according to Piaget.

Piaget proposed cognitive structures that underlie the ability to process information such as schemas, assimilations, accommodations, and adaptations. Cognitive tasks relative to each stage of growth are explained in relation to each of these constructs, along the developmental pathway. Specific age groups are said to be representative of certain levels of tasks within each one of these concepts, all of which may vary as a function of the child's unique maturation.

Schemas Schemas are the cognitive beliefs or images that develop as thought processes when a person assimilates newly acquired information. A child must develop a basic schema before comprehending more complex concepts, such as the categories associated with a basic element. For example, a schema of a bird must be formed mentally before a child can comprehend the concept of categories of birds, such as eagles or sparrows. Piaget proposed that basic concepts must be mastered as a prerequisite for the comprehension of more advanced concepts. These concepts are referred to as cognitive schemas.

Equilibrium Piaget (1952) believed that when a child is faced with new information, he or she will attempt to find equilibrium between what is known and the newly presented information. When confronted with information that requires a new method of analysis or adaptation, the child experiences a state of disequilibria, which continues until the new information is assimilated into formerly known concepts. This process occurs with each new piece of information; and as concepts become more difficult to comprehend, new cognitive processing skills are acquired that allow the child to integrate the material and return to a state of cognitive equilibrium.

Assimilation, Accommodation, and Adaptation As a child matures and absorbs increasingly complex information, advanced cognitive skills are assimilated. A growing child not only learns new concepts, but also develops cognitive processing skills that, in turn, expedite comprehension of more advanced materials. This can be illustrated in the school setting when reading skills must be acquired. A child first learns the alphabet, then moves on to words, then sentences, and then comprehension of the stories. Each task requires a more advanced manner of cognitive processing. As a child is exposed to reading materials, comprehension of more advanced reading materials is possible. Educators develop reading programs based on these theoretical concepts, often described by the reading level of textbooks. Similarly, school curriculum increases in complexity as a child achieves the cognitive maturity to deal with more advanced materials and concepts.

Adaptation, according to Piaget, is the process of adjusting to new information, situations, and events that occur. On a regular basis, children are forced to accommodate new events each day. In order to internalize new information, an individual may need to adapt a cognitive mode that is not preexisting. Similarly, assimilation is the process whereby new information is assimilated into preexisting schemas or associations. For example, when a child sees a bluejay, he or she can assimilate that information based on his or her existing information about the concept of a bird. Thus, cognitive adaptations and assimilations occur regularly as new information is absorbed.

Accommodation refers to modifying existing knowledge or schemas to meet the requirements of a new event, experience, or object. When new information enters the sensory nerves, be it through auditory, visual, or other means of sensory intake, that information must be processed mentally. If no schema exists for that object, event, or idea, a person has a difficult time grasping the concept. For example, a toddler who manages to stand alone while holding onto a sofa will slowly realize that he or she must hold on to the sofa to sustain the upright position. Eventually, the child will reach out automatically for support when standing alone, thereby accommodating behavioral skills to achieve the task.

Cognitive Stages of Development

Each stage of cognitive development introduces new schemas and categories of intellectual reasoning that range from simple insight learning (during infancy) to advanced formal applications (adulthood). Based on these stages of learning, children can only comprehend information that corresponds to their level of cognitive maturation. It is not possible for children to comprehend concepts beyond their cognitive stage of development unless the cognitive structure to do so is developed.

Sensorimotor Stage: Birth–2 Years During the sensorimotor stage, infants explore the external world via touching, tasting, and hearing. They are said to develop object permanence, based on the concept that items or people do not disappear just because they are out of sight, such as when a mother leaves the room. Flavell (1982) noted that object permanence is observed, for example, when an item is hidden from a child's view, and the child cries because the object appears to have disappeared. The child cannot comprehend that the object will be returned to sight until he or she has acquired object permanence.

Preoperational Stage: 2–7 Years During the preoperational stage of development, a child learns to use symbols for communication in language acquisition. New worlds are opened for the child as language permits the exploration of new concepts and schemas. Although language is acquired at this stage, concepts such as conservation, number, volume, and quantity are not well understood. For example, if both a narrow, cylindrical container and a short, wide container were filled with water and shown to the child, invariably a child at this stage would identify the tall cylinder as having the most liquid, although they hold similar quantities. This may explain why many children argue with siblings over who has the biggest glass of milk or largest piece of cake when, in fact, the glasses or pieces of cake are the same in volume. In an abusive setting, an impatient parent might severely punish a child for arguing with a sibling over something like this.

At this age, inanimate objects such as stuffed animals or toys may be idealized as being alive. Narcissism is a common attribute in children at this stage of development. These children demand to have what they want, when they want it, as is common during the "terrible twos." Outside of their own existence, young children have limited perceptions of the world. Most of their thoughts and ideas revolve around their own wants and desires, readily expressed through tantrums, tears, and obstinate insistence. For a conscientious parent, this time of child rearing can be demanding; but for the ill-prepared or abusive parents enraged by a child's outburst, punitive actions may involve severe beatings or, in extreme cases, life-threatening measures. All the while, the toddler was simply responding within normal developmental ranges.

Concrete Operational Stage: 7–12 Years As a child moves into the concrete operational stage, preoperational tasks are accomplished and the child can process information using concrete cognitive concepts. Children now understand concepts in literal terms. Although less narcissism is apparent and these children are beginning to consider the viewpoints of others to a degree, a rigid or functional perception of facts persists. Children in this stage understand concepts like sitting in a chair at a table to eat, but it may not be apparent to them that the chair and table are both pieces of furniture. A child functioning within the concrete stage of development requires consistent and structured settings as rather fixed and rigid concepts are adhered to. For example, if a child is told not to talk to strangers, that concept may be well understood. But then, when mother is observed talking to the check out person at the grocery store, the child becomes confused. In the young child's mind, there is no such thing as extenuating circumstances; you either do or do not talk to strangers.

Formal Operations Stage: Preteen–Adulthood Abstract concepts are mastered during the formal operations stage of development; consequently, more advanced relationships and concepts can be processed. Preteens can master scientific notions such as algebra and logic-based concepts. During this stage, preteens or teens can propose hypotheses and perform critical thinking tasks to analyze problems, all skill levels that should prepare the teenager for adulthood. For instance, while a young child may be dependent upon an abusive caregiver, remain loyal to that caregiver (for numerous reasons, perhaps partly due to a concrete functional mind-set), and view the situation from only one fixed perspective (that of dependency), a preteen or adolescent who develops cognitive formal operations can critically evaluate an abuse situation and perhaps seek help, given the emotional propensity to do so.

Age Variations Across Children

Although Piaget (1952) emphasized stages of cognitive development representing specific age ranges, each stage is not mutually exclusive. That is, overlaps and variations exist within the stages of cognitive development. For instance, an advanced 9-year-old may be capable of performing formal operations. Similarly, a lower intellectually functioning child may reach the age of 15, yet be capable of performing only concrete operations that are normally associated with much younger children; thus, a lower mental age of functioning would be evident.

Implications for Treatment of Sexual Abuse

Diagnosing the impact of child sexual abuse on a child at various stages of intellectual development differs considerably from one child to the next. Cognitive interpretations of the event are unique for each individual, partly based on maturation of cognitive skills (Finkelhor, 1984; Kuehnle, 1996; Oates, 1996; Stattler, 1998). Piaget's theory offers the professional a theoretical model from which to conduct assessments of the child's cognitive processing when treatment is needed following a sexually abusive experience. Treatment modalities, rapport building, and case management should all be conducted within the child's ability levels. All treatment plans should incorporate age-appropriate techniques relative to the child's cognitive processing abilities (Deblinger & Heflin, 1996).

KOHLBERG'S THEORY
OF MORAL DEVELOPMENT

Kohlberg's theory of moral development is discussed here with emphasis on moral development following a child sexual abuse experience. Kohlberg (1969; Kohlberg & Power, 1981) proposed a three-level, six-stage sequence of moral development that applies to all cultures, and therefore may have universal applications. For the most part, theorists believe that children do not develop moral reasoning until about the age of 7, although inherent variations do occur. Moral development is highly dependent upon familial and social influences within the child's environment.

Level I: Preconventional Level, Stages 1 and 2

According to Kohlberg (1969), the preconventional level of morality consists of two stages ranging from age 4 to 7 and 8 to 10 consecutively. During stage 1, children aged 4 to 7 respond to right and wrong or good and bad because of external sanctions that might be applied, such as punishment or coercion of others. Emphasis is placed on the physical consequences of a child's actions; for example, a child will acquiesce to a caregiver's demands due to fear of punishment rather than from any sense of right and wrong. Children submit to superior power and, for the most part, avoid confrontation. Given their tendency to want to please adults, young children may readily comply with a perpetrator's coercive actions, particularly during abusive incidents under a perceived threat of harm or punishment.

In stage 2, ranging from age 8 to10, of the preconventional level of moral development, instrumental relativity develops slowly and is often sporadically observed as the new mode of responding to the environment. This stage is characterized by a self-motivated drive, such as when a child improves behavior just before Christmas to receive more gifts. Behaviors are connected to concepts; if *A* is done, then *B* will occur. Consequently, children perceive little or no choice when an offending adult coerces, threatens, or harms a child during an abusive event. If the child tells (*A*), then harm to self or others may occur (*B*). Thus, during abuse, young children may have a rigid view of the situation both cognitively and morally; they are too young to perceive alternative options, as they are fixed in concrete cognitive and moral thinking.

Level II: Conventional Level, Stages 3 and 4

The conventional level of moral development is also comprised of two stages, stages 3 and 4, and ranges across ages 10–13. During stage 3 of the conventional level of moral development, conformity to social order and moral principles occurs. A child loyally adheres to these principles if he or she is so predisposed. Actions are justified by reinforcement from group involvement, that is, most often, peer pressure. Preteens and adolescents submit to social order, to whatever behavior appears to be "normal" within their social circle. If the influencing group advocates drugs, sex, and alcohol, the adolescent will succumb to peer pressure to maintain his or her group membership.

Conformity is a subjective concept that ranges across a continuum of acceptable behaviors, based on the perceived intention of a behavior. For example, statements like "He meant well" may be heard among friends who accept immoral behaviors from others. Adolescents subjected to an abusive environment may certainly accept perverse morality to gain acceptance from perpetrators who are significant to them. Teenagers' needs for acceptance, belonging, and enhanced self-identity render them vulnerable to masked acts of seduction from pedophiles who befriend them by providing feigned friendships, liquor, pornographic films, drugs, and other enticements. In some instances, adolescents who reveal sexual abuse experience a great deal of guilt about betraying the offender when a disclosure is made. One 13-year-old boy stated, "But he was also my friend, and now I sent him to jail." This boy may have believed that the perpetrator meant well.

Stage 4 of moral development emphasizes law and order, wherein authority, accepted rules, and maintenance of social order predominate. The concepts of duty and respect for authority evolve, and they foster a sense of moral obligation toward adult responsibilities. Clear delineation of right from wrong exists among most individuals. For instance, while a young child who is sworn to secrecy during abuse may remain true to that commitment with rigid compliance, an adolescent may disclose the abuse because a more advanced perspective of right and wrong is developed. For the most part, adolescents and adults function at the conventional level of moral reasoning.

Level III: Postconventional, Autonomous, or Principled Level, Stages 5 and 6

Postconventional morality should evolve around age 13, if at all. It represents a higher form of moral reasoning and again is comprised of two stages, stages 5 and 6. Postconventional morality is usually fostered by social reference and chosen peer groups. Individuals adhere to moral issues driven by internalized identity, more so than to morals that are enforced upon them by external forces such as parents. Stage 5 involves social contact and legal orientations. Rights are examined, and critical thinking is applied to moral situations. Rightful acts become personalized in that they result in self-congruence with internal value systems. A social conscience develops during this phase, prompting socially conscientious decision making, rather than the self-serving decision-making behaviors often found among younger children.

Stage 6 involves the development of universal ethical principles of orientation. Rights and wrongs are differentiated in accordance with ethical principles based on logic and consistency. Abstract concepts such as universality, human rights, respect, and the dignity of others are internalized.

Oprah Winfrey, the famous talk show host, displayed higher moral reasoning when she appeared before the U.S. Senate to support legislation to authorize the creation of a national registry of sexual offenders that would enable employers of day care centers to run background checks on potential employees (Mills, 1991). Her efforts resulted in an endorsement for the mandate that became a subsection of legislation known as the National Child Protection Act (Pub. L. No. 102-95).

Contemporary Theories

Some researchers have proposed that gender differences emerge across moral development. For example, Gilligan (1982) reported that males view moral decisions based on individual rights and self-fulfillment, whereas women tend to weigh moral decisions in support of interrelationships. Others, however, have disputed Gilligan's precepts of gender-specific morality development (Walker, 1989). Additionally, a consistent association between one's moral beliefs and one's moral actions has not been confirmed; it is possible for one to develop advanced stages of moral reasoning, and yet act immorally. This phenomenon is often apparent among convicted perpetrators who actually led a highly moralistic life, including adherence to religious rituals and participation in the community as a caring leader, while simultaneously abusing young children. Religious leaders who are convicted of child sexual abuse serve as clear examples of this moral parody (McManus, 1995; Skolnick, 1994).

SUMMARY

Social sciences are still in their infancy as compared to hard physical sciences such as medicine. The complexities of the human mind continue to plague professionals regarding the diagnosis, treatment, and outcomes for those who have experienced emotionally stressful phenomena. A review of psychological theories in this chapter should serve as a basis to explore childhood development as it occurs under the additional duress of childhood abuse, specifically sexual abuse. Due to the complexity of the childhood abuse syndrome, therapists must keenly understand the complex psychodynamics involved in resolving sexual abuse issues, unique to each individual. It is equally important to understand personality development across the life span, particularly how abuse may impact each developmental stage in a unique yet universal manner. The ill-prepared practitioner runs the risk of providing erroneous information to clients, so it is of paramount importance that a full understanding of the many facets of development and the impact of sexual abuse is comprehensively understood.

DISCUSSION QUESTIONS

1. After reading this chapter, can you express your own views of childhood development? What theoretical perspectives do you think are applicable in helping a child through recovery from sexual abuse? Explain your answer.

2. How would you describe Freud's psychosexual theory and its implications for understanding a child's reaction to abuse?

3. What concerns, if any, would you have about the manner in which Piaget developed his theory of cognitive development?

4. What influences in a child's life might contribute to moral development? When or how does a child develop an instrumental morality?

5. Choose one of the four theories discussed in this chapter and describe how the theory applies to a sexually abused child of 4 years of age versus 14 years of age.

6. Are you aware of any other theories that might apply when attempting to understand the emotional impact that child abuse has on a child? Explain.

7. Choose two of the four theories described in this chapter. Contrast and explain the strength and weaknesses of the two theories as applied to the impact of sexual abuse.

8. If confronted with a case of sexual abuse, what resources would you use to evaluate and assess the client while adhering to professional standards? Why?

PART II

Age-Specific and Treatment Issues Related to Sexual Abuse

7

Infant–Toddler Development

LEARNING OBJECTIVES

Chapter 7 will address the following learning objectives:

1. A brief review of theoretical concepts related to infant development

2. A discussion of developmental milestones and potential delays

3. A review of normal physiological development during infancy

4. A review of issues concerning infant evaluations and investigations

5. A discussion of symptomatic and pathological disorders in infancy

6. A discussion of gathering physical evidence in sexual abuse cases

INTRODUCTION

This chapter will focus on physiological and emotional development from birth, during infancy, and toddlerhood. Developmental milestones unique to the infant-toddler stage of development will be reviewed, with an emphasis on the impact of abuse on development. Discussions will focus on symptomology of sexual abuse found among infants, including identification of physical scarring and venereal disease, and other physical incidents representative of sexual assault. Technology issues in the medical field and documentation of abuse have greatly advanced, so these topics will be presented here. Finally, the chapter will review implications for claims of abuse at the hands of a parent or primary caretaker.

INFANT DEVELOPMENT

Skinner (1938, 1957) referred to infant learning as a process in which stimuli response leads to conditioned response, resulting in newly acquired behaviors. Whether the infant's act of crying is an instinctual, libido-driven impulse (Freud, 1923/1962) or a formally learned, conditioned response emitted on behalf of a desired reinforcement as proposed by Skinner as early as 1938, the essential question is whether or not the infant's needs are met in a way that permits healthy development of the organism.

A continuum of behaviors may occur when an infant must have needs met. These reactions may vary, partly based upon the child's own temperament (Frodi & Thompson, 1992), and partly based on the sensitivity of the caregiver (Ainsworth, Blehar, Walters, & Wall, 1978; Isabella, 1993). If the caregiver appropriately responds to the infant's cries, needs are satisfied and the infant continues with a sense of fulfillment and contentment. In cases of neglect and abuse, the mode of communication is driven by the infant's genetic predisposition, resiliency in light of stress, and compensatory behaviors to adjust under unfavorable conditions. If an infant senses tremendous stress, behavioral responses may range from passive submission and withdrawal of cries, to extreme and extended bouts of crying and discontent. If adverse conditions persist, an infant may eventually adopt a stressful mode of expressing needs such as excessive crying, abandon attempts to express needs, or adopt a combination of these communication styles. In any event, if caregivers remain insensitive to an infant's needs, the child may fail to thrive, resulting in physiological, psychological, and emotional deficits.

The manner in which infants receive cues about environmental responses to their cries shapes the manner in which the infant will express future needs. A cyclical learning pattern emerges. For example, if an infant seeks attention from a caregiver, cries for a feeding and immediately receives a bottle, the infant will cry in the same manner the next time a bottle is desired. Hence, a pattern of need and need fulfillment is developed. If all needs are met when expressed, a harmonious state of being exists, freeing the infant to use psychological energy to develop more advanced interactive behavior patterns. Infants' senses such as vision, hearing, and smell develop first, then continue to strengthen as the infant grows. Even on the first day of life, infants can feel pain. For the most part, they react to pain by instinctually pulling away from harm with abrupt reflex reactions.

Typically, physical development is from top to bottom, or, in medical terms, according to the cephalocaudal principle. The head, brain, and eyes develop early, but the skull that encases the brain is not fully formed. It is easy to harm infants by abruptly shaking, throwing, or roughly lifting them into the air, and certainly by inflicting a willful blow to the head or body. In extreme situations, shaking an infant can lead to the infant's death due to edema of the brain (American Association of Neurological Surgeons, 2000; Mills, 1998; Wyszynski, 1999).

Exposure to Violence

Infliction of pain or injury to a newborn infant is a vile act that is too repulsive for many individuals to acknowledge, but it does occur at alarming rates. The leading cause of death among children under 4 years of age is injuries purposely inflicted; 2,000 child deaths occur per year, which means that five children die every other day at the hands of an abusive caretaker (Johnson, 2000).

Death by Abuse

In severe cases of abuse, infants have been killed. In July 2000, a 9-month-old infant in Florida died from a severe blow to the chest at the hands of his father (Wexler, 2000). The child was found with broken ribs that punctured his heart, a broken collarbone, and a severely bruised lip and face. The father claimed the child had simply bumped into a door.

In another instance, a 17-year-old Denver mother allegedly wrapped her newborn infant in a plastic bag and buried the girl in a shallow grave (Sherry, 2000). Too scared to report the pregnancy to anyone, she had given birth, cut the umbilical cord, and fallen asleep. Later, in fear of her mother's return home, she had buried the baby in a plastic bag that was found by construction workers.

In a California case, a 15-year-old child weighed 44 pounds at the time of death in 1996 (Lui, 2000). Authorities arrested the parents for abuse. The parents pleaded that they had been devoted parents, but that the child had a disability that caused her to waste away. Authorities believed that the child's disability, if any existed, was not enough to cause such severe emaciation, particularly without benefit of medical attention.

A detailed account of abuse was revealed in the best-selling book *A Child Called It,* by David Pelzer (1998). The author notes how he was continually tortured, beaten, and starved at the hands of his mother. Only when he became a young teenager was he strong enough to break free of the daily torment inflicted by his mother.

DEVELOPMENTAL MILESTONES

Infants learn to use the upper parts of their bodies before their lower parts, continuing with a predetermined developmental process common among all infants. Physical growth progresses quickly and is dependent upon proper nourishment to attain age-appropriate weight gain and maturation. By the first 5 months of life, an infant's weight should double (Caplan, 1973; Edwards, Halse, & Waterston, 1994). By 1 year of age, infants should weigh five times their birth weight. Motor skills continue to develop, so that by 1 year of age, an infant should be walking independently or working toward achieving the ability to walk.

Major developmental milestones that are usually assessed for successful achievement include (a) talking by 1-2 years of age, (b) walking by age 1-3 years, and (c) potty-training by 2–3 years (Kaplan, 1991). A wide variation can occur in the age at which infants achieve these milestones due to cultural norms, environmental influences, and physiological concerns. When infants are examined, one of the first areas assessed as an index of healthy growth is the acquisition of developmental milestones (Papalia & Olds, 1995). If a developmental delay is observed, a more in-depth evaluation is warranted to investigate the source of the problem. Once medical disorders are ruled out, exposure to some form of emotional trauma, abuse, or neglect may be investigated. It is well documented that violence, trauma, or invasive abuse may inhibit natural maturation of any or all of the developmental milestones.

Language Skills

While language skills are acquired within a specific age range (9 months to 2 years), it is well known that developmental lags can occur without much cause for alarm. However, there are windows of time that pose serious concerns to caregivers if specific developmental goals are not achieved. If a child does not acquire speech ability by 2 1/2 years of age, a red flag is raised. Similarly, if a child remains labile during the first year when exploration through crawling, extended arm reaching, and attempts to walk independently are expected, diagnostic evaluations should be conducted. And finally, toilet training should be accomplished at this time, with relatively minor distress, if not outright enjoyment. Proper nurturance, attention, and encouragement can enhance the attainment of each developmental goal. For example, most parents will guide a wobbly child as the child's legs strengthen sufficiently to allow the child to stand alone, and they will encourage each new movement with claps and smiles, often prompting the infant to smile with pride at this new achievement. For neglected infants, however, little adult guidance, encouragement, or applause is provided to help them achieve these significant goals.

Toilet Training

Similarly, during toilet training, nurturing parents wait patiently as they guide their toddler through each step of learning proper potty procedures, until finally, the great day arrives when the infant independently indicates a need to eliminate urine and feces; and once more, the parents clap, cheer, and applaud the toddler for this new accomplishment. Abused children do not receive such grandiose treatment. For example, if an infant is injured during an invasive sexual abuse act in the anus area, sphincter muscles may become scarred or injured to the point of interfering with further development of the muscles. If damage is sufficient, bowel control and elimination can be impaired. In addition to experiencing the abusive act, the toddler may be further punished for not properly achieving a bowel movement.

Psychological ramifications of abuse can be extreme, depending upon the type of abusive treatment received by the infant or toddler. Some children respond to severe and harsh treatment for errors made in toilet training by becoming emotionally blocked, regressed, or withdrawn. Other children may respond to such treatment by becoming preoccupied with bowel movements or urination. Perhaps the most far-reaching consequences under harsh admonishments during toilet training are the feelings of shame, self-doubt, and reduced self-worth at not having successfully accomplished this developmental task.

Emotional Trauma

In addition to physiological trauma, infants suffer emotional trauma from repeated exposure to violence or other neglectful or abusive treatment. The ensuing reactions to that trauma are witnessed in the infant's emotional distress. In extreme cases, trauma may cause an infant to regress, to forget developmental milestones the infant had formerly attained. For example, an abused infant may not even try to stand up and walk, even though, prior to harsh treatment, walking skills were developed. Rather than striving to walk, the distressed infant may withdraw from further interactions with the environment. Although physiological strength is sufficiently acquired to permit walking, emotional trauma can cause the child to regress to an earlier emotional stage of development.

A traumatized child may show other signs of distress, such as excessive crying when confronted with a stranger, a hysterical response at the sight of an object that inflicted pain, or extreme fear of a situation, object, or person associated with the abusive act. Unless the child is under the supervision of a sensitive caregiver, these behavioral reactions may go unnoticed, and thus the aftereffects of a traumatic incident may perpetually undermine future development.

Advanced or Gifted Toddlers

In contrast to the infants and toddlers who fail to thrive, intellectually gifted toddlers have been known to acquire an outstanding vocabulary as early as 1 1/2 to 2 years of age, complete with reasoning and comprehension skills. These toddlers have the potential to participate in a verbally articulated examination, as long as the verbal content is appropriate for their level of comprehension. This may be done through the use of either primitive words or self-made terms, such as "peepee" for penis or "bum" for buttocks. Any reported abuse should be documented verbatim in the child's chosen words. A positive impact of working with highly verbal children is that they may be able to tell someone about the abuse, as awkwardly as it may be expressed. On the other hand, a pedophile in fear of exposure may use coercive techniques to silence such a toddler.

Verbal Communication

When a toddler is highly communicative and capable of verbalizing thoughts, it may be possible to compile a concise report of the actions surrounding the abuse experience. A toddler who is highly verbal and has an advanced vocabulary has a greater opportunity to reveal information about abusive interactions with others (Kuehnle, 1996). The report may be constrained by unique terms expressed because of the toddler's unsophisticated vocabulary. When a toddler uses unusual terms to express actions of abuse, it is essential to document the terms verbatim; in fact, acceptable interview techniques and evidentiary procedures endorse this procedure. The well-trained therapist must also be cognizant of professional standards for interviewing and techniques for reporting abuse (see guidelines provided by the APSAC and APA), particularly in cases where litigation is likely to follow. Mishandling of the preliminary interview procedures can result in erroneous dispensation of the case. Training in appropriate interview methods is essential; therefore, child sexual abuse (CSA) training programs should include ample material to provide therapists with accurate methodology (Hewitt, 1991; Kuehnle, 1996). Assessment techniques specific to child abuse are available from professional groups as noted above.

Attachment

The relationship between maternal sensitivity and infant temperament is paramount in the infant's development (Seifer, Schiller, Sameroff, Resnick, & Riordin, 1996). Researchers have found that the attachment qualities derived during infancy from the quality of care are instrumental in the quality of attachments formed in adult relationships (Ainsworth et al., 1978). Theoretical conceptions of attachment center around the quality of nurturing provided by an infant's primary caretakers.

Theoretical concepts concerning attachment also focus on varying aspects of the issues, such as formation of affectionate bonds (Bowlby, 1969), feelings of loss (Bowlby, 1980), and the mourning and grieving processes (Bowlby, 1983). According to Bowlby, attachment is a behavior that results from proximity to some preferred adult. An emotional need for attachment may be satisfied simply with a visual glance or momentary eye contact. Although attachment needs are distinct from feeding and sexual needs, they are equally important to the attached party. Once attachment behaviors are affirmed, they should lead to affectionate bonds, initially between child and parent, and eventually between adults.

Bowlby (1980) stated that psychopathology or emotional distress experienced by an individual is often embedded in affectionate bonds with the significant party in the reactive individual's life. Deviations in the reaction to loss are said to originate in the family of origin, due to unique patterns in which caretakers responded, or failed to respond, to infant needs. Similarly, personality disturbances that occur while processing the loss of a loved one stem from deviations in development; these disturbances can grow worse throughout infancy, childhood, and adulthood. Such deviations can manifest as either anxious, insecure attachments or denial of attachment, fueling alienation from others. Thus, intermittent acceptance or rejection from a caregiver often results in the development of anxious, ambivalent attachments, as the child never quite knows what to expect. Conversely, overindulgence of attention fosters overdependence in infants and children; they become unable to function independently and may place disproportionate demands upon others throughout life (Bowlby, 1980).

Mixed messages occur when caregivers alternate between professing love and displaying actions that are void of love and harsh or punitive. When affectionate bonds are broken, emotional reactions can include numbness, withdrawal from further affectionate bonds, and, in later life, a lack of willingness to form any additional attachments. Cognitive information must be processed, but often a moratorium on cognitive and emotional functioning occurs from the loss of an affectionate attachment that prevents an individual from completing this process.

Cognitive Processes and Cognitive Distancing

Bowlby (1980) proposed that mourning or loss is a two-part process of numbing and implementing change, in that individuals must modify their cognitions of affectionate attachment to realize a harmonious emotional existence. According to Bowlby, "the conceptualized models of attachment figures and of self, built during childhood and adolescence, are a function of experience during the early years of development . . . first, for the pattern of affectionate relationship he makes during his life and, secondly, for the cognitive biases he brings to any loss he may sustain" (p. 233). Individual biases that may thwart the mourning process or impede healing often include (a) a perceived role model associated with the attached party, (b) perceptions of a self-role in the loss, (c) anticipated treatment from others regarding loss, (d) reflections of past interpersonal events and the impact of each event on recovery from the loss, and (e) the extent to which an open approach toward acquiring new information is available.

Cognitive Processes During Loss   Aaron Beck (1976) also emphasized cognitive processes during loss. Depressive reactions occurring on a chronic basis, with or without actual loss of loved ones, are a direct reaction to how the individual thinks about self, the world, and the future. Therefore, depressive cognitive processes in depressive-prone individuals use cognitive schemas unique to their predisposition for onset of depression from loss. Although Beck suggested the presence of a predisposition toward depressive-prone tendencies, he did not explore the etiology of these characteristics as formed during childhood. Bowlby (1980), on the other hand, searched deeper into childhood experiences as a source of misguided schemas that undermine adult adjustments.

Behaviorists have studied parent-infant interactions by focusing on parent-generated responses, that is, cues emitted to the infant in the form of contingency reinforcements from parents that fuel an infant's behavior (Ainsworth et al., 1978). They have proposed antecedent actions or stimuli that provoke an infant's response, a concept that offers a rather simplistic explanation of infant behavior, dealing solely with the here and now. Hence, behaviorists view stimuli such as reinforcement or consequences of behavioral interactions as the main determinant for behavior, and for subsequent behavioral change in attachment related behaviors.

Trust Versus Mistrust

According to Erikson (1959), inconsistent behavioral patterns from caregivers will distort the development of trust in adulthood. When infants experience nurturance one moment but neglect or maltreatment the next, they may well develop a wide range of anxiety-provoked responses about interactions with others. Without a base of trust in the infant's cognitive schema, a host of residual emotional reactions may occur, ranging from mild to severe intensity such as anxious insecurity, distrust of others, and feelings of anger and hostility driven by a sense of abandonment. These may all be internalized by an infant, imprinted upon the infant's own unique personality traits, and carried throughout life as a direct result of neglectful or abusive parenting (Rosenberg, 1987).

Autonomy Versus Shame

Erikson (1959) claimed that from birth, infants continually develop a sense of autonomy, a sense of independence, and separate functioning from maternal influences. Infants learn to move independently by crawling at the age of 6 to 8 months and by walking at the age of 9 to 12 months. In abuse-free environments, infants receive guidance and encouragement to experiment with each newly learned step. A sense of autonomy develops that sets a precedence, or in Piaget's (1952) terms, a schema in the child's mind, for further learning and experimenting toward independence.

Prolonged Stress States

When abuse occurs during the infancy stage of development, trauma realized by the abuse riddles the infant with stress, which may or may not subside, dependent on factors unique to the child and the environment. Abused infants may internalize fears and anxieties that become generalized to all aspects of their interactions with others. A timid approach toward all activities can develop that serves to inhibit autonomous functioning, inhibiting ability to strive for new goals. At the infant stage, this may be manifested by a failure to assertively seek out basic needs that are normally achieved by crying, grabbing, or reaching activities (Taylor & Daniel, 1999; Ward, Brazelton, & Wust, 1999). Finally, perpetual abuse may result in an infant not only being physically injured, but also becoming psychologically withdrawn, full of self-doubt and hopelessness.

SYMPTOMATIC
AND PATHOLOGICAL DISORDERS

Any form of abuse directed toward an infant will have long-term effects on personality development (Wyatt & Powell, 1988). Verbal cues such as shouting, scolding, and unwarranted sanctioning often result in an infant's withdrawal from or avoidance of the source of verbal abuse. In extreme cases, excessive harshness results in a range of behaviors that are either internalized such as withdrawal from others, or externalized such as disruptive demands for attention to compensate for the perceived lack of attention and approval from others. Researchers noted that verbal as well as physical and emotional development can be delayed by exposure to abuse (Toth & Cicchetti, 1996).

Sense of Helplessness

The results of physical abuse of infants take numerous forms, ranging from minor bruises to more severe broken bones, internal injuries, and residual functional loss as is evidenced in medical records. But, secondary emotional scars leave marks long after the physical injuries have healed. Verbal assaults last a lifetime, forming the basis of negative cognitive schemas that are often internalized as a result of emotional abuse. Repeated and sustained abusive acts foster a sense of helplessness, worthlessness, and insignificance within an infant's psyche, all of which heighten the oppression of the child. Perhaps even more tragic is the fact that these early experiences render an infant more vulnerable to further abuse later in life from perpetrators who seek out helpless or victim-like children. The ultimate form of child abuse, of course, results in death of the infant (Berger, 1994).

Acute Versus Chronic Symptoms

When children display fear, excessive cringing or crying, or frightful expressions as overt signs of distress, it can be assumed that they associate fear with the object of their reactions. If infants are predisposed to react in an agitated manner, any acting out or mood changes may be deemed as routine or chronic behavior. Therefore, when a specific disruption occurs in a child's mood, the change is often subtle to the observer and may be undetected.

However, in instances of acute mood swings, when an infant's temperament changes from one of playful interaction to one of emotional withdrawal, apathy, or extreme crying, it may be assumed that some stimuli in the environment triggered that reaction, and the cause should be investigated. A caregiver who is at least sensitive enough to identify adverse reactions that may require attention would be alert to subtle mood changes in the infant. The impact of abuse on personality can range across many dimensions of behavior; abused infants may cry harder and develop a whiny, needy expression of their unmet needs, or they may totally withdraw and never acknowledge their needs.

Soft Versus Hard Evidence of Abuse

Soft signs of abuse, a term used in medical and forensic environments, refers to any behavioral change that cannot be objectively documented through the use of X rays, residual scars, or any other tangible physical evidence. Without *hard evidence,* such as medical documentation of the abuse or eyewitness accounts of the abuse, chances are that a conviction will not occur. In fact, many prosecutors may be hesitant to embark on legal proceedings without hard, physical evidence of the crime, even when multiple soft signs are apparent.

Some infants, by nature of their unique temperament, may emit few indicators of disturbance. This group of infants presents the most difficult diagnostic dilemma. Given a lack of hard evidence, even multiple soft signs of abuse are not enough to prosecute. If repeated abuse experiences go undetected and the child remains unprotected from the abuser, the prolonged and repeated abuse becomes increasingly detrimental to the child's welfare. This often occurs in cases of cult or ritualistic abuse where a child coerced into silence may endure multiple and long-term abuse experiences (Oates, 1996).

Sexually Transmitted Diseases

Forensic evaluators have been unable to pin down motivating factors for pedophilic behavior, although the overview of theoretically derived etiology presented in an earlier chapter shows that they have made efforts to do so. Infant sexual abuse is too repulsive a crime for anyone to conceptualize, but when an infant's genital area is infected, irritated, or ruptured, these physical manifestations may be more readily accepted as evidence that a sexual assault, molestation, or penetration has occurred. Physical cues of abuse are evident when an infant's genitals are excessively reddened, are unrealistically blistered, or exhibit tears or bruises on the surfaces (American Academy of Pediatrics, 1999). Examination often reveals that the infant has a sexually transmitted disease (STD), such as anogenital warts in children (Handley et al., 1993; Raimer & Raimer, 1992), genital human papillomavirus (HPV) infections (Moscicki, 1996), or another sexually transmitted disease (Shapiro, 1994), such as syphilis (Connors, Schubert, & Shapiro, 1998) or gonorrhea (Ingram, 1997; Siegried, Rasnick-Conley, Cook, Leonardi, & Montelcone, 1998). In addition, the examination often reveals rectal and genital trauma (Kadish, Schunk, & Britton, 1998) from the invasive use of objects (Gromb & Lazarini, 1998). Surprisingly, Lawson and Chaffin's (1992) study identified sexual abuse among children who were initially presented for what was thought to be normal childhood illnesses, which indicates the importance of thorough evaluations.

Long-Term Effect of Sexually Transmitted Diseases While immediate treatment can hasten a child's recovery from an STD, long-term consequences for the child may be significant. Moscicki (1996) notes that the majority of condylomatous lesions in children, HPV type 16 and 18, may persist for a short time in the genital region and may not represent acute morbidity; however, early onset of HPV may hasten the emergence of anogential concerns, as well as increase the risk of cancer. Similarly, Peclard and Taieb (1996) noted that some neonatal infections are revealed only once they have reached an advanced state. Additional hard evidence concerns are related to evidence of genital trauma (Pokorny, 1997) and exposure to AIDS (Meledandri, Cattaruzza, Zantedeschi, Signorelli, & Osborn, 1997).

Invasive Medical Examinations

A child may experience stress or trauma because of exposure to the colposcopic medical examination conducted when sexual abuse allegations are made (Berson, Herman-Giddens, & Frothingham, 1993). An infant may be retraumatized by the forensic investigation. Overall long-term effects of such events may contribute to the individual's symptomatic behaviors as an adult. When suspected physical or sexual abuse of children is reported to child protective services, it is often confirmed by the thorough medical examination that is provided. Long-standing physical abuse is most often revealed by the use of

X rays depicting multiple fractures and contusions that occurred years earlier, but were undetected during previous physical examinations (Kleinman, 1990).

If X rays confirm physical or sexual abuse in an older child, yet that abuse occurred years ago and continued for years without detection, it is likely that other siblings in the same family also are being, or were, abused. Intrafamilial abuse frequently involves more than one sibling, as evidenced in the following case.

> The father of seven brothers and sisters sexually abused each child for years. The father was so manipulative in silencing the children that, over the course of their youth, none of them knew the others were being abused. Rather, each child remained silent because of the father's threats of harm and abandonment. As adults, one female disclosed the abuse at age 35. Only then did the other siblings acknowledge that their father also had abused them and that they had remained silent because of the threats and coercive tactics used by their father.

Obviously, if a perpetrator can manipulate secrecy among several siblings, censoring the siblings from disclosing the abuse in the community is highly possible. This case contributes to the common belief that the incident rate of CSA is drastically underestimated as one pedophile may violate many children.

Delayed Idenfication of Abuse

While hard evidence of sexual abuse is required to expedite the prosecution of perpetrators, sexual abuse often leaves no visible physical evidence, perhaps for several reasons. First, infants cannot tell anyone about abuse. Consequently, sores or lesions that are inflicted in the course of the abuse may heal. Second, the type of sexual abuse or exploitative act may not result in physical lesions or bruises that are overtly evident. Third, eyewitnesses to the abuse may be unwilling to come forward, as in the case of negligible spouses who remain silent rather than face the consequences of reporting. And finally, the absence of hard evidence or obvious physical signs may cause the observer to misinterpret a behavioral change or emotional mood swing that is, in fact, due to abuse. Therefore, the abuse continues. Unfortunately, a greater incident rate of physical abuse is reported among more vulnerable infants, as compared to older children who might run or escape harm (Berger, 1994; Sherry, 2000; Wexler, 2000).

Nonoffending Parents

When a parent is alleged to have abused an infant, the nonoffending parent may respond with disbelief, denial, or evasion. The nonoffending parent is often shocked, devastated, and repulsed by the concept of abusing a child, and more so if the perpetrator is a loved family member or familiar friend. The repercussions that may constrict a spouse from reporting the abuse can include the breakup of the family, financial strain, and extended legal proceedings. Also, if the spouse experienced child abuse during his or her own childhood, extreme reactions may occur, due to a learned sense of helplessness. Such a spouse may either defend and protect the child or evade and avoid signs of abuse.

A child's claim of abuse may also be denied by the nonabusing spouse for the following reasons: (a) fear of confrontation with the perpetrator, (b) codependency on the perpetrator, or (c) simple unwillingness to disrupt the household to enact protective support for the abused child (Finkelhor, 1984). Consequently, the nonoffending parent often dismisses, avoids, or denies clues of the abuse, and, perhaps worse, may even punish the child for fabricating a story that is, in reality, true (Deblinger and Hefflin, 1996).

Gathering Physical Evidence

Soft signs of abuse cannot be substantiated as readily as hard signs, such as broken bones, punctures, or abrasions that are easily captured on film and later used as hard evidence in a court of law. When examining a nonverbal infant, it is often difficult to gather factual data about the abuse incident, particularly because molestation, exploitation, and outright sexual invasion of the infant do not always leave physical evidence on the child (Abel et al., 1987; Kempe et al., 1962; Pascoe & Duterette, 1981). Stressful reactions within infants may manifest in overt symptoms of acute anxiety or distress. Therefore, in the absence of an eyewitness testimony to the abuse, substantiation of a claim of sexual abuse requires multiple methods of assessment. Palusci et al. (1999) note that positive evidence of physical injury is associated with a higher rate of a "finding of guilt" of pedophilic behavior and subsequent prosecution of the perpetrator. Any number of reasons may account for an infant's acute mood change or disrupted schedule of eating and sleeping. Therefore, without hard evidence such as medical evidence of abuse, allegations can be readily disputed by the accused. In an instance of neglect and failure to thrive as a result of abuse, growth charts for normal expected body weight and height can easily be used for comparison. The American Academy of Pediatrics publishes growth charts that can be accessed online at

www.babysdoc.com/developmentpackage.htm.

Certainly, any surface bruises of an unexplainable nature are potential indicators of neglect or abuse.

When hard signs are apparent, a medical doctor must persist with a thorough physical examination. Infants being examined for sexual abuse are often subjected to highly invasive medical techniques and stress-provoking experiences that can be a source of additional trauma to the infant. While physical abuse or battering often can be detected by X rays, sonograms, magnetic resonance imaging (MRI), and other noninvasive techniques, sexual assault requires a medical examination that can be highly invasive.

Individualized Diagnosis

Levels of development and maturation vary widely among infants due to innate differences within infants, as well as in environmental influences. Abuse experiences impact each child differently (Kuehnle, 1996). Therefore, the following must be considered when diagnosing, treating, and providing a long-term prognosis for each abuse case: (a) the unique temperament of the child; (b) the nurturance received from the caregiver; (c) any additional trauma in the child's life; (d) the frequency and severity of abuse exposure; (e) any developmental dysfunction from organic, physiological, or neurological disorders identified in childhood; and (f) any other contributing factors within the child's environment.

A mental health specialist who is conducting a formal evaluation in an alleged sexual abuse case must investigate corroborative data, including an analysis of the alleged abuser's profile. In doing so, the specialist must adhere to professional standards, copies of which are available from professional organizations such as the American Professional Society on the Abuse of Children (APSAC, 1995) and the American Psychological Association (2001), and experts in child assessment techniques (Anastasia, 1988; Sattler, 2001).

Role of Medical Personnel

Medical doctors, like all child care workers, are mandated reporters of any form of suspected child abuse, including sexual abuse. However, as with other mandated reporters, medical professionals are often deterred from filing reports when hard evidence is not observed because of the implications for legal sanctions, the possibility of involvement in judicial proceedings, and their overall lack of preparedness. The protocol for medical personnel who suspect a case of child abuse requires that the child be detained and authorities be contacted immediately, particularly if the child is in immediate danger. Professionals should be familiar with the child abuse legislation in their state and the rulings unique to each district in which the practitioners are licensed. The American Academy of Pediatrics Association (1999) has published procedural protocols for substantiating abuse cases; in crisis cases, where bleeding is apparent, protocol requires medical personnel to secure biological trace evidence, such as "epithelial cells, semen, and blood, as well as to maintain a 'chain of evidence,'" within 72 hours of alleged abuse (p. 2).

In cases of suspected abuse by a parent, medical doctors must detain parents and children and not allow them to leave the medical facility until child investigative teams arrive. Usually a child abuse investigator arrives with a youth officer who is trained in dealing with child abuse matters. The youth officer, in accordance with departmental investigative procedures, may intervene and, if warranted, remove the infant from parental control, often resulting in the child being placed in an emergency shelter. Collaboration with medical personnel, mental health experts, law officials, and sexual abuse experts is essential (Finkelhor, 1994; Hanson & Bussiere, 1998; Kempe et al. 1985; Quinsey, Harris, Rice, & Cormier, 1998).

SUMMARY

While physical symptoms provide hard evidence of sexual abuse, enhanced methods of detecting subtle soft signs of abuse must be developed. Given the dynamics of human nature, this is a difficult task requiring an examination of short- and long-term infant reactions. Based on the severity and destructive nature of abusive treatment, long-term ramifications for the infant's well-being are extensive. Without the ability to verbalize facts, infants are vulnerable to repeated incidents of abuse and exploitation. Although infancy is a time when infants should pass through the developmental stages identified by Erikson, Piaget, and Kohlberg without detrimental experiences, increased abuse rates continue to plague child welfare.

Even with extensive federal funds allocated for medical care, investigation, prosecution, and intervention programs, the incident rate of CSA continues to rise. Professionals may not always be adequately prepared to deal with CSA, as most graduate programs and mental health licensing agencies do not require abuse-specific training courses other than a few hours of continuing education courses. More intervention programs are sorely needed, and child abuse service programs need to be continually reevaluated and new ones developed across the country.

Many citizens believe they need not get involved, as long as no abuse occurs in their family. This is an evasive approach to an ever-growing societal problem, however. Because of the long-term, often debilitating, effects of childhood abuse and sexual abuse, abusees may be forced into a life of oppression, rather than prospering as children in a safe environment that will prepare them for adulthood. Perhaps it is the unwillingness of others to get involved in prevention programs that allows predators to prey upon unprotected children. The longer the problem remains secondary in societal urgency, the longer it will plague society.

All citizens reap the consequences of child abuse, not just the abusee. Abuse causes a societal loss of potential human resources, in addition to the victim-related costs such as medical assistance, intervention programs, and follow-up services. Public tax monies are spent on lengthy prosecution processes, often for repeat offenders. Once convicted, prisoner maintenance expenses mount, including security facilities in which to house the perpetrators. These funds might be better spent on research, preventative programs, and more accessible intervention services to curtail this tragedy that subliminally diminishes national human resources.

All children are entitled to a protected childhood filled with security, warmth, and love. It does not take much to make an infant smile, gurgle, reach out for a familiar face, or play with a favorite toy. In light of an infant's vulnerable state, all citizens have a responsibility to intervene when a child is in harm's way.

DISCUSSION QUESTIONS

1. Contrast and review the elements of Freud's theory of psychosexual development with those of Skinner's learning theory. What implications does sexual abuse have on the child's development in light of these theoretical conceptions?

2. Can you identify a learning activity that you have observed among infants that supports Skinner's learning theory? Describe how that activity might change under the duress of abuse.

3. Behavioral responses to adverse stimuli may vary significantly across infants. Can you identify some reasons why this might be true?

4. What procedures or methods do you view as essential when an infant is examined for alleged abuse? How is the diagnostic process affected?

5. How can developmental milestones be affected if abuse is experienced? Can you provide examples of case histories that reflect this?

6. What complications hinder assessment of physical injuries due to abuse? What is being done about it in your community or nationwide?

7. How would you proceed if you suspected infant abuse? Base your answers on the probability that you are a regular citizen, a professional child care worker, or a licensed professional mental health care worker. Are there differences among the three? Why?

8. What programs in your community offer services for infants? Can you name two referral agencies or professionals who might be called in when abuse is suspected? What are the referral procedures?

8

Preschool-Age Development

LEARNING OBJECTIVES

Chapter 8 will address the following learning objectives:

1. A discussion of developmental theories specific to preschoolers

2. A discussion of developmental milestones and potential delays

3. A review of physiological development in preschoolers

4. A discussion of issues in abuse case investigations in preschools

5. A review of symptomatic and pathological disorders in preschoolers

6. A discussion of dilemmas in intrafamilial and extrafamilial abuse

INTRODUCTION

Child development theories are presented here as they relate to the impact of sexual abuse during the preschool-age period, ages 2–5. Discussions focus on how preschoolers' personalities are shaped by the completion of *normal* developmental tasks for this age period, as well as on how preschoolers' developmental progress can be impacted when preschoolers experience neglect, abuse, or sexual abuse at the hands of their primary caretakers.

During the preschool stage of development, children's minds are basically open and receptive to all new stimuli from the environment. Through visual, tactile, and auditory channels, preschoolers internalize sights, touches, and sounds, often for the first time. Their world enlarges as social interactions increase, partly because newly acquired language skills empower them. Preschoolers become most assertive in investigating, probing, and experimenting with each new phenomenon confronted in their environment. New information must be processed in a manner that is acceptable within the social environment that is unique to each child, given various cultural, social, and ethnic influences (Kaplan, 1991).

Parents guide or shape a child's behavior by applying sanctions for undesirable behaviors and reinforcements for acceptable behaviors. For example, a parent may cheer with pleasure when a child speaks a word or phrase for the first time, yet slap the child's hand and show disapproval when the child reaches toward a sharp object or an electrical outlet. Each reprimand not only serves as an external regulatory monitor, but also shapes that preschooler's personality for future interactions. Excessively harsh or assaultive punishment for unacceptable behaviors evokes a distressed state in the child, along with other emotional reactions that can adversely impact the child's progression through the developmental stages.

DEVELOPMENTAL TASKS

During the preschool years, a child becomes increasingly independent of family members in observing, experiencing, and internalizing environmental stimuli. The young child no longer functions on an oral-sensory mode as during infancy; rather, all sensory systems develop in preparation for more advanced activities. Although an awareness of self and self-needs persists within preschoolers, they now look outside themselves and absorb basic premises about their environment. In Piaget's (1952) words, they develop schemas of objects, events, and persons that serve as a base for more advanced learning.

Piaget (1952) refers to early learning patterns as the preoperational stage of development, usually spanning ages 2–7. During this stage, a child uses symbols to identify objects, events, and people. A child might use the word *out* to say "I want to go outside to play," or the word *hurt* to convey that something has injured the child. Children at this stage are fixed and rigid in their concept mastering, in that once a concept is learned, they believe it applies to many circumstances. Therefore, they may apply the concept to inappropriate or incorrect objects and events. For example, upon learning that a bird flies, children at this stage will often refer to airplanes as birds.

Only more advanced concept mastering will allow a child to realize that various objects, not just birds, fly as children place all new concepts into preexisting categories, or schemas. Eventually, with proper reinforcement, a child cognitively builds new schemas to accommodate the concept of airplanes.

Piaget refers to this process as the process of assimilation, whereby cognitive processes allow the child to realize that two kinds of objects fly, birds and airplanes.

When a child learns to say goodbye, the word *bye-bye* is repeated each time someone walks into or out of a room, perhaps sounding like a parrot. Children of this age usually cannot yet discriminate between concepts of coming or going. Even if another word, such as *hello,* is provided, a young child may adhere to the simplest word like a broken record, repeating it over and over. Similar learning paradigms exist when preschoolers are taught about safety issues.

Learning Safety Concepts

Using Piaget's (1965) model of learning, it is perhaps possible to understand why a child has difficulty mastering the concept of good people and bad people, a concept that may require several phases of learning. First, a child must understand the symbol for adults, and then learn the differences between females and males. Then a child must comprehend the concept of different types of people, such as good and bad, or friends and strangers. On one hand, parents wish to instill healthy respect for others and social mannerisms in their children; on the other hand, they must somehow teach the child to reject, shout at, or run away from any stranger who attempts to hurt them. Children are told that it is okay to be friendly with family and friends, but to remain silent and distant if a stranger approaches them. Children have a difficult time discriminating between friends and strangers, particularly if a stranger approaches a child with a playful or friendly manner.

My own nephew Keith, a highly verbal 4-year-old with a large vocabulary, provided an excellent example of this. At 4, Keith was quite personable and friendly, and he knew me well as his aunt. On a visit to my home, I asked Keith if he wanted to play with a set of blocks that were in the other room. He immediately put his hand into mine as we walked toward the other room. Suddenly, he stopped walking and looked up at me and asked, "Aunt Felicia, are you a stranger?" He knew he should not go with a stranger, but he could not yet differentiate between adults who were strangers and those who were family members.

Once a child develops a cognitive concept, symbols associated with that concept are used to enhance memory recall, and thus a child can recount an earlier event such as a birthday party or a visit to Santa. Direct sensory stimuli are not necessary to evoke memory streams of tastes, emotional reactions, and visual images; symbolic thought patterns occur as a result of the child's cognitive maturation. The child's ability to progress to advanced levels allows the child to form more complex schemas built upon earlier learned schemas.

Symbolic Functioning

According to Piaget (1962), a child applies symbolic functioning to carry out deferred imitation, symbolic play, and language enhancement. Deferred imitation occurs when a child imitates a behavior observed at an earlier time. For example, a child may imitate a dog barking and walking on all fours. Symbolic play bridges a gap between concrete experience and abstract thought, such as when a child pretends that he or she is making a cup of tea and drinking it, although the stove may be a box and a round object may substitute for a tea cup. Play activities allow a child to organize thoughts while developing a means of control and empowerment (Landreth, 1991; Webb, 1991).

Language expression is more developed during the preschool years than in earlier years. Children can interact with others in play activities and sustain verbal conversation for longer periods of time than was possible as a toddler. As the child progresses in cognitive maturation with each accomplishment, the child's sense of self-identity also emerges. Many play activities mirror activities modeled by primary caretakers or peers. As children receive praise (whether from doting parents or peers) for properly executed play activities, they begin to realize that they are capable and that social interactions can be a source of pleasure. Consequently, the child develops a new eagerness to seek attention from others. This is a positive developmental accomplishment, but it can make the child more susceptible to a perpetrator's engaging play.

Adaptive Responding

When neglectful or abusive parenting occurs, preschoolers learn to adapt and make the adjustments that are necessary for survival. According to Freud (1923/1962), a human organism's first instinct is one of physical and psychological survival. Even young children learn early that certain behaviors, such as cries for help or whining, will provoke a response from caregivers. If that response is appropriate, the child should instinctually learn socially acceptable behaviors to sustain basic needs in a healthy manner, that is, without developing negative self-concepts or self-deprecating behaviors. However, if caregivers excessively punish the child for his or her requests, a child may have to find ways to accommodate the situation: good, bad, or indifferent. This accommodation may not be healthy, such as when a child shuts down emotionally and is no longer capable of expressing needs or desires.

Even though a child can emotionally accommodate self-survival under the duress of abuse and perhaps ease the pain of the moment, the temporary or situational accommodation does not negate the trauma realized from the abuse. Unlike the accommodation that applies to cognitive learning in Piaget's theory, the emotional adjustments that work to accommodate the abusive situation, such as denial, minimization, or dissociation, have lasting negative effects on the child.

Accommodation in Abusive Situations

As noted earlier, when children are confronted with new ideas or concepts that do not fit into a previously acquired schema, they must accommodate them and assimilate them into a new schema. During an abusive experience, children must also accommodate thoughts and feelings as a means of coping. Preschoolers are, by nature, open, trusting, and naïve creatures who are dependent upon caregivers for all their physiological and psychological needs. If a child is confronted with a situation that is unpleasant, hurtful, or even painful, the child may withdraw from the interaction, feeling confused and hurt.

When a caregiver smacks and hurts a child but then picks up and holds the child in a loving and remorseful manner in the next moment, the child can experience a great amount of anxiety. With older children, the same interaction occurs when a caregiver inflicts a severe beating, only to give them a few dollars to spend and a verbal apology within moments after the abuse. In an attempt to hide hurt feelings and accommodate the situation, the child may appear to make peace with the situation, but high levels of emotional confusion and distress are experienced.

In this instance, accommodation can take many forms, based on the unique aspects of the child's personality and the environmental circumstances. At times, accommodations may be outwardly expressed through behaviors, ranging from rigid defensiveness to overt anger acted out on others. These reactions may be consciously or unconsciously developed to maintain the peace; an example is the development of an attitude like "I can't get it, so who needs it?" The ramification of this type of interaction is that the child sublimates emotional needs to keep the peace. Eventually, the child builds a wall of protection around his or her emotional needs and rarely publicly acknowledges his or her own needs. As abusive treatment increases in frequency and intensity, the child eventually adorns a tough shell of protection, often viewed by others as hardened or detached interactions with adults.

Accommodations during abuse address two dimensions of existence, physiological survival and the maintenance of emotional equilibrium. For example, imagine a child who anticipates that her alcoholic father expects the bed to be made perfectly or else he will severely beat her. The child may repeatedly make the bed until it appears acceptable to the demanding parent; thus, physiological safety is protected. A child who is frequently abused may even acquiesce to demands by the abuser that the child smile after a beating, hug the abuser, or sit on the abuser's lap in loving adoration, all of which the child will do to avoid further harsh treatment.

The abused child who accommodates to keep the peace at all costs may do so out of fear of the perpetrator, true helplessness, or perhaps even the hope of receiving a much-needed act of warmth. Thus, although the child is mistreated during the transaction, he or she responds to the demand for an emotional reaction in one way externally, while an opposing emotional reaction is occurring internally (Oliveri, Cockriel, & Dugan, 1993). Once again, the child's emotional needs are sublimated, and the child is helpless to defend him- or herself. Denial of needs and learned helplessness soon become an inherent part of the child's personality that may carry over into interactions with others outside the home.

Effect of Inadequate Parenting Skills

A child exposed to inadequate parenting behaviors develops a greater propensity for long-term emotional deficits. Whether poor parenting includes physical, emotional, or sexual abuse, neglect, or abandonment, the child suffers emotional consequences. The abused child's most frequent reaction is to suppress emotional needs that would be neglected or exploited by caretakers if they were to be expressed. A loss of self-worth emerges when attempts to express needs and wants are ignored or violated by others. Eventually, the child stops acknowledging his or her own needs, particularly when the child has been forced to repress them within a nonresponding family setting. The child may appear to be out of touch with his or her own emotions. Behavioral reactions may manifest in such a child as a tendency to withdraw or distance him- or herself from others. Eventually, the child is perceived as being content with less attention, and his or her feelings are ignored even more often than before.

Conversely, some children who experience abuse react with a more aggressive expression of needs. These expressions may be manifested in disruptive behaviors or clowning and self-ridiculing behaviors, all conducted in an attempt to gain attention, albeit negative attention. Maladjusted behavior patterns develop as the child learns that these actions serve to gain some form of attention from others, even if the response from others is less than desirable. Therefore, the true need for attention is never met, yet the cycle of need and unresolved need continues. The child assertively pursues attention, often by annoying others, but receives only harsh treatment or punishment that restricts the child's emotional development rather than enhancing it. Once again, a wedge is driven between a child's emotional needs and the fulfillment of those needs. Hence, a cycle of expressive need and need deprivation continues to plague the child, shaping his or her personality, perhaps with increased potential for maladjustment in adulthood.

Increased Child Vulnerability

In many ways, it is this cycle of unmet needs that renders a child unable to process the normal developmental tasks essential at each age of development. For example, when a child cries out for attention but is rejected, ignored, or punished harshly for crying, heightened distress dominates the child's thought processes. Consequently, instead of enjoying a problem-free, safe, and secure environment that allows the child to thrive, one that maximizes the development of personality traits, the child is forced to grapple with events, feelings, and emotions related to survival of the abuse. Emotional growth that is essential for a well-balanced adult life is blocked. Hence, the abuse experienced during the preschool and early childhood years creates a double jeopardy; not only is the child abused or neglected, perhaps suffering pain at the time of the abuse, but also the adverse psychological trauma that is experienced negates the development of core personality traits essential for healthy emotional adjustment in adulthood. Once preoccupied with emotional pain, the child is deprived of the opportunity to develop more positive schemas of self and essential interactive skills, and thus the child is placed at risk for later adjustment. For preschoolers, abuse experiences mean that vital social learning is restricted, rendering the children void of an otherwise pleasant time of life.

Conflicting Messages

Confusing cognitive and emotional reactions occur when a trusted person (i.e., father, stepfather, uncle, etc.) uses tactics like playing games or buying toys to break down defenses and, once trust has been gained, abuses or harms the child. Many ambiguous concepts are at work in this situation, as demonstrated by the following questions. Will the child willingly go to outreached arms or remain distant and fearful of all adults? Was the interaction pleasurable, as when toys or attention were received, or painful and demeaning, as when the abuse occurred? Did the action feel funny or good? Should the child tell others or remain silent? Although a preschooler may not be capable of expressing such questions verbally, the insecurity and confusion the child experiences may become manifest in highly anxious behaviors. If the child does not receive intervention, the inadequate coping skills the child develops to deal with the experience will continue into adulthood.

In cases of parental sexual abuse, a child's emotional needs for parental approval render him or her ready to acquiesce to the demands of the trusted adult. Because the child also relies on the parent figure for basic survival needs, little recourse exists for the child. Regardless of the method of entrapment or the rationale for the abusive event, the child will inevitably harbor confused and contradictory messages. Without a cognitive basis, or in Piaget's terms, a cognitive schema, for processing such complex dynamics, distorted views of self and others evolve.

DEVELOPMENTAL MILESTONES

Developmental milestones for children of this age group are focused on preparation for learning social skills and self-initiative. The newly arrived preschooler must be capable of walking, talking, and, most importantly, be toilet trained. Physiological maturation of muscular and neurological systems highly influences successful achievement of each milestone. Caretakers must be knowledgeable of the maturation process to appropriately guide, encourage, and support each child's unique developmental pathway.

For example, it does no good to force a child to try to walk until the child's skeletal system and muscle tone mature sufficiently to support the action of walking independent of adult assistance. Without skeletal maturation, it would be an impossible achievement. It is common and acceptable to help guide a child's first steps. However, any attempts to force walking prematurely by abrasively forcing a child to stand, only to have him or her fall down in defeat, are inappropriate and stress-provoking for the young child.

Similarly, perhaps the most frustrating stage of preschool development is the achievement of toilet training, as addressed briefly in the previous chapter. Because it is incumbent for preschoolers to be toilet trained before being accepted into a preschool, many working parents feel pressure to accomplish this task as early as possible. If the child's sphincter muscles have not matured sufficiently to gain control of the matter, accidents will occur.

Unfortunately, children have suffered beatings because of soiled pants. Caregivers have accused the children of not obeying by eliminating feces in their pants rather than into the toilet. If a child has developmental lags, it is not within the child's realm of functioning to be able to "obey." If the child's sphincter muscle control has not sufficiently matured, most often the problem is physiological. One such case occurred in a Florida county where a 25-year-old man was charged with the murder of a young child (Zielbauer, 2000). Apparently angry with the child for soiling his diapers, the man wrapped the boy in a blanket so tightly that the boy remained immobile on a bed, where he remained unattended. Shortly after being placed on the bed, the young boy choked on his own vomit and died, needlessly harmed under the care of a parent.

As physical maturation occurs, emotional maturation and personality attributes are also acquired. A preschool-aged child may excel or be impeded in attaining developmental milestones, based partly on environmental influences. For children to master the skills inherent in each milestone, they must strive to achieve them, which requires a sense of initiative. If a child had been sanctioned or reprimanded during earlier attempts to achieve a goal, a depressive sense of hopelessness may curtail the child's goal-seeking activities.

Overindulgence by doting adults can be equally detrimental to initiating independence in children. For example, a caregiver may hold the spoon or fork at feeding time and put the food into the child's mouth rather than allowing the child to feed him- or herself to avoid the mess the child would make when eating independently. This kind of behavior encourages dependency traits, and children treated this way will always look for others to meet their needs, rather than taking the initiative to fulfill their needs themselves.

Self-care skills, such as feeding, dressing, and fulfilling other bodily needs, are perhaps the most important tasks that preschoolers must accomplish. The typical preschooler will make mistakes and be messy while learning these skills, and will require a longer time to do them than an older child or an adult would. Preschoolers will wet or soil their pants prior to mastering toilet training. In learning to brush their teeth or bathe themselves, they will be awkward and messy. Their acquisition of vocabulary will be achieved at a rate that is unique to each child's skill level, and only when the child has matured sufficiently in his or her physiological development.

Patience is essential for anyone guiding children along developmental pathways during this period. If a caregiver is punitive or negligent when guiding a child who is working on these accomplishments, that child not only may stop striving to achieve but also may regress to earlier stages of development. Exposure to trauma, neglect, or abuse may influence a child's unique manner of attaining age-appropriate goals in different ways. Obviously, child development classes can inform parents of contributing factors for attaining developmental milestones, but in most cases, classes are not mandated unless abuse has already occurred.

Physiological Development

Physiological development differs significantly across children. If a child is severely below the average norms of skill achievement, the child may be experiencing a developmental delay or, in more severe cases, an actual childhood disorder of a more permanent nature. Distinguishing between the two, a *delay* versus a *disorder,* requires a diagnosis by a specialist in the appropriate field. Usually the diagnosis is made in accordance with the diagnostic codes in the *Diagnostic and Statistical Manual of Mental Disorders,* 4th edition-Text Revision (*DSM-IV-TR;* APA, 2000).

Standards in the *DSM-IV-TR* refer to developmental disorders as "disorders usually first diagnosed in infancy, childhood, or adolescence" (APA, 2000, p. 39). Developmental disorders—such as attention-deficit disorders; mental retardation; learning disabilities; motor skills disorders; communication disorders; and pervasive developmental disorders such as autism, Rhett's or Asperger's disorder—require expert intervention, including special needs services in school. Some theorists have noted that, because of their greater need for attention and approval from others, special needs children are five times more vulnerable to child predators for sexual abuse or exploitation (Hewitt, 1999; Tharinger, Russian, & Robinson, 1989; Waterman & Ben-Meir, 1993).

Developmental delays, on the other hand, may also be first viewed during early childhood, but they are of a temporary nature. As the child matures, symptoms should diminish, and the child may very well catch up with his or her peer group. For preschoolers, developmental delays may be seen in learning to run and jump, developing increased verbal and social skills, and the acquisition of other self-help tasks. If a pediatrician, parent, or school personnel note a developmental delay, they can recommend remediation activities specific to the deficient area, but the child should eventually mature sufficiently to illuminate or significantly minimize the problem.

When a child is exposed to trauma, the child's emotional reactions can induce, mimic, or actually cause what appears to be a developmental delay. The child may curtail his or her striving to acquire new skills because of emotional reactions such as fear, depression, or a sense of helplessness. In addition, even though a skill may have been previously learned, a traumatic incident can regress the child to an earlier stage of life or the child can become emotionally blocked and simply stop performing specific skills. In more severe cases, actual pathology may present, such as under conditions of shock, coma, or dissociation. The amount of neurotransmitters known as catecholamines has been found to change in the bodies of sexually abused children. This class of neurotransmitters can provoke excessive states of stress and hyperarousal (De Bellis & Putman, 1994; Putnam & Trickett, 1997), thus causing a secondary physiological reaction in response to stress.

Verbal Skills

Piaget (1962) noted that children conceptualize symbols rather than words when they begin to speak. Consequently, one word may provide the symbol for a normal seven-word sentence, such as when a child states the word *peepee,*

which is symbolic fc
can express brief thr
ferent children. So
potty," while highly
stating the need in
Any astute caregi
ineffective careg
Therefore, a chi
within an ineff

Verbal skill
a preschooler
evaluation, v
cuted, the c
The topic c
a child's as
Goodman
Kuehnle,

violates any trust that has been built bet
no way of comprehending what has h
been hurt at the hands of a trusted
Concepts such as love versus
perpetual problem for the chil
giver's behavior also provoke
may love the abuser, yet h
lines of delineation bet
emotional reactions su
traumatized child.

Social theo
proposed
they i
obse
ac

Erikson's ﹍﹍

Erikson (1968) noted that from age
trying new things. Thus, a normally developing
iment with a series of failures and successes while learning
out the fear of punitive treatment by caregivers. As a child attempts ﹍
learns new concepts, and strives to attain new feats appropriate to his or her
age, it is essential for a nurturing caregiver to encourage, reinforce, and guide
the child's progress. Because even siblings progress through the developmental
stages at varying rates of speed, each child within a family must be provided a
unique forum in which to accomplish the prescribed tasks. A child should have
the latitude to explore and progress at a unique rate of speed, tempered with
whatever degree of guidance, support, and encouragement is required to
enhance that child's success. Sexually abused children, especially very young
ones, often internalize the abuse experience with feelings of shame, guilt, and
reduced self-worth (Hewitt, 1999; Tharinger, Russian, & Robinson, 1989), all
of which serve to undermine future efforts to achieve and restrict initiative-
seeking activities.

Paradoxical Messages

When caregivers present paradoxical messages by switching parenting tactics,
by providing nurturance and guidance on some occasions but responding with
threats and abuse on others, a child's stress level mounts. Insecurity increases,
as the child never knows what to expect or under what conditions he or she
might be hurt. This is true whether the abuse is physical, verbal, or sexual.
Preschoolers and young school-aged children often manifest such stress in
somatic complaints of tummy aches, headaches, nauseousness, and so on. A
parent who vacillates between positive nurturance and sexual abuse of a child

ween them. Very young children have
appened; all they know is that they have
dult.

nate and trust versus mistrust may present a
who receives paradoxical messages. The care-
paradoxical responses within the child. The child
ate the behavior; in most instances, however, the
ween the two emotions become blurred. Confused
bsequently pose an added source of stress for an already
s the child grows, these feelings intensify.

Behavioral Implications

ists (Bandura, 1986; Beck, 1976; Beck & Freeman, 1990) have
that individuals internalize behaviors that are socially learned, that is,
ternalize behaviors that are modeled in the environment simply by
ving how others behave. A preschooler who is intimidated by witnessing
s of violence (displays of anger, aggression, or assault) may not only be ter-
orized and frightened, but may also eventually adapt similar emotional reactions toward others. Some children who witness or experience sexual abuse
during their early years act out sexually inappropriate behaviors with their
peers, even at the preschool years. Preschoolers have been known to verbalize
sexual knowledge that is not age-appropriate, touch peers in sexually suggestive manners, and perform acts suggestive of other sexualized behaviors.
Treatment issues become blurred, as treatment should be provided for both
areas of abuse—abuse imposed upon the child/abusee as well as the child's abusive acts imposed upon others (Hollin & Howells, 1991; Ryan & Lane, 1991).
It should be noted, however, that not all children who experience abuse
respond by acting out on other children with sexually assaultive behaviors.

Conversely, a child who witnesses a nonoffending parent avoiding and
withdrawing from confrontation with the abuser, allowing the abuse to continue, may adapt similar evasive behaviors that render him or her helpless in a
situation of conflict. Emotional reactions also may be internalized, whereby
the child retreats and withdraws from interactions with others. In either case,
a child who witnesses violence or abuse of others may be traumatized by the
event. The trauma may be manifested in any number of emotionally distressed
reactions, including nightmares, anxious feelings, and hypersensitivity, to name
just a few.

PRESCHOOL ABUSE INCIDENTS

Child abuse inflicted upon preschool-aged children was not highly documented prior to the early 1980s. However, during the 1980s, two tragic cases
emerged, one involving the McMartin Preschool in California, and the other
involving the Papoose Palace Preschool in Nevada. These cases now serve as a

focus of study to extend our knowledge of the impact of abuse on preschoolers (McCord, 1993). An overview of both cases is provided below.

McMartin Preschool

The first case, at the McMartin Preschool in Manhattan Beach, California, occurred in an oceanfront community south of Los Angeles. The McMartin Preschool made national headlines during a lengthy trial in which the school was alleged to be responsible for the sexual abuse of approximately 400 children. The McMartin Preschool was founded by Peggy McMartin in the 1950s and gained a reputation of excellence, resulting in a waiting list of potential students. Ms. McMartin's daughter, Peggy Buckey, had become the administrator, and she, in turn, had employed her 25-year-old son, Raymond Buckey, who was the person accused of allegedly abusing the children (Eberle & Eberle, 1993).

In 1983, a mother reported her 2-year-old son's allegations of abuse to the local police department, prompting them to send letters to other families to investigate similar statements from their own children. Victims came forward in abundance, media attention on the incidents escalated, and local community health agencies were bombarded with children requiring physical examinations and mental health services (Eberle & Eberle, 1993; McCord, 1993). Dr. Roland Summit, a psychiatrist at the University of California, Los Angeles Medical Center, was called upon to assist with services for the children, families, and professionals who required assistance in dealing with the voluminous and complex issues that emerged as a consequence of the ensuing investigations (McCord, 1993). The first trial resulted in an acquittal, reportedly due in large part to leading questions that had been used to interview the child victims. Several jurors noted that while the majority of the 65 child testimonies were believable, suggestible influences recorded on taped interviews were sufficient to thwart a guilty verdict (Ceci & Bruck, 1995).

During the early 1980s, little was known about the appropriate means of handling child interviews, handling the media, and providing treatment for child victims of heinous acts that had become, or soon would become, public knowledge. Community pressure and a frenzy of allegations resulted in arrests, and the McMartin Preschool closed in 1984.

Papoose Palace Preschool

A similar case, involving the Papoose Palace Preschool, emerged during 1983 in Reno, Nevada. A 10-year-old's mother reported her son's allegations that abuse had occurred while he was in preschool. Investigators contacted other boys implicated in the experience. Detective Birch interviewed approximately 50 children, who revealed that sexual abuse had taken place over a period of 5–6 years when the boys were students at the preschool. The school owner's 28-year-old son pleaded guilty within 3 weeks of the investigation, and he was subsequently sentenced to four life prison terms (McCord, 1993).

Although the children in this case were saved from a lengthy trial and traumatic interviews, current theories on the long-term effects of sexually abusive acts suggest that the aftereffects of their abuse will remain with them throughout their lives (Abel et al., 1987). Preschool-aged children are very vulnerable because they are unable to verbally express themselves proficiently and are easily intimidated by a perpetrator's coercive threats to ensure silence. The incident rate of preschool-age sexual abuse ranges from 18–33% of children under age 6, but many estimate that cases are underreported (DeJong, Hervada, & Emmett, 1983; Mannarino, Cohen, & Gregor, 1986; Waterman & Lusk, 1986). Waterman and Lusk (1986) have noted that parents are reluctant to have their children come forward due to fear that they will undergo extensive court testimony, the family will endure stressful hardships, and the children will be further exploited through the court process.

SYMPTOMATIC AND PATHOLOGICAL DISORDERS

Preschoolers often exhibit regressive behaviors in response to sexual abuse, including a reemergence of baby talk, bed wetting, and hyperactivity, as well as inappropriate sexualized behavior (Hewitt & Friedrich, 1991; Pascoe & Duterte, 1981; Reams & Friedrich, 1994). Other responses to sexual abuse include excessive anxiety, fear, nightmares, and separation anxiety (Adams-Tucker, 1982). Mannarino, Cohen, and Gregor (1986) observed somatic complaints among abused preschoolers, such as increased symptoms of nightmares, as well as anxiety, sadness, and clinging behaviors. In addition to regressive symptomology, abused preschoolers have displayed high-risk behaviors, impaired parent-child relationships, developmental delays, and an excessive need for adult approval.

Zivney, Nash, and Hulsey (1988) noted specific patterns of symptomology in children abused prior to the age of 7, such as diminished self-concept, impaired cognition, and primitive object relations, that were not identified to the same degree in older children. Sexualized behaviors may occur that include verbal references to the genitalia of others, masturbation when under stress, and acting out toward peers in sexually inappropriate manners, as in the following case.

> In a rural Head Start program, Timmy, a 4-year-old child, was referred for mental health services after he was witnessed gyrating and masturbating into his matt at naptime. The same child accosted a 4-year-old female student in a sexually inappropriate manner. Upon investigation by child protective services, the father was arrested for alleged sexual abuse of the child, and later he admitted his guilt.

Emotional Symptoms

Emotional symptoms most frequently identified with the experience of sexual abuse include depression, fear, anxiety, anger, and hostility (Finkelhor & Browne, 1986); distorted self-concept (Finkelhor, 1986; Hermin, 1981); anxiety including phobia and panic disorder (Briere, 1984; Sgroi, 1982b); post-traumatic stress disorder (Eth & Pynoos, 1985); depression (Brown, Cohen, Johnson, & Smailes, 1999; Yates, 1982); and anger, denial, or exacerbation (Conte & Schuerman, 1987b; Gomes-Schwartz, Horowitz, & Cardarelli, 1990). One instrument that is frequently used to identify behavioral concerns is the child behavior checklist (CBCL; Achenbach & Edelbrock, 1983). The checklist can be completed by parents, counselors, or teachers when assessing global symptomology (Friedrich, Beilke, & Urquiza, 1988). Sexual problems are often rated as more severe on the CBCL for sexually abused children. Internalizing behavior patterns such as fearfulness, self-hurting or cutting, inhibition, depression, or excessive self-control have been reported, while externalizing behaviors reported include aggression and antisocial and disruptive behaviors (Waterman & Ben-Meir, 1993). Many other behavioral rating scales are available to evaluate emotional and behavioral functioning among children and adolescents (Rapoport & Ismond, 1996).

Intrafamilial Abuse Symptomology

Symptomology is said to escalate when intrafamilial abuse occurs. Father-daughter incest is said to account for approximately 60–80% of cases (Greenfield, 1996). Friends, family members, and other relatives can easily access children for abuse, as trust is already built; the children become an easy mark for familiar persons. Finkelhor, Williams, and Burns (1988) conducted a national study of preschool incident rates and noted that 5.5 out of 10,000 preschool students are abused outside of the home versus 8.9 per 10,000 who are abused in their own home. These figures may vary from earlier figures due to the method of sampling and criteria for inclusion; nonetheless, findings are reinforced across studies. It would appear that a child has a higher probability of falling prey to abuse within his or her own home than elsewhere.

Intrafamilial Symptom Severity The severity of symptoms is related to the child's relationship with the perpetrator. For instance, children who experience intrafamilial abuse are said to present higher rates of symptomology than children who are abused by nonfamily members. The frequency and intensity of abusive acts greatly heighten the emotional distress following abuse when families belong to a cult. Perhaps not surprising, children exposed to multiple perpetrators, as in cases of ritualistic abuse, present increased and more intense symptomology (Kuehnle, 1996; Prendergast, 1993). Among 17% of children sampled in one RSA study, significant adverse effects were found among preschool children who experienced invasive sexual abuse acts, multiple perpetrators, pornographic activities, and participation in or observations of ritualistic abuse (Finkelhor et al., 1988).

Family Dynamics Intrafamilial sexual abuse, due to the implied reference to the family unit, poses different but equally complex dynamics as compared to sexual abuse from someone outside the family, as in cases of extrafamilial abuse. Transgenerational abuse is said to perpetuate the unending cycle of intrafamilial abuse, in which children are enmeshed into the dysfunctional dynamics of the family system (Ney, 1992) [A child who has been manipulated into collusion with family members through seductive charm or a caring façade may experience a greater sense of betrayal than a child who is coerced into compliance by open threats of harm by strangers.]

When a parent has violated a child, issues of heritage, identity, and basic survival needs, as well as betrayal and mistrust, complicate the child's overall recovery from the abuse. These concerns can increase the child's vulnerability to stress and anxiety. When disclosure eventually occurs, the child may have to contend with disbelief from other family members, humiliation at having family secrets exposed, and financial hardships in cases where families are disrupted. Often the abusee must endure further retaliation from the nonoffending parent.

Treatment Following Disclosure Nonoffending family members often treat a child who has disclosed abuse with contempt and disbelief, particularly if disclosure results in removal or arrest of the perpetrator. The remaining parent may be ineffective and resent the newly imposed hardships placed upon the household, thus taking it out on the child. In many instances, the child is ostracized from and harassed by the family. If the child develops a perception of self-blame, guilt, or sense of inadequacy because of the adverse treatment from the nonoffending parent, symptomology may increase significantly and extend to chronic proportions. Progress in recovery is prolonged when family members are unsupportive, as the child must attempt to process the emotional effects from secondary abuse, that of being ostracized and chastised from the family. In cases of ongoing abuse, the child and any other siblings may be removed from the family, only to be subjected to other types of alienation in crisis centers or foster homes. Therefore, once disclosure is made, ensuing dynamics must be processed in treatment to the degree that the child is capable.

Extrafamilial Abuse Symptomology

Extrafamilial abuse among children exploited by *child sex rings* has been examined by researchers. Symptomology in these cases is consistent with post-traumatic stress disorder (PTSD) at the time of disclosure (Burgess, Groth, & McCausland, 1981; Burgess, Hartman, McCausland, & Powers, 1984). Memories and flashbacks of threats have been reported, with additional symptoms of guilt, crying spells, sleep disturbance, moodiness, and somatization. A 2-year follow-up of 62 children exploited in sex rings noted that only 26% of the children were able to achieve successful psychosocial integration (Burgess, Groth, & McCausland, 1981). Three levels of symptomology were found across the remaining children: (a) avoidance or repression of the event; (b) re-experiencing of the trauma, resulting in chronic PTSD; and (c) adaptation or identification with the perpetrator's actions by means of acting out on others with antisocial actions. School-related behaviors ranged from a higher propensity for stress or vulnerability to chronic low-level symptoms during social interactions with others at school. In one study, Grosz, Kempe, and Kelly

(20(ͦ ͨd th⸗⸗ ͦ ͦ ͦ·milial perpetrators caused signifi-
can

C͢ used in stranger abuse
th ͦm, 1995; Prendergast,
1⸗ ͦ be more invasive and
r͢ ͦ ͦde by strangers against
e... ͦ secrecy or, worse yet,
force the child ɪ₦ₜₒ ₗₑₚ₋ ͦ going basis. Types of sexual abuse may include prostitution, pₒᵣₙₒ₉ and many other forms of
exploitive sexually related activity. Although most individuals find it difficult to
imagine harming a young child, or anyone else for that matter, perpetrators
who use harsh tactics, manipulative entrapment, and possibly kidnapping routinely violate small children.

Ritualistic Sexual Abuse Ritualistic sexual abuse (RSA) is reported to be by
far the most injurious form of sexual abuse (Gough, Kelly, & Scott, 1993). It
is defined by Kelly (1989) as "repetitive, and systematic sexual, physical, and
psychological abuse of children by adults as part of cult or satanic worship"
(p. 503). This type of abuse leaves children with more severe and increased
symptomology, including extensive traumatization (Faller, 1987; Finkelhor et
al., 1988). Oliveri, Cockriel, and Dugan (1993) noted that the overall impact
of ritualistic abuse on children includes (a) emotional reactivity and hypervigilence to threats and harm; (b) increased use of emotional barriers and adaptations to protect the inner self; (c) encapsulated experiences and confused
realities with potential for paradoxical perspectives about environmental
expectations; (d) disrupted ego formation, self-concept, and potential to bond;
(e) distorted expression of a range of emotions; (f) expression of anchor memories that trigger reemergence of negative emotional reactions from the past
abuse; and (g) a distorted perspective of self-involvement in the abuse and
identification with the abuser, thereby perpetuating negative emotional
reactions.

Disclosure Studies that have examined the patterns of disclosure of abuse
(Nagel, Putnam, & Noll, 1997) have noted that children can narrate about the
abuse, but the disclosure may come out in fragments across many interviews
(McCord, 1993). Increased recall does occur, particularly when the child talks
about the abuse voluntarily during subsequent interviews. Disclosure also
occurs in fragmented statements across counseling sessions for children of
preschool age (Waterman, Kelly, Oliveri, & McCord, 1993). While some
researchers question the validity of preschoolers' memory skills (Ceci & Bruck,
1995; Ney, 1995), abrupt or abbreviated recall does not negate the fact that the
child may still have experienced abuse. So, it is imperative that therapists are
acquainted with legislative requirements for acceptable interview techniques
such as the use of nonleading questions and other interview strategies
(Kuehnle, 1996).

Gender Issues When boys are accosted by an opposite-sex pedophile, such as a mother, they report a sense of abandonment because of the lack of parental protection in a manner consistent with expected mother roles. Boys are also more reluctant to disclose abuse due to embarrassment and fear of disbelief from others; however, boys are victims of sexual abuse at a much higher rate than that which is currently reported (Hunter, 1990). Girls also experience a sense of abandonment from mothers who fail to protect them from perpetrators, even when it is the father or stepfather who abuses. In addition, girls report a greater sense of intimidation from coercive male figures (Pendergast, 1993), although male children manifest symptoms of fear, intimidation, and anxieties as a result of the coercive tactics used by the abuser.

Assessment and Evaluation Assessment and evaluation of sexual abuse are beyond the scope of this book. However, as with all mental health issues, assessment strategies used to identify and diagnose trauma disorders are extensive and should comply with professional ethics and guidelines from professional organizations. Standards and guidelines are offered by the American Professional Society on the Abuse of Children (APSAC), the American Psychological Association (APA), and the National Association of School Psychologists (NASP). Test development standards such as the *Standards for Educational and Psychological Tests* (American Educational Research Association et al., 1996) are also available from professional resources. If rating scales are used, they must be technically validated and reliable in accordance with the standards. On-line resources with which to identify and review test instruments and rating scales include the Buros Mental Measurements Web site (www.buros.com) and the National Clearinghouse on Child Abuse and Neglect Information (NCCANI) Web site (www.calib.com/nccanch). Court-related procedures, such as those provided by Kuehnle (1996) and Ney (1995), must be adhered to when evaluating a sexual abuse case as well as standardized test administration (Anastasia, 1988; Sattler, 1998).

SUMMARY

More in-depth research is needed to examine the symptomology experienced by child victims. Therapists must be cognizant of the many factors that contribute to the uniqueness of each case of sexual abuse as noted throughout this chapter. More definitive diagnostic procedures are needed, particularly to address evaluation issues concerning nonverbal or developmentally challenged children. While play therapy techniques are recommended for the treatment of small children (Landreth, 1991; Webb, 1991), play activities need to be age-appropriate and paced at the child's level of cognitive processing. Therapeutic processes need to be coordinated relative to the child's level of comprehension, intellectual processing skills, and emotional maturity (Sattler, 1998). For example, McCord (1993) noted that many preschool-aged children emit fragments of information over several weeks, perhaps due to a need to feel safe and secure in the counseling session; therefore, a great deal of patience is required to provide sufficient time for the child to process accordingly. Untimely confrontation tactics during treatment can cause a child to shut down and withdraw from further interactions with the therapist, thus reinforcing the need for individualized treatment plans.

Similarly, therapists should be familiar with judicial requirements and rules of evidence within their county of jurisdiction, as well as federal and state legislation referring to sexual abuse (see www.calib.com/nccanch). To maintain updated resources and procedural knowledge in dealing with a problem as specialized as childhood sexual abuse, it is incumbent upon the therapist to be professionally prepared. Conference programs presented by professional groups, local community programs, professional journal reading, and attendance at continuing education programs are essential to enhance service delivery to children in need.

DISCUSSION QUESTIONS

1. Review two research articles concerning preschool sexual abuse occurring in the past 10 years and prepare an annotated bibliography for both. Be prepared to discuss them in class.

2. Research your local newspaper data bank for articles on local issues relative to the sexual abuse of a preschool-aged child. What cases or findings were reported, and how might they impact the local community?

3. Conduct a confidential interview with a parent of a preschooler. Examine the parent's perceptions about preschool child care and safety concerns, if any, for his or her child. Record the parent's conclusions and share your findings with the class.

4. Conduct a literature review on any aspect of preschool child abuse and how it impacts the family (i.e., interviews, court proceedings, child testimony, etc.). How do your findings compare to previous research on the matter?

5. If you were a preschool owner, what precautions could you take to screen employees? What resources are available to help with the screening?

6. What safety factors are encouraged in your community for young children? If possible, gather this information by interviewing a local youth officer, child care worker, or educator involved with the preschool-aged group.

7. Design a preschool setting with safety precautions to offset any threats to child safety. For example, how would you investigate potential employees, monitor child care, and initiate preventive programs?

8. What community resources could you use if you were suddenly confronted with a case of CSA? Briefly describe services provided at each resource.

9

Early Childhood Development

LEARNING OBJECTIVES

Chapter 9 will address the following learning objectives:

1. The impact of increased socialization on early childhood development

2. Theoretical concepts of emotional development during early childhood

3. Physiological and sociological developmental milestones of early childhood

4. Symptomatic and pathological disorders in abused children of elementary school age

5. A review of school-related issues of elementary school-aged children

6. A review of coping mechanisms found among elementary school-aged children

INTRODUCTION

Early childhood is a time when a child's world enlarges, environmental demands increase, and more time is spent outside of the family than ever before. For a child who has attended preschool and successfully achieved developmental milestones, school readiness should be apparent, with a typical age range of 4 years–8 months to 6 years. Prescreening is usually conducted in late spring or midsummer for students newly registered to attend kindergarten. Parents must relinquish control and supervisory tasks during school hours, leaving the care of their much-coveted children to others. Both children and parents must adapt to drop off and pick up with other parents, adherence to bus schedules, and broadened social boundaries.

Peer Influences

Attending kindergarten often represents a child's first exposure to peers from different environmental conditions, socioeconomic status, and, in many instances, from more fulfilling home lives. Children in the typical kindergarten setting compare themselves to their peers based on appearance, skill attainment, and cognitive functioning. Self-concepts are developed based on how children *measure up* to their peers, hold up under teacher evaluations, and how much encouragement they receive from concerned caregivers. During the kindergarten experience, a child functions within what Piaget (1952) referred to as the preoperational stage of cognitive development.

A typical 5-year-old child should have successfully accomplished a series of tasks formerly controlled by external sanctions from his or her parents. Now the child must also adhere to community and school rules concerning self-regulatory behaviors, such as not running in the hallway, completing assigned homework, participating in social play with other children, and so on. If preschool was attended, this task will be easier; however, for children who have never been exposed to structure outside of the home, adjustments may be either difficult or pleasurable, depending on how the child believes he or she measures up to the others. Although parental influences are important, other social influences now play a significant role in shaping the child's personality.

If the child is successful and has achieved some form of recognition for his or her efforts, self-esteem should increase, as will self-confidence. However, for a child who experiences a series of academic or school-related failures, perhaps due to emotional distress from neglect or abuse, self-esteem can be greatly diminished, as can be self-confidence. If a child believes he or she cannot succeed, then the child will make little or no effort to do so. If abuse is also experienced during this time, diminished self-worth is compounded significantly. A sort of double indemnity occurs, as both personal and social adjustments suffer; and as these feelings are perpetually experienced and internalized, they become fixed aspects of personality development.

As maturity continues, a child passes through the preoperational stage into the stage of concrete operations (Piaget, 1952), usually between the ages of 7 and 12. A child of this age can conduct logical operations and focus on the here and now. Social sanctions for misbehaviors may be internalized at this stage of development; children learn to behave because they know they should, rather than because of some external source of punishment.

THEORETICAL CONCEPTS

Several theories emerged over the years and are presented here, including Freud's (1923/1949) psychosexual theory, Bandura's (1986) social learning theory, Bem's (1985) gender theory, and Erikson's (1962) psychosocial theory. The discussion focuses on how each phase of development is impacted by abuse as an infant matures into a preschooler. Examination of the core theoretical conceptions of childhood helps to illustrate the potential effects that sexual abuse, molestation, or assault may have on each phase of development during the preschool years of maturation.

Psychoanalytical Theory

Psychoanalytic theory was the earliest formal theory to conceptualize the acquisition of sexual identity. Psychoanalytical theories focus on the subconscious and libido-driven needs that are of an innate nature within human beings. Mental wellness is said to be at least partly dependent on successful fulfillment of sexually oriented needs. As a child develops, the establishment of a centered ego state is dependent on successful resolution of a series of emotional tasks derived from those sexual needs. *during the 3-6 yr. old stage*

Freud (1923/1949) proposed that a child must work through coveted desires for the opposite-sex parent in a healthy manner if satisfactory sexual identity is to occur in adulthood. He describes these processes as the Oedipus complex for boys and the Electra complex for girls, both of which occur during the phallic stage of development, from ages 3 to 6 (Freud, 1962). According to Freud, a boy who covets his mother as the first female in his life and resolves this attraction for her in a healthy manner should eventually be released from that attachment and be capable of forming healthy relationships with other women as an adult. Similar dynamics underpin the resolution of the Electra complex for girls, who are said to covet their fathers. Conversely, if a child's experience during the phallic stage of development is negative, harmful, or traumatic, residual emotional conflicts will impair intimate relationships as an adult.

Freud's (1909/1936) exposition of this concept is exemplified in his psychoanalytical interpretation of *Little Hans,* a classic case study in psychoanalytical theory. Any event that threatens a child–parent relationship during this crucial stage of development will impair future interactions with opposite-sex partners. So, based on Freudian concepts, progression through the phallic stage of development is pivotal for a child to establish adult intimacy.

In Freud's theory, a child is in the latency stage of development between the age of 6 and puberty. A child of this age is not developing sexually based on physiological changes, but has internalized events experienced during the phallic stage. According to Freud, children in the latency stage learn to interact with each other as peers or simple playmates, not as objects of sexual intimacy.

Social Learning Theory

Social learning theorists (Bandura, 1986; Beck, 1976; Beck & Freeman, 1990) propose that socially learned behaviors serve to develop the gender identity of children (Bandura, 1960). According to early aspects of social learning theory, children identify with the same-sex parent, acquiring reinforcement when similar characteristics are imitated and family members applaud. For example, when a boy watches his father work with tools and then attempts to imitate his father's behavior, the son usually receives reinforcement and praise from family members. Similarly, when a girl undertakes nurturing activities, such as playing with dolls or imitating her mother's application of makeup, onlookers often praise the behavior. Eventually, the child internalizes the activities and adapts a role of preferred sexual identity (Bem, 1977, 1985).

Gender Theory

Gender theory is a cognitive social approach toward gender identity acquisition proposed by Sandra Bem (1983, 1985). A cognitive pattern of *gender-specific* behavior is said to develop as early as 2 to 3 years of age. As a child matures and adapts a role, gender identity is molded by environmental and cultural influences. Bem proposes that gender schemas can be changed based on roles espoused by environmental influences. For instance, cultural influences may attribute female-identity characteristics to activities involving domestication, such as child care, homemaking, and nurturance-related activities, whereas other cultures may endorse female participation in activities that are traditionally thought of as male activities, such as serving in the military. Theorists have proposed that if a female aspires toward male-dominated career choices, she may emulate personality traits normally attributed to males (Bem, 1983). According to Bem (1997), a healthier example of gender role development is one of androgyny, whereby a child takes on characteristics of both genders in balance. Bem purports that an androgynous individual would typically possess male-identified personality traits such as assertiveness, dominance, and self-reliance, as well as typically female-identified traits such as compassion, sympathy, and empathy toward others.

Undoubtedly, gender identity is a complex concept that is affected by biological, environmental, cultural, familial, and media influences, making the validity of a single theoretical perspective over another impossible to isolate. Recent studies have not supported these findings, noting that more similarities than differences exist across male and female cognitive characteristics (Bem, 1985; Hamburg, 2000; Kernberg, 2000).

Development of gender identity after experiencing sexual abuse as a child has not been well studied, but it has been noted that sexual identity, sexual intimacy, and intimate relationships are problem areas for many adults who were abused as young children (Classen & Yalom, 1995; Harris & Landis, 1997). Same-sex abuse versus opposite-sex abuse is an area that has received more attention in recent research. However, no conclusive studies have yet isolated characteristics of abuse incidents and the generalizability to all children, particularly in the realm of establishing gender identity.

Personal Attributes

Any child may experience trauma in a unique manner, dependent upon the severity of abuse as well as the child's personal reaction to the event. Personal attributes of the child obviously impact final reactions to the abuse. For some children, a simple touch or molestation can be devastating, while other children may have more resilient propensity to cope with severely harmful experiences. Several researchers have investigated numerous aspects of personal reactions and how these reactions may be manifested among children, particularly in light of the child's gender. A few concepts relative to personal attributes will be discussed here, including aggression and fear (Bauer, 1976; Patterson, DeBaryshe, & Ramsey, 1989), empathy (Carlo, Knight, Eisenberg, & Rotenberg, 1991), and issues of developing moral reasoning (Gilligan, 1982; Kohlberg, 1969; Zahn-Waxler, Radke-Yarrow, Wagner, & Chapman, 1992).

Aggression and Fear   Aggression is one personality attribute that is normally associated with gender-specific traits. For instance, fears are said to be expressed more readily by girls than boys (Bauer, 1976), and aggression is said to occur more often in boys than in girls (Patterson, DeBaryshe, & Ramsey, 1989). Patterson et al. (1989) noted that in homes where parenting styles model aggressive behaviors, children usually internalize aggressive behaviors and, in turn, act them out on peers. Once more, environmental influences interact with the development of specific personality characteristics. A high correlation has been found between parental displays of anger and a child's subsequent aggressive behaviors toward others, regardless of the gender of the child (Arroyo & Eth, 1995; Lehmann, 1997).

Empathy   Carlo, Knight, Eisenberg, and Rotenberg (1991) investigated personality characteristics in reference to empathy. They sought answers to questions like "What makes some children sympathetic to another child's suffering, while some children enjoy bullying and degrading others?" Carlo et al. (1991) examined prosocial behaviors directed toward others, defined as an ability to empathize with others, and found that altruistic children tended to be mentally advanced, in comparison with their peers, which enabled them to envision how another child might feel. A more developed moral sense was also identified among more altruistic children (Zahn-Waxler, Radke-Yarrow, Wagner, & Chapman, 1992). Subsequently, Hart, DeWolf, Wozniack, and Burts (1992) reported that family role models play a significant role in altruistic behaviors among children.

Moral Reasoning   Moral reasoning develops extensively during the elementary school years, as portrayed by Kohlberg's (1969) theoretical model of six stages of moral reasoning. Level I, the preconventional stage of moral reasoning, is said to evolve between the ages of 4 and 10. At first, children decide what is good or bad based on external influences; they are simply obedient to demands from others. As children mature, however, they become capable of independently reasoning and identifying right from wrong. Piaget (1952) referred to this process as moral realism, which suggests that moral rules exist as a fixed element of nature. Children want to be "good" because they believe in the concept of good.

Gilligan (1977, 1982), on the other hand, claimed that moral development is gender-specific, in that ethical and moral decision-making skills differ between men and women. Gilligan emphasized that morality is a personality quality or unique moral asset, rather than stating that one gender is superior or inferior to the other. In Gilligan's view, males construct moral views that are embedded in a sense of justice and rights, whereas females develop a sense of morality that is embedded in sensitivity, responsibility, and the ability to care for others. Researchers have also investigated the concept of moral development based on justice versus caring and found no gender-related differences in moral development (Kohlberg, Snarey, & Reimer, 1984; Walker, 1989, 1991).

When perpetrators approach children, children's propensity to be "good" and to please adults renders them more susceptible to the perpetrators' advances, particularly during the stage of development in which they adhere to moral views based on external suggestions. If Kohlberg et al. are correct, gender-specific moral beliefs may not affect a child's response to and recovery from abuse; rather, the child's response to and recovery from abuse will be associated with societal and cultural influences and the attitudes about abuse that are prevalent in the child's environment.

DEVELOPMENTAL MILESTONES

Development milestones represent any progressive stage of cognitive, physical, and social development that enables the child to progress to more advanced stages of maturation. It is essential that a therapist understand the normal progression of child development, in order to identify the full impact of an abusive event on the child. The following text briefly summarizes the stages through which a child progresses during normal child development; subsequent discussion will demonstrate how symptomatic issues impair these essential developmental processes.

Cognitive Milestones and Psychosocial Development

Cognitive milestones represent those developmental stages that enhance the thought process in a child. A primary milestone is language acquisition, such as when a child utters single words, then forms a three-word sentence, and then progresses to the point of listening to and conversing with another individual. This verbal exchange represents the child's ability to cognitively process and communicate an event to others as a manner of responding to that event (Erikson, 1962). When a child is exposed to adverse or harmful incidents, the manner in which those events are processed and the particular stage of development the child is in when the events occur have significant implications for psychosocial development throughout life.

Initiative Versus Guilt Erikson's (1962) developmental task for children aged 3 to 6 is the emergence of initiative versus guilt; however, the development of a sense of initiative versus guilt is complicated for children exposed to abusive treatment. The emotional impact of abuse may hinder a child from completing this developmental task, resulting in numerous adverse ramifications for overall emotional well-being later in life. It is well documented that some children who experience sexual abuse develop feelings of guilt and self-blame, particularly if the child's disclosure resulted in a parent's arrest or a family breakup. Once internalized, those feelings of guilt and diminished self-worth can override the child's attempts to take initiative toward life tasks, such as learning to read, write, and complete arithmetic.

According to Erikson, early childhood is a preparation time during which a child should successfully complete activities, tasks, and events as a precursor to learning more advanced tasks for later in life. Teachers, parents, and loved ones need to provide the child with encouragement and reinforcement to proceed if he or she is to develop a sense of initiative. Abused, neglected, and abandoned children lack this significant prerequisite for developing a sense of initiative. If age-appropriate tasks cannot be performed adequately, a child may experience embarrassment and discouragement. Once a child is discouraged, he or she may no longer attempt tasks that are now associated with failure. Rather, such children withdraw from school-related activities and no longer attempt to achieve.

Erikson (1969) noted that guilt is the opposite of initiative. If this holds true, any activity that diminishes a sense of initiative would then exacerbate a sense of guilt. So not only do these children abandon any attempt at new activities they think are beyond their ability, but they also develop a sense of guilt about their attitude. Such children feel estranged, distanced, and alienated from the social milieu associated with industrious activities. Further emotional duress ensues if parents are punitive, chastising, or ridiculing, as is often the case in abusive households.

The consequences for any future productivity of a child in such a situation are far-reaching. Not only is the child deprived of positive social reinforcers and the development of basic skills related to early learning, but the child's success experiences are also negligible. The child is deprived of the opportunity to thrive within a new social environment essential for self-affirmation, that of the school. In an attempt to gain social reinforcement and positive attention, the child is now more vulnerable to accepting social interactions from perpetrators; therefore, the problem grows in complexity.

Industry Versus Inferiority According to Erikson (1968), another important stage of psychosocial development in early childhood relates to industrious qualities, represented by productivity in school-related activities. To prepare for adulthood, the child needs to master new skills in the school environment. If a child is to undertake industrious attitudes toward learning, the child's mind must be free of emotional stress that can otherwise inhibit, constrict, or reduce the potential to achieve. If feelings of inferiority, in accordance with Erikson's model, are internalized because of sustained abuse issues, normal development is at risk. When a child is made to feel deprecated, inferior, damaged, or bad because of abuse experiences, the child's feelings of diminished self-worth, once more, override his or her potential to achieve.

Significant emotional trauma or distress impedes a child's ability to learn the advanced curricula presented in later grades. Therefore, a cumulative effect widens the gap between the child's ability and the materials that are actually learned, fueling a series of failures. Eventually, when the child falls behind classmates sufficiently, the child may stop trying. Secondary emotional reactions may emerge, including depression, withdrawal, and alienation from the school setting. The problem is cumulative: The child experiences emotional distress due to abuse, falls behind in childhood tasks, and then self-worth and self esteem are further diminished, sometimes to the point of immobilization or emotional blockage.

Skill Acquisition Eckenrode, Laird, and Doris (1993) noted that academic achievements represent the most salient developmental task for this age group. In addition to making strides in academic achievement, success at this age sets precedence for emotional well-being, due to a sense of productivity, and subsequent fulfillment in adulthood. Long-term consequences of perpetual abuse are extensive; consequently, early identification of children under the influence of maltreatment and neglect is essential.

Within the school setting, symptoms from abuse can be manifested in many reactions, ranging from withdrawal and alienation to acting out and disruptive behaviors, from underachievement to overachievement, or from psychological to physiological symptoms. Somatic complaints are often identified and associated with distress due to abuse (Kuehnle, 1996; Vevier & Tharinger, 1986), as are reduced school grades, (Batchelor, Dean, Gridley, & Batchelor, 1990), emotional dysfunction (Prendergast, 1993), and, in extreme cases, psychotic reactions such as dissociation or hallucinations (Classen & Yalom, 1995). Regardless of the identified response to abuse, reduced industriousness can be generalized as a common response in sexual abuse survivors who are attempting to cope with the experience.

Self-Identification Self-identification develops in early childhood as children adopt characteristics, beliefs, and attitudes of other people in their environment. In addition to developing an inner belief or value system, children also develop a gender identity during this stage of development. Although gender identity is one of the first characteristics people often associate with newborns, children develop knowledge of gender identity when they are in socialized settings that allow for gender comparisons. During this stage of broadened social exposure, a child's personality takes on advanced concepts of gender differences (Bem, 1983; Erikson, 1969).

Personal identification is particularly affected when a child's own parent is the abuser. Many survivors of abuse have attested to their difficulties in realizing that their own parent inflicted abusive harm on them. Diminished self-worth often occurs following any abuse incident, but parent-child abuse further obscures a child's self-image. Behaviors normally expected from parents, such as providing the child with support and guidance, are replaced with incidents of abuse and harm realized in the home (Sternberg et al., 1993). This finding is magnified if a same-sex parent was the abuser, which may trigger issues of self-identification and sexual identity for the child. Children who survive sexual abuse but incur diminished self-worth may struggle with depression and pessimism throughout their lives (Harter, 1986, 1998).

Physiological Development

Emphasis is placed on physiological development during early childhood, as motor skills mature during this time. Researchers have noted that boys tend to run, jump, and throw objects with greater strength and efficiency than girls can (Malina, 1996). Some researchers note that boys actually have two extra years of physiological development than do girls (Graber & Brooks-Gunn, 1996). Using video games, researchers have also determined that boys have better spatial skills than girls (Subrahmanyam, Kraut, Greenfield, & Gross, 2000), but girls have been found to excel in reading and writing (Finn, Pannozzo, & Voelkl, 1995). Although researchers often oppose these findings, school records indicating achievement differences across genders appear to substantiate them in many settings.

Physiological Changes Recent growth norms (Beausang & Razor, 2000; Hamill, 1977; Kuczmarski et al., 2000; Tanner, 1991) demonstrate that the early onset of menses now occurs among girls between 8 and 10 years of age, which clearly contradicts Freud's definition of puberty development as 14 and older. Recent studies also indicate that the sexual abuse of a child can induce physiological changes that mirror the changes that normally occur during preadolescence but are now being seen in early childhood girls (DeAngelis, 1995; Putnam & Trickett, 1997).

Unfortunately, prepubescent children are not always sensitive enough to their own body changes to seek help; for example, in a self-report study, many girls who were found positive for vaginal disorders could not identify such problems (Kahn, Goodman, Kaplowitz, Slap, & Emans, 2000). Consequently, undetected abuse fosters advanced medical problems such as surgery (Morgan, 1999) and cancer-provoking anogenital warts (Padel, Venning, Evans, Quantrill, & Fleming, 1990). Once more, in addition to being traumatized by the abuse, a child may be retraumatized during invasive medical procedures.

Participation in Sports Organized sports are an important factor in the lives of children at this age, more so than at any other age, perhaps because of the increased sense of competition between young children. However, for a withdrawn child who may be experiencing abuse of some form, physiological concerns may override any sense of striving in sports-related activities. School districts enforce physical education requirements, but not all children respond with enthusiasm (Darren, 2001; Nester, 2001). Instances of sexually related harassment and outright assaults on peers in the locker room showers have been reported (Dibrezzo & Hughes, 1998; Huber, 1996). Prendergast (1993) noted that many abused children fear removing their clothes during gym because the abuse will be evident if their naked bodies are exposed.

Often when abuse takes place during childhood, individuals wait to reveal it until they are much older or, perhaps, in a safer setting in which to disclose it. This was the case with a young man named Jim.

As a 19-year-old senior, Jim, while attending counseling sessions for college adjustment problems, recounted an incident of sexual exploitation that had occurred earlier in his life. He stated that, while in a sixth-grade gym class, several larger students took away his gym shorts and towel in the showers, while the other students stood around him and cheered about his penis size. As they were shouting, several boys thrust their own penises into Jim's face, indicating that he should "take it in to know what a real one feels like." The physical education teacher was in his office the whole time, while the boys laughed and shouted.

Jim had never reported the incident to anyone, obviously due to his embarrassment over the event. Many instances of harassment during physical education classes have been reported several years after the events occurred because at the time of abuse, fear of retribution from the abuser was significant.

SYMPTOMATIC AND PATHOLOGICAL DISORDERS

If a child is exposed to abuse (physical, emotional, or sexual), the impact of that abuse may manifest in numerous behavioral and emotional symptoms. In severe cases, pathological disorders may evolve. Perhaps most evident are behaviors observed in a school setting, a setting that is highly structured in terms of behavioral demands, where any departures from normal functioning are readily documented. The following text will address symptomatic observations often associated with, although not exclusively, child abuse of some form. As with all diagnostic procedures, alternative plausible explanations should be ruled out prior to making a final conclusion as to the cause of behavioral changes.

School-Related Behaviors

School-related behavioral changes associated with abusive or traumatic events in a child's life are well documented. These behavioral changes range from internalized reactions such as withdrawal, denial, and depression, to externalized behaviors such as aggression, anger, and disruptive outbursts (Chaffin, Wherry, & Dykman, 1997; Eckenrode et al., 1993; Kuehnle, 1995; Sgroi, 1982b). An abused child's grades may decline sharply following an abuse incident, drawings in art class may become sexually explicit in nature, and the child may regress to behaviors normally occurring at an earlier age (Prendergast, 1993). The following case scenario illustrates these findings.

Laura, a 9-year-old third grader, was referred to the school psychologist because of behavioral concerns noted by her teacher. Laura retreated to a fetal position under her desk, began intensely sucking her thumb, and had to be coaxed out from under the desk. When a collaborative evaluation was conducted, it appeared that many other symptoms normally associated with childhood sexual abuse were apparent. Laura was afraid of the sound of the toilet flushing, she projected a foul odor that was later diagnosed as gonorrhea, and her overall emotional behavior was comparable to that of a much younger child. Her communication skills were regressed, and her withdrawal from interactions with others had been more pronounced in recent past weeks.

Information was collected collaboratively from Laura's pediatrician, baby-sitter, and relatives and family members. It appeared that Laura's father had primary custody of Laura, as her mother had abandoned her at an early age. There had been prior accusations of abuse by Laura's father, but they had been dismissed for lack of evidence, so he steadfastly disputed the claims of sexual abuse once more. However, medical evidence of gonorrhea strongly supported suspicions that sexual abuse had occurred. Protective services removed Laura from her father's home. She was immediately placed into intervention services, and a permanent intervening residence was sought. Medical services treated the gonorrhea. Within two weeks of these interventions, Laura's demeanor began to improve. Her schoolwork improved, and slowly she began to interact with classmates in an age-appropriate manner.

While many school-aged children who are referred to counseling are viewed as having adjustment disorders due to acting out or severely withdrawn behaviors, the initial diagnosis may simply mask posttraumatic stress disorder (PTSD). Therefore, identifying symptoms is only the first step to appropriate intervention. Effective treatment requires an analysis of the etiology of the behavioral symptoms. Harsh or traumatic experiences with sexual abuse may result in pathological and clinically based symptoms such as dissociative disorders, psychosis, and severe mood disorders (Classen & Yalom, 1995; Prendergast, 1993). Severe disturbances among young children have become increasingly commonplace (Almquist et al., 1999), although these are not always related to sexual abuse alone.

Reduced Self-Esteem

Diminished self-esteem is a core symptom found among children who have been sexually abused, and one that renders a child more vulnerable to subsequent symptomology. Reduced self-esteem is a prerequisite to developing a sense of powerlessness, which then results in many secondary complications. One ramification of powerlessness is that a child is more prone to react passively or submissively when interacting with others, including child predators.

Similarly, once a child adapts an inner belief system, or internalizes, negative feelings about self, he or she may be more approachable by perpetrators. Sexual abuse prevention programs that are intended to enhance a child's ability to defy potential advances from a perpetrator are conducted in school systems throughout the United States. These programs cover several aspects of sexual abuse. Elementary school programs address the concept of "bad" and "good" touches (Swan, 1984), coping strategies (Chaffin, Wherry, & Dykman, 1997; Runtz & Schallow, 1997), and parental attitudes (Wurtele, Kvaternick, & Franklin, 1992). However, if a child is approached by a perpetrator, he or she must defy the approach with confidence and strong will, which requires a strong sense of self and healthy self-esteem.

Social Skills

Social skill development is not an automatic process for children; rather, socialization evolves from continual supportive encouragement and successful interactions with environmental influences (Johnson, 1995). For children exposed to ongoing intrafamilial neglect or abuse, the opportunity for positive reinforcement is sparse, if present at all. Secondary issues such as trust, withdrawal, distancing, and depression overshadow interactions with others.

Therefore, in addition to the primary crisis issues in dealing with the abuse itself, secondary personality concerns arise that impede socialization with others. Without an ability to form successful relations with others, all spheres of adult life are affected including personal, social, and career. Hence, a domino effect arises from the aftermath of abuse. Both short-term crisis issues and long-term coping issues require effective interventions. Long-term prognosis is always enhanced if significant others, such as parents, provide emotional support for the child.

To investigate the risk factors associated with depression and maltreatment among school-aged children, Levendosky, Okun, and Parker (1995) examined 68 children to predict social competence and social problem-solving skills, as rated by self, parent, and teacher. Five measures were used including (a) the Child Behavior Checklist (CBCL; Achenbach & Edelbrock, 1983), (b) the Ratings of Child's Competence (RCC; Harter, 1985), (c) the Children's Depression Inventory (CDI; Kovacs, 1985), (d) the Self-Perception Profile for Children (SPPC; Harter, 1985), and (e) the Home Interview with Child (HIWC; Dodge & Somberg, 1987). A multiple regression analysis generated significant associations between depression and a child's self-ratings of social competence (Levendosky et al., 1995).

In Levendosky et al.'s study, it appeared that even mild indications of depression impacted the children's social competence skills, while maltreatment, in and of itself, did not, in the absence of depression, predict diminished social competence scores. However, an added component was identified when both depression and maltreatment were indicated: Social competence scores were diminished. The authors inferred that this indicates an additive model, in that maltreatment combined with depression contributes to a greater reduction in social competence (Levendosky et al., 1995).

Physical Versus Sexual Abuse

Eckenrode et al. (1993) investigated the impact of different types of abuse (physical, emotional, and sexual) on childhood functioning. Physical abuse was associated with children having reduced academic achievement, while sexual abuse was associated with children having adverse internalizing and external-izing behaviors. Perhaps not surprising, physical abuse was also associated with children having behavior or discipline problems. However, classification of abuse was not clear, nor was the classification of multiple types of abuse expo-sure, such as exposure to physical, verbal, and sexual abuse.

Claussen and Crittenden (1991) reported multiple-abuse experiences among 89% of abused school-aged children studied via physician records, all of which involved both physical and psychological maltreatment. Eckenrode et al. (1993) found that children who experienced physical maltreatment exhibited a significantly greater number of discipline problems; however, their 420 heterogeneous subjects ranged from kindergarten to twelfth grade, making differentiation of symptoms difficult. Each age group was found to be vulnerable to additional stressors related to their respective grade levels, maturation rates, peers, and family dynamics. Significant symptomology was found among subjects who experienced multiple types of abuse, including problems with low academic achievement and behavioral concerns, both externalized and internalized.

Distress Hibbard and Hartman (1992) noted that behavioral disorders may not be specific to the incident of sexual abuse but, rather, may be related to distress. Behavioral disorders were investigated among groups of students using an experimental group ($n = 81$ sexually abused) and a control group ($n = 90$ nonclinical). Differentiated abuse was reported among the subjects as: (a) 42% experienced repeated abusive episodes, (b) 20% exhibitionism, and (c) 74% genital fondling. What was alarmingly consistent with previous reports was the finding that 32% of the perpetrators were fathers or stepfathers, while 46% represented other family members. Clinically significant behavioral concerns were found among the sexually abused group of students; these included symptoms of depression, mood swings, demands for attention, assaulting oth-ers, poor academic adjustment, sleep disorders, strange behavioral symptoms, anxiety, and secrecy tendencies.

Cohen and Mannarino (1988) noted that parents rate children higher for incidence of behavioral symptoms on the CBCL than children self-report. These discrepancies might be explained by parental bias in rating, variations in symptomology that occur among groups, or children's minimization and self-denial of their own reactions. Inconsistencies in parent-child symptom report-ing emphasize the need for collaborative data collection that includes other, perhaps more objective, sources such as teachers, baby-sitters, or clergy.

Subtle Behavioral Symptoms Professionals emphasize early identification of behavioral symptoms following incidents of sexual abuse for several reasons. Physical evidence is often lacking, whereas symptomology is often presented in subtle behaviors, including psychosomatic and behavioral problems. Researchers have noted that sexualized behaviors might arise from diminished inhibitions relative to the exposure to abuse (Prendergast, 1993; Ryan & Lane, 1991), whereas somatic complaints might be rooted in fear and anxiety pro-voked by the abuse (Summit, 1983). Associations between high-stress factors and the impact of that stress on physical and somatic complaints are well documented among adults (Droga, 1997; Werner, Joffe, & Graham, 1999). Children experience a similar emotional-physiological connection, perhaps to a greater degree than adults do, as evidenced by increased visits to the school nurse when stressful events, such as divorce, death, or other emotionally charged situations, occur at home.

Depression and Severity Depression is highly associated with survivors of abuse. Frequently it is cited as the most commonly reported long-term effect of sexual abuse (Finkelhor, 1990). To investigate this further, Koverola, Pound, Heger, and Lytle (1993) examined 39 girls, ages 7–12, in the initial stages of disclosure of abuse; two-thirds of the girls disclosed a history of sexual abuse, which was substantiated via physical examinations and full evaluations. Two-thirds of the girls met *DSM-III-R* criteria for depression, indicating that depression may arise following sexual abuse as early as the initial disclosure period, and lasting well into adulthood. Of these children, 62% reported severe sexual abuse, delineated as the following: occurring more than once a week, involving vaginal or anal intercourse and oral sex or digital penetration.

While depression was not found across all girls who experienced sexual abuse, it did occur in the majority of the sample group. It was suggested that other factors tend to moderate the potential to develop clinical depression. Given these findings, the authors suggested that early intervention for depression might hasten the long-term sequelae of depression so often experienced among adults who were abused as children. Koverola et al. recommended that therapists should focus the intervention on reinforcing family members' support of the child following disclosure in an attempt to minimize adverse long-term reactions such as depression.

Multiple Perpetrators or Repeated Abuse Nash, Zivney, and Hulsey (1993) noted that greater psychological disturbances in abused children are associated with multiple perpetrators, the onset of abuse prior to age 7, and periods of intense or frequent abuse episodes repeated more than three to four times per month. Nash et al. (1993) also stated that recovery is enhanced if the household is stable and family members support the child's recovery needs. Fleming, Mullen, and Bammer (1997) found significant correlations between CSA and mentally ill or emotionally ineffective mothers. Children left without maternal supervision were at the highest risk for repeated abuse by a male household member, as were children with alcoholic fathers who repeatedly abused while under the influence of alcohol.

Family Dynamics and Dysfunction

Preexisting dysfunctional family systems may be partially responsible for anxiety symptoms identified in sexually abused children; examples of such dysfunction include domestic violence, alcoholism, and other adverse family problems (Harris & Landis, 1997; Prendergast, 1993). Sustained stress found among abused children may exist because of the manner in which family members respond to a child's disclosure of sexual abuse and the subsequent ramifications of disclosure, such as intense legal proceedings, family breakups, and financial devastation (Pope & Brown, 1996). The speed of the child's recovery and the severity of the child's symptoms are affected by the amount of support from the family, particularly the family's reaction upon the child's disclosure and the amount of emotional support offered by the family throughout the recovery period.

Isolation Social isolation has often been reported among sexually abused women, and it may serve as a risk identifier among younger children (Harris & Landis, 1997). Socially isolated girls have less chance for contact outside the home, and thus may be more vulnerable to abusive advances from a family member. Harris and Landis's findings were consistent with earlier findings, showing an association between sexual abuse and a noncaring, ineffective, or deceased mother; social isolation; violence; and abuse from an alcoholic father. Combined factors of alcoholism, violence, and emotionally barren environments render children more vulnerable to high-stress factors, in addition to increasing their potential to suffer abuse.

Domestic Violence Sternberg et al. (1993) investigated the relationship of domestic violence to childhood depression and other behavioral problems. Questionnaires completed by caregivers showed that the effects of domestic violence on childhood development varied in magnitude and nature based on the type of violence and the reported symptoms. Children who witnessed violence or were violently abused themselves indicated greater adjustment problems than nonabused children. Young children showed a wide range of stress–related symptoms from being directly abused as well as from witnessing spousal abuse. Zaslow and Hayes (1986) also found gender differences, in that boys were found to be more vulnerable to stress following traumatic life events, but gender differences were not emphasized in the Sternberg et al. study.

In Sternberg et al.'s (1993) study, the overall anxiety and significantly higher symptomology resulted regardless of the type of violence (emotional, physical, or sexual abuse, or domestic violence) to which the children were exposed. Symptomatic behaviors included general anxiety, disruptive behavior, and externalizing aggressive outbursts. Added stress factors included being housed in a shelter, feeling humiliated by the arrest of family members for domestic violence, and experiencing a sense of loss of parenting from one or both parents during the critical periods following the violent event.

Severe Pathology Family of origin variables have been examined among adult survivors who were sexually abused as children (Draucker, 1996). Not surprising, women who sustained abuse as young children described their families as more dysfunctional than did their nonabused counterparts. The abused group yielded specific psychological difficulties with bodily functions and stress–related psychopathology or dissociation. Impairment was indicated in terms of a damaged sense of self, painful self–introspection, and egocentricity.

Farmer (1989) further described eight factors associated with abusive families, identifying specific interactional elements such as: denial, inconsistency and unpredictability, lack of empathy, lack of clear boundaries, role reversal, closed family system, incongruent communication, and too much or too little conflict. Farmer suggested interventions such as imaginary reparenting. Comprehensive therapy for survivors must address both the unique impact of sexual abuse and the influence of multidimensional aspects of early family life. For school-aged children enmeshed in multiple dysfunctional systems at home, it is essential that each element be examined and focused on during therapy.

Denial of Abuse Denial is a trait that often permeates dysfunctional families when sexual abuse occurs. Trepper, Niedner, Mika, and Barrett (1996) identified four types of denial: (a) denial of facts, (b) denial of impact, (c) denial of responsibility, and (d) denial of awareness. Denial of facts is evidenced in most instances when perpetrators deny committing the offense. Nonoffending spouses deny the impact of the abuse more often than the facts. Victims also often deny the impact of the abuse, perhaps to minimize the impact on family members, particularly those who are nonsupportive. Denial of responsibility occurs when, for example, a nonoffending parent suspects abuse but does nothing to investigate or intervene with the problem. Then denial of awareness, that is, denial that any problem exists at all, supports the denial of responsibility. These elements of interactions in dysfunctional families may occur at a conscious or unconscious level of functioning. Several other unhealthy dynamics often permeate family functioning. Marital discord, lack of cohesion, and general marital unhappiness were reported by 82% of the nonabusive spouses, and another 92% of the sample rated communication skills as highly negative, remiss, or incongruent (Trepper et al., 1996).

Symptomology Found in Schools

Tharinger, Russian, and Robinson (1989) observed significant behavioral symptomology among school children known to have experienced sexual abuse. Symptomatic behaviors included both internalized behaviors (e.g., somatic complaints and withdrawn, depressive, and lethargic behaviors) and externalized behaviors (e.g., disruptive classroom behavior, tearful outbursts, harassment of other children, and inappropriate sexual acts toward others). Additional problems arose during social interactions, such as fighting in the playground, on the bus, or during lunch periods. Other issues that resulted from the abuse included teasing from peers, ostracism from cliques, and an overall detachment due to withdrawal tendencies.

Intelligence Several researchers have examined intelligence factors using the Wechsler Intelligence Scale for Children (WISC), both the original WISC and the subsequently revised WISC-R (Basta & Peterson, 1990; Meiselman, 1978; Weinberg, 1976). Although Lusk (1993) found that sexually abused children had a mean IQ score of 109.9, while non-sexually abused students had an average IQ score of 117.6, it appeared to be a matter of subject selection rather than due to sexual abuse itself. Therefore, one cannot infer that the lower IQ scores of the sexually abused group were a consequence of the abuse, although they could have been due to diminished intellectual capacity as a result of impaired attention span, depression, or withdrawal reactions to the abuse. These areas of cognitive functioning and possible impairment are certainly worthy of further investigation.

Lusk (1993) also compared IQ scores of nonabused children with those of children who experienced ritualistic sexual abuse and found no significant difference in the scores, although the nonabused children did emit slightly higher scores. Again, cautious interpretations of these data need to be made, as any number of moderator factors may account for similar results. Also, when using group averages as a unit of analysis, extreme individual scores may distort group averages, a concept often defined as an outlier in data that may distort final outcomes.

Achievement Researchers have investigated achievement factors among children who have experienced abuse and have found a decline in these children's academic scores (Achenbach & Edelbrock, 1983; Conte & Schuerman, 1987; Eckenrode, Rowe, Laird, & Brathwaite, 1985). Eckenrode et al. found depressed math and reading scores among sexually abused or neglected children on the Iowa Test of Basic Skills (ITBS), a standardized achievement test. The lowest scores were found among children who had experienced ritual sexual abuse (RSA), although the scores were not significantly different. Overall, however, significant differences in school performance were found among the children who had experienced RSA; these children fell within the 30th percentile range on the CBCL interview form, based on their mothers' ratings (Achenbach, 1991a), as compared to the group of non–sexually abused children who rated in the 50th percentile range. No empirically significant differences were found among the sexually abused and nonabused children using group averages as a unit of analysis. A more in-depth examination of subsets of abused children based on type, frequency, and duration of abuse is warranted to provide a finite evaluation of the source of abuse and the impact on academic functioning.

Attitude Lusk (1993) examined school attributes concerning attitude, school performance and behavior, self-esteem, attention and concentration, attributions of locus of control, and overall intelligence and achievement across children who were sexually abused (SA) as compared to children who experienced ritualistic sexual abuse (RSA). Several instruments were used, including the Wechsler Intelligence Scale for Children-Revised (WISC-R; Wechsler, 1984) (now the WISC-III; Wechsler, 1991), the Child Behavior Checklist (CBCL; Achenbach & Edelbrock, 1983), the Peabody Individual Achievement Test (PIAT; Dunn & Markwardt, 1970), the Self-Perception Profile for Children (Harter & Pike, 1984), the Behaviors After Diagnostic Interview (BADI; Lusk, 1993), and the Why Things Happen questionnaire (Connell, 1985), an instrument with indicators of locus of control used with children who may perceive a loss of power as a result of abuse.

Cognitive and school-related effects were evident among children exposed to ritualistic sexual abuse. Lusk noted that literature to date focused on emotional and behavioral indicators rather than cognitive functioning, thus he suggested that treatment plans incorporate areas of school-related functioning for the abused child. Further recommendations included performing a review of school records and the child's class work and homework performance, conducting classroom observations, and collecting behavior ratings from teachers involved with the student. It was further found that long-term effects in the cognitive realms of functioning may persist even after emotional concerns are stabilized, particularly in areas of attention and concentration (Lusk, 1993). Given the cumulative process of educational programs, it is reasonable to assume that a child's educational process is likely to be interrupted by the emotional distress realized from abuse experiences.

School-Related Behavioral Symptoms Residual effects of child victimization impact emotional and intellectual adjustment in school, as evidenced through decreased grades, poor attendance, withdrawal and evasive behaviors, as well as acting out, disruptive, and sexualized expressions (Batchelor et al., 1990; Byers, 1990; Tharinger, Russian, & Robinson, 1989). Additionally, intensified emotional reactions often occur among special needs children, who are five times more vulnerable to perpetrators' advances (Batchelor et al., 1990; O'Day, 1983; Slater & Gallagher, 1989; Tharinger et al., 1989). Further examination of the impact of sexual abuse on school achievement and grades is needed. Cumulative records of former grades can serve as an index of functioning prior to the occurrence of sexual abuse. A multidisciplinary team of specialists, including school psychologists, school nurses, and counselors, can readily provide services to children; however, without further training, many school personnel are reticent to be involved in sexually related matters that may result in court testimony (Tharinger et al., 1989).

As mandated reporters, school personnel should adhere to federal, state, and local legal mandates, as well as to the school district's policy for handling child abuse reports. Many schools call for an emergency "child study team" meeting when abuse allegations or crises arise. Even with a multidisciplinary team involved, however, the staff member who first observed symptoms of abuse or first heard the child's disclosure should report it to the proper authorities as soon as possible, since it is the initial observer of suspected abuse who is responsible for seeing that a report is placed with protective services.

Disclosure in the School Setting The National Resource Center on Child Sexual Abuse (1994) noted that the average age of disclosure is 9. Clearly, this places a child within access to school personnel at the time of disclosure, so all school personnel need to be qualified to proceed appropriately in the event that a child discloses to them. Spontaneous disclosures need to be referred to the appropriate personnel in the school building, and any discussion or interview with the child following the disclosure should be documented verbatim. Interviews should be held in compliance with standardized interview formats for incidents of sexual abuse (Faller, 1998; Kuehnle, 1996). When a formal abuse report is made, a designated school official should be notified in case follow-up meetings with child protective teams, parents, or other staff members are needed. If staff members are not trained to deal with sexual abuse issues, they should make appropriate community referrals. The procedural steps of abuse reporting should comply with the school district's policy manual, as well as with legal mandates.

Coping Strategies

Coping strategies have been studied among groups of school-aged children, with varying results across groups, depending on intrapersonal and environmental elements. The factors relating to the type, duration, and frequency of abuse do not appear to offer a definitive prediction model as to recovery outcomes for children. Any one case of abuse is often riddled with complex intrapersonal and environmental interactions, such as the details of the abuse, the context and follow-up of disclosure, the quality of the intervention services, and final case dispensation. Beitchman, Zucker, Hood, daCosta, and Akman (1991) stated that using behaviors noted by the abusee as outcome predictors is erroneous due to the broad and unique range of influences in any given case of sexual abuse (Chaffin, Wherry, & Dykman, 1997). Although this may be true if a researcher intends to generalize findings to others, it may be a misnomer if findings are to be applied to show improvements in a specific single-case study. Single-case study design, which can yield insightful findings to enhance a specific client's treatment, is perhaps the most overlooked procedure in scientific research but is definitely appropriate in sexual abuse cases due to the unique elements and dynamics within each case.

Four-Factor Coping Mechanism Model Chaffin, Wherry, and Dykman (1997) sampled 84 sexually abused children between the ages of 7 and 12, and identified four distinct coping mechanisms that a child might employ in reaction to an abusive experience. Criteria for inclusion in the study was reported as: a clear disclosure of abuse, lack of emotional support from the nonabusing parent, and a verification of abuse by either a professional or the abuser him- or herself. An interview and the following five measurement instruments were used to collect data: (a) the Abuse Dimensions Inventory (ADI; Chaffin, Wherry, Newlin, Crutchfield, & Dykman, 1997), (b) the Children's Impact of Traumatic Events Scale-Revised (CITES-R; Wolfe, 1996), (c) the Child Behavior Checklist (CBCL; Achenbach, 1991a, (d) the Teacher Rating Form (TRF; Achenbach, 1991b), and (e) Kidcope (Spirito, Stark, & Williams, 1988). Upon conducting a principal component factor analysis, Chaffin et al. (1997) identified four distinct coping patterns: avoidant, internalized, angry, and active/social. Unexpectedly, children who used an avoidant coping style displayed fewer behavioral symptoms, a finding that contrasts with the avoidant coping style for adolescent and adult survivors of sexual abuse.

Short- and Long-Term Coping Lanktree and Briere (1995) reported that avoidant coping strategies may work sufficiently in the short duration, but more serious problems, such as anxieties surrounding sexuality, may evolve in the long term. They further suggested that internalized coping strategies, such as self-blame, resignation, and isolation, might generate more complex adjustment problems in long-term coping, depending upon how ingrained these strategies are as stationary attributes of the abusee. Negative reactions from significant others were said to be associated with greater internalization problems, including guilt. Children who exhibited active/social coping strategies were said to emit the fewest behavioral symptoms; however, children using active/social coping mechanisms also were associated with less severe acts of sexual abuse. The authors cautioned that, although they identified a four-factor model of coping mechanisms, it is not a clear linear model to be used for prediction of recovery or treatment outcomes, due to the complexity of child sexual abuse cases.

Social Support and Coping Runtz and Schallow (1997) examined the association of social support and coping mechanisms in terms of long-term prognosis, and noted an extensive range of variables that influence recovery. They investigated additional risk factors that influence recovery including: relationship to the offender (Browne & Finkelhor, 1986), emotional support from the nonoffending parent (Spaccarelli & Kim, 1995), cognitive processing of the event (Wyatt & Mickey, 1987), amount and severity of internalized emotions (Wyatt & Newcomb, 1990), and spiritual perspective in terms of finding meaning within the experience (Roth & Newman, 1993). All researchers agree that the healing process is complex, incorporating numerous interpersonal and intrapersonal variables unique to each individual who is abused.

Life Stressors

Life stress factors, which impact recovery, have been investigated in an effort to identify coping strategies (Heller, Swindel, & Dusenbury, 1986) for sexually abused girls (Conte & Schuerman, 1987), adults abused as children (Gold, Milan, Mayall, & Johnson, 1994), and child victims of neglect, poverty, and violence (Mrazek & Mrazek, 1987). Spaccarelli (1994) investigated risk and protective factors, as well as developmental and environmental factors, including child-parent relationships that may serve to enhance resilience following disclosure. Coping strategies used as a child directly impact an individual's long-term recovery as an adult, regardless of whether the abuse was emotional, physical, or sexual. Building positive coping skills within a child can not only be instrumental in assisting with immediate adjustment problems but also serve as a basis for dealing with any recurrent distress that is experienced.

SUMMARY

Researchers agree that issues involved in sexual abuse cases are complex. Although coping skills can be developed to address short- and long term stressors, individual treatment plans are warranted for each abusee. When dealing with elementary school–aged children, treatment plans may need to incorporate school-related programs to address academic concerns in addition to the typical emotional issues prevalent in sexual abuse cases.

Ramifications of disclosure should be discussed with children in an age-appropriate manner, in an attempt to help them cope with anxieties associated with investigative procedures. A child's feelings must be respected as the child passes through a traumatic experience that may be publicly exposed through the judicial process.

Further research is warranted to identify, diagnose, and treat sexual abuse survivors of all ages, but certainly for school-aged children. Research is also needed to identify appropriate outcome variables in cases of sexual abuse assessment, and more standardized data collection techniques should be developed. Although a common core of symptoms can be found among children who experience sexual abuse, generalizations and stereotypical biases are not applicable when treating sexually abused clients. Each case is unique and holds new challenges for even the most seasoned sexual abuse expert. School-aged children who are abused may view the school as a safe setting and often disclose abuse to school personnel via direct and indirect disclosure. All school personnel need to be apprised of the complex issues, judicial regulations, and professional standards applicable to child sexual abuse cases, as all are child mental health providers.

DISCUSSION QUESTIONS

1. What major developmental events occur in a child's life between the ages of 5 and 12? How might such events impact a child's reaction or response to an abuse experience?

2. What theoretical overview of child development most coincides with your own beliefs about elementary school-aged children?

3. How might a child's acquisition of self-esteem be impacted by a traumatic or abusive experience at an early age?

4. Review Erikson's psychosocial theory of development and discuss how a child might develop conflicts between initiative and guilt as proposed by Erikson's theory.

5. Research two or three professional journal articles relating to the development of self-identity. Discuss your findings in class.

6. What impact might a sexually abusive experience have on a child's academic achievement? How and why does the experience have this effect?

7. Is it possible that physical development can be altered or impacted by traumatic experiences? Provide a rationale for your response.

8. What behavioral symptoms in the school setting have been identified as being related to abuse? How can symptoms of abuse be identified or diagnosed within a school setting, if at all?

9. What ancillary resources are available to school personnel in your community?

10. Dysfunctional families adversely impact a child's overall development. How might you identify a child in need, and what community intervention services can be offered for families in need?

10

Preadolescence and Adolescence

LEARNING OBJECTIVES

Chapter 10 will address the following learning objectives:

1. A discussion of the impact of internal turmoil that evolves during adolescence

2. A presentation of theoretical concepts on developmental milestones of adolescence

3. A review of physiological and sociological developmental tasks in adolescence

4. A discussion of symptomatic and pathological disorders in adolescents who have experienced child abuse

5. A review of high-risk activities that impact adolescents following abuse

6. A discussion of emotional concerns that differ according to gender

INTRODUCTION

This chapter will address issues unique to adolescent development. Comparisons will be made between the adolescent turmoil commonly experienced by nonabused youth versus the turbulence experienced by sexually abused youth. This chapter will also discuss the process of identity formation based on numerous theoretical perspectives, and will provide illustrations of how identity formation becomes increasingly complicated when sexual abuse is experienced. Finally, this chapter will present physical and cognitive growth patterns of adolescents in light of abuse experiences, with an emphasis on the symptomatic and pathological issues that are most frequently identified among adolescent populations.

TURBULENCE OF ADOLESCENCE

Turbulence among youth has been a perpetual problem, regardless of cultural norms or customs (Muuss, 1996). Adolescence is and always has been a turbulent time of life. It is a time when children are expected to cross the bridge to adulthood. They must form long-term life plans and make productive career moves such as choosing a school of higher learning and identifying a major course of study. It is also a time when age-appropriate intimate relationships with peers should occur as part of developing a sense of sexual identity. Accomplishing these tasks is not easy for any child, but adolescents who have experienced sexual abuse as children may find self-identity, self-concept, and sexual identity much more difficult to master.

Internal Turmoil

Internal turmoil and emotional upheavals are common occurrences among this age group. In addition to the conscious emotional struggles that adolescents must transgress to achieve adulthood, especially in light of the demands placed on them by adult caregivers, adolescents struggle internally to arrive at the most expedient solution to all of the developmental dilemmas of adolescence. As time passes, adolescents eventually cross the bridge into adulthood, whether or not they are prepared. If abuse is experienced, developmental tasks may be prematurely curtailed, distorted, or delayed in response to the abuse. The adolescent may develop a sense of frustration and powerlessness, whereby self-identity is diminished further, all of which undermines fulfillment in life as an adult.

Risk-Taking Activities

Adolescence is a stage of development in which children gain a more independent self-identity, sufficient enough to move away from family influences and gain an extended range of friends and social interests. Social acceptance from peers is critical at this time. Consequently, the need to be accepted intensifies the adolescent's propensity to perform actions that ingratiate him or her into a chosen peer group. The adolescent may participate in high-risk activities simply to gain peer approval or acceptance. Behaviors such as substance abuse, driving a car when under the influence of alcohol, premature sexual exploration, and running away from home may all be activities to which an adolescent succumbs when influenced by peers because of the need for peer approval.

Peer group pressure also may provoke adolescents into activities of sexual abuse or exploitation, as when teens are recruited or coerced into pornographic or prostitution rings by trusted adults. Teens who have run away from an abusive household, perhaps without the opportunity to form a fully integrated ego, become easy prey for a manipulative pimp or pornographer. Thus, teens who are unable to find solace in their abusive homes are revictimized in even more severe ways, and so develop a life cycle of perpetual and continual hardships.

PHYSIOLOGICAL DEVELOPMENT

Significant growth gains can catapult an adolescent into a full-grown body while mentally he or she is still like a young child. Any middle or high school teacher will attest that it is not unusual to see a young boy of 13 or 14 years of age leave school in June at average height, only to return in September having gained 6 inches or more in height. To observers, this boy may now be viewed as a man, as people have an unfortunate tendency to interpret such physical growth spurts as a sign of maturity, even though physical maturity and mental maturity are not synonymous. Thus, observers, including parents, may make unrealistic demands on teens to act maturely in accordance with their appearances, while internally the child/adolescent struggles to appear cool, mature, and in control. Peers also make different demands on their counterparts when physical changes compel attention from others. For instance, when a young girl develops breasts at an early age, she may experience severe teasing, sexually inappropriate gestures, or outright sexual assault from aggressive peers as well as from adults, all of which add to internal pressures from physiological and hormonal changes that provoke new emotions and physical needs.

Frightening Physical Changes

For teens who have experienced sexual abuse, physical changes that occur during puberty may be most unwelcome if not outright traumatic. When a young boy ejaculates for the first time or when a young girl menstruates for the first time, formerly repressed fears or anxieties may emerge. The more severe the abuse was, the more likely it is that the transition from childhood to adolescence will be emotionally stressful. As pleasurable feelings of sexual arousal from hormonal changes occur, feelings of guilt, shame, and self-doubt may also emerge. Genital changes may be unwanted if it is believed that a larger penis or enlarged breasts will draw more attention from predators. In severe cases, emotional reactions can propel the teen into serious pathology such as conversion disorders, dissociation, self-hurting or cutting, suicidal ideation, or suicide attempts.

Male Growth Spurts

Growth spurts may vary among boys and girls across a period of five or six years. While some boys show significant gains in height and weight at age 12, other boys remain short but then catch up in height well after high school graduation. During puberty, males may also experience nocturnal emissions or ejaculations without a provocative dream or stimuli, which can be frightening to the unprepared male. One young man perceived that he was dying of cancer and his body was erupting when, in fact, he had merely experienced his first ejaculation. This can be frightening to any young boy, but can be traumatic for a sexually abused boy. Memories of abuse may provoke or precipitate dreams and nightmares. When violence was also associated with a sexual assault, more intense emotional reactions may result in thoughts of suicide, as in the case of John.

> John had been repeatedly forced to help masturbate an uncle since the age of 6; consequently, he found his own genital maturation, including spontaneous ejaculation, most repulsive. He experienced destructive thoughts, shame, and suicidal ideation for many years. John also avoided participation with opposite-sex peers out of fear of potential sexual involvement.

In addition to robbing him of childhood innocence, sexual abuse had robbed this young man of the opportunity to develop normal experiences in preparation for adult intimate relationships.

Menarche

Girls experience menarche and breast development during puberty; however, a wide variation occurs across girls in regard to the age of menarche. Some experience puberty and menses as early as 10 or 11 years of age, while others are well into their teens before their first period. Similar differences occur in timelines to developing breasts and a shapelier figure. While some girls welcome womanly body changes, others dread them. If a young girl is receptive to these events, it can be a happy time, one that is enthusiastically received. However, some girls dread any outward signs of womanhood, as they associate these signs with unwanted sexual abuse experienced at an earlier age.

The following case illustrates the intensity of reaction and long-term impact of sexual abuse, particularly with the onset of menarche.

> Two cousins sexually violated Ginny at age 12. The attack was violent, resulting in the emission of blood from her genital area. A few years later when her period began and every month afterward, she was retraumatized at the sight of blood from her period, as she associated it with the sexual assault. This continued for over 10 years; she struggled with it well into her twenties. Normal daily functioning was curtailed due to severe bouts of depression and suicidal thoughts. The trauma of her attack was severe and long-standing, thrusting her into emotional crisis each time an otherwise normal body function occurred.

Advances from Others

Although pedophiles may be drawn to children of all ages, regardless of age, size, or physical maturity, some seek out young preteens and naïve adolescents. As girls approach womanhood, sexual advances or assaults may occur at the hands of family members, such as a father, stepfather, uncle, brother, or cousin; and if preliminary advances and flirtatious comments are made to her, puberty may be most foreboding. Extrafamilial abuse can occur from community members, such as a neighbor, classmate, or community leader who uses his or her position to prey upon young children—particularly if that individual is consumed with the newly developing preteen or early adolescent. Male and female adolescents must contend with newly awakened physiological changes that can precipitate discomfort with their own bodies. If these changes coincide with abusive assaults, emotional reactions are heightened. What should be an enjoyable and inspired time of life—physical maturation in preparation for adulthood—becomes a shameful and undesired hardship.

Heightened Self-Consciousness

Self-conscious tendencies permeate an adolescent's thoughts at this stage of growth. Routine physical changes such as voice changes, new body hair, sexual development, and overall appearance are often embarrassing enough to cause behavioral and emotional reactions from teens. Events are intensified, magnified, and exaggerated when they threaten any perceptions of self-image and self-identity. Often adult onlookers or parents interpret the adolescent's behavior as being overly dramatic or histrionic, but to the growing adolescent, the emotional reactions are sincerely painful. This sense of embarrassment is magnified when teens are immersed in issues as sensitive as sexual abuse, particularly if they are exposed to public ridicule under taunting or judging eyes. The abusee who is undergoing legal proceedings, complete with unwanted public attention, has his or her personal psyche and self-identity threatened even more than the abusee who is not involved in court litigation.

DEVELOPMENTAL MILESTONES

During adolescence many changes take place in all realms of growth—physiological, emotional, and mental. Milestones that occur at this time significantly affect development and are quite evident to the observer, as their impact invokes significant changes from childhood to young adulthood. Height, shapeliness or increase in muscular physique, vocal chord changes, and outward signs of puberty all alert others that a child is transgressing into adulthood. But perhaps the single most crucial change is the one that develops internally, that is, the development of a self-identity.

Theories on Identity Formation

According to Erikson (1968), the adolescent's main task at this stage of life is to resolve the identity crisis. If this is not accomplished, the adolescent may be restricted to an adult life riddled with confusion. Inherent in accomplishing this task is the identification of a career, personal values, and a corresponding lifestyle. Skills acquired during earlier stages, such as the industry versus inferiority stage, prepare individuals for fulfilling work in adulthood. Often adolescents who have experienced abuse cannot deal with power or authority figures in the workplace, as they represent images of the adults who abused them. Abusees have reported instances of panic attacks when a supervisor and superior entered the room or when anyone else in the work setting resembled images of the abuser. Many teens avoid confrontation in the workplace because of learned helplessness resulting from the abuse. Such abusees may become resigned to a life of underachievement and an ineffective job history, all of which could have been avoided if the adolescent had been given adequate opportunity to attain a solid sense of self and become grounded in ego-strength.

Marcia's Identity Theory Marcia (1980) broadened Erikson's concept of identity formation by using a two-dimensional concept of identity: *conferred* identity, which consists of facts that cannot be changed, such as parents and siblings; and *self-constructed* identity, which includes chosen aspects of identity, such as career choice, lifestyle, and personal belief systems. Marcia's (1980) early propositions of identity included four identity states: achievement, moratorium, foreclosure, and diffusion. Each identity status is associated with negative or positive implications, dependent upon the accomplishment of focused goal setting and adherence to goals cumulating in the attainment of a chosen career. According to Marcia, *identity achievement* is accomplished if both *choice* and *goals* are in place, whereas *identity foreclosure* occurs when a choice is made too early, for example, choosing the same career as a parent's due to overidentification with that parent, and thus career goals are established without sufficient exploration of alternatives. *Identity diffusion* occurs when career choices are decided but goals are not acted on, resulting in a drifting or vague concept of career aspirations. Finally, *moratorium* arises when the adolescent remains in crisis throughout adulthood, thereby never forming a true sense of positive well-balanced identity.

Theories of Kroeger and Waterman Kroger (1993) and Waterman (1993) have offered more contemporary theories of identity formation. According to Kroger, conflict arises at each stage of development, and the manner in which that conflict is resolved is instrumental in the formation of an identity. She proposed that this concept of conflict resolution leading toward emotional growth of the individual is universal and that all individuals experience conflicts as part of normal development. Conflicts of adolescents entail gaining greater independence during adolescence, leaving their parents' home, and finding a self-identity that is fulfilling or integral to self.

Waterman (1993) emphasized the development of an expressive identity, one that is the result of accumulated attributes and behaviors. He questioned why some individuals are more tolerant of others and can more easily express empathy, responsiveness, conscientiousness, and similar traits toward others. He noted that identity is continually reevaluated, modified, or altered based on a continual set of interactions with environmental influences. Final resolution of identity occurs only upon successful integration of internalized personalized characteristics such as anxiety, self-esteem, moral reasoning, and patterns of behavior (Waterman, 1993). In order to advance or commit to a chosen life path, personal beliefs and ideologies must be adhered to, all of which are dependent upon values and beliefs internalized throughout childhood. Still other theorists (Grotevant, 1993) believe that an identity crisis can reappear if personal or environmental changes occur. Needless to say, many factors can hinder or enhance the resolution of an identity crisis.

Regardless of which theoretical underpinning is used to comprehend the concept of identity formation, any adverse or traumatic incidents in a child's life impede this essential developmental task. When physical, verbal, or sexual abuse is encountered, acquisition of self-identity is greatly hampered, particularly if problematic family dynamics are prevalent. For a sexually abused teen, fear of physical harm, confused sexual identity, and preoccupation with self-doubt, self-blame, guilt, and shame all deter exploration and acquisition of personal skills needed to accomplish self-identity.

Ego–Identity and Cognitive Awareness Because ego–identity is not strongly rooted during this age, adolescents may respond to certain actions, events, and persons in a variety of ways, as they attempt to find their own value systems and preferred lifestyles. Indecision and self-doubt are commonplace among teenagers, who are trying to bridge the distance between parental expectations and personal aspirations. Consequently, although they may cognitively know the difference between right and wrong, adolescents may not always have the self-confidence, inner determination, and assertiveness to react appropriately. This renders them more vulnerable to adverse influences in their social environment as they struggle to identify self-needs and aspirations. If ego–identity is completed in a healthy manner, ego formation becomes an inherent personality trait (Achenbach, 1991b; Kroeger, 1993; Loevinger, 1993), and increased assuredness should follow. However, the propensity to develop serious mental health issues is intensified and personality disorders may occur if the ego is not sufficiently integrated. For the child exposed to sexual abuse, ego formation becomes increasingly complex due to perceptions of self, both realistic and unwarranted, that arise from the abuse (Davies, 1995).

Loevinger's Theory of Ego Development Loevinger (1990) proposed that ego development evolves differently among young children but is consistent with early life experiences. If an advanced ego state develops at an early age, the propensity to achieve more advanced ego states throughout life is increased. Conversely, if integrated ego states do not emerge in early years, the potential to remain in a regressed ego state is imminent.

Loevinger (1976) defined six stages of ego development, with three overall transitional phases proposed as the prosocial, impulsive, and opportunist stages of development.

The *prosocial* stage of ego development involves preoccupation with inanimate objects rather than people, and gratification of self-needs dominates the personality. Next is the *impulsive* stage, similar to what is seen in toddlers; if this behavior is apparent during adolescence, it is considered a problem. Serious maladjustment would be recognized if either the prosocial or impulsive ego state were to dominate during adolescence. Self-control evolves during the transitional stage of development referred to as *opportunist* or, more recently, *self-protective*. An adolescent may behave or conform due to penalties invoked by others rather than because the behavior is moralistically right or wrong.

If Loevinger's (1976, 1990) concepts are applied to sexual abuse, then, during the opportunistic phase, an abused teen might seek help or remain silent about the abuse in light of the perceived consequences anticipated from others in the environment. If earlier impulsive ego states emerge, perhaps manifested in risky behaviors, or if a prosocial stage emerges where objects preoccupy the teen, then withdrawal, avoidance, or dissociation may be observed in the abused teenager.

Ego-Identity and Peer Acceptance   Toward junior high and into high school, the stage of *conformity* sets in, and an adolescent's behavior becomes motivated by the need for acceptance. Preoccupation with superficial appearances predominates, and the adolescent's view of self is keenly associated with the approval of others. Interpersonal relationships may be developed based on observed behaviors rather than on emotional intimacy or spiritual kinship. Stereotypical and rigid opinions may be developed solely based on the adoption of another person's point of view. Consequently, an adolescent at this age is more prone to acquiesce to a persuasive adult's malintended attention. It may be viewed as *cool* to smoke, take drugs, play hooky from school, drive under the influence, and/or participate in sexual adventures and risky activities for the sole purpose of gaining approval from a perpetrator who feigns friendship.

Ego Development and Critical Thinking   Fortunately for most parents, the conscious *self-awareness* stage emerges during the adolescent age period (Loevinger, 1990). As an adolescent internalizes moralistic values, a sense of right or wrong emerges, in and of itself, rather than because punishment may occur for wrongdoing; thus a stronger ego state emerges. Persuasive peers or adults may not penetrate the adolescent's adapted beliefs by acts of seduction regardless of how heavily they mask their attempts with feigned friendliness. Distinctions can be made between normative behaviors and inappropriate acts. Personality traits of critical awareness, interpersonal differences, and alternative problem-solving skills are apparent in an individual who has achieved an ego-state that encompasses self-awareness.

Conscientious traits are said to evolve mainly in the most grounded, ego-centered individual. Tolerance of others results in a more universal view of people, life, and life situations. Feelings and motives rather than superficial appearances become the motivating forces for actions and behaviors. Personality traits become stabilized, represented by traits of empathy, self-respect and respect of others, and the ability to comprehend complex concepts and dilemmas (Loevinger, 1976; Muuss, 1996).

Psychosexual Development

Perhaps most controversial is Freud's (1925/1953) conceptualization of what he calls the *genital* stage, originating in puberty and extending into young adulthood. For any adolescent, male or female, who has experienced abuse, this phase of development may be increasingly painful to process. New feelings emerge that may provoke emotional trauma related to the abuse. Since intimacy is a normal developmental process that is sometimes intensely fueled during this stage, early sexual experiences of an unpleasant or outright traumatic nature may sorely distort, and once more rob an adolescent of, the normal developmental process.

Freudian Concepts According to Freud (1925/1953), distinct qualities are delineated for males and females, all attributed to a predestined, biologically driven, process of maturation. Freud proposed that an adolescent must determine his or her own sense of self-worth during this time, simultaneously with the awakening of hormonal influences that energize the libido. Sexual urges experienced during the phallic stage, yet dormant during the latency stage, now reemerge, supposedly with a harmonious resolution of the Electra or Oedipus complex so that fulfilling intimate relationships can be formed with opposite-sex peers. Needless to say, any unresolved issues from childhood will negatively impact successful passage through the genital stage and subsequent sexual identity.

Cognitive Development

Cognitive development matures to more advanced levels during adolescence. At this stage of development, cognitive structures acquired from life experiences should assist the adolescent in conducting more advanced thought patterns. In doing so, critical thinking skills, abstract reasoning, and complex problem-solving skills should evolve.

Critical Thinking Piaget (1962) noted that as cognitive development skills mature during adolescence, comprehension of abstract concepts increases. Reasoning skills are extended to problems of logic, critical thinking, and internalization of societal values and beliefs. Problem-solving skills include the ability to explore alternatives to problems and to accommodate situational differences, and decision making should be approached with increased confidence and adherence to personal convictions.

Adolescents should rely on internal reasoning skills for completing behavioral tasks, rather than parental guidance as in childhood. Reflective introspection also may be possible now. If an adolescent experienced sexual abuse at an earlier age, concepts related to that event can be cognitively processed, perhaps for the first time since the abuse occurred. Any misperceptions about the abuse may become evident, and ensuing emotional distress from these misperceptions can be addressed in therapy. Verbal expression should be sufficiently developed to articulate feelings about abuse as well. Any lingering thoughts about the abuse, such as self-blame or guilt, can be processed in a more therapeutic manner. Cognitive therapy techniques such as reframing, desensitization, and creative imagery can be introduced into the healing process with more effective results than was possible when the child was younger.

Even though adolescents are capable of cognitive reasoning skills, however, they may not be *emotionally* ready. Emotional willingness or readiness to deal with abuse issues must be assessed individually for each client, and the progress may not be linear in fashion. Setbacks due to intense reactions are common. For some, the entire experience was so traumatic that the mere thought of discussing it with anyone is terrifying regardless of what advanced cognitive skills are developed. If another party forces a child to speak about the event when, in fact, he or she may not be emotionally ready to deal with it, more severe emotional harm can occur.

SYMPTOMATIC AND PATHOLOGICAL DISORDERS

Emotional concerns that remained dormant during early childhood may manifest in adolescence as extreme behavioral reactions, either internalized externalized, to those problems. Internalized behavioral dysfunction is most often associated with withdrawal, depression, and self-hurting acts, whereas externalized behaviors are viewed as disruptive, aggressive, oppositional, and extreme antisocial conduct disorders (Achenbach, 1991b). When a group of sexually abused children were sampled, internalizing and externalizing behaviors were found equally across both sexes. On the Child Behavior Checklist (CBC; Achenbach, 1991b), 35% males and 46% of females scored significantly for internalizing behaviors, whereas 36% males and 39% females responded with elevated scores for externalizing behaviors. The following sections will address numerous symptomatic behaviors that may or may not be directly related to childhood sexual abuse.

Eating Disorders

Eating disorders are perhaps the most highly associated disorder originating during the adolescent time period. Estimates of adolescent females experiencing some form of eating disorder, be it bulimia, anorexia, or obesity, are as high as 20–30%. All of these disorders are related to a distorted perceptual view of actual physical attributes, and they have been found to be highly associated with locus of control (Waller, 1998). If that control has been jeopardized by the impact of abuse by an adult, an adolescent may have a greater propensity toward developing an eating disorder. While theorists are not in agreement about the etiology of these disorders, serious medical consequences can evolve due to diminished protein and mineral intake vital to healthy living (Jenny, 1996; Korte, Horton, & Graybill, 1998; Waller, 1998). Because extensive weight loss can mask or inhibit an adolescent female's normal development of a womanly figure, it has been suggested that females experience eating disorders as a means of hiding their womanhood in an attempt to feign off any unwanted sexual advances.

About 95% of all anorexia patients are girls, although recently boys are showing an increased rate of incidents of anorexia. Because adolescence is a time when growth spurts occur that make demands on the physical strength of the body, increased need for iron, zinc, and other vitamins exists; yet, when eating disorders occur, physical demands on the body increase, thereby jeopardizing healthy development.

Because of the potential lethality of eating disorders, expert treatment requires the involvement of a multidisciplinary team that is well versed on the disease and its possible ramifications in terms of overall health impairment. For example, if anorexia persists, long-term physical impairments, such as lack of menses, reduced strength in the heart lining, and loosening of the sphincter muscles, can result. Death results in about 2–5% of all anorexia cases. Unfortunately, the relapse rate for individuals experiencing anorexia or bulimia is high. Strober, Freeman, and Morrell (1997) noted that approximately 25% of clients with severe eating disorders move into chronic relapses, with many of these ending in death.

Depression

Depression is perhaps the most widely cited disorder associated with adolescence. While many teens experience some form of or minor bouts with depression, chronic depression manifests itself in acting out behaviors as well as withdrawn behaviors. Acute and chronic symptoms associated with depression include types of self-harm (or cutting), severe withdrawal, and suicidal ideation or attempts. Acting out behaviors may also include self-hurting behaviors such as reckless driving, high-risk activities, and excessive aggressiveness.

Moran and Eckenrode (1992) examined the etiology of depression, citing self-esteem and locus of control as predictors for developmental outcomes under the influence of abuse. Cognitive theorists (Bonner, Walker, & Berliner, 1999; Deblinger & Heflin, 1996; Dobson & Craig, 1996; Knell, 1993; Perry & Azad, 1999; Verduyn & Calam, 1999) propose that if self-esteem and internal locus of control are diminished, distorted cognitions may be at the root of depressive thoughts. For example, girls with high self-esteem and a reliance on an internal locus of control may be more resilient in coping with an abusive experience; therefore, prognosis for their recovery may be optimistic. Girls with low self-esteem and an external locus of control are at greater risk for depression following abuse experiences.

Moran and Eckenrode (1992) suggested that the younger a child is at the onset of abuse, the greater the risk for severe long-term adjustment and emotional problems. Self-esteem develops during early childhood, based on the quality of the child's interactions with primary caregivers. If intrafamilial abuse starts at a young age, a basis for self-esteem is not established, whereas if abuse occurs during adolescence, the adolescent can fall back on a foundation of self-esteem that was developed as a child (Moran & Eckenrode, 1992).

Often depression is masked in disruptive behaviors and acting out disturbances. Because of the problems arising when an adolescent acts out, concerned caretakers often overlook the fact that underlying depressive thoughts are actually precipitating the behavioral disruption. In many instances, severe punishment is enforced, propelling the teen into even more severe withdrawal or episodes of anger. Diagnosis is often difficult to make because of the closely aligned characteristics of depressive disorders and aggressive, oppositional, and conduct disorders (Rapoport & Ismond, 1996).

Emotional Distress

Researchers note a higher incident rate of suicide attempts, severe emotional distress, and mental health disorders among abusees as a result of residual effects of the abuse. At the same time, however, many adolescents are not at all ready to discuss such highly sensitive and painful issues as sex, sexuality, and sexually abusive treatment. The following example emphasizes the need to pace counseling activities in coordination with the specific adolescent's needs.

> Alice was a 13-year-old high school freshman who had been sexually molested two years earlier by a member of the clergy who had offered to assist her and her mother during a financial crisis. During visits to her home, he took her on shopping trips, spent time talking to her, and took her to numerous community events for children. Eventually, on one such outing, he molested her in his car. The abuse continued over many visits, during which he would drive Alice to a park and proceed to molest her. He threatened her into silence by noting that no one would believe her because he was a minister. He also threatened to stop helping her family financially if she revealed "their secret."
>
> Eventually Alice's distress over the matter reached the point where she sought help and disclosed the abuse to a school counselor. During Alice's freshman year of high school, the court case became the focus of much attention, given that the defendant was a high-profile community leader and minister. Although the authorities assured Alice that files would remain confidential at the time she pressed charges, community grapevines soon released victim identification. Classmates cruelly ridiculed her on the school bus each day for almost two weeks before Alice brought their behavior to the attention of a school psychologist. Administrators took disciplinary actions against the bullies, and the school psychologist immediately notified Alice's mother, whose response was, "Talk to her and take care of that sexual thing, will ya?"
>
> By this time, the whole school was aware of the situation and the girl was gravely embarrassed and humiliated. Alice was not verbalizing feelings about any sexual concerns; rather, she made numerous statements

about her embarrassment and humiliation within the school and community. She suffered from a depleted sense of self-esteem along with acute depressive symptoms. Coping techniques were discussed during therapy, but in many ways, peer pressure and extreme embarrassment were as devastating to Alice as was the abuse itself. Essentially, she was retraumatized by the entire episode. It took several months of intense rapport- and trust-building before she felt safe enough to verbalize her feelings about the sexual abuse at all.

Substance Abuse

Alcohol and substance abuse, which exacerbates emotional states, is currently a prevalent problem among 14–20% of high school-aged children. Teens who participate in early drug use often continue to use as adults (Kandel & Rosenbaum, 1990). National statistics indicate that tobacco, alcohol, and marijuana are the drugs most frequently used by adolescents (Children's Defense Fund, 2000). Since marijuana and alcohol are frequently used to seduce adolescents into increasingly abusive behaviors by pedophiles who attempt to win the trust of their victims, any teen who uses drugs is placed in a highly vulnerable position for sexual assault and exploitation.

Scher and Twaite (1999) found significant score differences on a measure of alexithymia, or inability to consciously experience and communicate feelings, among teens recovering from substance abuse who had been abused as children compared to nonabused teens recovering from substance abuse. Alexithymia was significantly higher when the sexual abuse first occurred after the victim had reached the age of 12, when a perpetrator of the sexual abuse was a father or stepfather, and when the abuse involved oral, vaginal, and/or anal penetration. Results were interpreted as indicating that the development of alexithymic symptoms may represent another defense that victims employ to insulate themselves from painful affect, along with dissociative symptoms and substance abuse. These findings may further substantiate that the use of drugs might be a form of self-medication to avoid dealing with painful elements of abuse.

Frey (1995) referred to adolescents who were sexually abused and used drugs as individuals with dual diagnosis disorders. The combination of reduced self-esteem from past abuse and the reduced inhibitions from drug use magnifies the propensity to be abused further; therefore, such teens are placed in *double jeopardy*. The twelve-step program is used in treatment for both substance-related and abuse-related issues, so it is not unusual for an adolescent diagnosed with a dual disorder to attend multiple twelve-step programs. Frey (1995) recommended that adolescents be substance-free before participating in treatment for sexual abuse. Then again, some adolescents are in denial of substance abuse issues, yet are willing to talk about their sexual abuse issues. Consequently, therapists must be well informed about dual diagnosis therapy issues if effective treatment is to be realized at a pace relative to the adolescent's functioning.

One aspect of recovery is that an abusee's relapse into drug use can trigger other aspects of recovery. Therefore, the achievement of optimal recovery calls for an ongoing cyclical process of treatment rather than a linear progressive path of recovery. Although this cyclical process of recovery may be applicable to all abusees, it is more apparent when substance abuse complicates the healing process. The benefits of using a twelve-step process in therapy are dependent on the availability of community programs such as AA for the abusee to attend long after therapy has ended.

Sexual Disease

Over 12 million sexually transmitted diseases (STDs) are diagnosed each year. Many incidents are diagnosed in individuals under the age of 25, with chlamydia representing the most prevalent STD. Teenagers currently represent the highest population for acquiring the AIDS or HIV virus. High school surveys concerning sexual activity revealed that over two-thirds of the high school females reported sexual activity without the use of condoms. Although health education stresses hygiene and the use of protection with condoms, many teens believe either that "it won't happen to me" or that pharmacological intervention will "cure the disease." Venereal diseases are diagnosed at alarming rates in sexually abused adolescents. A sexually abused adolescent who acts out with promiscuous sexual behaviors is at the highest risk for STD diagnosis. Similarly, runaways and kidnapped adolescents who are entrapped in sex slave rings are obviously at high risk to acquire an STD.

Thompson, Potter, Sanderson, and Maibach (1997) studied 83 patients found to have STDs and noted that low self-esteem, feelings of powerlessness, and more frequent sexual encounters coupled with drug use were factors found among all clients. The authors attributed these findings to a higher propensity to participate in nonpositive sexual experiences and a lower propensity to use condoms during sex. Other researchers examined 107 young patients referred for STDs and found vaginal discharge as the most frequently cited complaint, particularly among patients 5 years of age or younger. Evidence of abuse was identified in 67% of the patients, with gonorrhea being the most common STD. Multiple STDs were found in 10 of the clients (Argent, Lachman, Hanslo, & Bass, 1995). Kenney, Reinholtz, and Angelini (1998) studied a larger group of 1,994 women aged 18–22 and found that high-risk behaviors were more predictive of STDs than previous sexual abuse history; these authors proposed further health education classes in school in an attempt to deter risky sexual behaviors among teens.

Pregnancy

Teen pregnancy rates increased tremendously throughout the 20th century; figures were cited showing that four-fifths of all pregnancies occurred to unmarried women, with over 50–70% of the deliveries occurring to girls under the age of 19 (Children's Defense Fund, 2000). Stevens-Simon and McAnarney (1994) investigated the possibility of former abuse among single teenage parents. Based on a sample of 127 girls aged 12 to 18, 33% reported that they were sexually abused prior to the pregnancy; thus an association between early sexual abuse and premature sexual activity in adolescence was indicated (Rainey, Stevens-Simon, & Kaplan, 1995). Previously abused girls were also found to (a) be prone to high stress and anxieties throughout their pregnancy, (b) neglect prenatal care, (c) deliver babies with lower weight, and (d) remain at high risk for substance abuse.

Newborn babies of sexually abused adolescents thus represented a high-risk group for future developmental difficulties due to poor prenatal care in general. It was also found that a 25% probability rate existed that an HIV active mother would pass the disease on to her unborn baby unless she were treated with AZT during pregnancy, which then reduced the risk to a 5% probability rate of transmitting the disease to the baby (Edelman, 1999). Even with medication, AIDS-infected newborns were placed at further risk due to the impact of such drugs on the developmental process of the unborn fetus. Obviously, these are far-reaching ramifications, and ones that occur, in part, because of the sexual abuse of female children who become infected with the AIDS virus while pregnant and pass it on to their infants.

EMOTIONAL DISORDERS
AND GENDER DIFFERENCES

Females who have been sexually abused experience a multitude of symptoms ranging across a continuum of mild to severe reactions. Researchers acknowledge that incident rates of abuse may range from 25–65% across females, and symptomology and pathology found in abused females is well documented. However, sparse information has been available to assist the male child who has been sexually abused.

Incident rates of sexual abuse of males are reported at about 14–25%, depending on the reporting source, although some believe the percentage is much higher. During the 1990s, researchers intensified their focus on the residual effects of sexual abuse in males. Males are said to experience more intense debilitating emotional reactions than had previously been anticipated (Hunter, 1990). Black and DeBlassie (1993) report an incident whereby two older boys continually sexually assaulted a younger boy, Matthew, over a period of three years. Although he was initially devastated by the abuse, Matthew did not report it, and he experienced emotional reactions from it well into adulthood. Only when the emotional difficulties began to interfere with his daily functioning did he report the abuse to a college counselor.

Boys may avoid disclosure of abuse out of fear of societal stigmas, homophobic concerns, further ridicule if the abusee is a homosexual, or any other issue that is unique to males (Hunter; 1990; Porter, 1986; Singer, 1989). Long-term or extended periods of abuse often provoke more intense emotional effects (Deblinger & Heflin, 1996). This may be due to the additional trauma of not being able to break free of the abuse, extended periods of duress, and continual lack of protection from other adults (Hunter, 1990). Also, the earlier the age at which sexual abuse begins, the more devastating it can be for any child–male or female. Examination of hospital room records of boys treated for sexual abuse problems indicated an average age of 9.7 for their first assaults. "Violent assaults under life-threatening coercion . . . , public humiliation as in ritualistic abuse . . . , and use of bondage or other physical restraint also adds to the trauma" (Hunter, 1990, p. 46).

Emotional Reactions Across Genders

Briere et al. (1988) noted that child sexual abuse has a similar impact on boys and girls. Even molestation can be highly traumatic for males as well as for females, at times triggering severe symptomology. Males may experience a greater sense of paranoia and mistrust of others and more school difficulties, reduced socialization, and excessive sexual activity including masturbating excessively (Black & DeBlassie, 1993). Other researchers have noted that males may experience a sense of powerlessness that, in turn, is aggressively acted out on others; hence, they may become the perpetrators (Hunter, 1990; Rogers & Terry, 1984). Repeating a sexual assault on others, however, occurs in only 30% of males abuse victims (Strean, 1988). Although females experience the same sense of powerlessness, withdrawal and evasive behaviors are readily viewed among females, in contrast to the more aggressive actions emitted by males.

Males appear to repress or normalize the abuse experience (Myers, 1989) more than females, which results in denial of the emotional impact and the invalidation of emotions. Females may report abuse more readily than males; however, this does not imply that females do not invalidate or deny their own emotional reactions as well. The long-term impact of invalidating feelings is that the individual may also deny or suppress feelings in adult relationships, thus hindering the potential for fulfilling adult relationships.

Fear of homosexual implications occurs for many adolescents as they explore their own sexual identity, but no causal relationship is indicated between childhood sexual abuse and adult homosexuality. Also, fear of reprisal from other males in light of homophobic relations compels male victims of male sexual abuse to remain silent about the abuse. Same-sex abuse assaults leave males with many residual emotional concerns, similar in complexity to those of females, but different in terms of content. This fact may be even more relevant for the homosexual male, who may have fewer support resources in his environment. Researchers note that homosexual males have been found to be more vulnerable to sexual abuse than heterosexual males (Dimock, 1988).

Violence as Precursor to Delinquency

Hunter (1990) indicated that coercive and violent force was used to sexually assault over 60% of the boys sampled. If a parent has assaulted a child and the child tells the nonoffending parent, additional harsh treatment may be inflicted upon the child, particularly when the nonoffending parent is in denial. Rather than receiving the supportive protection to which any child is entitled, the child is blamed for making up lies or dramatic stories. Subsequently, the child is forced to remain silent until he or she matures enough to seek help on his or her own. By then, long-term exposure to physical and psychological injury can extenuate severe and chronic emotional distress. Continued exposure to violent or abusive behaviors may represent a strong factor in prediction of juvenile delinquency (Englander, 1997; Rencken, 1989).

Rencken (1989) noted that in addition to the negative attributes normally associated with abuse, such as loss of trust, security, and innocence along with ambivalent and conflicting feelings and defensive behaviors, several other family dynamics impact later propensity toward violence. When sexual abuse takes place within the family, family systems in general do not prepare the child or teen to deal with life-enhancing attributes such as appropriate coping skills, ability to communicate effectively, and avoiding isolation from others. Rather, sexually abusive families are rigid and controlling, encourage secrecy, and manipulate power structures within the interrelationships of the family. Clearly such dynamics leave an adolescent at risk for greater frustration in adulthood, with the only recourse to vent anger or anxiousness through violence. Englander (1997) also notes that teens with a history of family violence are drawn to violent activities.

For teens who have experienced sexual abuse since early childhood, running away may be the only foreseeable escape from a painful life (Gary & Campbell, 1998; Hunter; 1990). Once teens are on the street, however, predators easily prey upon them for purposes of sexual assault, exploitation, or forced prostitution (Shaw & Butler, 1998). In one study, approximately 50% of detained youth reported abusive acts within six months prior to detainment, and they further stated that they had run from home to avoid further emotional, physical, or sexual abuse. Hence, the runaway becomes vulnerable to acts of sexual abuse or exploitation, and may be forced into juvenile delinquent acts.

Delinquency

As early as 1957, Bender noted that identification with the aggression expressed by adults in their household was a common factor among teens with delinquent behaviors. Young children who internalize aggressive behaviors, perhaps through social learning (Bandura, 1989), are more likely to act out their anger and aggression in defiance on others. Once an adolescent is on the streets, exposure to further exploitation, sexual offenses, and sexual assault increases significantly. One study (Ryan & Lane, 1991) revealed that 45% of juvenile child molesters were abused as children, while 16% of juvenile rapists and prisoners convicted of indecent exposure had experienced physical and sexual abuse.

Research on adolescent perpetrators (Ryan & Lane, 1991) noted that the average age of first sexual predator behavior is 14 and that the most frequent assault, other than opposite-sex rape, is same-sex sodomy. Complexities arise in treating perpetrators of sexually deviant acts of delinquency due to the fact that the predator may be both abusee and abuser. Educational information needs to be shared with the perpetrator so that concepts of sexual abuse and subsequent sexual offenses can be clarified within his or her own realm of understanding. Treatment programs are essential if the adolescent abuser is to overcome the propensity to abuse others and to avoid becoming an adult perpetrator of sexually deviant crimes (Hanson & Bussiere, 1998; Quinsey, Harris, Rice, & Cormier, 1998; Ryan & Lane, 1991).

Baker (1991) noted that delinquency is a dual accountability problem. While the adolescent must take responsibility for his or her actions, society must also make attempts to reach troubled youth. He proposed that first offenders be treated differently than repeat offenders, which may occur now on a case-by-case basis.

Aggressive and Self-Destructive Acts

Females who act out aggressively may manifest behaviors of sexual promiscuity, juvenile delinquency, aggressive acts, and other juvenile delinquent behaviors but may or may not report that they have been sexually abused (Hanson, Resnick, Saunders, Kilpatrick, & Best, 1999). Needless to say, this makes it difficult to activate intervention programs to overcome the negative effects of abuse so that further at-risk behaviors will not evolve. Prostitution is a high probability as females become increasingly vulnerable to the manipulative behaviors of pimps, abusers, and pedophiles. A propensity for self-destructive behaviors in general, such as cutting, substance abuse, and other high-risk activities, may, in turn, increase vulnerability toward severe psychopathology or such personality attributes as those found in borderline disorders (Brown, Cohen, Johnson, Smailes, 1999). Abusive dating relationships have become a more frequent problem among adolescent females, leading to harmful situations such as physical beatings, date rape, and stranger rape (Kilpatrick, 1992). Many of these behaviors set precedence for further involvement in unhealthy adult relationships.

When the perpetrator is a parent or sibling, the impact of the abuse is significantly greater, requiring total family therapy (Trepper, Niedner, Mika, & Barrett, 1996). This may be noted in the case of June.

> June was a 14-year-old freshman who had been sexually abused by her father since the age of 5 or 6. June reported being sexually molested, fingered, and coerced to perform sodomy upon her father at least once a week or more throughout the years. To ingratiate himself into her trust, he would do kind deeds, give her special attention in front of family members who thought he was so devoted to her, and coax her to sit on his lap when others were present as well. But he would sneak into her room late at night when others were asleep.
>
> June reported that she frequently fought off her father's attacks; however, when she did so, his mannerism changed from mild coaxing to forceful physical entrapment. There were many nights, said June, when tears streamed down her face while he finished, but he never responded to her tears; he just kept manipulating her physically. She also reported that afterward she would cry herself to sleep, burying her sobs in her pillow because she had been threatened and told not to awaken anyone.

The father's threats took the form of physical coercion as well as verbal threats of abandonment. June's father threatened her into silence by telling her that he would put June away for telling lies, so she would never see her siblings or mother again; that if June's mother heard such filthy lies she would surely have a nervous breakdown, be taken away to a hospital, and never be seen again; and that June would be put into an orphanage for disturbed children. Her father had already intimidated June, as she had witnessed his physical wrath when he beat the male children of the family. Other times, he had destroyed furniture and punched holes in the walls during angry outbursts. She did, indeed, see him as a powerful person capable of inflicting harm onto his loved ones.

June described her mother as a chronically depressed person who spent most of her time bedridden or under medication from doctors. By the time June reached adolescence, she no longer could tolerate her father's abuse but saw no recourse other than suicide. Ironically, the night she took an entire package of sleeping pills, her mother, who usually did not check on her at night, came into her room for some reason and found her sleeping next to an emptied package of sleeping pills. Instead of being rushed to specialists for help, the family doctor was called, and she was forced to stay awake by being taken along with her parents and siblings, in 10-degree winter weather, to observe the lighting of the town's Christmas tree.

Even though no mental health specialist was consulted, June's suicide attempt must have made an impact on her father, for he never abused her again. No one in the family ever discussed her suicide attempt or her reasons for attempting suicide.

Suicide Incidents

Associations between suicide attempts during adolescence and sexual abuse are evident (Molnar, Shade, Kral, Booth, & Watters, 1998), as noted in a study of 775 street youth aged 12–19. Molnar et al. (1998) found that 70% of females sampled reported sexual abuse, while 24% of males reported sexual abuse. Of the total sample, 48% of females reported suicide attempts, while 27% of males reported suicide attempts. Based on reported attempts among previously sexually abused teens versus nonabused teens, it was suggested that prior sexually abused teens are at a two to four times higher risk for attempted suicide.

It appears that, upon reaching the teen years, if a child has experienced or continues to experience sexual abuse, the ultimate method of ending that abuse is suicide. Many adolescents develop a sense of helplessness due to extended abuse and oppressive treatment and see no way out of the situation, other than death. This is particularly true for adolescents having no means of emotional support in their environment due to neglect, abuse, or abandonment of parental care.

Another reason suicide attempts may escalate during adolescence is that during the teen years, males and females are to accomplish the developmental task of establishing their own sexual identity. As a child moves into preadolescence and then adolescence, experimentation with intimacy of opposite-sex peers is a natural precursor toward and preparation for adult intimate relationships. However, flashbacks and memory recalls of the abuse may arise when a sexually abused teen is faced with an intimate encounter with a same-age peer.

Flashbacks and memory recalls can be frightening and intimidating to the adolescent for several reasons. First, memories themselves may be frightening as the teenager recalls life-threatening comments, threats, and coercive statements made by the perpetrator; thus, the adolescent is forced to re-experience scary emotions. Second, the adolescent may be reminded of feeling shame and embarrassment about the abuse, and thus feel unworthy of a same-age sexual relationship, even though it is a normal process. Third, pain may have been experienced during earlier abuse, resulting in a perceived association between sex, pain, and the current relationship. And finally, repulsion for the abusive sexual act can distort perceptions of and anticipation for same-age sexual acts, so that the adolescent abandons any attempt to obtain a healthy same-age sexual relationship within his or her peer group.

If these feelings are intense enough to propel the adolescent into depression, self-blame, and withdrawal from others, suicide may be viewed as a means of ending the emotional turmoil. Although adolescents may be well aware of mental health services accessible in their school or community, embarrassment over the incident of abuse may prohibit them from seeking out that help. Also, such adolescents face any other life stressors encountered at this time with reduced coping ability to work through emotional distress.

Sibling Abuse

Perhaps most traumatic, yet understudied, is sibling abuse. Numerous case histories have revealed that the effects of either same-sex or opposite-sex abuse between siblings are harsh and long-term (Greenwald & Leitenberg, 1989). Usually offending siblings make more extreme coercive threats and use more violence to overpower their victims than do nonsibling abusers. Also, the type of sexual abuse may be more severe; often humiliation is maximized, and in some cases friends are called in to participate (Classen & Yalom, 1995; DiGeogio-Miller, 1998; Harris & Landis, 1997). Fear and anxieties are higher among abused siblings, as the abuse is more aggressive and acted out more frequently due to easy access to the sibling for victimization. In many cases, parents either do not believe the disclosure from abused siblings or minimize the effect, interpreting complaints from the abusee as mere sibling rivalry. Some victims have reported that they did not tell because no one would have believed them; other siblings have reported feeling guilt and shame at experiencing sexual urges toward a sibling, if that was the case.

Disclosure

During the adolescent years disclosure may take many forms. Although preschool children often disclose spontaneously and school-age children may make direct disclosures, teens have more difficulty speaking about their abuse

(Nagel, Putnam, & Noll, 1997). Often abused adolescents vent anger manifested in aggressive acts or sexual assaults of others. In many instances, a disclosure occurs only after a concerned friend confides in a school counselor or staff person. In other instances, teachers make referrals after seeing warning signs in the classroom, such as vivid descriptions of abuse in an English classroom assignment or indicators of concern in a child's artwork in art class. In such cases, an astute teacher usually makes a referral to the school psychologist, social worker, or counselor.

Dating

Violence in the dating scene increased rapidly in the late 1990s. For adolescents who have experienced child abuse, a greater probability of experiencing abuse in dating relationships exists. Researchers have noted a 50% increase in the probability of an abused child accepting abuse in subsequent dating relationships. This frequency in accepting abusive dating relationships is not found among nonabused teenagers (Browne & Finkelhor, 1986; Sappington, Pharr, Tunstall, & Rickert, 1997).

In a study conducted by Sappington et al. (1997), college girls ($N = 133$) were surveyed and reported varied patterns of abusive relationships during adulthood. Forty-nine percent of the girls who had not been abused had incurred substance abuse problems and/or mood disorders, whereas 62% experienced date abuse but not childhood abuse, and 86% reported childhood abuse but not date abuse. But 97% of the girls abused as children also experienced date abuse. It was found that a combination of child abuse and subsequent date abuse was associated with an increased risk of psychological problems (Sappington et al., 1997). However, no association was found between child abuse and the length of time a girl stayed in an abusive dating relationship. The authors noted that reduced self-esteem and anger problems may serve as mediators that increase exposure to date abuse and emotional abuse as a young adult. Verbal abuse, physical abuse, and sexual abuse all rendered a girl more vulnerable to accept abuse as an adult. In many instances, verbal abuse alone was enough to lower self-esteem and, therefore, heighten the tolerance level of future abuse from others.

SUMMARY

The adolescent stage of development is filled with developmental tasks that enhance ego development. At one end, an adequate ego development allows adolescents to identify and maintain boundaries for acceptable actions from others. Conversely, teens who have been abused as children display a greater vulnerability toward abusive acts by others. Symptomology differs based on gender; for the most part, girls display more internalized behaviors such as depression and withdrawal, whereas boys display more externalized behaviors such as acting out and aggressive displays of anger. Reactions following a sexual abuse incident vary in significance based on type of abuse, intensity, frequency, and duration. Similarly, the identity of the perpetrator and his or her relationship to the abused teen may significantly impact recovery.

Adolescents who transgress the teen years with a reservoir of inappropriate cognitive beliefs of others, internalized self-blame, diminished self-esteem, and a distorted sense of trust for others will most likely experience greater adjustment problems as adults. The high school setting may represent the most feasible opportunity for a teen to receive the counseling needed to resolve inherently important issues prior to embarking on an adult life. It is incumbent that efforts be made to increase the availability of intervention programs to reach teens at this pivotal point in their lives. If intervention services are not acquired at this time, significant adjustment problems may permeate adult life in work, social, and personal areas.

DISCUSSION QUESTIONS

1. Discuss the topic of peer pressure. What social forces impact teens more than any other age group? Elaborate on your response.

2. What life stressors, if any, occur for teens facing the new millennium that earlier generations did not have to endure?

3. List gender-specific issues that may make a teen predisposed to accepting inappropriate behaviors from others.

4. What theorist's views do you agree with in terms of adolescent development—Freud, Erikson, or perhaps Loevinger? Why? Discuss your conclusions.

5. How does an abusive experience impact one's cognitive functioning, if at all? Elaborate on your response.

6. Critical thinking is an important skill that should be developed during adolescence. How is it impaired by exposure to abuse? Can it be strengthened following abuse? Explain.

7. Describe the difference between males and females in regard to coping with abuse. How might their responses differ?

8. Elaborate on how and why the ramifications of abuse are so extensive, particularly for an adolescent.

9. What community resources are available in your community to address the needs of adolescents who have been abused?

10. You are confronted with a sexually abused adolescent. What are your professional, moral, and ethical concerns?

11

Adulthood

LEARNING OBJECTIVES

Chapter 11 will address the following learning objectives:

1. A presentation of a brief overview of theoretical perspectives on adult survivors of abuse

2. A discussion of theoretical concepts of adult tasks of accomplishment indicative of well-being

3. A review of diagnostic issues and the *DSM-IV-TR* categories of CSA for focus of treatment

4. A review of symptomatic and pathological disorders often associated with CSA

5. A discussion of the severity of symptoms found among adult survivors of CSA

6. A review of compound issues that complicate adult adjustment following CSA

INTRODUCTION

This chapter provides a brief overview of current concerns for adult adjustment following sexually abusive treatment during childhood. Perspectives are proposed regarding physiological and psychological etiology of symptoms, a descriptive account of symptoms, and personality attributes that expedite the therapeutic process. Diagnostic criteria provided in the *Diagnostic and Statistical Manual of Mental Disorders,* 4th edition-Test Revision (*DSM-IV-TR;* APA, 2000) are presented, including the use of V codes for delineation of abuse categories for focus of treatment as well as diagnosis of severe pathology. Symptom severity and complexity are discussed, including high-risk sexual activities and/or dual diagnosis with substance abuse, along with compound stressors commonly found in adult populations. Finally, concerns for child-rearing practices are presented given histories of sexual abuse or ritualistic abuse and lack of positive role models for appropriate parenting behaviors among some CSA survivors.

THEORETICAL PERSPECTIVES

Theoretical perspectives on the etiology of symptoms that arise as a consequence of early child sexual abuse are offered in this section, which covers many divergent conceptualizations of the problem. Initially Freud (1895) referred to a women's hysteria as symptomatic of earlier abuse, although labeling of symptoms following abuse no longer carries with it a stigma of non-normal behavior, under the circumstances. Since Freud's early writings on hysteria, many other theories have evolved to identify, diagnose, and treat symptoms emanating from a sexually abusive incident, several of which will be presented in the following text.

Psychoanalytical Concepts

Freud's early conceptualizations of childhood sexual abuse are revealed in his seminal work, *The Aetiology of Hysteria* (Freud, 1896), wherein he describes numerous psychologically derived symptoms among women who claimed sexual abuse during childhood. It was proposed that women who experienced hysteria did so because of early childhood sexual abuse, presumably with the father. Memories would be repressed into the unconscious, only to emerge through hysterical neurosis or in physiological disorders that Freud referred to as *conversion disorders.*

A second term that was associated with child sexual abuse, *infantile sexuality,* presented in Freud's (1923/1936b) early writings, received notable rejection from medical and other professional communities. The term was criticized for denoting a distorted view of child sexual abuse, implying that the child was at fault for participating willingly or for provoking sexual interactions with adults. Although Freud's conceptualizations were initially rejected, in part due to the puritanical views of his time, diagnostic terms such as *conversion disorder* remain a psychiatric disorder today (*DSM-IV-TR;* APA, 2000), which serves as testament of Freud's contribution to understanding the depth and magnitude of the long-term impact of childhood trauma.

Psychologically Induced Symptoms

Blum (1996) proposed the term *seduction trauma,* which focused on psychic trauma and development of future pathology. Psychic trauma was associated with alteration of self, object representations, and new self-identifications, and was later related to vulnerability for additional trauma and unconscious conflict. Blum related these concepts to psychoanalytical interpretations of psychopathology with a history in pathogenic parent-child relationships. Although this theory reiterates many of Freud's early propositions of traumatization, some aspects of reported pathological behavior may be difficult to take at face value. For example, Blum suggested that while fear of a situation arises, an unconscious desire to recreate the trauma exists; therefore, adult trauma events reoccur. This implies that the adult consciously seeks out adverse traumatic incidents throughout life, which may be a misattribution of adult maladjustment, given the complex dynamics surrounding CSA.

Physiological Perspectives

Somatization effects as a result of CSA have been explored as a secondary effect of the emotional distress and disorientation realized by many abusees (Reilly, Baker, Rhodes, & Salmon, 1999). Reilly et al. cited two physical diseases without organic etiology, epilepsy and Crohn's disease, where patients reported histories of sexual abuse; yet other patients who did not report prior histories of abuse had organically driven diseases in similar categories. It was further noted that although the abused adults were more emotionally distressed, distress alone did not account for physical ailments that appeared to be much more deeply ingrained in the psychological structures of the patients.

Dugan, Nagin, and Rosenfeld (1999) explored another physiologically based theory for the aftereffects of childhood abuse, wherein a cyclical effect was found with neurotransmitters released under stressful or coping conditions. Norepinephrine, dopamine, serotonin, and gamma-amniobutyric acid (GABA) were said to mediate levels of manifested stress. For example, GABA levels may increase when relaxed states are encouraged through coping strategies and memory is enhanced and stabilized. Theoretical models were suggested to account for stress, coping, memory, and potential risks for substance abuse as reactions to trauma. Coping was said to promote resiliency leading to recovery, whereas failure to cope with trauma-related issues may lead to posttraumatic stress disorder (PTSD) or more severe pathological concerns, due in part to exacerbated physiological changes in body structure.

Attachment Theory

Liem and Boudewyn (1999) suggested that multiple maltreatment and loss experiences in childhood foster vulnerability to CSA and adult problems in self and social functioning. They found that multiple losses and adverse experiences fostered high levels of depression and lower levels of self-esteem and self-blame among adult college students identified as having been sexually abused as children, as compared to those who were not. CSA survivors reported more sexual, physical, and emotional abuse realized in adulthood as well as in childhood, whereas women not reporting earlier CSA did not report poor adult relationships. Although the authors attribute these difficulties to attachment theories, it would appear that alternative explanations may better explain reported findings such as poor judgment, poor boundary setting, and self-doubt in relation to self and social settings.

Accommodation Theory

Summit (1983) coined the term *accommodation theory* in reference to the manner of coping style a child uses to accommodate abusive situations. Helplessness, secrecy, entrapment, and conflicting emotional reactions were described as common elements found across CSA survivors. Because of coercive or authoritative demands to remain secretive, obey, and comply, children find themselves trapped into submitting or acquiescing to their abusers' assaults. During adolescence, acting out behaviors may emerge, including delinquent, hypersexual, and countersexual activities, or internal stressors may provoke suicidal thought, hysteria, or psychosis. Observers may assume such behavior as grounds to discredit disclosures, and thereby leave the child with self-blame for ensuing family discord or destruction. Finally, the abused child-adolescent is left with unresolved concerns that heighten any sense of helplessness, hopelessness, and alienation. All the while, the child must accommodate the situation without validation of emotions and acknowledgment of self—a pattern that may continue throughout life, thus leading to diminished fulfillment in adulthood.

Resiliency Theory

Resiliency theory focuses on the personal strengths and attributes of the abusee, perhaps more so than character theory, since many elements can impact one's resiliency to distress. This theory is relevant for understanding the prognosis for recovery and treatment, but it must encompass a broader range of aspects of recovery in addition to the abusee's personality traits. Anderson (1997) noted that resiliency was viewed in children and adults who responded to trauma with creative intelligence and insightfulness, and perhaps entertained a spiritual goal-oriented approach to healing. While all of these qualities would enhance recovery from any disorder, overcoming childhood trauma may require a still greater determination to heal, as well as a focus on family systems dynamics. Anderson emphasized the benefits of relationships with at least one supportive family member as instrumental in resilient characteristics during recovery.

Lam and Grossman (1997) found similar attributes among a sample of 199 women; these authors called the attributes *protective factors*. Women who scored high in protective-self factors appeared to recover from CSA with significantly greater effectiveness. Since recovery rates differ significantly across abusees for many reasons other than individual attributes of resiliency, it would appear that a broader conceptualization of the entire abuse experience is essential to understanding the totality of the phenomenon of CSA.

Piers (1999) considered preexisting character traits of the individual as paramount to recovery from abuse. Piers suggested that individual perceptions and mannerisms impact the way symptomatic behaviors evolve, and that multiple abuse experiences and loss experiences in early childhood would interfere with attachment relationships as an adult. Maladaptive behavior was attributed to conflicted character attributes rather than to the abuse itself; thus, Piers's theory did not center on aspects of abuse or trauma, as did Liem and Bourdewyns' theory (1999). Greater instances of depression and reduced self-esteem were found among child sexual abuse survivors, while self-blame was found to be related more to poorer adult adjustments in social functioning. Whether or not a predisposition for adult pathology may exist in the absence of CSA is difficult to discern, given CSA's onset during early childhood.

Regardless of the theoretical perspective used to understand, explain, or treat adult survivors of CSA, the CSA survivor's path of recovery is often complex and painful. Throughout the recovery process, adults are expected to maintain the typical roles of adulthood, yet they have been cheated of the opportunity to prepare for them. The following sections address the normal development of adulthood and the complications that plague adult adjustment for those who have been exposed to CSA.

DEVELOPMENTAL TASKS OF ADULTHOOD

Adults are expected to engage in intimate relationships, find a productive lifestyle, usually via a career or vocational interest, and contribute to society in a productive manner (Erikson, 1968). For the self-accomplished adult, self-identity and ego development are intact, making these accomplishments possible. To attain this state of life, one must accomplish a series of tasks during childhood.

If all developmental tasks are accomplished during childhood, the essential foundations should exist for the adult to achieve self-fulfillment. But if adverse incidents occur during childhood, the residual emotional issues often impair or jeopardize the adult's well-being. Energy and attention that should have been focused on learning and skill acquisition in preparation for adulthood was spent on generating psychological energy to survive the sexually abusive experience.

Family Pathology

Briere (1984) referred to a post-abuse syndrome, which prolongs the healing process, that arises due to complicated family dynamics and inflicted traumatic experiences. Role confusion within the family, rigid authoritarian homes, and ineffective parenting styles are all said to pose multiple problems for abuse survivors. Additionally, since children are more reluctant to report intrafamilial abuse, abusive treatment is often prolonged (Williams, 1993). Emotional reactions to the abuse—such as fear of harm in the face of frightening threats, a sense of loyalty to the perpetrator, or perhaps a perceived need to keep the family together—bind the child into secrecy, yet increase the individual's vulnerability to further abuse for years to come (Harris & Landis, 1997).

Wind-Weissman and Silvern (1994) examined the quality of care that was provided in the home of the sexually abused children to assess its impact on future adjustment. Degree of parental support was said to mediate long-term depression and reduced self-esteem. Significant differences were found between abused adults who experienced a positive and warm environment at the time of abuse and those abuse survivors who did not experience familial warmth as children. Although parental support can reduce the risk of long-term depressive reactions, the trauma that stems from the abuse is still debilitating to the abusee, in and of itself.

SYMPTOMATIC AND PATHOLOGICAL DISORDERS AND THE *DSM-IV-TR*

Professional groups recognized the serious impact of childhood abuse during the late 1970s and early 1980s; research articles appeared, and treatment models were explored. But perhaps the greatest stride in the recognition of sexual abuse as a problem was made when the *Diagnostic and Statistical Manual of Mental Disorders,* 4th edition (*DSM-IV;* APA, 1994) included categories of child abuse and child sexual abuse in the V codes section; these categories are still included in the newer *DSM-IV-TR* (APA, 2000). Earlier editions of the *DSM* did not specifically address issues of child abuse or sexual abuse, although post-traumatic stress disorder (PTSD) was included in the 1994 edition. PTSD is often assigned as a diagnostic category for abused persons due to the traumatic impact of abuse, which is similar to that found among combat soldiers during war. PTSD is often diagnosed if the following two items occur:

1. The person experienced, witnessed, or was confronted with an event or events that involved actual or threatened death or serious injury, or a threat to the physical integrity of self or other.

2. The person's response involved intense fear, helplessness, or horror. Note: In children, this may be expressed instead by disorganized or agitated behavior. (*DSM-IV-TR,* 2000, p. 467)

Witnessing Trauma

DSM-IV-TR diagnostic criteria include the observation and witnessing a threatening event, not only experiencing it. Examples of PTSD cases are found worldwide, as illustrated by the discussion of the following case at the 1996 International School Psychologists Association (ISPA) in Eger, Hungary (Ferrara, 1996a). In the 1990s, during the Bosnian invasions, a young 14-year-old boy was forced to watch his mother and sister being raped by soldiers, as well as being forced to watch the death of his father. Afterward, his sister was taken away and never seen by family members again. Only he and his mother remained. Traumatized by the event, the boy was propelled into a catatonic state; he was placed in an institution in Copenhagen after he and his mother escaped. The boy's mother experienced severe PTSD exacerbated by cultural belief systems, since rape is an ultimate source of shame for Bosnian women. According to Bosnian cultural and religious beliefs, family members are expected to kill (referred to as an *honor killing*) any female family member who is violated (raped) by invading soldiers, or to at least sever ties with the raped woman forever, since the raped woman has brought disgrace to the family. The mother's depression was severe, understandably so given the multiple traumatic events and losses she had experienced. (This practice is currently being resisted by progressive leaders throughout third world countries.)

V Codes in the *DSM-IV-TR*

While PTSD is the overall diagnosis for mental distress, V codes (APA, 2000) that identify more specific concerns are assigned to enhance the focus of treatment. Thus, in cases of sexual abuse, the *type* of abuse and the client's *relationship* in the abuse is easily identified, making treatment planning more efficient. Categories within the V codes are as follows: (a) physical abuse of a child, b) sexual abuse of a child, (c) neglect of a child, (d) physical abuse of an adult, and (e) sexual abuse of an adult. A separate code exists to identify the focus of treatment, that is, whether the client is the offender or the victim. PTSD diagnosis emerged with the publication of the *DSM-IV* (APA, 1994), with symptom criteria noted, in part, as "physiological reactivity on exposure to internal or external cues that symbolize or resemble an aspect of the traumatic experience" (APA, 1994, p. 210).

Comorbidity

Comorbidity or *dual diagnosis* exists if additional disorders are present at the time PTSD is diagnosed (Freeman & Fallot, 1997; Harris & Landis, 1997). Complications such as chronic or acute mood disorders, dissociation, agitation and attention-deficits, sleep disorders, and numerous other mental health disorders may require treatment or may alter the route of recovery. Secondary symptoms can exacerbate symptomology, impede recovery, or demand an intensive treatment plan such as hospitalization or pharmacology (Classen & Yalom, 1995; Fox & Gilbert, 1994; Freeman & Fallot, 1997; Roesler &

McKenzie, 1994). Often the path of recovery requires attention to each disorder in proportion to the impact it has on the course of treatment. If substance abuse is apparent, it, rather than the sexual abuse, may become the focus of treatment. Conversely, when substance abuse is under control, greater attention can be placed on recovery issues concerning sexual abuse (Harris & Landis, 1997).

Prioritizing Symptoms

It is essential that the abusee receive a holistic treatment plan that addresses all areas of concern within the client's environment. For many individuals, when mental health agencies are initially contacted, numerous presenting problems may arise. Financial hardships, family disorder, home and shelter needs, and sometimes medical concerns are all part of the environmental stressors that can impede the healing process (Classen & Yalom, 1995; Wind-Weissman & Silvern, 1994). A priority of symptoms for treatment must be identified, although this may be difficult, particularly in cases of dual diagnosis including organically induced problems due to substance abuse, dissociative disorder, or psychosis (Allers, Benjack, White, & Rousey, 1993; Fox & Gilbert, 1994).

Additionally, without adequate personality development and sufficient ego-strength, a greater propensity for adult mental health issues exists (Harris & Landis, 1997; Heller, Swindel, & Dusenbury, 1986). High-risk behaviors that undermine adult well-being include not only the initial traumatic event, but also the secondary issues that arise because of that traumatic event. Both internalized and externalized behaviors further impede the individual's well-being, such as substance abuse, dissociation, avoidant behavioral traits, and aggressive acting out traits. Underlying all of these issues is the individual's ability to express and communicate a multitude of emotions that permeates the abused person's psyche (Finkelman, 1995a; Fox & Gilbert, 1994).

Adult Life Stressors

Adult coping skills also vary based on individual personality characteristics. Life stressors often mount as a person proceeds into adulthood. New demands are made upon the individual. Mid-life divorce, loss of loved ones, death of a spouse or child, loss of employment, financial hardships, and physical impairment all pose additive stress for the adult as the years pass. Victimization from domestic violence or abuse requires tremendous emotional effort to overcome singularly, but when placed in the context of multiple losses or life stressors, the impact is devastating for the individual (Classen & Yalom, 1995; Harris & Landis, 1997; Sternberg, Lamb, Greenbarm et. al., 1993).

As life stressors mount along with the long-term trauma from abuse, a cumulative effect of added stressors may propel an individual into serious emotional dysfunction. An individual who experiences mounting hardships that become unbearable and whose mental health deteriorates to the point of becoming nonfunctioning may realize dire consequences, including loss of finances, shelter, and loved ones. For example, such individuals may, at the lowest point under full stress, lose their jobs due to nonfunctioning, and then in turn lose their shelter and be forced to join the homeless population (Harris & Landis, 1997; Roesler & McKenzie, 1994). If this happens, the daily stressors of life on the street, such as concern for safety and fear of physical harm, add to the individual's already debilitating stress level from abuse. For many homeless individuals, health issues also mount, as medical attention is neglected and their overall quality of life declines significantly, and so the downward spiral continues.

Coping Mechanisms

To assess the magnitude of adult dysfunction following childhood abuse, Varia, Abidin, and Dass (1996) examined 173 individuals. They classified coping mechanisms displayed by each subject: *Minimizers* downplayed symptoms of abuse, while *Acknowledgers* accepted and admitted that abuse occurred. Both coping styles were related to poor adult adjustment. However, the group that minimized the occurrence was found to have more serious adjustment difficulties. Information as to length of time at admittance or stage of recovery was not available.

Shedler, Mayman, and Manis (1993) focused on defensive deniers who maintained a facade of good adjustment and mental health, but who were psychologically distressed and continued to deny their own needs. Perpetual denial of feelings was said to result in an inhibited ability to form intimate relationships in later life. However, it was noted that the perception of abuse, whether the abuse was nonharming or detrimental, did not follow a consistent pattern across groups, suggesting that personal characteristics, environmental influences, and other unique variables contribute to the magnitude and intensity of adverse reactions.

SEVERE PATHOLOGY

Briere (1989) noted that female survivors of CSA comprised 50–60% of female psychiatric patients who were surveyed at random as they applied for treatment. Complications for multiple mental health issues were found at disproportionate rates among CSA survivors as compared to nonabused females. Harris and Landis (1997) noted that pathological symptoms include self-hurting behaviors, suicide attempts, dissociation, PTSD, severe depression, multiple personality disorder (MPD), and a greater propensity for traumatic life events than are found in general populations without abuse experiences. Flashbacks, nightmares, distress, and abstract symbolization of elements of the trauma are commonly occurring reactions to CSA. Physiological responses also occur, including trauma-invoked agitated states of irritability, hypervigilance, anger, and abrupt startles or spontaneous reflect actions due to unexpected stimuli triggering memories of the abuse.

Psychogenic Paralysis

Psychogenic paralysis (Bisagni, 1995; Brenman, 1985) is a disorder that is similar to what Freud referred to as a conversion disorder. The *DSM-IV-TR* (APA, 2000) defined "somatoform disorders as disorders with a history of onset prior to age 30 that occur over a period of several years and result in significant impairment in social, occupational, or other important area of functioning" (p. 490). These disorders have no organic etiology yet range from minor impairments to severe loss of sensory or motor functioning, resulting in blindness, paralysis, convulsions, and similar deficits. Complaints of pain may be grossly exaggerated in light of physical findings (APA, 2000).

Conversion disorder (CD) is defined as "one or more symptoms affecting voluntary motor or sensory functioning that suggest a neurological or other general condition" (APA, 2000, p. 498). These illnesses cannot be attributed to a physiological disorder, but are often preceded by significant stressors. Differentiation is made from factitious disorders that are usually feigned for some external reward, such as to win a court case for injury, as CD operates solely at the subconscious level of processing. Extreme cases of conversion disorder have been documented; these are said to occur when emotional trauma is so significant that the individual splits off the pain onto the physical self. The following case scenario illustrates this occurrence.

> A woman who shall be called Jane to protect confidentiality revealed, at a local sexual assault center, her highly traumatic experience. She related a case history that included paralysis that she had acquired in her early 30s but for which doctors could find no physiological reason. When Jane was a child, Jane's father had violently threatened her, including pointing a shotgun at her in "jest." He was a wealthy, successful businessman who was viewed as a powerful individual—not to be crossed. Because of his infamous public reputation, he was able to easily hide or conceal his private behaviors behind a grand public persona. He sexually abused Jane for many years. She felt no one would believe her and she was helpless under his powerful reputation and socially affluent position. Eventually she married and was able to escape his victimization, but the psychological torment from the abuse became manifested in paralysis of her legs. She remained bedridden for some time. Only after years of therapy did the source of the paralysis surface. Once the issues surrounding her abuse were unlocked from her subconscious, therapeutic interventions helped her resolve emotional issues, and eventually she was able to walk again.

Thus, the far-reaching effects of sexual abuse can, and do, cause significant physiological impairment, either as primary injury from invasive treatment or as secondary symptom manifestation such as that which fuels psychogenic illnesses.

Dissociative Identity Disorders

Dissociative amnesia, denial, and expression may not be admitted to openly in the beginning of therapy, making treatment effectiveness more difficult (Harris & Landis, 1997). Dissociative identity disorder (DID) can result from exposure to highly traumatic events and may be a necessary defense mechanism for survival from an unavoidable event, particularly when physical removal from harm is not possible as when a small child is helplessly trapped and must endure abuse from a perpetrator. When dissociative or avoidant behaviors are evident, concrete tasks are most effective during treatment to keep the client focused in the present. Scott (1999) noted a pronounced need for structure when working with group members diagnosed with DID and recommended a series of group session guidelines and processes.

In terms of identifying predictors of propensity to develop DID, Gold, Hill, Swingle, and Elfant (1999) studied 118 women using the Dissociative Experiences Scale and the Dissociation Subscale of the Symptoms Checklist 90—Revised. The authors found that several characteristics of the abuse experience were significantly predictive of DID: age of onset, coercive and objective sexual acts, and concurrent multiple perpetrators. It was noted however, that wide variations exist among characteristics of DID and more research in this area is needed.

Neurological aspects of DID were investigated by Joseph (1999), who noted that ongoing stress caused by prolonged abuse can initiate physiological changes in the hippocampus region of the brain, an area attributed to long-term memory storage. Learning deficits and memory loss may occur as a result of this systemic change, although exact causal influences for these deficits may be attributed to other pathological illnesses such as mood disorders or psychosis that may occur concurrently with DID.

Other researchers have observed a propensity for some abusees to be at risk for abusing others, in part as a result of dissociative states related to their former abuse (Harris & Landis, 1997; Ryan & Lane, 1991). Others have noted that the mere process of pregnancy can trigger formerly suppressed memories of past abuse. Bonding issues between abused mothers and newly born infants can become an issue if attributes of distance or detachment from others are a prevalent part of the mother's personality. Quality of child care may suffer if dissociation occurs when the mother is in charge of her child.

Compound Stressors in Adulthood

During the adolescent years, ego identity should emerge (Erikson, 1969; Loevinger, 1990). If ego development is accomplished, as an adult an individual has a strong enough sense of self to set guidelines for future goals as well as the ability to set boundaries for acceptable treatment from others. However, Wolfe (1999) noted that a self-deprecatory attitude evolves among adults who were abused; thus, they are predispositioned to view life events in a more negative stance, including assigning self-blame, self-guilt, and self-shame when other events in life are not fulfilled.

If a trusted parent disbelieved when the individual disclosed the abuse during childhood, as an adult the individual may have buried his or her pain deeply into the subconscious. All the while, however, memories of the abuse and of the parent's rejection have festered beneath the surface, sabotaging future goals and aspirations. Adjustment difficulties may arise, ranging from mild interpersonal deficits or adjustment disorders that can be managed to severe mental illness that demands intensive intervention services (Classen & Yalom, 1995; Harris & Landis, 1997; Prendergast, 1993).

Residual Source of Stress Jumper (1995) conducted a meta-analysis of childhood sexual abuse and adult adjustment, and found that significant relationships existed between sexual abuse and symptomology, including depression and self-esteem issues, later in life. Fulfilling interpersonal relations usually arise from mutual respect between people who share common interests and personal values. But an adult who encountered abuse as a child has been deprived of a model of positive relations upon which to build future relationships. Rather than setting clear guidelines and behavioral expectations of others, such an adult may accept abusive treatment even under duress. Similarly, the learned helplessness that was felt during childhood becomes an intrinsic personality characteristic (Draucker, 1996; Mrazek & Mrazek, 1987). Due in part to that learned helplessness, such adults continue to accept undesirable treatment from others because they do not possess the communication skills to circumvent or defy such treatment and because their diminished self-worth is exacerbated (Kluft, 1990; Kovacs, 1985; Koverola, Pound, Heger, & Lytle, 1993; Stevens-Simon & McAnarney, 1993).

Feelings of helplessness, lack of control, and nonassertive action toward others render many abused adults, although not all, powerless in light of adverse advances from others. Consequently, rather than confronting the perpetrator, the child, and later the adult, learns to submit and accommodate to abusive situations. Although these defensive actions occur as a means of psychic survival to an event that cannot be thwarted, at least not in the abusee's perception, these passive behaviors only serve to heighten the victim's vulnerability and sense of powerlessness (Conte & Schuerman, 1987; Dolan, 1991).

As this pattern continues into adulthood, it becomes the only frame of reference that a victim has from which to form adult intimate relationships. Abusive dating relationships may arise, and thus a sequence of abuse perpetuates into adulthood. Multiple types of abuse, such as verbal, physical, and sexual, intensify the debilitating impact of abuse, as does the impact of multiple perpetrators (Classen & Yalom, 1995; Harris & Landis, 1997). The case of Janice serves to describe this phenomenon of being conditioned to accept abusive treatment.

> Janice was a 37-year-old Caucasian woman who was raised in a trailer camp by an alcoholic mother, abandoned by the father. She reported that her mother frequently brought home strange men, several of whom sexually abused Janice. She recounted numerous instances of being teased, molested, or sexually abused by her mother's companions while her mother was too drunk to intercede on her behalf. As Janice got older, she would wander about the trailer camp to avoid the strangers she came to resent so intensely. On two separate occasions at the age of 12, she was

raped by older adolescent boys, but was too frightened to report the rapes and did not believe anyone would care anyway.

Janice's school attendance and peer relations were poor from elementary school on. She often fought with peers, argued during playtimes, and even struck out at the teachers on occasion. She could recall no friends or classmates she considered to be close friends. Most children teased her because her clothes were used and worn and her hair was often knotted and unkempt. By the time she reached high school, excessive absences and poor grades left her with little motivation to complete school. Janice quit at 16; a series of minimum skill level jobs filled her time, and she lived in poverty. While working as a waitress, she met Stan who had also quit school and had a juvenile police record. Charmed by his attention and free spirit, Janice immediately paired up with him.

By age 17, she delivered a daughter, Rose. From the beginning, she and Stan lived together in a low-cost project apartment under much financial hardship. He frequently drank alcohol and displayed violent outbursts, shouted degrading insults at her, smashed various furniture, walls, and doors. When she complained, he threatened to harm her and Rose if she did not do whatever he told her to do. Janice complied by remaining passive in an attempt to appease him, although she often fell asleep in fear of what he would do next.

Janice reported that during one tirade, after Stan had drunk almost a fifth of liquor, he stormed through the apartment, room by room, in a rage, breaking and smashing every wall hanging, knick-knack, or vase in his path. At that time, she held her 3-year-old Rose in one hand and covered her stomach (she was eight and a half months' pregnant) with the other hand, hoping to protect the unborn child. When Stan finally stopped breaking and destroying the household belongings, probably from exhaustion, Janice and little Rose were cowering in a corner of a bedroom. She described how the five-room apartment was covered with broken ceramics at least three inches thick in all rooms.

Stan then turned to Janice, grabbed their daughter from her arms, and began shaking her harder and harder. Janice reached out to stop him and protect her daughter, but Stan pushed Janice hard onto the floor, at which time a pain shot through her abdomen. Stan continued to hit Rose with a newfound rage. Janice described how the girl's howling screams quickly withered down to barely audible whimpers, as her tiny body now lay limp on the floor beside her mother. Stan stormed from the apartment, leaving both females heaped on the floor.

Concerned neighbors called the police when they heard the screams. Emergency services were called for baby Rose, who later died in the emergency room. As the police questioned Janice about the identity and whereabouts of her boyfriend Stan, Janice became silent with a new fear. She would not reveal his true identity and even gave police a phony name. Stan was never found, as he remained on the run, fully realizing he was a fugitive from the police. Janice did not cooperate with police and would not provide detailed information about Stan's family members, his possible whereabouts, and so on.

Three weeks later, Janice gave birth to her second child, and she was arrested as an accomplice to the murder of her daughter and for interfering with the search for and arrest of Stan. Following a trial, during which community opinion in heated debates was split as to her role in her daughter's death, Janice was sentenced to eight years' imprisonment for interfering with an arrest and for the death of her daughter.

If Janice had not been abused by her mother's boyfriends as a young teen, would she have been so passive in her interactions with Stan? Would she have had the courage to assert herself? Or is courage the issue? What aspects of personality are required to maintain healthy boundaries with others?

Initial Disclosure Wind-Weissman and Silvern (1994) examined parenting styles and found that parental support at time of disclosure and early intervention for prevention of further abuse from the perpetrator were associated with less pathology in adulthood. Adults who perceived their parents as caring and empathetic when they disclosed the abuse had relatively high self-esteem and low depression. Distinguishing between nonsupportive and supportive parenting is often difficult because of the numerous moderating variables toward self-esteem, but crossover effects are possible between the two parenting styles when examining responses to disclosure of abuse. Nonsupportive parenting has been associated with depression and low self-esteem in adulthood. Anderson (1997) recommended finding individual strengths of children and adults who have been abused to help them work through the resulting emotional distress.

Substance Abuse One study found that substance abuse increases vulnerability toward sexual abuse by about 50%, as compared to non–substance abusing persons, a finding that is consistent with the sexual abuse history of women in other drug treatment centers (Ross, Kronson, Koensgen, Barkman, Clark, & Rockman, 1992). Trauma often (a) obscures accurate diagnosis, (b) increases risk factors for harm, (c) results in emergency room trauma, and (d) makes post-trauma risk difficult to assess adequately when substance abuse is prominent. The connection between sexual abuse and revictimization is readily acknowledged among researchers (Goodman & Bottoms, 1993; Walker, 2000). Bryer (1990) noted that the prevalence rates of 59–63% among psychiatric patients versus nonclinical women signifies the problem. Bryer stated that "physical and sexual abuse and victimization and its sequelae . . . may be one of our most profound health problems" (p. 259).

Males who experienced childhood sexual abuse have been found to partake in substance abuse more often than females (Hunter, 1990; Myers, 1989; Singer, 1989). Bisexual men are said to experience greater vulnerability to contracting HIV infections as well. Male outcome studies are sparse; thus, information about female outcomes from sexual abuse is more available than information about males. Of the case histories reviewed, however, many males who were abused report participation in high-risk activities, substance abuse, and sexually exploitative acts at alarming rates. Also, on tests of depression, self-esteem, trauma symptoms, sexual dysfunction, PTSD, and dissociation, male and female responses have indicated similar score patterns for pathology among abuse survivors as well as substance abuse problems.

Male Survivors Post-traumatic stress disorder was found to be significantly associated with male childhood sexual abuse in a study that controlled for non-sexual trauma effects (Roesler & McKenzie, 1994). High correlations were also found between sexual abuse and dissociation, whereas use of force was the most significant contributor to adult pathology. Problems with sexual dysfunction occurred equally as frequently among males and females who were sexually abused as children. Prevalence rates of CSA among homosexual males are higher than rates among heterosexual men, although such findings imply nothing more than a high association, not causality of alternative lifestyles (Bartholow, Doll, Joy, et al., 1994). It was inferred that sexual abuse among males may have more significant adverse effects in adulthood.

Male survivors of abuse are more apt than females to encounter or display violence in the community rather than internalizing symptomology. Five developmental dimensions of care concerns are addressed for males: (a) self-esteem and self-worth; (b) self-protection; (c) self-direction; (d) mutuality, trust, and interdependence; and (e) responsibility and accountability. Freeman and Fallot (1997) posit that self-esteem issues range from shame to projections of grandiosity, and treatment addresses issues of self-perception in projecting bravado feelings of invulnerability.

Direction toward life issues manifest in vague goals and aspirations or, in contrast, very controlled precepts of goals in life. Regarding *mutuality*, a term used by Freeman and Fallot (1997), aspects of personality ranged from dependency to independence, whereby the person overcompensates with extreme acts of independence. Women experience similar reactions; however, men may display different or more aggressive behaviors associated with this concept. Finally, problems arise concerning responsibility, defined as taking initiative versus taking a passive approach toward life.

Sexual Dysfunction Sexual dysfunction was investigated among 168 women and 28 men, and findings indicated an increase in the occurrence of sexual dysfunction among males who were sexually abused as children (Roesler & McKenzie, 1994). However, sexual dysfunction and the number of male subjects were low, so conclusions may warrant further research. Use of force was found to be more highly associated with subsequent post-traumatic stress disorder.

Sarwer and Durlak (1996) examined sexual dysfunction among 359 married adult women involved in sex therapy. The authors found that 75–94% of the women who had experienced invasive sexual abuse, such as intercourse, experienced sexual dysfunction as an adult. In this study, sexual dysfunction was defined as hypoactive sexual desire disorder (HSDD). Distinctions were made that another 37% of subjects who also had experienced invasive sexual abuse did not experience reduced sexual desires. Inconsistent findings were also indicated in earlier studies. Becker, Skinner, Abel, Axelrod, and Cichon (1984) noted that 50% of female survivors of abuse experience a lack of sexual desire in adulthood.

HIV Allers, Benjack, White, and Rousey (1993) examined the association of early childhood sexual abuse and subsequent chronic depression, sexual compulsivity, revictimization, and substance abuse as a prerequisite to high-risk sexual behaviors and HIV contraction. The authors inferred that unidentified and untreated survivors of sexual abuse might be at greater risk for HIV infection due to the possibility of early involvement in high-risk sexual activities. They suggested enhancements of cooperative HIV educational plans and outreach programs to engage substance abusers and survivors of childhood sexual abuse, and they recommended that HIV clinicians obtain in-depth interview data, including responses to items inquiring about child sexual abuse incidents, because of the high associative rates found among HIV-positive patients. Due to the potential to infect newborns, Edelman (1999) suggested that mothers-to-be should be tested for HIV as a routine measure.

Parenting Issues

Parenting future children is an area of concern for many survivors of abuse for several reasons. Many abusees who were abused by a biological parent fear identification with the abusing parent's attributes, while others express concern about inheriting a gene or other trait associated with the abuser. If the abusee experienced ritualistic abuse or severe and prolonged abuse at the hands of parent figures, positive role models for parenting were nonexistent.

Concerns for Parenting Skills Feelings of inadequacy for parenting their own children are frequently expressed by survivors of abuse. Some express concern about intense feelings of anger that may erupt and potentially be used against a child in a moment of displaced rage provoked by memories of past abuse. Self-doubt, misperceptions, and misinformation give rise to concern among survivors about their propensity to abuse others or that others may now abuse their children. Distrust and fear of others may become generalized to all persons in the vicinity of their children so that survivors suspect all adults of being abusers. If this fear becomes obsessive, it may result in unnecessary monopolization or overprotection of children, and intervention services may be needed to resolve unrealistic concerns.

Parenting After Ritual Abuse Ritualistic sexual abuse (RSA) poses more complex problems for survivors who were submitted to repeated heinous abuse experiences (Nash, Zivner, & Hulsey, 1993). Self-doubt about ability to parent subsequent offspring persists, as many survivors of family-based RSA readily acknowledge that poor role models for parenting skills create a sense of loss

(Kelly, 1989; Wind-Weissman & Silvern, 1994; World Health Organization, 2000b; Wyatt & Mickey, 1987). Not only does the child grow into adulthood without a secure sense of self and a loving, nurturing environment, but as adults, such survivors approach daily tasks of caring for their own children with major concerns (Burgess, Groth, McCausland, & Powers, 1984; Burgess, Harman, McCausland, & Powers, 1984; Wind-Weissman & Silvern, 1994).

Insecurities about proper parenting skills and the lack of an appropriate parental role model often undermine adult survivors' peace of mind about the quality of care they may provide for their own children. Intervention strategies for treatment should address these fears, which in many cases can be remedied by attending child development classes along with counseling sessions. Not only will parenting skills be enhanced, but successful approaches to parent-child problem solving can be a confidence-building act that enhances self-esteem of the abusee, who is now a loving parent aspiring to be the best parent possible.

SUMMARY

Adults who are victimized by abuse at an early age are robbed of more than innocence; they are also robbed of spirit, soul, and body. Thus, a travesty of nurturance needed in childhood permeates an entire lifetime as vital personality attributes become endangered, distorted, or totally immobilized. The ability to form and enforce protective boundaries is depleted (Hamacheck, 1988; Heller, Swindel, & Dusenbury, 1986; Hibbard & Hartman, 1992). Emotional needs that should have been fulfilled are depleted, if not outright nonexistent; and finally, spiritual beliefs and inspirational hope that should vitalize and sustain the human spirit for a lifetime are left riddled with doubts and circumspection. Essentially, then, the overall impact of abuse permeates all aspects of adult life. Emotional needs go unattended, unacknowledged, or perhaps are regressed or fixated to mirror those of a young child riddled with underdeveloped qualities (Russell, 1986; Shedler, Mayman, & Manis, 1993; Strean, 1988; Trepper, Niedner, Mika, & Barrett, 1996; Wyatt & Newcomb, 1990; Wyatt & Powell, 1988).

Treatment issues must not only address current states of crisis and emotional needs, but also focus on rehabilitative activities to enhance quality of life. Career options may be explored, social activities can be sought out, and personal goal setting should be structured. While these activities may appear to be superfluous in terms of recovery from CSA, each new step taken toward enhanced quality of life offers success experiences. In turn, these activities allow clients to take control of issues and, therefore, are empowering for survivors of CSA.

DISCUSSION QUESTIONS

1. Research a theoretical perspective related to CSA etiology, pathology, or recovery. Be prepared to discuss the strengths and weaknesses of the theory.

2. How can personal belief systems impact the recovery process? Elaborate.

3. Erikson cited productivity as a developmental task for adults. How does child abuse interfere with that task?

4. What additional life stressors impact adults that may hinder their ability to cope with past abuse? Discuss.

5. What factors may necessitate psychiatric hospitalization during adulthood for survivors of abuse?

6. What factors impact the prognosis for someone who experiences severe adjustment problems due to CSA?

7. Research an article on the topic of adult psychopathology associated with abuse, and be prepared to discuss it.

8. Dissociative identity disorder is strongly associated with survivors of abuse. Research several articles on DID. Discuss your findings and supply an annotated bibliography.

9. Explain comorbidity or dual diagnosis. What does it involve and why is it difficult to treat? Provide examples.

10. Research a topic of your choice related to sexual abuse and symptomology. Bring an article to class, and be prepared to discuss your findings.

12

Treatment Issues

LEARNING OBJECTIVES

Chapter 12 will address the following learning objectives:

1. An overview of adult therapy issues related to sexual abuse
2. A discussion of the use of goals in the therapy process
3. A discussion of benefits and issues to consider in using group therapy
4. An examination of special considerations in treating patients who have been sexually abused
5. An overview of adolescent services and issues related to sexual abuse
6. A discussion of issues to consider in child therapy and issues of sexual abuse

INTRODUCTION

This chapter will address several issues relevant to treatment services for adults, adolescents, and children. Adults who are dealing with former child abuse for the first time, often at middle age, are also vulnerable to other life stressors such as financial hardships or failed relationships. Since adult survivors of abuse may have acquired distorted perceptions that have become embedded in personality attributes as a consequence of the abuse, change during therapy may be more difficult for them than for younger children who are able to work through emotional issues immediately following the abuse. Also, more intense demands are made on adults, for example, adequate functioning is expected daily in work and home settings, which may render them too tired or overwhelmed to deal with therapy issues.

The discussion of problems during adolescence includes issues of youth at risk, who are more vulnerable to sexual abuse and most likely to require treatment. Special problems of youth that result in ethical and moral dilemmas for therapists, such as drug use and abortion, are also presented.

The examination of child service delivery focuses on a unique set of issues relevant to minors, such as conducting evaluations and the use of various treatment modalities. Procedures for interviewing children for reported sexual abuse incidents are reviewed, including legal ramifications for record keeping and the use of standardized procedures.

ADULT THERAPY ISSUES

If coping mechanisms are not sufficiently developed by adulthood, secondary emotional problems will persist throughout life. Propensity for substance abuse, revisited trauma, and adverse activities will increase as life stressors mount, more so for the survivor of abuse than for a nonabused adult. Greater potential to develop mental illness may be indicated based on the higher incident rate of child sexual abuse among residential patients in psychiatric institutions as compared to the general population (Bagley, Wood, & Young, 1995; Fox & Gilbert, 1994; Jumper, 1995; Wilsnack, Vogeltanz, Klassen, & Harris, 1997; Zlotnick, Ryan, Miller, & Keitner, 1995).

Lack of Early Services

Among older survivors, 40 years of age and over, childhood sexual abuse may be recalled for the first time, due to any number of reasons that abusees repress and suppress such events. Treatment for sexual abuse was not easily accessible or available when they were children in the 1950s and 1960s. In fact, child counseling services were seldom provided as regularly as they are today. School-related services blossomed only with the 1976 enactment of the Education for All Children Handicapped Act (Pub. L. No. 94-142). Therefore, children were compelled to remain silent throughout their youth and well into adulthood. Many individuals in their 50s, 60s, and 70s are still struggling through mixed emotions, ambivalent feelings toward parents, and unresolved feelings of diminished self-worth, all due to sexual abuse they experienced as children (Faller, 1987; Farmer, 1989; Gelinas, 1989; Harris & Landis, 1997; Macoby, 1992; Pope & Brown, 1996; Porter, 1986; Porter, Heitsch, & Miller, 1994; Russell, 1986; Sappington, Pharr, Tunstall, & Rickert, 1997; Sarwer & Durlak, 1996; Varia, Abidin, & Dass, 1996).

Delayed Recall

The emergence of repressed memories is not unusual in later years of life for several reasons, a fact that ignites much controversy among professionals (Ceci & Bruck, 1995; Courtois, 1999; Ney, 1995; Pope & Brown, 1996; Roesler & McKenzie, 1994). First, as stressful life events accumulate (e.g., loss of a child, divorce, financial hardships, illnesses, etc.), the weight of such burdens takes a toll on psychic energy. Resiliency is reduced, and memories or recalled images of negative events emerge. Ironically, while it can be an opportunity to process unresolved emotional turmoil, treatment can be a painful, distressful, and emotionally unraveling process. If the adult maintains a fast-paced, highly demanding lifestyle (as most do today), focus and concentration are required to maintain that pace. Once therapy begins, any emotional disruption or distress that jeopardizes daily functioning may be resented, resulting in premature termination of the therapy process.

Ramifications of the abuse, such as self-blame, guilt, high-risk activities, and any other harmful behavior, may have been diverted if interventions were obtained at an early age. Early intervention is imperative (Mrazek & Mrazek, 1987; Sgroi, 1982b; Summitt, 1983; Wyatt & Mickey, 1987; Wyatt & Newcomb, 1990). Maximum recovery for some abusees may simply entail developing sufficient coping mechanisms to allow the individual to overcome residual emotional effects when they erupt. Memories never completely go away and can be triggered by a seemingly innocuous event. Thus, the most an individual can hope for is to gain control over his or her emotional reactions to the memories, indicating that in the future, when memories occur, the emotional pain will no longer be intense enough to hinder daily functioning. That is not to say that the memories are not painful in and of themselves. The fact that one has been violated as a child by a family member, trusted clergy, friend, or relative (as occurs in over 90% of cases) remains deeply embedded in memory (Allers, Benjack, White, & Rousey, 1993; Berlinger & Wheeler, 1987; Shedler, Mayman, & Manis, 1993; Varia, Abidin, & Dass, 1996).

TREATMENT GOALS

Treatment often requires a multidisciplinary approach to case management. Mental health services, housing, medical care, judicial advice, and numerous other community services must be coordinated to address problems that can complicate the recovery process. Basic safety and survival needs must be addressed in cases of potential harm to the client via current exposure to the offender or other detrimental influence. Collaborative efforts with community services are frequently needed; therefore, therapists should always have a community resource directory available to them. Once the essentials are addressed and diagnostic issues are resolved, treatment plans, with a range of interventions, should be developed individually for each client.

A wide range of treatment modalities and therapeutic tasks can be introduced to the treatment milieu. As with any therapy process, rapport and trust building are essential prerequisites for effective outcomes for therapeutic relationships. Assurances of confidentiality and anonymity are needed, as most individuals revealing abuse for the first time are extremely anxious and distressed, perhaps filled with self-blame feelings of guilt. Such feelings are heightened if the offender was a parent figure, often fueling unresolved identity issues and feelings of abandonment (Davies, 1995; Lasch, 1977; Runtz & Schallow, 1997).

Educational Component

Informational and educational materials about sexual abuse should be provided to dispel distorted facts or perceptions about sexual abuse, self, or offender behavior. Coping skills can be developed to deal with residual emotional concerns but need to be learned and practiced (Runtz & Schallow, 1997). Creative outlets often help with expressing emotionally charged sentiments. Some individuals do well with expressive writing such as journaling and poetry or story writing. Others may find comfort in helping other abusees through support group assistance or mentor programs initiated in local community centers or health agencies.

Formal coping strategies may include relaxation techniques, withstanding flashbacks that trigger emotional upheavals, maintaining a balanced life with rest and exercise, and certainly finding a positive outlet for expressing or venting anger or any other highly charged emotional reaction, perhaps through physical activities such as walking or jogging. Finally, because childhood abuse—physical, emotional, or sexual—fosters a sense of helplessness, exercises that empower the abusee are essential. Each positive behavior and success experience contributes to the enhancement of the abusee's self-esteem.

Thus, once a formal evaluation has been completed, overall treatment goals should represent a collaborative effort of community and therapeutic services. Treatment plans may require active client participation both in and out of the office; for example, a client may need to attend community education programs on parenting or anger management, or see substance abuse specialists if warranted. At the same time, all procedures must be geared to the client's ability to process information.

Symptom Identification

Messman-Moore, Long, and Siegfried (2000) stressed the importance of identifying the source of repressed memories, often manifested in overt behavioral symptoms such as reduced intellectual functioning (e.g., language and cognition) in severely ill individuals. Loftus noted that the differentiation between physical, sexual, and verbal abuse is difficult, in part because of the existence of all three forms of abuse in one family. Symptom identification and overlap complicate treatment planning and the prognosis for recovery (Classen & Yalom, 1995; Freeman & Fallot, 1997; Gold, 1986; Hermin, 1981).

Rundell, Ursano, Holloway, and Silberman (1989) noted that depression often accompanies PTSD among sexual abuse survivors, but that symptoms associated with PTSD are notably more significant than is related by the *DSM-*

IV-TR categories. Schizophrenic and psychotic features may occur simultane-ously with PTSD, as has been identified with postcombat soldiers. The result of misdiagnosis is obviously failure to identify and treat the appropriate disor-der. Rundell recommended intensive case management with crisis interven-tion, if needed, along with client participation in support groups.

Torrey and Drake (1994) noted that serious illnesses such as schizophrenia or psychoses obviously need to be identified as early as possible, which may be difficult when the client is seen only on an outpatient basis. Symptoms may take time to surface if the client is not sensitive or aware of self-symptoms suf-ficiently to make a self-report. Immediate short-term planning may be neces-sary if the client is in crisis and requires hospitalization, medication, or another form of structured intervention. Long-term planning may evolve after initial diagnosis and interventions are completed, depending on the client's progres-sion through the crisis stage.

Circumspection should be used throughout the therapy process, as each individual may react differently to the same treatment technique. Often the therapeutic process elicits an onset of new memories and recalled images. Furthermore, dissociation may become reinstated as the recall of memories can become increasingly difficult for the individual to cope with. However, reac-tivated memories can be discussed and reinterpreted with the client so that less emotional pain is equated with each memory (Classen & Yalom, 1995; Harris & Landis, 1997).

Pacing the Healing Process

Effective therapeutic relationships should allow for pacing of sensitive or con-frontational issues that may provoke high amounts of stress for the client. As issues are revealed during the process, each verbalization of an act, a feeling, or a need is quite painful for someone who has kept these issues buried for many years. To acknowledge that abuse took place at all forces an abusee to come to terms with the fact that something is wrong and must be dealt with. Mixed feelings of relief, fear, and repulsion occur when past experiences surface and are exposed in an open forum.

The process of revealing details of the abuse to others can be very painful and emotionally traumatizing. Regardless of whether the abuse took place one week before or twenty years earlier, recall is painful. Particularly at the onset of therapy, an abusee may very well be in a crisis state and need to work at a slow and unique pace when recounting the abuse. Statements about the abuse may be made in sporadic accounts, or a flood of tearful statements may need to be verbalized immediately. Therapists must be in tune with the unique pro-cessing style of the abusee in the therapeutic setting. Setbacks may also occur, as the progression of therapy is rarely straightforward. There will be good days and bad days.

Different aspects of therapy present new challenges for an abusee. Attending the initial therapy session may be so anxiety-provoking that the abusee will take weeks or months to simply schedule an appointment.

Disclosure to family members can be frightening and immobilizing and provoke new emotional concerns in case of anticipated abandonment and rejection. Attending a group session versus individual therapy can pose new threats, as now more public acknowledgment of the abuse is required, although group therapy may also be beneficial as members become cohesive and supportive. Acknowledging abuse from either one or several perpetrators can be too threatening for the abusee to deal with, and revealing past acts in which the abusee was forced to participate is very painful, sensitive, and deeply embarrassing to the abusee.

Because each step toward healing is so stressful and anxiety-provoking, it is essential that pacing of events be dispersed throughout therapy. When great strides are not made during a specific period of time and the abusee is experiencing extensive anxiety and dismay with the healing process, relaxation and coping exercises may relieve excessive distress.

Hypnosis techniques are extremely effective to assist an abusee to relax through highly stressful episodes of recall (Ferrara, 1998a; Maldonado & Spiegel, 1995). Creative imagery can also be helpful in allowing the client to gain a sense of control over self-reactions to painful memories. But any therapist choosing to use these techniques should be well trained and licensed or certified in hypnosis in accordance with legislative requirements within the respective state of service. Therapists should also be well versed on the controversies concerning the use of hypnosis in treatment and recovered memories (Brown, Scheflin, Hammond, 1998; Courtois, 1999; Kluft, 1998).

Although some abusees may express a desire to speed up the healing process, caution should be used in pacing revisited memories, depending on the client's emotional state at the time. Distancing activities can reduce the stress experienced during periods of high tension, as they allow the abusee to cognitively process information without feeling the emotional pain. One technique is for the abusee to read about others in similar situations, for example, in a dramatic nonfictional account of abuse such as that found in *Conquered Legacy: A Healing Journey* (Ferrara, 1998a). Other techniques such as journaling, artwork, poetry writing, and other creative therapies serve to distance the abusee from the emotional pain provoked with each memory recall.

Distancing Techniques

Distancing the emotional pain by enhancing relaxation makes the recalled images less threatening; if necessary, the therapy process can be stopped and relaxation can be reintroduced. Maldonado and Spiegel have recommended several hypnosis techniques for assisting PTSD clients (Maldonado & Spiegel, 1995; Spiegel, 1989, 1990). Relaxation can be enhanced tremendously using the hypnosis process during therapy. Distancing, a technique that is enhanced during hypnosis, provides a sort of safety net in which the client can explore each memory without the emotional pain connected with that memory. State legislation and professional associations' materials concerning hypnosis should be consulted for applicable regulations in any given jurisdiction.

Therapeutic Goals

Classen and Yalom (1995) noted two main goals for therapy. First, memories should be brought into conscious awareness so the client can achieve congruency between past memories and current self-perceptions; and second, the client needs to accept that he or she must restructure cognitive thoughts into a more positive light. Six subgoals were also noted: (a) confronting traumatic memories, (b) condensing traumatic events to overcome them, (c) resolving states of confusion over painful memories, (d) resolving issues with unconditional acceptance, (e) concentrating focus to enhance daily functioning, and (f) achieving control and empowerment by gaining a sense of control over spontaneous recall via learned coping techniques. Each of these suggestions should be carried out within a pace that mirrors that of the client and in a way that addresses issues in an age-appropriate manner.

Contracting and Goal Setting

Harris and Landis (1997) offered the following suggestions to enhance the therapeutic process. First, contract with the client to delineate areas of responsibility and commitment to the counseling process and clarify terms. For example, acknowledge up front that "self-trashing" comments will not be allowed and that if a self-derogatory statement is made, the client will have to follow it with a more positively worded statement about self. Second, inform the client ahead of time about each new step in the counseling process to alleviate the client's fear and stress. Third, ask before dealing with issues of sexual abuse, as this affords the client a sense of control of sensitive issues that are often painful to speak about, and be sure any activities are agreed on before introducing them into the session. Fourth, remember that clients have a right to say *no* to services and that informed consent should always be established prior to introducing new materials, activities, or homework assignments.

The therapeutic relationship is imperative to recovery, particularly when a heightened sensitivity toward others exists. Therapists should watch their demeanor, facial expressions, and body language, as the client may interpret all discussions in a hypersensitive manner. Communication styles are important and should be both complementary to client needs and conducted in a professional manner. Therapists should perform self-assessments to determine whether they communicate in an authoritarian, democratic, or laissez-faire manner, as the therapist's communication style can mean different things to different clients. Privacy issues should be addressed as in any therapy session, but particularly in light of the sensitive nature of sexual abuse. If hospitalization is required, it should be addressed in a voluntary manner to enhance the client's sense of control over circumstances, provided that no life-threatening emergency is imminent.

Byers (1990) noted that the therapist-client relationship is the key to effective therapy. Additionally, if a client is not highly verbal, alternative methods of communication (e.g., expressive therapies such as art, poetry, dance, etc.) should be considered. If alternative techniques are applied, however, they should always fall within the acceptable guidelines of standards set by professional organizations such as the American Psychological Association (APA), National Association of School Psychologists (NASP), American Counseling Association (ACA), and American Professional Society on the Abuse of Children (APSAC).

GROUP THERAPY

Group counseling is highly recommended, as it serves many purposes over and above individual counseling. Torrey and Drake (1994) noted that groups serve to engage the client in alliances with others. Personal adaptive functioning can be improved since group members tend to encourage self-help skills as well as attitude toward recovery in general, all of which build opportunity for success experiences that, in turn, build confidence levels. Another benefit of the support group setting is that social relationship skills can be improved in a safe and secure setting; thus, environmental support can be enhanced with group members as they bond with one another (Classen & Yalom, 1995; Harris & Landis, 1997).

Improved Self-Worth

Members of support groups can develop a greater sense of worth as others listen, acknowledge, and validate their emotional reactions stemming from the abuse. Similarly, verbal feedback from group members can clarify distorted cognitions that may restrict healing or be a source of anxiety for abusees. Finally, new relationships can be formed that are based on trust in an area where there was none. A shared experience fosters bonding between participants, which in turn may serve as a bridge to expedite the healing process more efficiently than individual counseling. Also, as bonds occur among members, the thought that they were the only one this ever happened to is disbanded. Role-playing can be easily adapted whereby group members can work through dysfunctional family issues. More specific details on group membership and skill building are available through resources such as Classen and Yalom's (1995) material on goal setting (discussed earlier) and suggested hierarchy of treatment planning.

Structure and Rules

Abbott (1995) noted that group therapy offers great benefits to clients if appropriate criteria for inclusion is established, structured group rules are developed, and potential topics are gathered. Structural details, such as time and length of meetings, size and duration (short- or long-term) of the group, and the facilitator's role, are clarified up front. Procedural issues, such as whether a dynamic free-floating topic area will be implemented or static topics will be discussed, must be resolved. Methods for handling disruptive behaviors, illnesses, and crises that may arise should be stated up front. Any information regarding necessary violations of confidentiality (e.g., mandated reporting of abuse and "duty to warn" issues) should be announced at the initial group meeting.

Selection

Pregroup screening of clients is essential to ensure that the group setting is appropriate for them. When severe mental illness such as psychosis or schizophrenia is apparent in a client, participation in group sessions may not be appropriate. Similarly, during the crisis stage of therapy, group participation may be too direct or too frightening; a client may need to develop more emotional stability before a group format can be effective.

Gender issues need to be acknowledged in case a male or female participant has residual issues related to his or her offender's gender. While there are times when mixed groups work quite well, this issue should be explored during an intake interview for potential group members so they can make informed choices about whether they would prefer same-sex or mixed-sex group participation. Many women have difficulty sitting across from male counterparts, even those who have been victimized just as they were. Survivors of sexual assaults that were conducted with violence (e.g., rape) may have different responses from other participants.

On the other hand, for individuals at more advanced stages of recovery, opposite-sex group members can serve as a healing force in regard to gender-related issues of fear, anxiousness, and stress. Once a male counterpart is viewed as nonthreatening or even compatible, fearful reactions to males in general may be reduced (Classen & Yalom, 1995; Freeman & Fallot, 1997; Singer, 1989).

Cultural issues should be considered in view of whether language barriers, ethnic beliefs, or other cultural social norms may prohibit group participation (Zaslow & Hayes, 1986). Many cultures find the need for psychotherapy a disgrace; therefore, participating in support groups to discuss emotional or family concerns is in direct opposition to cultural values.

Meeting Plans

Preplanning should address meeting procedures, pacing, topics to be discussed, and any ground rules related to maintaining a respectful and safe setting for all members. Rules for dealing with missed meetings or rescheduled meetings should be apparent to all participants. Introduction procedures such as use of first names only, tone of the meeting (e.g., casual versus formal), structure of meeting content (e.g., fixed or flexible materials for discussion), and any other relevant issues should be presented at the initiation of the group. This allows group participants to feel safer, as they know what to expect. It would be especially difficult for participants to attend a meeting without proper preparation when such a highly personal matter as sexual abuse is the topic of discussion (Classen & Yalom, 1995; Faller, 1987).

Individual subsets of group members may emerge as participants become increasingly cohesive over time. Handling of personal information and retention of confidential data on each member must be properly guarded; therefore, privacy rules should be reiterated. If matters are discussed outside the group meeting room, clear guidelines should be established to protect all members; an example would be establishing a no-tolerance policy for gossip, adverse comments, and derogatory remarks that might harm another member.

Termination of Groups

Perhaps most crucial for effective treatment is a discussion of termination procedures. Once group cohesiveness is established, many individuals may not wish to stop the group sessions. Panic can set in, and any progress that has been made may be regressed under sufficient anxiety. Therefore, proper preparation of group members should occur prior to the actual termination of the group. Resources for follow-up should be provided. If subsequent groups are not available, follow-up care will need to be arranged. Regardless of the dispensation methods or the progress of the group members, participants usually feel a void when a group ends (Faller, 1987; Ferrara, 1998a; Fox & Gilbert, 1994).

SPECIAL CONSIDERATIONS

Although a set of core therapy procedures may be universally effective, due to the vast and diverse needs of individual clients, an effective therapist must be familiar with the wide range of treatment theories and modalities. However, prior to implementing new procedures, it is also imperative that a background research be conducted to ensure that the techniques have been validated within professional standards. Professional associations are an excellent resource, as are professional databases that publish peer-reviewed articles on new treatment methods. When initiating new techniques, particularly if legal proceedings are imminent, be sure that they meet the standards of the rules of evidence used in the respective jurisdiction.

Twelve-Step Programs

Fallot (1997) proposed a spiritual method of establishing well-being comprised of a twelve-step program based on object-relations theory, combined with spiritual influences. Self-acceptance is gained by a sense of comfort and soothing of the psyche, embedded in a spiritual approach to issues. Self-affirmation is attained within the twelve-step series of philosophies.

Frey (1995) recommended similar programs when treating clients diagnosed with dual disorders, defined as chemical dependency combined with sexual abuse recovery. Because of the potential for one disorder to interrupt progress in a second disorder, treatment is often nonlinear, in that setbacks can and do occur. Recurrence of flashbacks can trigger repeated substance abuse, and a person who has been substance-free can be propelled back into drug or alcohol use if flashbacks become more intense, frightening, or too stressful to deal with (Shedler, Mayman, & Mannis, 1993; Spaccarelli, 1994).

Multidisciplinary collaboration may be essential; for example, substance abuse programs or drug testing can be contracted for during the therapy process. Hinterkopf (1998) suggests spirituality interventions as well.

Male Survivors of Abuse

Freeman and Fallot (1995) recommended focus on several elements they considered essential to counseling programs working with adult male survivors of sexual abuse. Five dimensions were noted; these involve efforts in building: (a) self-esteem and self-worth, (b) self-protection skills, (c) self-direction (as in purposeful inner efforts), (d) mutuality in trusting relationships, and (e) responsibility or accountability in making efforts toward recovery. Although most of these elements are self-explanatory in relation to all aspects of CSA, the concept of mutuality is rather unique to Freeman and Fallot's treatment program. Mutuality is described here, within the emphasis on treating males, as the ability to work through trust issues with others, develop equally balanced interactions, and examine interdependence attributes that may impact the propensity for abuse among males.

The authors suggested a set of oppositional concepts that should be addressed in therapy. For instance, concepts of *self-protection* or vulnerability versus *invulnerability* are addressed with the optimal outcome of empowering males toward reduced aspects of vulnerability. Self-direction topics address issues of *impulsive behaviors* versus *overcontrol* or rigid control, in that males are helped to find a balanced adjustment between sporadic acts that may result in harmful activities (e.g., one-night stands) and restricted behaviors that diminish spontaneity. Treatment topics encourage healthy relationships. Responsibility issues address finding a balance between reacting with a *lack of responsibility (for self)* versus behaving in an *overresponsible* manner. Whether or not these issues are exclusive to males has not been determined, but in the therapeutic arena, these areas of concern were most apparent among males (Freeman & Fallot, 1995).

Dissociative Identity Disorder (DID)

Symptoms of dissociative identity disorder (DID) may not be revealed to the therapist during the early phases of treatment (Harris & Landis, 1997). DID often results in response to excessive exposure to stress and feelings of lack of control realized during abusive experiences. When dissociative or avoidant behaviors occur during therapy, the client must be brought back to reality, which is often done through the use of concrete tasks and structured therapy techniques. DID may not be responsive to pharmacological treatment and, therefore, needs to be closely monitored. If a client with DID is placed within a group setting, the group should be comprised of members with similar attributes; otherwise, the setting may be very intimidating for the member with DID. If a dissociative episode occurs, it should be addressed with the client, who should be provided with suggestions for coping with the aftermath of the episode in ways to minimize stress-provoking reactions.

Computer-Based Services

With the age of the Internet, self-help groups have found a new forum. Anyone can easily sign onto a chat room, listserv, or privately owned bulletin board at any time of the day or night, but the use of such groups needs to be carefully evaluated. Some serious pros and cons exist in regard to using cyberspace for working through residual issues from child sexual abuse. Granted, it is enticing to have contacts available whenever an emotionally upsetting event triggers memories or middle-of-the-night nightmares, but as consumers of special services, abusees should be apprised of the relevant issues involved in cyberspace and how it might render them vulnerable for further abuse.

Case histories presented earlier illustrated how easily pedophiles can mask their true identities and arrange to meet with someone who is vulnerable and approachable. When personal information is exchanged through the Internet, there is no guarantee that it will be kept confidential. The given identity of the party who is communicating with the abuser may or may not be authentic. In a period of grave concern, such as when an abusee is in crisis, the party receiving the Internet messages may not be cognizant of the seriousness of the sender's condition, and thus make erroneous recommendations that may harm the individual.

In layperson support groups on the Web, there is no way of knowing the qualifications of the members or whether they are sincere. Since 80% of communication is said to come from nonverbal language such as facial expressions and body language, much is lost in the exchange and words can easily be misinterpreted. In addition to the danger of meeting an insincere or harmful party, there is also the risk of an individual assuming a helping relationship with someone who may actually be in need of more critical services. For instance, if a group member makes suicidal comments, how can he or she be helped via the Internet, particularly if an actual attempt has been made?

Of course, there may also be benefits to be reaped in finding a friend to speak to at all hours of the night, and under anonymous conditions that require no face-to-face meeting. In support groups formed with other survivors of abuse, very positive and insightful information may be exchanged. When a main bulletin board system is used, the owner or originator of the bulletin board monitors all messages that are exchanged and uploads them once a day. Usually the initiator of the group process also sets the rules for the group, such as what types of messages can be uploaded and what criteria are used for new members to join. While a cohesive group membership can emerge even when members live thousands of miles apart, usually a subgroup forms based on mutual interests, needs, or goals. If cyberspace support groups are recommended, criteria for evaluating the authenticity of the group may be warranted (Dubrovsky, Diesler, & Sethna, 1991; Finn & Lavitt, 1994).

ADOLESCENT THERAPY SERVICES

Adolescents sometimes require more intense therapy services, in that community agencies often need to be collaborated with, due in part to the turbulent behaviors that surface during adolescence. As noted in previous chapters, issues seem to escalate during the adolescent years. When working with at-risk youth who have been sexually abused, many other social-psychological issues complicate the therapeutic process.

McWhirter et al. (1998) emphasize four problem areas that are unique to adolescent populations: dropping out of school, substance abuse, teenage pregnancy, and delinquency. Each problem area places an adolescent at greater risk for emotional difficulties, but the jeopardy of severe pathology exists when these areas are coupled with previous child sexual abuse. Pathological reactions may range across mood disorders, dissociative disorders, acting out behaviors, and greater risk for suicide attempts. If delinquent behaviors have resulted in pending judicial proceedings, further complexities arise due to anticipated revictimization in the judicial process.

Substance Abuse

Substance abuse issues become blurred during therapy in regard to when it is necessary to reveal an adolescent's active use or possession of drugs. If suicide risk is high and drug use is present, duty to warn may prevail (Schinke, Botvin & Orlandi, 1991); however, if no other risk of harmful behavior is imminent, breaking confidentiality to report drug use may sabotage the therapeutic relationship.

Treatment options vary across institutions, ranging from the use of twelve-step programs and cognitive therapies such as reality therapy to the use of community substance abuse programs such as NARC. The interdependent nature of drug use and former child sexual abuse is substantial, so the same premise applies as when dealing with adults: When a dual diagnosis exists, as the client makes progress in therapy with one facet of the problem (sexual abuse), the other facet (drug use) may become exacerbated due to the high degree of stress experienced during therapy. Thus, a highly regulated, structured treatment plan is extremely important when substance abuse problems coexist with sexual abuse issues during adolesence.

Abortion

Additional issues arise in the counseling arena in cases involving teen pregnancy (Musick, 1993). A disproportionate number of young women who become pregnant during adolescence report sexual abuse during childhood (Rainey, Stevens-Simon, & Kaplan, 1995). It was noted that 50–60% of adolescents who give birth have a history of sexual abuse, representing double the percentages found among nonabused adolescents. It was noted that chaotic home life does not prepare the youth for self-disciplined behaviors in areas of sexual activity, reduced self-esteem renders them more vulnerable, and sometimes victims are impregnated by their abusers (Browne & Finkelhor, 1986; Rainey, Steven-Simon, & Kaplan, 1995).

Although initial premises for counseling may be for recovery from sexual abuse, if pregnancy factors complicate recovery from sexual abuse, abortion issues may become a focus of counseling. Although the U.S. courts decided in *Roe v. Wade* (1973) in favor of confidentiality for abortion issues regardless of minor status, recent rulings may differ in state jurisdictions; therefore, the abortion laws in the jurisdiction of the offense should be reviewed.

Venereal Disease

Venereal disease among adolescents is continually increasing. Although many minimize the harm of diseases such as gonorrhea, chlamydia, and other curable diseases, the more lethal diseases such as AIDS and advanced syphilis cannot be overlooked. For victims infected by their perpetrators, an added factor leading toward emotional illness exists, as frequently depression, self-blame, and anger are involved. For youth who have not sought medical attention, the chances of developing complications are magnified. These issues must be addressed in the therapy process, since they complicate the prognosis for successful interventions as well as pose ethical dilemmas for the therapist.

An example of such an ethical dilemma is that posed by a client who reports that he or she is infected with a sexually transmitted disease (STD), yet is sexually active. If duty to warn the third party is favored (*Tarasoff v. Regents of the University of California,* 1976), confidentiality will be broken. On the other hand, if the disease is serious, as in the case of a positive HIV diagnosis, duty to warn may prevail due to the lethal implications of AIDS if an infected party is actively pursuing unsuspecting partners (DiClemente, 1992).

Youthful Offenders

If an adolescent survivor of childhood sexual abuse becomes a perpetrator (Ryan & Lane, 1991), the question of how to proceed in therapy presents dilemmas. Counselors may have a duty to warn, in which case confidentiality must be broken between the adolescent and therapist, and any potential for a therapeutic relationship will be nullified (Barbaree, Marshall, & Hudson, 1993). For example, if other minor children are at risk for abuse, duty to warn supersedes other aspects of maintaining confidentiality and a mandated report must be made. Youthful offenders also pose unique therapy issues in that resolving the therapy may require techniques to address their own childhood sexual abuse as well as to develop and use self-control to circumvent any urge to harm another. Boundary settings that were never realized by the adolescent may now need to be established both for the client and for any potential victims.

In terms of treatment issues, in addition to dealing with the immediate issues of abuse and possible incarceration for abusing another, youthful offenders need some alternative educational intervention in preparation for adulthood. Problems of poor self-esteem sorely compromise productive behaviors and the attainment of goals for academic achievement. Not only is self-esteem diminished due to the abuse they experienced as children, but the self-esteem of these youth is also diminished with the recognition that they are unwanted in the community because of their reputations as sex offenders. Unless this devastated self-esteem is somehow elevated, any attempts to educate or rehabilitate the youth may be thwarted. It is by all means in society's best interest to promote intervention services for this population, if for no other reason than to divert the possibility of them offending again with other child victims. Yet, across the United States, youthful offenders receive minimal intervention services, if any.

Suicidal Behavior

Suicide is noted to be the third leading cause of death for young people between the ages of 15 and 24, with white males accounting for 73% of all suicides in 1998 (Centers for Disease Control and Prevention, 2001). Dysfunctional families are often associated with suicidal behavior among youth (Fergusson & Lynskey, 1995), as well as with child sexual abuse (Finkelhor, 1986). Violence in the home is highly associated with suicidal adolescents; Blumenthall (1990) found that suicide attempters were three to six times more likely to have experienced sexual or physical abuse in the home.

Loss and separation of loved ones due to separation, divorce, or death (Marttunen, Aro, & Longquist, 1993) are also highly associated with suicidal behaviors. Given the multiple losses that occur when a child discloses abuse to others, particularly if the offender was a parent who is removed from the home at the time of disclosure, a sexually abused child may be in a heightened depressed or suicidal state. When the disclosure is met with disbelief, denial, and rejection of the adolescent, feelings of loss are magnified. Given these findings, it is imperative that an abusee be prepared emotionally for anticipated reactions from others so that traumatic reactions in light of potential rejection can be minimized. At the same time, evaluation of the lethality of any depressive states, verbal comments, and peculiar behaviors should be conducted and behavior carefully monitored. Contracting with students is helpful in gaining a commitment to return to therapy, or crisis interventions can be called if suicidal thoughts strengthen in intensity.

School Dropouts

Although schools are not deemed to be the gatekeepers for the psychological welfare of a child, emotional well-being is an essential prerequisite to productive academic learning. When behavioral disruptions occur or students act out in the face of authority, the "cure" for this misbehavior is to suspend the student from school. Once repeated suspensions result in failing grades and, eventually, repeating of grades due to extensive failures, the student perceives defeat and thus acts accordingly, playing to the label of "troublemaker," "bad character," and so on. Once the student falls behind in schoolwork, making it impossible to continue, depression usually sets in, with an ultimate motion to alienate self from the only structured activity that is accessible for help. Ironically, the very intervention that is proposed to prepare a child for life is exactly the source of irretrievable failing and eventual dropping out of school, thus rendering the student who drops out in jeopardy for failure throughout life.

For the sexually abused child who runs away from home, who is too depressed to complete school assignments, or is sexually assaulted to the point of withdrawal from interactions in school, no hope for intervention exists. The school setting is usually the only source of help for at-risk students, yet it fails them miserably; dropout rates have hit the 40% mark across the United States. Many of these dropouts have struggled to survive dysfunctional family settings. Impaired academic functioning is related to suicide (Lewinsohn, Rhode, & Seeley, 1994), and the added intervening variable of abuse heightens the suicide risk significantly, with obvious compound causes.

Sexual Abuse Prevention Programs

Although sexual abuse preventive programs are conducted in elementary schools under the "good touch–bad touch" approach, the concept of bringing sex education classes, Planned Parenthood, and other sexually related programs into the high school setting provokes highly explosive controversy within a community. Ironically, as teen pregnancies continue to rise and the incident rates for sexual abuse stand at 20–40% of all children (Durlak, 1994; Sarwar & Durlak, 1996), school settings remain shrouded in a veil of denial. For sexually abused students who may be at high risk for further sexually exploitive behaviors, the school setting may pose the only feasible intervention alternative.

Although school counselors exist in public schools, the ratio of counselors to students is totally ineffective, and antiquated laws insist that the counselor's role is reserved for academic achievement rather than to provide psychotherapy for students. Yet, if students are referred to community agencies for therapy services, it is likely that transportation problems or the parents' schedules will prohibit them from attaining those services. Essentially, the school setting is the most effective setting in which to address students' counseling needs. Furthermore, it is readily acknowledged that early intervention may circumvent serious disorders in adult life (Durlak, 1994). In addition, there is an academic question here: How does a student get academically charged if emotional crises occur daily, and yet they go on unattended?

CHILD THERAPY ISSUES

Mental health specialists working with sexually abused children should have mastered basic counseling techniques with this age group as well as an understanding of developmental norms for children. Familiarity with issues related to medical, educational, and psychological areas of concern are also relevant to providing effective therapy with children, so a community resource guide should be readily accessible to make family referrals if needed. While many experts have developed theoretical conceptions on how to proceed in therapy with children (Axline, 1947; Freud, 1928), recent play therapy techniques (Landreth, 1991; Webb, 1991) and cognitive behavioral play therapy (Knell, 1993) may be most effective in the counseling setting.

Unique needs of children demand special approaches to therapy, along with the ability to adapt services to meet any special needs that may arise. Building rapport is easy if the context is playful, but when essential issues surface, a more structured set of behaviors is expected from the professional. Documentation of specific behaviors, comments, and actions is essential to substantiate facts submitted on written reports, particularly if court proceedings are expected. Similarly, it is essential that a child's needs are met throughout the counseling session not only to build rapport but also to enforce a sense that the child is in a safe setting at all times.

Even though the focus is on a child as the client, parental involvement is essential if effective interventions are to be completed. Treatment plans may include assisting parents in developing behavior management techniques, and perhaps monitoring those techniques over time. The main point is, the child cannot be serviced in isolation; caretakers must be involved in a supportive role in accordance with the treatment strategies prescribed by the therapist.

Office Setting

An office setting can enhance the counseling relationship, particularly when working with children. Office furniture and accessories should be conducive to child activities, with an emphasis on furniture that is suitable to their own body structure. Lighting should be arranged to provide focus on the tasks at hand, rather than the office at large. Any excessive toys or distractions in the room should be put out of sight so they can be brought out one at a time. An array of toys that elicit behaviors ranging from nurturance to aggression should be available; for most purposes, an array of puppets can achieve this goal, yet offer soft materials to minimize the possibility of injury. For instance, a therapist might use bunnies or kittens to represent soft images and grizzly bears or snakes to represent more aggressive images. Some therapists believe that drums or overtly loud and aggressive activities may allow a child to vent anger, but these objects and activities may actually provoke no constructive behaviors from the child. Safety issues related to toys that induce rambunctious behaviors should also be considered, and by all means, a child should never be left alone in the office, even for a second. If any segment of the session provokes excessive stress in the child, every effort must be made to calm the child and make the interactions as pleasant as possible.

Initial Session with a Child

Establishing rapport with children is an essential component of effective therapy. Upon initial meetings, children may not understand why they are seeing a counselor (Thompson & Rudolph, 1999); they may be there simply at parental urging. If a child does not assent to counseling (orally agree with the process), little effectiveness will occur. Resistance to counseling can be identified by several behavioral characteristics, such as refusal to talk, avoidance of eye contact, late or missed appointments, negative body language, open opposition to all suggested activities, and other resistant behaviors.

Relationship building is constructed with children the same as with adults. A friendly, warm, genuine, and empathetic approach toward the child should be used. If resistance prevails, shared games or activities may provide a distancing format so that preoccupation with self-consciousness can be circumvented. As the child engages in play activities, clear boundaries of acceptable behaviors should be established, and reestablished whenever necessary. If unacceptable behaviors occur, the child should be confronted about them with firm but warm and fair guidelines. Children will continually test the limits of what they can do in the office, so consistency in setting acceptable boundaries is essential.

Record Maintenance

Permission records, releases, and any legal paperwork related to a child's file should be kept in a forensic multidepartmental folder so that paperwork can be easily accessed when needed. Legal guidelines concerning confidentiality, court testimonies, and the release of records to other professionals must be adhered to. For instance, in most states, if a release of information is received from another organization or therapist, any records with notes pertaining to family members other than those named in the subpoena must not be released. Most states also have a time limit for the purging of psychological records; if in doubt on how to proceed, contact your state licensing boards for a review of pertinent laws.

Conducting Interviews with Children

When interviews are conducted following disclosures or accusations of abuse from others, rigid guidelines must be followed. If the parent is not the perpetrator, then parental permission is required; prior to beginning sessions with any minors, a parental signature is a must. Releases for information exchanges between specialists such as pediatricians, day care workers, or teachers must be obtained and all relevant documents carefully reviewed. Forensic interviews or expert testimony work should be conducted within the legislative requirements of the respective district, and the rules of evidence must be adhered to (Faller, 1998; Kuehnle, 1996; Melton, Petrila, Poythress & Slobogin, 1997; Peole & Lamb, 1998; Sattler, 1998).

When conducting child interviews of a forensic nature, it is imperative to adhere to professional standards, legal guidelines (Melton, Petrila, Poythress, & Slobogin, 1997), and at the same time maintain rapport and integrity during the questioning process (Faller, 1998; Kuehnle, 1996). First, assuming the child is verbal, it is essential to evaluate the child's (a) memory skills, (b) cognitive processing, (c) social and motivational facets, (d) likelihood of accurately recalling past events, (e) ability to verbalize articulately, (f) unique needs and special techniques or approaches that could be used to meet them, and, above all, (g) the emotional impact on the child as a potential witness. Further assessment of the child's autobiographic recall abilities should be made, and cues for proper wording should be constructed in the child's own words. Effects of cognitive questioning should be evaluated in terms of the child's recall performance. For instance, the use of leading questions may sway the final response of the child. The interview should be conducted in a safe place, and the child should be comfortable in the setting. If the child gives any indication of experiencing high stress levels or retraumatization, alternative questioning arrangements should be made to avoid revictimization of the child.

Yuille, Hunter, Joffe, and Zaparniuk (1993) suggested using a stepping-stone interview approach, beginning with the most open, least leading question possible, and then proceeding to the next level of questioning if needed. Every opportunity should be given to allow the child to respond with a free narrative style before forming more structured questions. Kuehnle (1996) provides a series of questions to assess the veracity of a child's statements; she cites Myers's (1992) list of indicators of reliability concerning: spontaneity, appropriate terminology, consistency, non–age-appropriate sexual language, details about sexual abuse, fear of punishment upon disclosure, state of mind and emotion, child's correction of the interviewer, gestures that support claims of abuse, source of motivation to fabricate, if any exists, and quantity and quality of previous questioning.

Anatomically Correct Dolls

The use of anatomically correct dolls has been controversial since its first inception in court proceedings (*In re Amber B.,* 1987), wherein an appeals court reversed a trial court's decision based on the fact that the dolls represented a new scientific method of proof and that they were not accepted across the respective scientific communities. Subsequent courts, however, have admitted testimony based on behaviors emitted on dolls during evaluations. Any therapist contemplating the use of dolls to evaluate children should be aware of the controversies surrounding this technique. Anatomically correct dolls are widely used throughout the scientific community in child abuse evaluations, and professional groups such as the American Professional Society on the Abuse of Children (1995) have published guidelines on their use during forensic evaluations. Any therapy tool or article used during evaluation or treatment of CSA should meet the *Frye* test for admittance in court as being reasonably accepted among professional groups (see Melton et al., 1997).

SUMMARY

The World Health Organization (2001b) noted that child abuse is a major public health problem, with an estimated 40,000,000 children aged 0–14 around the world suffering from abuse and neglect. Yet, given all of the advancements in social science, this remains an area of complexity in terms of procedural, therapeutic, and resolution paradigms. While all admit that the long-term impact of abuse can play havoc on an abusee's life, and that the problem is recognized in a large percentage of the population, little emphasis is placed on preparing professionals to address these wide-ranging needs, other than occasional workshops or conferences that may, or may not, be attended by professionals.

This is an odd state of affairs considering that approximately 30–40% of the general population will experience some form of sexual abuse in their childhood based on combined estimates expressed by researchers (Briere & Conte, 1993, 59%; Finkelhor, Hotaling, Lewis, & Smith, 1990, 27% females and 16% of males surveyed; Herman & Schatzow, 1987, 63%), wherein over one-third noted they did not disclose the abuse as a child. Given the probability that these individuals may seek out intervention services as children or adults, it would be pragmatic to prepare mental health professionals to handle such complex mental health issues in the appropriate manner. University programs need to increase course offerings on the complex dynamics of abuse-related mental health issues; one or two hours of training in continuing education programs do not adequately prepare professionals to intervene in such cases. Similarly, licensing boards put little emphasis on abuse-specific course requirements across the United States.

Ironically, billions of dollars are spent on special needs programs to enhance academic achievement of the 12% of students who require individualized programs (National Center for Educational Statistics, 2001). Yet, minimal comparative federal dollars are spent to prepare professionals on abuse-specific dynamics to provide intervention at the elementary and secondary school level for the nearly 40% of students (as noted earlier) who will experience some form of abuse. Mind you, of course, that this intervention not only can minimize a child's distress but also, in the long run, indirectly enhances academic achievement for the many victimized children attempting to keep up with academic functioning. Is there something wrong with this picture? How wide must the gap become between service need in the mental health arena and program availability? Doesn't it stand to reason that if a child is not emotionally protected and nurtured, cognitive achievement pales in focus as compared to the greater need to survive harm?

DISCUSSION QUESTIONS

1. Design a treatment plan for an elementary school-aged child who has been sexually abused by a neighborhood friend who occasionally babysat for her. The child has not been interacting with others since the day her mother walked in on the abuse event, started screaming at the man, and hit him until he ran from the house. What therapeutic techniques could be used to encourage the child's communication? Be sure to include a treatment plan for working with the parents as well. Make your plans as detailed as possible, exploring all alternative strategies and involving as many community programs as warranted. Include a rationale statement for each suggestion.

2. You have just been assigned to a new high school in your school district. Within the first few weeks, two different students have come forward and asked for help with their "friend" who has been sexually abused. You are not sure about what to expect in the way of administrative support, but you feel you must do something to address the issue of abuse with the students. How will you proceed? Design a system for handling such cases, either an intervention program for dealing with students and parents, or a consultation program for providing the teachers with training and support. Be creative; use your imagination, and assume that the administration has now given you a free rein.

3. A 24-year-old male client has attended three weekly sessions in your private office. Each time he started to speak about important issues, but then stopped short and withdrew. As his therapist, you encourage him as much as possible, but you feel there is a need to build more trust before he will reveal personal information that is too painful for him to speak about. How would you approach the matter and, at the same time, assess his level of functioning? Design a treatment plan with an emphasis on trust-building exercises, include homework assignments that would allow him to get in touch with his feelings through less threatening techniques such as journaling or letter writing. Be creative, but adhere to professional standards. Be sure to cite resources and references included in your summary.

References

Abbott, B. R. (1995). Group therapy. In C. Classen & I. E. Yalom (Eds.), *Treating women molested in womanhood* (pp. 95–107). San Francisco: Jossey Bass.

Abel, G. G., Becker, J. V., Mittelman, M., Cunningham-Rather, J., Rouleau, J. L., & Murphy, W. D. (1987). Self-reported sex crimes of nonincarcerated pedophilias. *Journal of Interpersonal Violence, 2*(1), 3–25.

Abel, G. G., & Rouleau, J. L. (1990). The nature and extent of sexual assault. In W. Marshall, D. R. Laws, & H. E. Barbaree (Eds.), *Handbook of sexual assault: Issues, theories, and Treatment of the Offender* (Applied Clinical Psychology Series, pp. 115–142). New York: Plenum Press.

Achenbach, T. M. (1991a). *Integrative guide for the 1991 CBCL/4–18 YSR and TRF Profiles.* Burlington, VT: University of Vermont Department of Psychiatry.

Achenbach, T. M. (1991b). *Manual for the Child Behavior Checklist 4–18 and 1991 Profile.* Burlington, VT: University of Vermont Department of Psychiatry.

Achenbach, T. M. (1991c). *Manual for the Teacher's Report Form and 1991 Profile.* Burlington, VT: University of Vermont Department of Psychiatry.

Achenbach, T. M., & Edelbrock, C. S. (1983). *Manual for the child behavior checklist and child behavior profile.* Burlington, VT: University of Vermont, Psychiatry Department.

Adams-Tucker, C. (1982). Proximate effects of sexual abuse in childhood: A report on 28 children. *American Journal of Psychiatry, 139,* 1252–1256.

Addams, J. (1935). *My friend Julia Lathrop.* New York: MacMillan.

Ainsworth, M. D., Blehar, M. C., Walters, E., & Wall, S. (1978). *Patterns of attachment.* Hillsdale, NJ: Erlbaum.

Allen, J. G., Keller, M. W., & Console, D. A. (1999). *EMDR: A closer look.* New York: Guilford.

Allers, C. T., Benjack, K. J., White, J., & Rousey, J. T. (1993). HIV vulnerability and the adult survivor of childhood sexual abuse. *Child Abuse and Neglect, 17,* 291–298.

Almquist, F., Puura, K., Kumpulainen, K., Tuompo-Joansson, E., Henttonen, I., Huikko, E., Linna, S. L., Ikaheimo, K., Aronen, F., Katainen, S., Piha, J., Moilancen, I., Rasanen, E., & Tamminen, T. (1999). Psychiatric disorders in 8–9 year old children based on a diagnostic interview with the parents. *European Child and Adolescent Psychiatry, 8,* 17–28.

Amber B., *In re,* 191 Cal. App. 3d 682, 685 (1987).

American Academy of Pediatrics. (1999). Guidelines for the evaluation of sexual abuse of children: Subject review. *Pediatrics, 103,* 186–191.

American Academy of Pediatrics. (2000a). *Gender identity.* [On-line]. Available: www. medem.com/MedLb/article_detaillb.cfm

American Academy of Pediatrics. (2000b). *Growth and development: 5–6 years.* [On-line]. Available: www.medem.com/MedLb /article_detaillb.cfm

American Academy of Pediatrics. (2000c). *Pre-pubertal development.* [On-line]. Available: www.medem.com/MedLb/article _detaillb.cfm

American Academy of Pediatrics. (2000d). *Sexual abuse: What is child sexual abuse?* [On-line]. Available: www.medem.com/MedLb /article_detaillb.cfm

American Anthropological Association. (1971). *Principles of professional responsibility.* Washington, DC: Author.

American Association of Neurological Surgeons. (2000). *Shaken baby syndrome—A potentially deadly concern.* [On-line]. Available: wysiwyg://76/http://www .Medem.com/Med1.b/article_detaillb.cf.

American Educational Research Association, American Psychological Association, &

National Council on Measurement in Education. (1996). *Standards for educational and psychological tests.* Washington, DC: American Psychological Association.

American Medical Association. (2000). *Health-related quality of life and symptom profiles of female survivors of sexual abuse.* [On-line]. Available: www.medem.com/MedLb /article_detaillb.cfm

American Professional Society on the Abuse of Children (APSAC). (1995). *Practice guidelines—Use of anatomical dolls in child sexual abuse assessment.* Chicago: Author.

American Psychiatric Association (APA). (2000). *Diagnostic and statistical manual of mental disorders* (4th ed., Test Revision [DSM-IV-TR]). Washington, DC: Author.

American Psychiatric Association (APA). (1994). *Diagnostic and statistical manual of mental disorders* (4th ed. [DSM-IV]). Washington, DC: Author.

American Psychological Association. (1981). *Ethical principles of psychologists.* Washington, DC: Author.

American Psychological Association. (2001). *Professional, ethical, and legal issues concerning interpersonal violence, maltreatment, and related trauma.* A report of the ad hoc committee on legal and ethical issues in the treatment of interpersonal violence. Washington, DC: Author. [Available on-line: www.apa.org /pi/pii/professional.html]

American Sociological Association. (1981). *Code of ethics.* Washington, DC: Author.

Anastasia, A. (1988). *Psychological testing.* New York: MacMillan.

Anderson, C. (1995). Childhood sexually transmitted diseases: One consequence of sexual abuse. *Public Health Nursing, 12*(1), 42–46.

Anderson, K. M. (1997). Uncovering survival abilities in children who have been sexually abused. *Families in Society, 78*(6), 592–599.

Anderson, L., & Shafer, G. (1979). The character disordered family: A community treatment model for family sexual abuse. *American Journal of Orthopsychiatry, 49,* 436–445.

Anonymous. (1835). *Grandmother's advice to young mothers.* Unknown: Author. [On-line]. Available: University of Florida, Special Collections, Gainesville, FL, Call No. 23h10628.

Anthony, S. B., Harper, I. D., & Husead, E. (1902). *The history of women's suffrage.* Rochester, New York: Greenwood Press.

Argent, A. C., Lachman, P. I., Hanslo, D., & Bass, D. (1995). Sexually transmitted diseases in children and evidence of sexual abuse. *Child Abuse and Neglect, 19*(10), 1303–1310.

Armstrong, I. (1978). *Kiss daddy good night.* New York: Hawthorne.

Arroyo, W., & Eth, S. (1995). Assessment following violence-witnessing trauma. In E. Peled, P. G. Jaffe, & J. L. Edelson (Eds.), *Ending the cycle of violence: Community responses to children of battered women* (pp. 27-42). Thousand Oaks, CA: Sage.

Attwood, K. C. (2001). The efficacy of spiritual healing. *Annals of Internal Medicine, 134*(12), 1150–1151.

Atwood, R., & Howell, R. (1971). Pupillometric and personality test scores of female aggressing pedophiliacs and normals. *Psychonomic Science, 22,* 115–116.

Axline, V. (1947). *Play therapy: The inner dynamics of childhood.* Cambridge, MA: Houghton Mifflin.

Baby M., *In re,* 537 A.2d 1227, 1241.

Bachman, F. F., Green, S., & Wirtanen, I. D. (1970). *Youth in transition* (Vol. II). Ann Arbor, MI: University of Michigan, Institute for Social Research.

Bagley, C., Wood, M., & Young, L. (1994). Victim to abuser: Mental health and behavioral sequels of child sexual abuse in a community survey of young adult males. *Child Abuse and Neglect,* 683–697.

Baker, F. (1991). *Saving our kids from delinquency, drugs, and despair.* New York: Cornelia & Michael Bessie Books.

Bandura, A. (1960). *Relationship of family patterns to child behavior disorders. Progress report.* Stanford, CA: Stanford University Press (USPH Research Grant M-1734).

Bandura, A. (1986). *Social foundations of thought and action: A social cognitive theory.* Englewood Cliffs, NJ: Prentice-Hall.

Barbaree, H. E., Marshall, W. L., & Hudson, S. M. (Eds.). (1993). *The juvenile sex offender.* New York: Guilford.

Barker, L. H., & Howell, R. J. (1994). Munchausen Syndrome by Proxy in false allegations of child sexual abuse: Legal implications. *Bulletin American Academy Psychiatry Law, 22*(4), 499–510.

Bartholow, B. N., Doll, L. S., Joy, D., Douglas, J. M., Bolan, G., Harrison, J. S., Moss, P. M., & McKirnan, D. (1995). Emotional, behavioral, and HIV risks associated with sexual abuse among adult homosexual and bisexual men. *Child Abuse and Neglect, 18*(9), 747–761.

Bass, E., & Davis, L. (1994). *The courage to heal: A guide for women survivors of child sexual abuse.* New York: Harper & Row.

Basta, S. M., & Peterson, R. F. (1990). Perpetrator status and the personality characteristics of molested children. *Child Abuse & Neglect, 14*(4), 555–566.

Batchelor, E., Dean, R., Gridley, B., & Batchelor, B. (1990). Reports on child sexual abuse in the schools. *Psychology in the Schools, 27,* 131–138.

Bauer, D. (1976). An exploratory study of developmental changes in children's fears. *Journal of Child Psychology and Psychiatry, 17,* 69–74.

Beahrs, J. O., Cannell, J. J., & Gutheil, T. G. (1996). Delayed traumatic recall in adults: A synthesis with legal, clinical, and forensic recommendations. *Bulletin of American Acadamy Psychiatry Law, 24*(1), 45–55.

Beales, B. W. (1985). The child in seventeenth-century New England and the Chesapeake colonies. In J. M. Hawes & N. Ray Hiner (Eds.), *American childhood: A research guide and historical handbook* (pp. 15–57). Westport, CT: Greenwood Press.

Beausang, C. C., & Razor, A. G. (2000). Young western women's experiences of menarche and menstruation. *Health Care Women International, 21*(6), 517–528.

Beck, A. T. (1976). *Cognitive therapy and emotional disorders.* New York: International University Press.

Beck, A. T., & Emery, G. (1985). *Anxiety disorders and phobias: A cognitive perspective.* New York: Basic Books.

Beck, A. T., & Freeman, A. (1990). *Cognitive therapy of cognitive disorders.* New York: Guilford.

Becker, J. B., Skinner, L. J., Abel, G. G., Axelrod, R., Cichon, J. (1984). Sexual problems of sexual assault survivors. *Women and Health, 9*(4), 5–20.

Beitchman, J., Zucker, K., Hood, J., daCosta, G., & Akman, D. (1991). Short-term effects of child sexual abuse. *Child Abuse and Neglect, 15,* 537–556.

Bem, A. P. (1997). *Personality theories: Development, growth, and adversity* (2nd ed.). Boston: Allyn Bacon.

Bem, S. L. (1974). The measurement of psychological androgyny. *Journal of Consulting and Clinical Psychology, 42,* 155–162.

Bem, S. L. (1983). Gender schema theory and its implications for child development: Raising gender-aschematic children in a gender-schematic society. *Signs, 8,* 598–616.

Bem, S. L. (1985). Androgony and gender schema theory: A conceptual and empirical integration. In T. B. Sondregger (Ed.), *Psychology and gender.* Lincoln, NE: University of Nebraska Press.

Bender, L. (1957). What are the influential factors that predispose the youth of our society to delinquency and crime? In F. J. Cohen (Ed.), *Youth and crime.* New York: International Press.

Berenson, A. B. (1995). A longitudinal study of hymenal morphology in the first 3 years of life. *Pediatrics, 95*(4), 490–496.

Berger, A. M. (1980). The child abusing family: Methodological issues and parent-related characteristics of abusing families. *American Journal of Family Therapy, 8,*(3), 53–66.

Berger, K. (1994). *Psychopathologic correlates of incarcerated female infanticides, filicides, and homicides on the MMPI-2 basic scales: A preliminary study.* Unpublished doctoral dissertation. Springfield, MO: Forest Institute.

Berlin, F. S. (1982). A biomedical perspective. In J. Greer & I. Stuart (Eds.), *Sexual aggression: Vol. 1. Current perspectives on treatment, and Vol. 2. Victim Treatment.* New York: Van Nostrand Reinhold.

Berlin, F. S., & Meinecke, C. F. (1981). Treatment of sex offenders with antiadrogenic medication: Conceptualization, review of treatment modalities and preliminary findings. *American Journal of Psychiatry, 138,* 601–607.

Berlinger, L., & Wheeler, J. R. (1987). Treating the effects of sexual abuse on children. *Journal of Interpersonal Violence, 2,* 415–434.

Berson, N. L., Herman-Giddens, M. E., & Frothingham, T. E. (1993). Children's perceptions of genital examinations during sexual abuse evaluations. *Child Welfare, 72*(1), 41–49.

Bisagni, F. (1995). The stone womb: A case of psychogenic paralysis.In M. Sidoli & G. Bovensiepen. (Eds.), *Incest fantasies and self-destructive acts: Jungian and post-Jungian psychotherapy in adolescence* (pp. 187–204). New Brunswick, NJ: Transaction Publishers.

Black, C. A., & DeBlassie, R. R. (1993). Sexual abuse in male children and adolescents: Indicators, effects, and treatments. *Adolescence, 28*(109), 123–133.

Blinn, L. M., & Pike, G. (1989). Future time perspective: Adolescents' predictions of their interpersonal lives in the future. *Adolescence, XXIV*(94).

Blum, H. P. (1996). Seduction trauma: Representation, deferred actions, and pathogenic development. *Journal of American Psychoanalytic Association, 44*(4), 1147–1164.

Blumenthall, S. J. (1990). Youth suicide: Risk factors assessment, and treatment of adolescent and young adult suicidal patients. *Psychiatric Clinics of North America, 13*(3), 511–556.

Blumstein, A., & Cohen, J. (1992). The UCR-NCS relationship revisited: A reply to Menard. *Criminology, 30*(1), 115–125.

Boland, B., Conly, C. J., Warner, L., Sones, R., & Martin, W. (1986). *The prosecution of felony arrests.* Washington, DC: Bureau of Justice Statistics.

Bonner, B. L., Walker, C. E., & Berliner, L. (1999). Treatment manual for cognitive-behavioral group therapy for children with sexual behavior problems. Report published by the National Clearinghouse on Child Abuse and Neglect Information. [On-line]. Available: www.clib.com/nccanch

Bools, C., Neale, B., & Meadow, S. (1991). Co-morbidity associated with fabricated illness (Munchausen by proxy). *Archives Disabled Children, 67,* 77–79.

Borg, W. R., Gall, M. D., & Borg, P. (1997). *Educational research: An introduction* (6th ed.). New York: Longman.

Bowen, L. D. K. *A study of bastardy cases.* Chicago: Juvenile Protective Association.

Bowlby, J. (1969). *Maternal care and mental health.* New York: Schocken Books.

Bowlby, J. (1980). *Attachment and Loss: Vol. 3. Sadness and depression.* New York: Basic Books.

Bowlby, J. (1983). Attachment and loss: retrospect and prospect. *American Journal of Orthopsychiatry, 52,* 664–678.

Bradford, J. M. W., & Kaye, N. S. (1999, January). Pharmacological treatment of sexual offenders. *American Academy of Psychiatry and the Law Newsletter,* 16–17.

Bradwell v. Illinois, 83 U.S. [16 Wall.] 130, 141, 21 L.3d 442 (1873).

Bremner, R. (1970). *Children and youth in America.* Cambridge, MA: Harvard University Press.

Brenman, E. (1985). Hysteria. *International Journal of Psycho-Analysis, 66,* 423.

Breuer, J., & Freud, A. (1950). *Studies in hysteria.* Boston: Beacon Press. (Original work published 1895).

Briere, J. (1984). *The effects of childhood sexual abuse on later psychological functioning: Defining a post-sexual abuse syndrome.* Paper presented at the Third National Conference on Sexual Victimization of Children, Washington, DC.

Briere, J. (1989). *Therapy for adults molested as children.* New York: Springer.

Briere, J., & Conte, J. (1993). Self-reported amnesia for abuse in adults molested as children. *Journal of Traumatic Stress, 6*(1), 21–31.

Briere, J., Evans, D., Runtz, M., & Wall, T. (1988). Symptomatology in men who were molested as children: A comparison study. *American Journal of Orthopsychiatry, 58*(3), 457–461.

Briggs, L., & Joyce, P. R. (1997). What determines post-traumatic stress disorder symptomology for survivors of childhood sexual abuse? *Child Abuse and Neglect, 21*(6), 575–585.

Broadhurst, D. D. (1986). *Educators, schools, and child abuse.* Chicago: National Committee for Prevention of Child Abuse.

Brown, J. (1995). Treating sexual dysfunction in survivors of sexual abuse and assault. In M. Hunter (Ed.), *Adult survivors of sexual abuse: Treatment innovations.* Newbury Park, CA: Sage.

Brown, J., Cohen, P., Johnson, J. G., & Smailes, E. M. (1999). Childhood abuse and neglect: Specificity of effects on adolescent and young adult depression and suicidality. *Journal of the American Academy of Child and Adolescent Psychiatry, 38*(12), 1490–1496.

Brown, D., Scheflin, A. W., & Hammond, D. C. (1998). *Memory, trauma treatment, and the law.* New York: W. W. Norton.

Browne, A., & Finkelhor, D. (1986). A review of the research. *Psychological Bulletin, 99*(1), 66–77.

Bruch, C. (1988). And how are the children? The effects of ideology and mediation on child custody law and children's well-being in the United States. *International Journal of Law and the Family, 2*(106), 116–121.

Bryer, J. (1990). *The effects of child sex abuse on children, adolescents and adults.* East Lansing, MI: National Center for Educational Research Information Clearinghouse (ERIC Document Reproduction Service No. ED 327 773).

Bryk, F. (1974). *Circumcision in man and woman: Its history psychology and ethnology.* New York: AMS Press.

Burgess, A. W., Groth, A. N., & McCausland, M. P. (1981). Child sex initiation rings. *American Journal of Orthopsychiatry, 51,* 129–133.

Burgess, A. W., Hartman, C. R., McCausland, M. P., & Powers, P. (1984). Response patterns in children and adolescents exploited through sex rings and pornography. *American Journal of Psychiatry, 141,* 656–662.

Burton, L. (1968). *Vulnerable children.* London: Routledge & Kegan Paul.

Callie, R. M. (2000). *National crime victimization survey. Criminal victimization 1999, changes 1998–99 with trends 1993–99.* Washington, DC: U.S. Department of Justice, Office of Justice Programs.

Campell, J. C. (Ed.). (1995). *Assessing dangerousness: Violence by sexual offenders, batterers, and child abusers.* Thousand Oaks, CA: Sage.

Caplan, F. (Ed.). (1973). *The first twelve months of life: Your baby's growth month by month.* New York: Perigee Books.

Capuzzi, D. (1994). *Suicide prevention in the schools: Guidelines for middle and high school settings.* Alexandria, VA: American Counseling Association.

Carlo, G., Knight, G. P., Eisenberg, N., & Rotenberg, K. J. (1991). Cognitive processes and prosocial behaviors among children: The role of affective attributions and reconciliations. *Developmental Psychology, 27*(3), 456–461.

Casal, J. (1980). Ethical principles for conducting fieldwork. *American Anthropologist,* (82), 28–41.

Ceci, S. J., & Bruck, M. (1995). *Jeopardy in the courtroom.* Washington, DC: American Psychological Association.

Centers for Disease Control and Prevention. (2001). Suicide in the United States. [On-line]. Available: www.cdc.gov/ncipc/factsheets/suifacts.htm

Chaffin, M., Wherry, J. N., & Dykman, R. (1997). School age children's coping with sexual abuse: Abuse stresses and symptoms associated with four coping strategies. *Child Abuse and Neglect, 21*(2), 227–240.

Chaffin, M., Wherry, J. N., Newlin, C., Crutchfield, A., & Dykman, R. (1997). The Abuse Dimensions Inventory: Initial data on a research measure of abuse severity. *Journal of Interpersonal Violence, 12*(4), 569–589.

Chambers, D. (1984). Rethinking the substantive rule for custody disputes in divorce. *Michigan Law Review, 83,* 477.

Child Abuse Prevention and Enforcement Act (Pub. L. No. 106-77), enacted March 10, 2000.

Child Abuse Prevention and Treatment Act (CAPTA) (Pub. L. No. 93-247) (1974), as amended (Pub. L. No. 104-235) (1996).

Child Abuse Prevention, Adoption and Family Services Act of 1988 (Pub. L. No. 100–294).

Child Abuse Victims' Rights Act (Pub. L. No. 99–504) (1986).

Children's Defense Fund. (2000). *Children in the states—2000.* Washington, DC: Author. [Available on-line: www.childrensdefensefund.org/states_2000_introduction.htm]

Clark, D. M., & Fairburn, C. G. (1997). *Science and practice of cognitive behavior therapy.* New York: Oxford University Press.

Clark, J. (1998). How did she get these warts? Anogenital warts and sexual abuse. *Child Abuse Review,* 7(3), 206–211.

Classen, C., & Yalom, I. E. (Eds.). (1995). *Treating women molested in childhood.* San Francisco: Jossey-Bass.

Claussen, A. H., & Crittenden, P. M. (1991). Physical and psychological maltreatment: Relations among types of maltreatment. *Child Abuse and Neglect, 15* (5–18).

Cohen, J. A., & Mannarino, A. P. (1988). Psychological symptoms in sexually abused girls. *Child Abuse and Neglect, 12,* 571–577.

Cohn, S. I. (1970). Connecticut divorce mechanism. *American Journal of Legal History, 44,* 35–54.

Communications Decency Act (Pub. L. No. 104–104) (1996).

Connell, J. P. (1985). A new multi-dimensional measure of children' perceptions of control. *Child Development, 56,* 1018–1041.

Connors, J. M., Schubert, C., & Shapiro, R. (1998, April). Syphilis or abuse: Making the diagnosis and understanding the implication. *Pediatric Emergency Care, 14*(2), 139–142.

Conte, J., & Schuerman, J. R. (1987). Factors associated with an increased impact of child sexual abuse: Perceived stigma, betrayal, powerlessness, and self-blame. *Child Abuse and Neglect, 20,* 447–455.

Courtois, C. A. (1999). *Recollections of sexual abuse: Treatment principles and guidelines.* New York: W. W. Norton.

Crewdson, J. (1988). *By silence betrayed. Sexual abuse of children in America.* Boston: Little, Brown.

Darren, C. T. (2001). Students' perceptions of the motivational climate, achievement beliefs, and satisfaction in physical education. *Research Quarterly for Exercise and Sport, 72*(2), 165–176.

Darwin, C. (1958). *The origin of species.* Richey, MT: Menter Printing. (Original work published 1859).

Davies, M. L. (1995). *Childhood sexual abuse and the construction of identity: Healing Sylvia.* Bristol, PA: Taylor & Francis.

DeAngelis, T. (1995). New threat associated with child abuse. *The APA Moniter, 26*(4), 1–3.

De Bellis, M. D., & Putnam, F. W. (1994). The psychobiology of childhood maltreatment. *Child and Adolescent Psychiatric Clinics of North America, 3*(4), 663–678.

Deblinger, E., & Heflin, A. H. (1996). *Treating sexually abused children and their nonoffending parents: A cognitive behavioral approach* (Interpersonal Violence, Vol. 16). Thousand Oaks, CA: Sage.

Deblinger, E., Steer, R. A., & Lippmann, J. (1999). Two-year follow-up study of cognitive behavioral therapy for sexually abused children suffering post-traumatic stress symptoms. *Child Abuse and Neglect, 23*(12), 1371–1378.

DeFrancis, B. (1969). *Protecting the child victim of sex crimes committed by adults.* Denver, CO: American Humane Association.

DeJong, A. R., Hervada, A. R., & Emmett, G. A. (1983). Epidemiological variations in childhood sexual abuse. *Child Abuse and Neglect,* 7(2), 155–162.

DeMause, L. (1974). The evolution of childhood. In L. DeMause (Ed.), *The history of childhood.* New York: Psychistory Press. (Original work published 1919).

Demos, J. (1986). *Past, present, and personal: The family and life course in American history.* New York: Oxford University Press.

Densen-Gerber, J. (1983). Why is there so much hard-core pornography nowadays? Is it a threat to society or just a nuisance? *Medical Aspects of Human Sexuality, 17,* 1–10.

DePanfilis, D., & Salus, M. K. (1992). *Child protective services: A guide for caseworkers.* (User Manual Series). Washington, DC: National Center on Child Abuse and Neglect.

Derdeyn, A. P. (1976). Child custody contest in historical perspective. *The American Journal of Psychiatry, 133*(12), 369.

De Young, M. (1982). *The sexual victimization of children.* Jefferson, NC: McFarland.

Dibrezzo, R., & Hughes, H. M. (1988). The abused and neglected child: Strategies for the teacher. *Journal of Physical Education, Recreation & Dance, 59*(1), 22–25.

DiClemente, R. J. (Ed.) (1992). *Adolescents and AIDS: A generation in jeopardy.* Thousand Oaks, CA: Sage.

DiGeogio-Miller, J. (1998). Sibling incest: Treatment of the family and the offender. *Child Welfare, 77*(3), 335–346.

Dimock, P. T. (1988). Adult males sexually abused as children: Characteristics and implications for treatment. *Journal of Interpersonal Violence, 3*(2), 203–221.

Dobson, K. S., & Craig, K. D. E. (1996). *Advances in cognitive behavioral therapy.* Thousand Oaks, CA: Sage.

Dodge, K. A., & Somberg, D. R. (1987). Hostile attributional biases among aggressive boys are exacerbated under conditions of threats to self. *Child Development, 58,* 213–224.

Dolan, Y. M. (1991). *Resolving sexual abuse.* New York: W. W. Norton.

Doulin, T. (2000, June 28). Man pleads guilty, admits shocking girl with cattle prod. *The Columbus Dispatch,* p. 4d.

Draucker, C. B. (1996). Family-of-origin variables and adult female survivors of childhood sexual abuse: A review of the research. *Journal of Child Sexual Abuse, 5*(4), 35–63.

Droga, J. T. (1997). Realities lost and found: Trauma, dissociation, and somatic memories in a survivor of childhood sexual abuse. *Psychoanalytic Inquiry, 17*(2), 173–191.

Drugan, R. C. (1992). Coping with traumatic stress interferes with the memory of the event: A new conceptual mechanism for the protective effects of stress control. In L. M. Williams and V. L. Banyard (Eds.), *Trauma and memory.* (pp. 245–256). Thousand Oaks, CA: Sage.

Dubois, E. E. (1981). *Elizabeth Cady Stanton, Susan B. Anthony: Correspondence writings, speeches.* New York: Schoeken Books.

Dubowitz, H., Black, M., Harrington, D., & Verschoore, A. (1993). A follow-up study of behavior problems associated with child

sexual abuse. *Child Abuse and Neglect, 17,* 743–754.

Dubrovsky, V. J., Diesler, S., & Sethna, B. N. (1991). The equalization phenomenon: Status effects in computer-mediated and face to face groups. *Human Computer Interaction, 6,* 119–146.

Dugan, L., Nagin, D. S., & Rosenfeld, R. (1999). Explaining the decline in intimate homicide: The effects of changing domesticity, women's status, and domestic violence resources. *Homicide Studies, 3*(3), 17–21.

Dunn, L. M., & Markwardt, F. C. (1970). *Peabody Individual Achievement Test.* Circle Pines, MN: American Guidance Service.

Durlak, J. A. (1994). *School-based prevention programs for children and adolescents.* Thousand Oaks, CA.: Sage.

Dworkin, A. (1981). *Pornography, men possessing women.* New York: Putnam.

Earls, T. (1982). Application of DSM-III in an epidemiological study of preschool children. *American Journal of Psychiatry, 139,* 242–243.

Eberle, P., & Eberle, S. (1993). *The abuse of innocence: The McMartin preschool trial.* New York: Prometheus Books.

Eckenrode, J., Laird, M., & Doris, J. (1993). School performance and disciplinary problems among abused and neglected children. *Developmental Psychology, 29*(1), 53–62.

Eckenrode, J., Rowe, E., Laird, M., & Brathwaite, J. (1995). Mobility as a mediator of the effects of child maltreatment on academic performance. *Child Development, 66*(4), 1130–1142.

Edelman, M. W. (1999). *Mother-to-be must get tested for HIV.* [On-line]. Available: www.childrensdefense.org/cwatch041398.html

Edlebrock, C., Costello, A., Duncan, M., Conover, N., & Kala, R. (1986). Parent-child agreement on child psychiatric symptoms assessed via structured interview. *Journal of Child Psychology and Psychiatry, 27,* 181–190.

Education for All Children Handicapped Act (Pub. L. No. 94–142) (1976).

Edwall, G. E., Hoffmann, N. G., & Harrison, P. A. (1994). Psychological correlates of sexual abuse in adolescent girls in chemical dependency treatment. *Adolescence, 24*(94), 279–288.

Edwards, A., Halse, P., & Waterston, T. (1994). Does poor weight gain identify children in need? *Child Abuse Review, 3*(2), 107–119.

Elders, M. J. (1998). Adolescent pregnancy and sexual abuse. *Journal of American Medical Association, 280*(7), 648–649.

Elliot, D. S., & Ageton, S. S. (1978). Reconciling differences in estimates of delinquency. *American Sociological Review, 45,* 95–110.

Elliott, D. M., & Briere, J. (1995). Posttraumatic stress associated with delayed recall of sexual abuse: A general population study. *Journal of Traumatic Stress, 8*(4), 629–643.

Elliott, M. (1993). *Female sexual abuse of children.* New York: Guilford.

Englander, E. K. (1997). *Understanding violence.* Mahwah, NJ : Lawrence Erlbaum.

English Poor Act of 1601 (see DeMause, 1974).

Erickson, J. M. (1997). *The life cycle completed.* New York: W. W. Norton.

Erikson, E. H. (1950). *Childhood and society.* New York: W. W. Norton.

Erikson, E. H. (1959). *The problem of ego identity. Identity and the life cycle.* New York: W. W. Norton.

Erikson, E. H. (1962). *Young man Luther.* New York: W. W. Norton.

Erikson, E. H. (1968). *Identity, youth, and crisis.* New York: W. W. Norton.

Erikson, E. H. (1969). *Gandhi's truth.* New York: W. W. Norton.

Erikson, E. H. (1981). The problem of ego identity. In L. D. Steinberg (Ed.), *The life cycle: Reading in human development.* New York: Columbia Press.

Espenschade, A. (1960). Motor development. In W. R. Johnson (Ed.), *Science and medicine of exercise and sports.* New York: Harper.

Eth, S., & Pynoos, R. S. (1985). Developmental perspective on psychic trauma in childhood. In C. R. Figley (Ed.), *Trauma and its wakeup* (pp. 36–52). New York: Brunner/Mazel.

Ewing, C. P. (1997). *Fatal families: The dynamics of intrafamilial homicide.* Thousand Oaks, CA: Sage.

Faller, K. C. (1987). *Child sexual abuse: An interdisciplinary manual for diagnosis case management, and treatment.* New York: Columbia University Press.

Faller, K. C. (1998). *Interviewing for child sex abuse.* New York: Guilford.

Faller, K. C., & Everson, M. D. E. (1995). Child interviewing. *Child Maltreatment, 1*(2), 83–177.

Fallot, R. D. (1997). Spirituality in trauma recovery. In M. Harris & C. Landis, *Sexual abuse in the lives of women diagnosed with serious mental illness* (pp. 337–356). Washington, DC: Hardwood Academic Publishers.

Family Privacy Protection Act of 1995 (Pub. L. No. 104–01), 104th Congress, 1st Session, Introduced March 2, 1996.

Farmer, S. (1989). *Adult children of abusive parents.* Chicago: Contemporary Books.

Federal Bureau of Investigation. (1989). *Uniform crime reports.* Washington, DC: U.S. Government Printing Office.

Fenichel, D. (1945). *The psychoanalytic theory of neurosis.* New York: W. W. Norton.

Ferguson, L. R. (1978). The competence and freedom of children to make choices regarding participation in research: A statement. *Journal of Social Issues, 34,* 114-121.

Fergusson, D. M., & Lynskey, M. T. (1995). Childhood circumstances, adolescent adjustment, and suicide attempts in a New Zealand birth cohort. *Journal of American Child and Adolescent Psychiatry, 34*(5), 612–621.

Ferrara, F. F. (1996a). *Child sex abuse: Professional issues for school psychologists.* Paper presented at the XIX International School Psychology Colloquium, Eger, Hungary, Europe.

Ferrara, F. F. (1996b). Construct validation of the Child Sex Abuse Attitude Scale (CSAAS) through Confirmatory Factor Analysis. East Lansing, MI: National Center for Research on Teacher Learning. (ERIC Document Reproduction Service No. ED 399 289).

Ferrara, F. (1998a). *Conquered legacy: A healing journey.* Tampa, FL: CEC Publishers.

Ferrara, F. (1998b). *Conquered legacy: A healing experience.* [CD-ROM]. Tampa, FL: CEC Publishers.

Ferrara, F. F. (1999). Validation of the Child Sexual Abuse Attitude Scale through confirmatory factor analysis. *Journal of Structural Equation Modeling, 6*(1), 99–112.

Fineman, M. L. (1988). Dominant discourse, professional language, and legal change in child custody decision-making. *Harvard Law Review, 101*(4), 727–730.

Finkel, M. A. (1988). The medical evaluation of child sexual abuse. In D. H. Schetky & A. H. Gree (Eds.), *Child sexual abuse. A handbook for health care and legal professionals* (pp. 82–103). New York: Brunner-Mazel.

Finkelhor, D. (1979). *Sexually victimized children.* New York: Free Press.

Finkelhor, D. (1984). *Child sexual abuse: New theory and research.* New York: Free Press.

Finkelhor, D. (1986). *A sourcebook on child sexual abuse.* Beverly Hills, CA: Sage.

Finkelhor, D. (1994). The extent of child abuse is not exaggerated. In K. de Koster & K. L. Swishwer (Eds.), *Child abuse: Opposing viewpoints* (pp. 25–33). San Diego: Greenhaven Press.

Finkelhor, D., & Browne, A. (1985). The traumatic impact of child sexual abuse: A conceptualization. *American Journal of Orthopsychiatry, 555*(4), 530–541.

Finkelhor, D., & Browne, A. (1986). Initial and long-term effects: A conceptual framework. In D. Finkelhor (Ed.), *A sourcebook on child sexual abuse.* Beverly Hills, CA.: Sage.

Finkelhor, D., & Hotaling, G. (1983). *Report to the National Center for Child Abuse and*

Neglect. Huntsville, AL: National Center for Child Abuse and Neglect.

Finkelhor, D., Hotaling, G., Lewis, I. A., & Smith, C. (1990). Sexual abuse in a national survey of adult men and women: Prevalence, characteristics, and risk factors. *Child Abuse and Neglect, 14,* 19–28.

Finkelhor, D., Williams, L., & Burns, N. (1988). *Nursery crimes: Sexual abuse in daycare.* Newbury Park, CA: Sage.

Finkelman, B. J. D. (Ed.). (1995a). *Child abuse: A multidisciplinary survey.* New York: Garland.

Finkelman, B. J. D. (Ed.). (1995b). *Child abuse legislation.* New York: Garland.

Finn, J., & Lavitt, M. (1994). Computer-based self-help groups for sexual abuse survivors. *Social Work with Groups, 17*(1/2), 21–44.

Finn, J. D., Pannozzo, G. M., Voelkl, K. E. (1995). Disruptive and inattentive-withdrawn behavior and achievement among fourth graders. *The Elementary School Journal, 95*(5), 421–435.

Firestone, D. (2001). Woman is convicted of killing her fetus by smoking cocaine. *New York Times* (Late Edition, East Coast), A12.

Flavell, J. H. (1982). On cognitive development. *Child Development, 53,* 1–10.

Fleming, J., Mullen, P., & Bammer, G. (1997). A study of potential risk factors for sexual abuse in childhood. *Child Abuse and Neglect, 21*(1), 49–58.

Folberg, J. (Ed.). (1984). *Joint custody and shared parenting.* New York: Guilford.

Ford, C. S., & Beach, F. (1951). *Patterns of sexual behavior.* New York: Harper & Row.

Foreman, D., & Farsides, C. (1993). Ethical use of covert videotaping techniques in detecting Munchausen Syndrome by Proxy. *British Medical Journal, 307,* 611–613.

Foster, C. (1994). On the trial of a taboo: Female circumcision in the Islamic world. *Contemporary Review, 264,* 244.

Fox, G. L. (1999). Families in the media: Reflections on the public scrutiny of private behavior. *Journal of Marriage and the Family, 61*(4), 821–831.

Fox, K. M., & Gilbert, B. O. (1994). The interpersonal and psychological functioning of women who experienced childhood physical abuse, incest, and parental alcoholism. *Child Abuse and Neglect, 18*(10), 849–858.

Frankel, K. A., Boetsch, E. A., & Harmon, R. J. (2000). Elevated picture completion scores: A possible indicator of hypervigilance in maltreated preschoolers. *Child Abuse and Neglect, 24*(1), 63–70.

Fraser, B. G. (1976). Sexual child abuse: The legislation and the law in the United States. In P. B. Mrazek & C. H. Kempe (Eds.), *Sexually abused children and their families.* Oxford: Pergamon.

Fraser, M. W., Nelson, K. E., & Rivard, J. C. (1997). Effectiveness of family preservation services. *Social Work Research, 21*(3), 138–153.

Frazer, S. (1973). *Pandora.* London: Pandora Press.

Frazer, S. (1989). *My father's house: A memoir of incest and of healing.* London: Virago.

Frederick, C. J. (1986). Post traumatic stress disorder and child molestation. In A. W. Burgess & C. Hartman (Eds.), *Sexual exploitation of clients by mental health professionals* (pp. 131–144). New York: Praeger.

Freedman, W. (1965). *Societal behavior: New and unique rights of the person.* Springfield, MA: Charles C. Thomas.

Freedom of Information Act of 1966 (Pub. L. No. 89–554), 5 U.S. C. § 552 (1982).

Freeman, D. W., & Fallot, R. D. (1997). Trauma and trauma recovery for dually diagnosed male survivors. In M. Harris and C. C. Landis (Eds.), *Sexual abuse in lives of women diagnosed with serious mental illness* (pp. 357–371). Washington, DC: Hardwood Academic Publishers.

Freeman, M. A., Bosnahan, C. S., & Colburn, G. B. (1972). *Attorney's guide to family law act practice* (2nd ed.). Berkeley, CA: California Continuing Education of the Bar.

Freud, A. (1928). *Introduction to the technique of child analysis.* New York: Schocken Books.

Freud, A. (1949). *The infantile genital organization of the libido.* (Collected Papers, Vol. 2). London: Hograth. (Original work published 1923).

Freud, A. (1964). *The psychoanalytic treatment of children.* New York: Schocken Books.

Freud, A. (1967). *The ego and the mechanisms of defense* (Rev. ed.). (Series: The Writings of Anna Freud, Vol. 2). New York: International Universities Press. (Original work published 1947).

Freud, S. (1936a). Analysis of a phobia in a five-year-old boy. In Sigmund Freud (Ed.), *The sexual enlightenment of children.* New York: Collier. (Original work published 1909)

Freud, S. (1936b). *The problem of anxiety.* New York: W. W. Norton. (Original work published 1923)

Freud S. (1949). *An outline of psychoanalysis.* New York: W. W. Norton. (Original work published 1940)

Freud, S. (1953). *Three essays on the theory of sexuality.* London: Hograth. (Original work published 1925)

Freud, S. (1960). *The ego and the id,* ed. J. Strachey. New York: W. W. Norton. (Original work published 1923)

Freud, S. (1965). *New introductory lectures on psychoanalysis.* New York: W. W. Norton. (Original work published 1933)

Freud, S. (1977). *Introductory lectures on psycho-analysis.* New York: W. W. Norton. (Original work published 1920)

Frey, C. L. (1995). *Double jeopardy: Treating juvenile victims and perpetrator for the dual disorder of sexual abuse and substance abuse.* Dubuque, IA: Islewest.

Friedrich, W. N., Beilke, R. L., & Urquiza, A. J. (1988). Behavior problems in young sexually abused boys. *Journal of Interpersonal Violence, 3,* 21-28.

Friedrich, W. N., & Reams, R. A. (1987). The course of psychological symptoms in sexually abused young children. *Psychotherapy: Theory, research, and practice, 24,* 160–170.

Friedrich, W. N., Urquiza, A. J., & Beilke, R. L. (1986). Behavior problems in sexually abused young children. *Journal of Pediatric Psychology, 11,* 47–57.

Frisbie, L. V., & Dondis, E. L. (1965). *Recidivism among treated sex offenders.* (State of California Department of Mental Health Series). California Mental Health Research Monograph No. 5. Sacramento, CA.

Frodi, A., & Thompson, R. (1985, October). Infants' affective responses in the strange situation: Effects of prematurity and of quality of attachment. *Child Development, 56*(5), 1280–1290.

Frude, N. (1982). The sexual nature of sexual abuse. *Child Abuse and Neglect, 6,* 211–223.

Furth, H. G., & Wachs, H. (1975). *Thinking goes to school.* New York: Oxford University Press.

Gardner, R. A. (1992a). *The parental alienation syndrome.* Cresskill, NJ: Creative Therapeutics.

Gardner, R. A. (1992b). *True and false accusations of child sex abuse.* Cresskill, NJ: Creative Therapeutics.

Gary, F. A., & Campbell, D. W. (1998). The struggles of runaway youth: Violence and abuse. In J. C. Campbell (Ed.), *Empowering survivors of abuse: Health care for battered women and their children.* Thousand Oaks, CA: Sage.

Gebhard, P., Gagnon, J., Pomeroy, W., & Christenson, C. (1965). *Sex offenders: An analysis of types.* New York: Harper & Row.

Gelinas, D. (1989). The persisting negative effects of incest. *Psychiatry, XXIV*(94), 279–288.

Gelles, R. J. (1978). Methods for studying sensitive family topics. *American Journal of Orthopsychiatry, 48,* 408–424.

Giardino, A. P., Finkel, M. A., Giardino, E. R., Seidl, T., & Ludwig, S. (1992). *A practical guide to the evaluation of sexual abuse in the prepubertal child.* Newbury Park, CA: Sage.

Gilchrist, I. (Ed.). (1974). *Medical experimentation on prisoners must stop: Documents generated during the course of a struggle.* College Park, MD: Urban Information Interpreters.

Gillespie, D. (1987). Ethical issues in research. In *Encyclopedia of social work* (18th ed). Washington, DC: National Association of Social Workers.

Gillespie, W. H. (1964). The psycho-analytic theory of sexual deviation with special reference to fetishism. In I. Rosen (Ed.), *The psychology and treatment of sexual deviation.* New York: Oxford University Press.

Gilligan, C. (1977). In a different voice: Women's conceptions of self and morality. *Harvard Educational Review, 47,* 481–517.

Gilligan, C. (1982). *In a different voice: Psychological theory and women's development.* Cambridge, MA: Harvard University Press.

Gilligan, C., Taylor, J. M., Tolman, D., Sullivan, A., Pleasants, P., & Dorney, J. (1992). *The relational world of adolescent girls considered to be at risk.* Cambridge, MA: Harvard University Press.

Gold, E. R. (1986). Long-term effects of sexual victimization in childhood: An attributional approach. *Journal of Consulting and Clinical Psychology, 54,* 471–475.

Gold, M., & Reimer, D. J. (1972). *Changing patterns of delinquent behavior among American 13- to 17- year-olds. Report No. 1 of the National Survey of Youth.* Ann Arbor, MI: University of Michigan, Institute for Social Research.

Gold, S., Milan, L., Mayall, A., & Johnson, A. (1994). A cross-validation study of the Trauma Symptom Checklist: The role of mediating variables. *Journal of Interpersonal Violence, 9,* 12–26.

Gold, S. N., Hill, E. L., Swingle, J. M., & Elfant, A. S. (1999). Relationship between childhood sexual abuse characteristics and dissociation among women in therapy. *Journal of Family Violence, 14*(2), 157–171.

Goldstein, J., Freud, A., & Solnit, A. (1973). *Beyond the best interest of the child.* New York: Free Press.

Goldstein, J., Freud, A., Solnit, A., & Goldstein, S. (1986). *In the best interest of the child.* New York: Free Press.

Goldstein, M. J., Kant, H. S., & Hartman. J. J. (1973). *Pornography and sexual deviance.* Los Angeles: University of California Press.

Gomes-Schwartz, B., Horowitz, J. M., & Cardarelli, A. P. (1990). *Child sexual abuse: The initial effects.* Newbury Park, CA.: Sage.

Goodman, G. S., & Bottoms, B. L. (Eds.). (1993). *Child victims, child witnesses: Understanding and improving testimony.* New York: Guilford.

Goodman, G. S., & Clarke-Stewart, A. (1991). Suggestibility in children's testimony: Implications for child sexual abuse investigations. In J. L. Doris (Ed.), *The suggestibility of children's recollections.* (pp. 92–105). Washington, DC: American Psychological Association.

Goodman, G. S., Qin, J., Bottoms, B. L., & Shaver, P. R. (1994). Characteristics and sources of allegations of ritualistic child abuse. Paper presented at California University, Davis, 1994. [Available on-line: www.calib.com/nccanch]

Gordon, L. (1988). *Heroes of their own lives: The politics and history of family violence.* New York: Penguin Books.

Gough, D., Kelly, L., & Scott, S. (1993). The current literature about organized abuse of children. *Child Abuse Review, 2*(4), 282–287.

Gove, W. R., Hughes, M., & Geerken, M. (1985). Are uniform crime reports a valid indicator of the Index crimes? An affirmative answer with minor qualifications. *Criminology, 23,* 451–501.

Graber, J. A., & Brooks, Gunn, J. (1996). Transitions and turning points: Navigating the passage from childhood through adolescence. *Developmental Psychology, 32*(4), 768–784.

Green, A. H., Coupe, P., Fernandez, R., & Stevens, B. (1995). Incest revisited: Delayed post-traumatic stress disorder in mothers following the sexual abuse of their children. *Child Abuse and Neglect, 19*(10), 1275–1282.

Green, L., & Parkin, W. (1999). *Sexuality, sexual abuse and children's homes: Oppression or protection? Violence Against Children Study Group, Huddersfield (England). Children, child abuse and child protection: Placing children centrally.* New York: Wiley.

Greene, M. A. (1902). *The woman's manual of law.* New York: Silver Burdett.

Greenfield, L. A. (1996). *Child victimizer's: Violent offenders and their victims.* Washington, DC: U.S. Department of Justice.

Greenwald E., & Leitenberg, H. (1989). Long-term effects of sexual experiences with siblings and nonsiblings during childhood. *Archives of Sexual Behavior, 18,* 389–399.

Gromb, S., & Lazarini, H. J. (1998, June 8). An unusual case of sexual assault on an infant: An intraperitoneal candle in a 20-month-old girl. *Forensic Science International, 94*(1–2), 153–158.

Grossberg, M. (1985). *Governing the hearth: Law and family in nineteenth-century America.* Chapel Hill, NC: University of North Carolina Press.

Grosz, C. A., Kempe, R. S., & Kelly, M. (2000). Extrafamilial sexual abuse: Treatment for child victims and their families. *Child Abuse and Neglect, 24*(1), 9–23.

Grotevant, H. D. (1993). The integrative nature of identity: Bringing the soloists to sing in the choir. In J. Kroeger (Ed.), *Discussions on ego identity.* Hillsdale, NJ: Erlbaum.

Groth, A. N. (1979). *Men who rape. The psychology of the offender.* New York: Plenum Press.

Groth, A. N., Hobson, W., & Gary, R. (1982). Child molester: Clinical observations. In J. Conte & D. Shore (Eds.), *Social work and child sexual abuse.* New York: Hayworth Press.

Groth, A. N., & Oliveri, F. J. (1989). Understanding sexual offense behavior and differentiating among sexual abusers: Basic conceptual issues. In S. M. Sgroi (Ed.), *Vulnerable populations. Sexual abuse treatment for children, adult survivors, offenders, and persons with mental retardation.* Lexington, MA: Lexington Books.

Halpern, D. F. (1986). *Sex differences in cognitive abilities.* Hillsdale, NJ: Erlbaum.

Hamacheck, D. E. (1988). Evaluating self-concept and ego development within Erikson's psychosocial framework: A formulation. *Journal of Counseling and Development, 66*(8), 354–360.

Hamberg, K. (2000). Gender in the brain. A critical scrutiny of the biological gender differences. (Review. Swedish.) *Lakartidningen, 97*(45), 5130–5132. [Available on-line: PUBMED, www.ncbi.nlm.nih.gov/htbinpost/Wntrez/query, ID No. 11116893]

Hammer, E. F., & Glueck, B. C., Jr. (1957). Psychodynamic patterns in sex offense: A four-factor theory. *Psychiatric Quarterly, 3,* 325–345.

Hammill, P. V. V. (1977). *NCHS growth curves for children vital health statistics: Series 11, data from the national health survey, No. 165.* (CHEW No. 78–1650). Washington, DC: U.S. Government Printing Office.

Handley, J. M., Maw, R. D., Bingham, E. A., Horner, T., Bharucha, H., Swann, A., Lawther, H., & Dinsmore, W. W. (1993). Anogenital warts in children. *Clinical and Experimental Dermatology, 18*(3), 241–247.

Haney, C., Banks, W. C., & Zimbardo, P. (1973). Interpersonal dynamics in a simulated prison. *International Journal of Criminology and Penology, 1,* 69–73.

Hanson, R. F., Resnick, H. S., Saunders, B. E., Kilpatrick, D. G., & Best, C. (1999). Factors related to the reporting of childhood rape. *Child Abuse and Neglect, 23*(6), 559–569.

Hanson, R. K., & Bussiere, M. T. (1998). Predicting relapse: A meta-analysis of sexual offender recidivism studies. *Journal of Consulting and Clinical Psychology, 66,* 348–362.

Harris, M., & Landis, C. L. (1997). *Sexual abuse in the lives of women diagnosed with serious mental illness.* Washington, DC: Hardwood Academic Publishers.

Hart, C. H., DeWolf, M., Wozniack, P., & Burts, D. C. (1992). Maternal and paternal disciplinary styles: Relationship with preschoolers' playground behavioral orientation and peer status. *Child Development, 63,* 879–892.

Harter, S. (1985). *Manual for the Self-Perception Profile for Children.* Denver, CO.: University of Denver.

Harter, S. (1998). The effects of child abuse on the self-system. *Journal of Aggression, Maltreatment and Trauma, 2*(1), 147–169.

Harter, S., & Pike, R. (1984). The Pictorial Scale of Perceived Competence and Social Acceptance for Young Children. *Child Development, 55,* 1969–1982.

Hazzard, A., Celano, M., Gould, J., Lawry, S., & Webb, C. (1995). Predicting symptomology and self-blame among child sex abuse victims. *Child Abuse and Neglect, 19*(6), 707–714.

Helfer, M. E., Kempe, R. S., & Krugman, R. D. (1997). *The battered child* (5th ed.). Chicago: University of Chicago Press.

Heller, K., Swindel, R., & Dusenbury, L. (1986). Component social support processes: Comments and integration. *Journal of Consulting and Clinical Psychology, 54,* 466–470.

Herman, J. L. (1992). *Trauma and recovery.* New York: Basic Books.

Herman, J., & Schatzow, E. (1987). Recovery and verification of memories of childhood sexual trauma. *Psychoanalytic Psychology, 4,* 1–4.

Hermin, J. (1981). *Father-daughter incest.* Cambridge, MA: Harvard University Press.

Hewitt, S. K. (1991). Therapeutic management of preschool cases of alleged but unsubstantiated sexual abuse. *Child Welfare, 70*(1), 59–67.

Hewitt, S. K. (1999). *Assessing allegations of sexual abuse in preschool children: Understanding small voices.* Thousand Oaks, CA: Sage.

Hewitt, S. K., & Friedrich, W. N. (1991). Effects of probable sexual abuse on preschool children. In M. Q. Patton (Ed.), *Family sexual abuse. Frontline research and evaluation.* Newbury Park, CA: Sage.

Hewlett v. George, 68 Miss. 703, 9 So. 885, 1891 LEXIS 22 (1891).

Hibbard, R. A., & Hartman, G. (1990). Genitalia in human figure drawings: Childrearing practices and child sexual abuse. *Journal of Pediatrics, 116,* 822–828.

Hibbard, R. A., & Hartman, G. (1992). Behavioral problems in alleged sexual abuse victims. *Child Abuse and Neglect, 16,* 755–762.

Hilbert, R. A. (1980). Covert participant observation. *Urban Life, 9,* 51–78.

Hill, S., & Goodwin, J. R. (1993). Demonic possession as a consequence of childhood trauma. *Journal of Psychotherapy, 20*(4), 399–402.

Hindelang, M. J., Hirschi, T., & Weiss, J. G. (1979). Correlates of delinquency: The illusion of discrepancy between self-report and official measures. *American Sociological Review, 44,* 995–1014.

Hinterkopf, E. (1998). *Integrating spirituality in counseling.* Alexandria, VA. American Counseling Association.

Hollin, C. R., & Howells, K. E. (1991). *Clinical approaches to sex offenders and their victims.* (Wiley Series in Clinical Approaches to Criminal Behaviors). New York: Wiley.

Horn, L., Chen, X., & Adelman, C. (1998). *Toward resiliency: At-risk students who make it to college project officer.* Washington, DC: U.S. Department of Education, Office of Educational Research and Improvement.

Horowitz, I. (Ed.). (1967). *The rise and fall of Project Camelot: Studies in the relationship between social science and practical politics.* Cambridge, MA: MIT Press.

Howells, K. (1979). Some meanings of children for pedophiles. In M. Cook & G. Wilson (Eds.), *Love and attraction.* Oxford, UK: Cropwood.

Howells, K. (1981). Adult sex interest in children. In H. M. Cook & K. Howells (Eds.), *Adult sexual interest in children* (pp. 55–94). New York: Academic Press.

Huber, J. H. (1996). Accused of sexual abuse: A potential dilemma for physical education teachers. *Journal of Physical Education, Recreation & Dance, 67*(9), 6–8.

Huizinga, D., & Elliott, D. S. (1984). *Self-reported measures of delinquency and crime: Methodological issues and comparative findings.* Boulder, CO: Behavioral Research Institute.

Humphreys, L. (1975). *Tearoom trade: Impersonal sex in public places with retrospect on ethical issues.* Chicago: Aldine.

Hunter, M. (1990). *Abused boys: The neglected victims of sexual abuse.* New York: Ballantine Books.

Ingram, D. L., Everett, V. D., Flick, L. A., Russell, T. A., & White-Sims, S. T. (1997). Vaginal gonococcal cultures in sexual abuse evaluations: Evaluation of selective criteria for preteenaged girls. *Pediatrics, 99*(6), 8.

Isabella, R. A. (1993). Origins of attachment: Maternal interactive behavior across the first year. *Child Development, 64*(2), 605–621.

Itzin, C. (1997). Pornography and the organization of intra- and extrafamilial child sexual abuse: A conceptual model. In F. Kantor & J. Jasinki (Eds.), *Out of darkness: Contemporary perspectives on family violence.* Thousand Oaks, CA: Sage.

Jenny, C. (1996). Medical issues in sexual abuse. In J. Briere, L. Berliner, J. A. Bulkey, C. Jenny, & T. Reid (Eds.), *The APSAC handbook on child maltreatment* (pp. 195–205). Thousand Oaks, CA.: Sage.

Jenny, C., Taylor, R. J., & Cooper, M. (1996). *Diagnostic imaging and child abuse: Technologies, practices and guidelines.* Washington, DC: Medical Technology and Practice Patterns Institute.

Jernegan, M. W. (1960). *Laboring and dependent classes in colonial America.* New York: Ungar.

Johnson, C. F. (2000, December). Death from child abuse and neglect. *The Lancelot Perspectives, 356,* 14.

Johnson, T. C. (1995). *Treatment exercises for child abuse victims and children with sexual behavior problems.* South Pasadena, CA: Toni Cavanaugh Johnson.

Jones, D. P. H. (1991). Ritualism and child sexual abuse. *Child Abuse and Neglect, 15* 163–170.

Jones, J. (1989). Race, sex, and self-evident truths: The status of slave women during the era of the American Revolution. In A. Hoffman & P. J. Albert (Eds.), *Women in the age of the American Revolution.* Charlottesville, VA: United States Historical Society by University Press of America.

Jones v. Stanko, 118 Ohio St. 147, 160 N.E. 456, 1928 Ohio LEXIS 367, 6 Ohio L. Abs. 79 (1928).

Joseph, R. (1999). The neurology of traumatic dissociative amnesia: Commentary and literature review. *Child Abuse and Neglect, 23*(8), 715–727.

Jumper, S. A. (1995). A meta-analysis of the relationship of child sexual abuse to adult psychological adjustment. *Child Abuse and Neglect, 19*(6), 715–728.

Kadish, H. A., Schunk, J. E., & Britton, H. (1998). Pediatric male rectal and genital trauma: Accidental and nonaccidental injuries. *Pediatric Emergency Care, 14*(2), 95–98.

Kaduson, H., & Schaefer, C. (1997). *101 favorite play therapy techniques.* Northvale, NJ: Jason Aronson.

Kaff, R. (1982). The tender years doctrine: A defense. *California Law Review, 76,* 335.

Kahan, B., & Crofts, Y. (1991). Munchausen Syndrome by Proxy: Clinical review and legal issues. *Issues in Child Abuse Accusations,*(1), 32–34.

Kahn, J. A., Goodman, E., Kaplowitz, R. A., Slap, G. B., & Emans, S. J. (2000). Validity of adolescent and young adult self-report of Papanicolaou smear results. *Obstetrics and Gynecology, 96*(4), 625–631.

Kandel, D. B., & Rosenbaum, E. (1990). Early onset of adolescent sexual behavior and drug involvement. *Journal of Marriage & the Family, 52*(3), 783–799.

Kandel, E. (1991). *Interrelationship of family and extrafamilial violence in a representative sample.* Durham, NH: University of New Hampshire, Family Research Laboratory.

Kaplan, P. S. (1991). *A child's odyssey* (2nd ed.). New York: West.

Karpman, B. (1954). *The sexual offender and his offenses.* New York: Julian Press.

Kelly, S. J. (1989). Stress responses of children to sexual abuse and ritualistic abuse in day care centers. *Journal of Interpersonal Violence, 4,* 502–513.

Kempe, R., & Kempe, C. (1984). *The common secret: Sexual abuse of children and adolescents.* New York: Free Press.

Kempe, C. H., Silverman, F. N., Steele, B. F., Droegemueller, W., & Silver, H. K. (1962). The battered child syndrome. *Journal of the American Medical Association, 181* 17–24.

Kempf, K. L. (1990). *Measurement issues in criminology.* New York: Springer-Verlag.

Kenney, J. W., Reinholtz, C., & Angelini, P. J. (1998). Sexual abuse, sex before age 16, and high-risk behaviors of young females with sexually transmitted diseases. *Journal of Obstetric, Gynecologic, and Neonatal Nursing (JOGNN), 27*(1), 54–63.

Kent, J. (1840). *Commentaries on American law* (4th ed.). New York: Author. [Available microfilm. Ann Arbor, MI: Xerox University Microfilms, 1974. 35mm. (American Culture Series, reel 590.5–591.1).]

Kernberg, O. E. (2000). The influence of the gender of patient and analyst in the psychoanalytic relationship. *Journal of American Psychoanalytical Association, 48*(3), 859–863. [Available on-line: PUBMED, www.ncbi.nlm.nih.gov/htbinpost/Wntrez/query, ID No. 11059400]

Kihlstrom, J. F. (1998). Exhumed memory. In S. J. Lynn & K. M. McConkey (Eds.), *Truth in memory* (pp. 3–31). New York: Guilford.

Kilpatrick, A. C. (1992). *Long-range effects of child and adolescent sexual experiences: Myth, mores, and menaces.* Hillsdale, NJ: Erlbaum.

Kimmel, A. J. (1988). *Ethics and values in applied social research.* Beverly Hills, CA: Sage.

Kitamura, T., Sakamoto, S., Yasumiya, R., Sumiyama, T., & Fujihara, S. (2000). Child abuse, other early experiences and depression: II. Single episode and recurrent/chronic subtypes of depression and their link to early experiences. *Archives of Women's Mental Health, 3*(2), 53–58.

Kleinman, P. E. (1990). Diagnostic imaging in infant abuse. [Review.] *American Journal of Roentgenology, 155*(4), 703–712. [Available: MEDLINE ID 90379101]

Kluft, R. P. (1990). *Incest-related syndromes of adult psychopathology.* Washington, DC: American Psychiatric Press.

Kluft, R. P. (1998). Reflections on the traumatic memories of dissociative identity disorder patients. In S. J. Lynn & K. M. McConkey (Eds.), *Truth in memory* (pp. 304-322). New York: Guilford.

Knell, S. M. (1993). *Cognitive-behavioral play therapy.* Northvale, NJ: Jason Aronson.

Knopp, F. H. (1982). *Remedial intervention in adolescent sex offenses: Nine program descriptions.* New York: Safer Society Press.

Kohlberg, L. (1969). Stage and sequence: The cognitive developmental approach to socialization. In D. A. Goslin (Ed.), *Handbook of socialization theory and research.* Chicago: Rand McNally.

Kohlberg, L. (1981). *Essays on moral development.* San Francisco: Harper & Row.

Kohlberg, L. (1985). Resolving moral conflicts with the just community. In C. Harding (Ed.), *Moral dilemmas.* Chicago: Precedent.

Kohlberg, L., & Kramer, R. (1969). Continuities and discontinuities in childhood and adult moral development. *Human Development, 12,* 93–120.

Kohlberg, L., & Power, C. (1981). Moral development, religious thinking, and the question of a seventh stage. In L. Kohlberg (Ed.), *The psychology of moral development: Essays on moral development* (Vol. 1). San Francisco: Harper & Row.

Kohlberg, L., Snarey, J., & Reimer, J. (1984). Cultural universality of moral judgment stages: A longitudinal study in Israel. In L. Kohlberg (Ed.), *The psychology of moral development: Essays on moral development* (Vol. 1). San Francisco: Harper & Row.

Kohm, L. M., & Lawrence, M. E. (1997). Sex at six: The victimization of innocence and other concerns over children's rights. *Brandeis Journal of Family Law, 36*(3), 361–406.

Koocher G. P., & Spiegel, K. (1990). *Children, ethics, and the law.* Lincoln, NE: University of Nebraska Press.

Korte, K. L., Horton, C. B., & Graybill, D. (1998). Child sexual abuse and bulimic behaviors: An exploratory investigation of the frequency and nature of a relationship. *Journal of Child Sexual Abuse, 7*(1), 53–64.

Kotelchuck, D. (Ed.). (1976). *Prognosis negative: Crisis in the health care system.* New York: Vintage.

Kovacs, M. (1985). The Children's Depression Inventory: A self-rated depression scale for school-aged youngsters. *Psychopharmacology Bulletin, 21* 995–998.

Koverola, C. (1992). Psychological effects of child sexual abuse. In A. Heger & J. Emans (Eds.), *Evaluation of the sexually abused child.* Boston: Oxford University Press.

Koverola, C., Pound, J., Heger, A., & Lytle, C. (1993). Relationship of child sexual abuse to depression. *Child Abuse and Neglect, 17,* 393–400.

Kraditor, A. S. (1970). *Up from the pedestal.* Chicago: Chicago University Press.

Kramer, S., & Akhtar, S. E. (1991). *The trauma of transgression. Psychotherapy of incest victims.* Northvale, NJ: Jason Aronson.

Kroeger, J. (1993). On the nature of structural transition in the identity formation process. In J. Kroeger (Ed.), *Discussions on ego identity.* Hillsdale, NJ: Erlbaum.

Kuczmarski, R. J., Ogden, C. L., Grummer-Strawn, L. M., Flegal, K. M., Guo, S. S., Weit, R., Mei, Z., Curtin, L. R., Roche, A. F., & Johnson, C. L. (2000). CDC growth charts: United States. *Advanced Data, 8*(314), 1–27.

Kuehnle, K. (1996). *Assessing allegations of child sexual abuse.* Sarasota, FL: Professional Resource Press.

Lahey, B., Applegate, B., Barkley, R., Garfinkel, B., McBurnett, K., Kerdy, K. L., Greenfill, L., Hynd, G., Frick, P., Newcornm, J., Biederman, J., Ollendick, T., Hart, E., Perez, D., Waldman, L., & Shaffer, D. (1994). DSM-IV field trials for oppositional defiant disorder and conduct disorder in children and adolescents. *American Journal of Psychiatry, 151*(8), 1163–1171.

Lam, J. N., & Grossman, F. K. (1997). Resiliency and adult adaptation in women with and without self-reported histories of childhood sexual abuse. *Journal of Traumatic Stress, 10*(2), 175–196.

Lamson, A. (1995). Evaluating child sex abuse allegations. *Family Violence and Sexual Assault Bulletin, 11*(3–4), 24–27.

Landreth, G. L. (1991). *Play therapy: The art of the relationship.* Bristol, PA: Accelerated Development.

Langevin, R. (1983). *Sexual strands: Understanding and treating sexual anomalies in men.* Hillsdale, NJ: Erlbaum.

Lanktree, C. B., & Briere, J. (1995). Outcome of therapy for sexually abused children: A repeated measures study. *Child Abuse and Neglect, 19,* 1145–1156.

Lasch, C. (1965). *The social thought of Jane Addams.* New York: W. W. Norton.

Lasch, C. (1977). *Haven in a heartless world: The family besieged.* New York: Basic Books.

Laughlin, H. P. (1970). *The ego and its defenses.* New York: Appleton-Century.

Lawson, L., & Chaffin, M. (1992). False negative in sexual abuse disclosure interviews: Incidence and influence of caretaker's belief in abuse in cases of accidental abuse discovery by diagnosis of STD. *Journal of Interpersonal Violence, 7*(4), 532–542.

Lehmann, P. (1997). The development of post-traumatic stress disorder (PTSD) in a sample of child witnesses to mother assault. *Journal of Family Violence, 12*(3), 241–257.

Lehnen, R. G., & Skogan, W. G. E. (1981). *The National Crime Survey: Working papers: Vol. I. Current and historical perspectives.* Washington, DC: U.S. Government Printing Office.

Leonard, H. L., & Topoal, D. A. (1993). Elective mutism. *Journal of the American Academy of Child and Adolescent Psychiatry, 2,* 695–707.

Lester, D. (1992). The murder of babies in American states: Association with suicide rates. *Psychological Reports, 71,* 1202–1204.

Levendosky, A., Okun, A., & Parker, J. G. (1995). Depression and maltreatment as predictors of social competence and social problem-solving skills in school-age children. *Child Abuse and Neglect, 19*(10), 1183–1195.

Lewinsohn, P. M., Rhode, R., & Seeley, J. R. (1994). Psychosocial risk factors for future adolescent suicide attempts. *Journal of Consulting and Clinical Psychology, 62*(2), 297–305.

Libbey, P., & Bybee, R. (1979). The physical abuse of adolescents. *Journal of Social Issues, 35*(2), 101–126.

Libow, J., & Schreier, H. (1986). Three forms of factitious illness in children: When is it Munchausen Syndrome by Proxy? *American Journal of Orthopsychiatry, 56,* 602–610.

Liem, J. H., & Boudewyn, A. C. (1999). Contextualizing the effects of childhood sexual abuse on adult self- and social functioning. *Child Abuse and Neglect, 23*(11), 1141–1158.

Liu, C. (2000, July 7). Parents get prison in starvation death. *Los Angeles Times,* 1.

Locy, T. (2000, August). Cyberstalking: Lost innocence. *U.S. News & World Report,* p. 38.

Loevinger, J. (1969). Theories of ego development. In L. Berger (Ed.), *Clinical-cognitive psychology: Models and integrations.* Englewood Cliffs, NJ: Prentice-Hall.

Loevinger, J. (1976). *Ego development.* San Francisco: Jossey-Bass.

Loevinger, J. (1990). Ego development in adolescence. In R. R. Muuss (Ed.), *Adolescent behavior and society.* New York: McGraw-Hill.

Loevinger, J. (1993). Measurement of personality: True or false. *Psychological Inquiry, 4,* 1–6.

Loftus, E. F. (1993). The reality of repressed memories. *American Psychologist, 48*(5), 518.

Loss, P., & Clancy, E. (1983). Men who sexually abuse their children. *Medical Aspects of Human Sexuality, 17,* 328–329.

Lourie, I. S. (1977). The phenomenon of the abused adolescent. *Victimology, 2,* 268-276.

Lucero v. Salazar, 117 N.M. 802, 877 P.2d 1105, 1994 N.M. LEXIS 233 (1994).

Lui, C. (2000, July 7). Parents get prison in starvation death. *Metro,* Pt. B, p. 1.

Lukianowicz, N. (1972). Incest. *British Journal of Psychiatry, 120,* 301–313.

Lund, N. (1985). Infanticide, physicians, and the law: The Baby Doe Amendments to the Child Abuse Prevention and Treatment Act. *American Journal of Law and Medicine, 11*(1), 1–29.

Lusk, R. (1993). Cognitive and school-related effects. In J. Waterman, R. J. Kelly, M. K. Oliveri, & J. McCord (Eds.), *Behind playground walls: Sexual abuse in preschools* (pp. 93–105). New York: Guilford.

Lystad, M. H. (Ed.). (1986). *Violence in the home: Interdisciplinary perspectives.* New York: Brunner/Mazel.

Macoby, E. E. (1992). Gender and relationships: A developmental account. *American Psychologist, 45*(4), 513-520.

Mahnke v. Moore, 197 Md. 61, 77 A.2d 923 (1951).

Malamuth, N. M. (1984). Aggression against women. In N. M. Malamuth & E. Donnerstein (Eds.), *Pornography and sexual aggression* (pp. 19-52). New York: Academic Press.

Maldonado, J. R., & Spiegel, D. (1995). Using hypnosis. In C. Classen & I. D. Yalom (Eds.), *Treating women molested in childhood.* San Francisco: Jossey-Bass.

Malina, R. M. (1996). Tracking of physical activity and physical fitness across the life-span. (Review). *Research Questions in Exercise Sport, 67*(3), 48–57. [Available online: PUBMED, www.ncbi.nlm.nih.gov/htbinpost/Wntrez/query, ID No. 8902908]

Mannarino, A. P., Cohen, J. A., & Berman, S. P. (1994). The relationship between pre-abuse factors and psychological symptomology in sexually abused girls. *Child Abuse and Neglect, 18,* 63–71.

Mannarino, A. P., Cohen, J. A., & Gregor, M. (1986). A clinical-demographic study of sexually abused children. *Journal of Interpersonal Violence, 10,* 17–23.

Mannarino, A. P., Cohen, J. A., & Gregor, M. (1989). Emotional and behavioral difficulties in sexually abused girls. *Journal of Interpersonal Violence, 4,* 437–451.

Mannix, M. (2000, August). The Web's dark side. *U.S. News & World Report, 129,* pp. 36–38.

Marcia, J. E. (1980). Identity in adolescence. In J. Adelson (Ed.), *Handbook of adolescent psychology.* New York: Wiley.

Marks, N. N., & Kumar, R. (1993). Infanticide in England and Wales. *Medicine, Science, and the Law, 33,* 329-339.

Marshall, S. P., & Smith, J. D. (1987). Sex differences in learning mathematics: A longitudinal study with item and error analysis. *Journal of Educational Psyhcology, 79,* 372–381.

Martin, E. F., & Esplin, P. W. (1997). The guessing game: Emotional propensity experts in the criminal courts. *Law and Psychology Review, 21,* 29.

Marttunen, M. J., Aro, H. M., & Longquist, J. K. (1993). Precipitant stressors in adolescent suicide. *Journal of the American Academy of Child and Adolescent Psychiatry, 32*(6), 1178–1183.

Maslow, A. H. (1954). *Motivation and personality.* New York: Harper & Row.

Mason, M. A. (1992). A judicial dilemma: Use of expert witness testimony in child sex abuse cases. *Journal of Psychiatry, 21,* 35–65.

Mason, M. A. (1994). *From father's property to children's rights.* New York: Columbia University Press.

Mason, M. A. (1998). Eighteenth century family and social life. *Journal of Social History, 96*(3), 29–30.

Mason, M. A. (1999). *The custody wars.* New York: Basic Books.

Mason, M. A., Skolnick, A., & Sugarman, S. D. (1998). *All our families.* New York: Oxford University Press.

Masters, W. H., & Johnson, V. E. (1979). *Homosexuality in perspective.* Boston: Little, Brown.

Mayhall, P. D., & Norgard, K. E. (1983). *Child abuse and neglect: Sharing responsibility.* New York: Wiley.

McCachy, C. H. (1968). Drinking and deviance disavowal: The case of child molesters. *Social Problems, 16,* 43–49.

McCord, J. (1993). A tale of two communities. In J. Waterman, R. J. Kelly, M. K. Oliveri, & J. McCord (Eds.), *Behind playground walls: Sexual abuse in preschools.* New York: Guilford.

McCoy, F. (2000). Child solicitation: A fall from grace. *U.S. News & World Report, 129,* pp. 42–43.

McGuire, R. J., Carlisle, J. M., & Young, B. G. (1965). Sexual deviations and conditioned behavior: A hypothesis. *Behavior Research Therapy, 2,* 185–190.

McIntrye, K. (1981). Role of mothers in father-daughter incest: A feminist analysis. *Social Work, 26,* 462–466.

McKelvey v. McKelvey, 111 Tenn. 388, 77 S.W. 664, 64 L.R.A. 991 (1903).

McKenna, K., Gordon, C. T., & Rappaport, J. (1994). Childhood onset schizophrenia: Timely neurobiological research. *Journal of American Academy of Child-Adolescent Psychiatry, 33*(6), 771–781.

McManus, E. L. (1995). Fallout from pedophilia. *Commonweal, 122*(5), 6–8.

McWhirter, J. J., McWhirter, B. T., McWhirter, A. M., & McWhirter, E. H. (1998). *At-risk youth* (2nd ed.). Pacific Grove, CA: Brooks/Cole.

Mead, M. (1954). Some theoretical considerations of the problems of mother-child separation. *American Journal of Orthopsychiatry, 24,* 24.

Mehl, A., Coble, L., & Johnson, S. (1990). Munchausen Syndrome by Proxy: A family affair. *Child Abuse and Neglect, 14,* 577–585.

Meiselman, K. C. (1978). *Incest: A psychological study of causes and effects with treatment recommendations.* San Francisco: Jossey-Bass.

Meledandri, G. Cattaruzza, M. S., Zantedeschi, E., Signorelli, C., & Osborn, J. F. (1997). Does child abuse influence subsequent sexual behaviour and risk of AIDS? *Journal of Epidemiology and Community Health, 51*(1), 10.

Melton, G. B., Kroocher, G. P., & Saks, M. J. (1983). *Children's competence to consent.* New York: Plenum Press.

Melton, G. B., Petrila, J., Poythress, N. G., & Slobogin, C. (1997). *Psychological evaluations for the courts* (2nd ed.). New York: Guilford.

Menard, S. F. (1984). The "dark figure" and composite indexes of crime: Some empirical exploration of alternative data sources. *Journal of Criminal Justice, 12,* 435–444.

Menard, S. F. (1988). UCR and NCD: Comparisons over space and time. *Journal of Criminal Justice, 16,* 371–384.

Mercein v. People ex rel. Barry, 25 Wend. 64, 1840 N.Y. LEXIS 279 (1840).

Messman-Moore, T. L., Long, P. J., & Siegfried, N. J. (2000). The revictimization of child sexual abuse survivors: An examination of the adjustment of college women with child sexual abuse, adult sexual assault and adult physical abuse. *Child Maltreatment, 5*(1), 18–27.

Mills, D. (1991, November 13). Oprah, children's crusader: The celebrity turns activist on an issue she knows all too well. *Washington Post,* p. B1.

Mills, M. (1998). Funduscopic lesions associated with mortality in shaken baby syndrome. *Journal American Association Pediactric Opthamology and Visual Sciences, 2*(2), 67–71.

Mills, M., & Morris, N. (1974). Prisoners as laboratory animals. *Society, 11*(5), 60–65.

Miner, M. H., West, M. A., & Day, D. M. (1995). Sexual preference for child and aggressive stimuli: Comparison of rapists and child molesters using auditory and visual stimuli. *Behavioral Research Therapy, 33*(5), 545–551.

Minkin v. Minkin, 336 Pa. 49, 7 A.2d 461, 1939 Pa. LEXIS 472 (1939).

Molnar, B. E., Shade, S. B., Kral, A. H., Booth, R. E., & Watters, J. K. (1998). Suicidal behavior and sexual-physical abuse among street youth. *Child Abuse and Neglect, 22*(3), 213–222.

Money, J. (1961). Sex hormones and other variables in human eroticism. In W. C. Young (Ed.), *Sex and internal secretions* (Vol. VIII). Baltimore: Williams & Wilkins.

Moore v. Dozier, 128 Ga. 90, 57 S.E. 110, 1996–1997 Ga. LEXIS 539 (1907).

Moran, P. B., & Eckenrode, J. (1992). Protective personality characteristics among adolescent victims of maltreatment. *Child Abuse and Neglect, 16,* 743–754.

Morgan, E. S. (1958). *The puritan dilemma: The story of John Winthrop.* Boston: Little, Brown.

Morgan, J. F. (1999). Surgery experienced as sexual abuse: A case of pre-pubescent sexual offending and hypospadias. *Clinical Child Psychology and Psychiatry, 4*(4), 543–550.

Morgan, R. (1978). The battered adolescent: A developmental approach to identification and intervention. In M. I. Lauderdale, R. N. Anderson, & S. E. (Eds.), *Child abuse and neglect: Issues on innovation and implementation* (Vol. II). Proceedings of the Second National Conference on Child Abuse and Neglect, April 17–20, 1977, National Center on Child Abuse and Neglect (DHEW), Washington, DC. (OHDS 78-301).

Morris, C. G. (1996). *Psychology: An introduction* (7th ed.). Englewood Cliffs, NJ: Prentice-Hall.

Morris, R. B. (1946). *Government and labor in early America.* New York: Harper Torchbooks.

Morris, R. B. (1958). *Studies in the history of American law with special reference to the seventeenth and eighteenth centuries* (2nd ed.). Philadelphia: J. M. Mitchell.

Morton, N. (1985). *The journey is home.* Boston: Beacon Press.

Morton, T. D., & Salus, M. K. (1994). *Supervising child protective service caseworkers.* (User Manual Series). Washington, DC: Department of Health and Human Services, National Center on Child Abuse and Neglect.

Moscicki, A. B. (1996). Genital HPV infections in children and adolescents. *Obstetrics Gynecology Clinical North America, 23*(3), 675–697.

Mrazek, P. J., & Mrazek, D. A. (1987). Resilience in child maltreatment victims: A conceptual exploration. *Child Abuse and Neglect, 3,* 357–366.

Muniz v. State, 2000 Fla. App. LEXIS 8142, 25 Fla. Law W.D. 1580 (2000).

Musick, J. S. (1993). *Young, poor, and pregnant.* New Haven, CT: Yale University Press.

Muuss, R. E. (1996). *Theories of adolescence* (6th ed.). New York: McGraw-Hill.

Myers, J. E. B. (1992). *Legal issues in child abuse and neglect.* Newbury Park, CA: Sage.

Myers, M. F. (1989). Men sexually assaulted as adults and sexually abused as boys. *Archives of Sexual Behavior, 18*(3), 203–215.

Nagel, D. E., Putnam, F. W., & Noll, J. G. (1997). Disclosure patterns of sexual abuse and psychological functioning at a 1-year follow-up. *Child Abuse and Neglect, 21*(2), 137–147.

Nash, M. R., Zivner, O. A., & Hulsey, T. (1993). Characteristics of sexual abuse associated with greater psychological impairment among children. *Child Abuse and Neglect, 17,* 401–408.

National Center for Educational Statistics (NCES). (2001). *Overview of public elementary and secondary schools and districts: School year 1999–2000.* Washington, DC: U.S. Department of Education, Office of Educational Research and Improvement.

National Center for the Prosecution of Child Abuse (NCPCA). (2000). *HIV testing for sex offenders.* (Child Abuse and Neglect State Statutes Series). Report published by the National Clearinghouse on Child Abuse and Neglect Information. [On-line]. Available: www.calib.com/nccanch/statutes

National Child Protection Act, Pub. L. No. 102-95.

National Clearinghouse on Child Abuse and Neglect Information (NCCANI). (1996). *Statistical fact sheet.* [On-line]. Available: www.calib.com/nccanch

National Clearinghouse on Child Abuse and Neglect Information (NCCANI). (1997). *Highlights from child maltreatment 1999.* [On-line]. Available: www.calib.com /nccanch/pubs/factsheets/constats.cfm

National Clearinghouse on Child Abuse and Neglect Information (NCCANI). (1998). *Child abuse and neglect: 1965 through October 1998.* [CD-Rom]. Washington, DC: NISCDiscover. [Available on-line: www.calib.com/nccanch]

National Clearinghouse on Child Abuse and Neglect Information (NCCANI). (2000a). *Incident rate of child abuse fact sheet.* [On-line]. Available: www.calib.com/nccanch /stats/index.cfm#about

National Clearinghouse on Child Abuse and Neglect Information (NCCANI). (2000b). *Reports from the states to the National Child Abuse and Neglect Data System (NCANDS).* [On-line]. Available: www.acf.dhhs.gov /programs/cb

National Clearinghouse on Child Abuse and Neglect Information (NCCANI). (2000c). *Mandatory reporters of child abuse and neglect.* (Statutes at a Glance Series). Washington, DC: Author. [Available: 1-800-FYI-3366].

National Clearinghouse on Child Abuse and Neglect Information (NCCANI). (2000d).

Definitions of child abuse and neglect. (Statutes at a Glance Series). Washington, DC: Author. [Available: 1-800-FYI-3366].

National Clearinghouse on Child Abuse and Neglect Information (NCCANI). (2000e). *Central registry expungement.* (Statutes at a Glance Series). Washington, DC: Author. [Available: 1-800-FYI-3366].

National Clearinghouse on Child Abuse and Neglect Information (NCCANI). (2000f). *Sex offender registration.* (Statutes at a Glance Series). Washington, DC: Author. [Available: 1-800-FYI-3366].

National Clearinghouse on Child Abuse and Neglect Information (NCCANI). (2000g). *Public notification of the release of sex offenders.* (Statutes at a Glance Series). Washington, DC: Author. [Available: 1-800-FYI-3366].

National Committee to Prevent Child Abuse. (1995). *Child abuse and neglect statistics from the National Committee to Prevent Child Abuse.* Chicago: Author. [Available on-line: www.vix.com/men/abuse/studies /children.html].

National Institute of Justice. (1987). *Data resources of the National Institute of Justice.* Washington, D.C: U.S. Government Printing Office.

National Resource Center on Child Sexual Abuse (NRCCSA). (1994). Advanced training curriculum emphasizes cutting-edge research, techniques, approaches. *NRCCSA News, 3,* 4.

National Resource Center on Child Sexual Abuse (NRCCSA). (1996). New statistics show child abuse and neglect is increasing. *NRCCSA News, 5*(2), 8.

Nester, W. S. (2001). Connecting physical education to the lives of urban high school students. *Journal of Physical Education, Recreation & Dance, 72*(4), 6–7.

Newsome v. Newsome, 557 So. 2d 511 (Miss. 1990).

Ney, P., & Peters, A. (1995). *Ending the cycle of abuse.* New York: Brunner/Mazel.

Ney, P. G. (1992). Transgenerational triangles of abuse: A model of family violence. In E. C. E. Viano (Ed.), *Intimate violence: Interdisciplinary perspectives* (pp. 15–25). Washington, DC: Hemisphere.

Ney, T. (1995). *True and false allegations of child sexual abuse.* New York: Brunner/Mazel.

Nicholas, S. C., Price, A. M., & Rubin, R. (1986). *Rights and wrongs.* New York: University of New York Feminist Press.

Nishith, P., Hearst, D. E., Mueser, K. T., & Foa, E. B. (1995). PTSD and major depression: Methodological and treatment considerations in a single case design. *Behavior Therapy, 26,* 319–335.

Noblitt, J. R., & Perskin, P. S. (2000). *Cult and ritual abuse: Its history, anthropology, and recent discovery in contemporary America.* Westport, CT: Praeger.

Nye, R. D. (1975). *Three views of man.* Monterey, CA: Brooks/Cole.

Oates, R. K. (1996). *The spectrum of child abuse.* New York: Brunner/Mazel.

Oberlander, L. B. (1995). Psychological issues in child sexual abuse evaluations: A survey of forensic mental health professionals. *Child Abuse and Neglect, 19,*(4), 475–479.

Ochberg, F. M. (1993). Posttraumatic therapy. In J. P. Wilson & B. Raphael (eds.), *Handbook of traumatic stress syndromes* (pp. 773-783). New York: Plenum Press.

O'Conner, S. (2001). *The orphan trains: The story of Charles Loring Brace and the children he saved and failed.* New York: Houghton Mifflin.

O'Day, B. (1983). *Preventing sexual abuse of persons with disabilities. A curriculum for hearing impaired, physically disabled, blind and mentally retarded students.* Santa Cruz, CA: Network Publications.

Oliveri, M. K., Cockriel, M., & Dugan, M. (1993). Clinical implications: Assault, levels of injury, and the healing process in cases of alleged preschool ritualistic abuse. In J. Waterman, R. J. Kelly, M. K. Oliveri, & J. McCord (Eds.), *Behind playground walls: Sexual abuse in preschools.* New York: Guilford.

O'Neill, W. (1967). *Divorce in the Progressive Era.* New Haven, CT: Yale University Press.

Padel, A. F., Venning, V. A., Evans, M. F., Quantrill, A. M., & Fleming, K. A. (1990). Human papillomaviruses in anogenital warts in children: Typing by in situ hybridisation. *British Medical Journal, 300*(6738), 1491–1494.

Palusci, V. J., Cox, E. O., Cyrus, T. A., Heartwell, S. W., Vandervort, F. E., & Pott, E. S. (1999). Medical assessment and legal outcome in child sexual abuse. *Archives of Pediatric Adolescent Medicine, 153*(4), 388–392.

Paniagua, F. A. (1998). *Assessing and treating culturally diverse clients: A practical guide.* Thousand Oaks, CA.: Sage.

Panton, J. H. (1978). Personality differences appearing between rapists of adults, rapists of children, and non-violent sexual molesters of children. *Research Communications in Psychology, Psychiatry, and Behavior, 3*(4), 385–393.

Papalia, D. E., & Olds, S. W. (1995). *Human development* (6th ed.). New York: McGraw-Hill.

Paperny, D. M., & Deisher, R. W. (1983). Maltreatment of adolescents: The relationship to a predisposition toward violent behavior and delinquency. *Adolescence, XVIII*(71), 499–506.

Pascoe, D. J., & Duterte, B. O. (1981). The medical diagnosis of sexual abuse in the premenarcheal child. *Pediatric Annals, 10*(5), 40–45.

Patterson, G. R., DeBaryshe, B. D., & Ramsey, E. (1989). A developmental perspective on antisocial behavior. *American Psychologist, 44*(2), 329–335.

Peclard, N., & Taieb, A. (1996). Sexually transmitted diseases in children. *La Revue du Praticien, 46*(16), 1979–1983. [Available online: PUBMED, www.ncbi.nlm.nih.gov /htbinpost/Wntrez/query, ID No. 8978205]

Pelzer, D. (1998). *A child called it*. Deerfield Beach, FL: Health Communications.

Pendergast, M. (1996). *Victims of memory: Sex abuse accusations and shattered lives*. Hinesburg, VT: Upper Access.

People v. Mercein, 3 Hill. 399, 410 (N.Y. 1842).

People ex rel. Sinclair v. Sinclair, 47 Misc. Rep. 230, 231(N.Y. 1905).

Perry, B. D., & Azad, I. (1999). *Post-traumatic stress disorders in children and adolescents*. Houston, TX: Baylor College of Medicine.

Piaget, J. (1952). *The origins of intelligence in children*. New York: International Universities Press.

Piaget, J. (1962). *Play, dreams, and limitations*. New York: W. W. Norton.

Piaget, J. (1965). *The child's conception of the world*. Totowa, NJ: Littlefield.

Piers, B. (1999). Mathew's moral vision. *Philosophy, Psychiatry, and Psychology, 6*(40), 317–319.

Piers, C. (1999). Remembering trauma: A characterological perspective. In L. M. Williams & V. L. Banyard (Eds.), *Trauma and memory* (pp. 57–65). Thousand Oaks, CA: Sage.

Pleck, E. (1987). *Domestic tyranny: The making of social policy against family violence from colonial times to the present.*. New York: Oxford University Press.

Pokorny, S. E. (1997). Genital trauma. *Clincial Obstetrics and Gynecology, 40*(1), 219–225.

Poole, D.A. and Lamb, M.E. (1998). *Investigative Interviews of Children*. Washington, D.C.: American Psychological Association.

Pope, K. S., & Brown, L. S. (1996). *Recovered memories of abuse: Assessment, therapy, forensics*. Washington, DC: American Psychological Association.

Porter, E. (1986). *Treating the young male victims of sexual assault: Issues and intervention strategies*. Syracuse, NY: Safer Society Press.

Porter, G. E., Heitsch, G. M., & Miller, M. D. (1994). Munchausen syndrome by proxy: Unusual manifestations and disturbing sequalae. *Child Abuse and Neglect, 18*(9), 789–794.

Prendergast, M., Taylor, E., Rapoport, J., Bartko, J., Donnelly, M., Zamekin, A., Ahearn, M. B., Dunn, G., & Weiselberg, H. (1988). The diagnosis of childhood hyperactivity: A U.S.-U.K. cross-cultural study of DSM-III and ICD-9. *Journal of Child Psychology and Psychiatry, 29,* 284–300.

Prendergast, W. E. (1993). *The merry-go-round of sexual abuse: Identifying and treating survivors*. Binghamton, NY: Haworth Press.

Preston, S. H., Lim, S., & Morgan, P. (1992). African-American marriage in 1910: Beneath the surface of census data. *Demography, 29*(1), 12.

Prohibition of Female Genital Mutilation Act of 1993 (Pub. L. No. 104–208).

Protection of Children Against Sexual Exploitation Act of 1977 (Pub. L. No. 95–225).

Protection of Children from Sexual Predators (Pub. L. No. 105–314), October 30, 1998.

Putnam, F. W., & Trickett, P. K. (1997). Psychobiological effects of sexual abuse: A longitudinal study. *Annals of New York Academy of Sciences, 21*(821), 150–159.

Quinsey, V. L., Harris, G. T., Rice, M. E., & Cormier, C. A. (1998). *Violent offenders: Appraising and managing risk*. Washington, DC: American Psychological Association.

Quinsey, V. L., Rice, M. E., & Harris, G. T. (1995). Actuarial prediction of sexual recidivism. *Journal of Interpersonal Violence, 10,* 85–105.

Rabkin, P. (1980). *Fathers to daughters: The legal foundations of female emancipation*. Westport, CT: Greenwood Press.

Racketeer-Influenced and Corrupt Organizations (RICO), 18 U.S.C. 146 (Pub. L. No. 107–15).

Rada, R. T. (1976). Alcoholism and the child molester. *Annals of New York Academy of Science, 273,* 492–496.

Radbill, S. X. (1980). Children in a world of violence. In C. H. Kempe & R. E. Helfer (Eds.), *The battered child*. Chicago: University of Chicago Press.

Raimer, S. S., & Raimer, B. G. (1992). Family violence, child abuse, and anogenital warts. In *Violence: A compendium from JAMA, American Medical News, and the specialty journals of the American Medical Association* (pp. 232–233). Chicago: American Medical Association.

Rainey, D. Y., Stevens-Simon, C., & Kaplan, D. W. (1995). Are adolescents who report prior sexual abuse at higher risk for pregnancy? *Child Abuse and Neglect, 19*(10), 1283–1288.

Rand, D. (1990). Munchausen Syndrome by Proxy: Integration of classic and contemporary types. *Issues in Child Abuse Accusations, 2,* 83–89.

Rand, D. (1993). Munchausen Syndrome by Proxy: A complex type of emotional abuse responsible for some false allegations of child abuse. *Issues in Child Abuse Accusations, 5,* 135–155.

Rapoport, J. L., & Ismond, D. R. (1996). *DSM-IV training guide for diagnosis of childhood disorders.* New York: Brunner/Mazel.

Reams, R., & Friedrich, W. (1994). The efficacy of time-limited play therapy with maltreated preschoolers. *Journal of Clinical Psychology, 50*(6), 888–899.

Regehr, H., & Glancy, G. (1997). Survivors of sexual abuse alleged therapist negligence. *Journal of American Academy Psychiatry Law, 25*(1), 49–58.

Reidy, T. J., Silver, R. M., & Carlson, A. (1991). Child custody decisions: A survey of judges. *Family Law Quarterly, 23*(75), 110.

Reilly, J., Baker, G. A., Rhodes, J., & Salmon, P. (1999). The association of sexual and physical abuse with somatization: Characteristics of patients presenting with irritable bowel syndrome and non-epileptic attack disorder. *Psychological Medicine, 29*(2), 399–406.

Reiniger, A., Robison, E., & McHugh, M. (1995). Mandated training of professionals: A means for improving reporting of suspected child abuse. *Child Abuse and Neglect, 19*(1), 63–69.

Rencken, R. H. (1989). Bodily assault: Physical and sexual abuse. In D. Capuzzi & D. R. Gross (Eds.), *Youth at risk: A resource for counselors, teachers, and parents* (pp. 71–95). Alexandria, VA: American Association for Counseling and Development.

Reyes, C. J. (1996). *Resiliency of young children: Self-concept, parental support, and traumatic symptoms after sexual abuse.* Paper presented at the 104th Annual Convention of the American Psychological Association, August 9–13, Toronto, Canada.

Robinson, A. J. (1998). Sexually transmitted organisms in children and child sexual abuse. *International Journal of STD and AIDS, 9*(9), 501–511.

Roe v. Roe, 324 S.E.2d 6691 (Va. Sup. Ct. 1985).

Roe v. Wade, 410 U.S. 179 (1973).

Roesler, T. A., & McKenzie, N. (1994). Effects of childhood trauma on psychological functioning in adults. *The Journal of Nervous and Mental Disease, 182*(3), 145–150.

Rogers, C. M., & Terry, T. (1984). Clinical intervention with boy victims of sexual abuse. In I. R. Stuart & J. G. Greer (Eds.), *Victims of sexual aggression: Treatment of chil-*

dren, women, and men. New York: Van Nostrand Reinhold.

Roller v. Roller, 37 Wash. 242, 68 L.R.A. 893 (1905).

Rosenberg, D. (1987). Web of deceit: A literature review of Munchausen Syndrome. *Child Abuse and Neglect, 11,* 547–563.

Rosler, A., & Witztum, E. (1998). Treatment of men with paraphilia with long-lasting analogue of gonadroptopin-releasing hormones. *The New England Journal of Medicine, 12,* 416–422.

Ross, C. A., Kronson, J., Koensgen, S., Barkman, D., Clark, P., & Rockman, G. (1992). Dissociative comorbidity in 100 chemically dependent patients. *Hospital and Community Psychiatry, 43*(8), 840–842.

Roth, S., & Newman, E. (1993). The process of coping with incest for adult survivors: Measurement and implication for treatment and research. *Journal of Interpersonal Violence, 8,* 363–377.

Roth, S., Newman, E., Polcovitz, D., Van der Kolk, B., & Mandel, F. S. (1997). Complex PTSD in victims exposed to sexual and physical abuse: Results from the DSM-IV field trial for Posttraumatic Stress Disorder. *Journal of Traumatic Stress, 10*(4), 539–555.

Rotter, J. B. (1966). Generalized expectancies for internal versus external control of reinforcement. *Psychological Monographs, 80*(1), 1–28.

Ruch, L. O., & Chandler, S. M. (1982). The crisis impact of sexual assault on three victim groups: Adult rape victims, child rape victims and incest victims. *Journal of Social Service Research, 5,* 83–100.

Rudolf, M. C., Cole, T. J., Krom, A. J., Sahota, P., & Walker, J. (2000). Growth of primary school children: A validation of the 1990 references and their use in growth monitoring. *Archives of Disease in Childhood, 83*(4), 298–301.

Rundell, J. R., Ursano, R. J., Holloway, H. C., & Silberman, E. K. (1989). Psychiatric responses to trauma. *Hospital Community Psychiatry, 40*(1), 68–74.

Runtz, M. G., & Schallow, J. R. (1997). Social support and coping strategies as mediators of adult adjustment following childhood treatment. *Child Abuse and Neglect, 21*(2), 211–225.

Russell, D. E. (1983). The incidence and prevalence of intrafamilial and extrafamilial sexual abuse of female children. *Child Abuse and Neglect, 7*(2), 133–146.

Russell, D. E. (1986). *The secret trauma: Incest in the lives of girls and women.* New York: Basic Books.

Russell, D. E., & Bolen, R. M. (2000). *The epidemic of rape and child sexual abuse in the United States.* Thousand Oaks, CA: Sage.

Ryan, G. D. (1991). The juvenile sex offender's family. In G. D. Ryan & S. L. Lane (Eds.), *Juvenile sexual offending: Causes, consequences, and correction.* Lexington, MA: Lexington Books.

Ryan, G. D., & Lane, S. L. (Eds.). (1991). *Juvenile sexual offending. Causes, consequences, and correction.* Lexington, MA: Lexington Books.

Sagatun, I. J., & Edwards, L. P. (1995). *Child abuse and the legal system.* (ed.). Chicago: Nelson-Hall.

Salazar v. Salazar, 582 So. 2d 374, 375 (La. App. 4th Cir. 1991).

Sappington, A. A., Pharr, R., Tunstall, A., & Rickert, E. (1997). Relationships among child abuse, date abuse, and psychological problems. *Journal of Clincial Psychology, 53*(4), 319–329.

Sarwer, D. B., & Durlak, J. A. (1996). Childhood sexual abuse as a predictor of adult female sexual dysfunction: A study of couples seeking sex therapy. *Child Abuse and Neglect, 20*(10), 963–971.

Sattler, J. M. (1998). *Clinical and forensic interviewing of children and families: Guidelines for the mental health, education, pediatric, and child maltreatment fields.* San Diego: Jerome M. Sattler.

Sattler, J. M. (2001). *Assessment of children: Cognitive applications* (4th ed.). San Diego: Jerome M. Sattler.

Savitz, L. D. (1982). Official statistics. In L. D. Savitz & N. Johnston (Eds.), *Contemporary criminology.* New York: Wiley.

Sawyer, R. (1986). *Slavery in the twentieth century.* New York: Routledge.

Saywotz, K. J., & Goodman, G. S. (1997). Interviewing children in and out of court: Current research and practical implications. In J. B. L. Berliner & J. Bulkley (Eds.), *APSAC handbook on child maltreatment.* Thousand Oaks, CA: Sage.

Scher, D., & Twaite, J. A. (1999). The relationship between child sexual abuse and alexithymic symptoms in a population of recovering adult substance abusers. *Journal of Child Sexual Abuse, 8*(2), 25–40.

Schinke, S. P., Botvin, G. J., & Orlandi, M. A. (1991). *Substance abuse in children and adolescents: Evaluation and intervention.* Newbury Park, CA: Sage.

Schroeder, P. (1994). Female genital mutilation: A form of child abuse. *New England Journal of Medicine, 331*(11), 739–740.

Schwab-Stone, M., Chen, C., Greenberger, E. (1999). No safe haven II: The effects of violence exposure on urban youth. *Journal of the American Academy of Child and Adolescent Psychiatry, 38*(4), 359–367.

Schwab-Stone, M., Fischer, P., Piacentini, J., Shaffer, D., Davies, M., & Briggs, M. (1993). The Diagnostic Interview Schedule for Children—Revised (SISC-R): II. Test-retest reliability. *Journal of American Academy of Child-Adolescent Psychiatry, 32*(3), 651–657.

Scott, W. (1999). Group therapy for survivors of severe childhood abuse: Repairing the social contract. *Journal of Child Sexual Abuse, 7*(3), 35–54.

Sedlak, A. J., & Broadhurst, D. D. (1966). *Executive summary of the third national incidence study of child abuse and neglect (NIS-3).* Washington, DC: Department of Health and Human Services. (Award No. 105-91-1800). [Available on-line: www.calib.com /nccanch/pbg/statinfo/nis3.cfm]

Seifer, R., Schiller, M., Sameroff, A. J., Resnick, S., & Riordan, K. (1996). Attachment, maternal sensitivity, and infant temperament during the first year of life. *Developmental Psychology, 32*(1), 12–25.

Sgroi, S. M. (1982a). Family treatment of child sexual abuse. *Journal of Social Work and Human Sexuality, 1*(1-2), 109–129.

Sgroi, S. M. (1982b). *Handbook of clinical intervention in child sexual abuse.* Lexington MA: D. C. Heath Co.

S.H. v. B.L.H., 572 A.2d 730 (Pa. 1990).

Shapiro, R. (1994). Evaluating sexually transmitted diseases in children. *APSAC Advisor, 7*(2), 11–14.

Shaw, I., & Butler, I. (1998). Understanding young people and prostitution: A foundation for practice? *British Journal of Social Work, 28*(2), 177–196.

Shedler, J., Mayman, M., & Manis, M. (1993). The illusion of mental health. *American Psychologist, 48*(11), 1117–1132.

Shengold, L. (1989). *Soul murder. The effects of childhood abuse and deprivation.* New Haven, CT: Yale University Press.

Sherry, A. (2000, July 7). Bail reduced in baby's death—Woman accused of burying infant. *The Denver Post,* B–05.

Sidoli, M., & Bovensiepen, G. E. (1995). *Incest fantasies and self-destructive acts: Jungian and post-Jungian psychotherapy in adolescence.* New Brunswick, NJ : Transaction Publishers.

Siegried, E., Rasnick-Conley, J., Cook, S., Leonardi, C., & Montelcone, J. (1998). Human papillomavirus screening in pediatric victims of sexual abuse. *Pediatrics, 101*(1, part I), 43–47.

Simons, M. (1993, January 11). France jails woman for daughter's circumcision. *New York Times,* A8.

Singer, K. I. (1989). Group work with men who experienced incest in childhood. *American Journal of Orthopsychiatry, 59*(3), 468–472.

Singer, L., & Reynolds, D. (1988). A dissent on joint custody. *Maryland Law Review, 47,* 497.

Skinner, B. F. (1938). *The behavior of organisms: An experimental approach.* New York: Appleton-Century.

Skinner, B. F. (1957). *Verbal behavior.* New York: Appleton-Century Crofts.

Skolnick, A. A. (1994). Massachusetts' new child abuse and neglect felony law repeals religious exemption. *Journal of the American Medical Association (JAMA), 271*(7), 489–491.

Slater, B., & Gallagher, M. (1989). Outside the realm of psychotherapy: Consultation for interventions with sexualized children. *School Psychology Review, 18*(3), 401–411.

Smith, A. E. (1947). *Colonists in bondage.* Chapel Hill, NC: University of North Carolina Press.

Smith, C., & Carlson, B. F. (1997). Stress, coping, and resilience in children and youth. *Social Service Review, 71*(2), 231–256.

Smith, D., Smight, S., & Doolittle, F. (1975). How children used to work. *Law and Contemporary Problems, 39*(3), 99.

Soukup, R., Wickner, S., & Corbett, J. (1984). *Three in every classroom: The child victim of incest—What you as a teacher can do.* Bemidji, MN: Minnesota Sexual Assault Program.

Spaccarelli, S. (1994). Stress, appraisal, and coping in child sexual abuse: A theoretical and empirical review. *Psychological Bulletin, 116,* 1–23.

Spaccarelli, S., & Kim, S. (1995). Resilience criteria and factors associated with resilience in sexually abused girls. *Child Abuse and Neglect, 19,* 1171–1182.

Speth, E. (1995, Summer). Factors affecting children's power to choose their caretakers in custody proceedings. *The Custody Newsletter, 12,* 2–27.

Spiegel, D. (1989). Hypnosis in the treatment of victims of sexual abuse. *Psychiatric Clinics of North America , 12*(2), 295–305.

Spiegel, D. (1990). Trauma, dissociation and hypnosis. In R. P. Kluft (Ed.), *Incest-related syndromes of adult psychopathology* (pp. 247–261). Washington, DC: American Psychiatric Press.

Spirito, A., Stark, L. J., & Williams, C. (1988). Development of a brief checklist to assess coping in pediatric patients. *Journal of Pediatric Psychology, 13,* 555–574.

Stanton, E. C. (1867). *History of woman's suffrage* (Vols. 1–6). Albany, NY: Weed Parsons.

State v. Bisagno, 246 P. 101 (Kan. 1926).

State v. Finley, 388 P.2d 790, 796 (Ariz. 1959).

State v. Finley, 108 Ariz. 420, 501 P.2d 4, 1972 Ariz. LEXIS 349 (1972).

State v. Hopkins, 177 Ariz. 161, 866 P.2d 143, 1993 Ariz. App. LEXIS 194, 147 Ariz. Adv. Rep. 59 (1993).

State v. McFarlin, 517 P.2d 87, 88, 1973 Ariz. LEXIS 482 (1973).

State v. Parker, 470 P.2d 461 (Ariz. 1970).

State v. Phillips, 102 Ariz. 377, 430 P.2d 139, 141 (1967).

State v. Salazar, 181 Ariz. 87, 88-92, 887 P.2d 617, 618-22 (1992).

State v. Weatherbee, 158 Ariz. 303, 762 P.2d 590, 1988 Ariz. App. LEXIS 134, 7 Ariz. Adv. Rep. 61 (1988).

Stein, D. J., Hollander, E., Anthony, D. T., Schneider, F. R., Fallon, B. A., & Liebowitz, M. R. (1992). Serotonergic medications for sexual obsessions, sexual additions and paraphilias. *Journal of Clinical Psychiatry, 53,* 267–271.

Sternberg, K. J., Lamb, M. E., Greenbarm, C., Cicchetti, D., Dawud, S., Cortes, R. M., Drispin, O., & Lorey, F. (1993). Effects of domestic violence on children's behavior problems and depression. *Developmental Psychology, 29*(1), 44–52.

Stevens-Simon, C., Kelly, L., Singer, D., & Nelligan, D. (1998). Reasons for first teen pregnancies predict the rate of subsequent teen conceptions. *Pediatrics, 101*(1), 6.

Stevens-Simon, C., & McAnarney, E. R. (1994). Childhood victimization: Relationship to adolescent pregnancy outcome. *Child Abuse and Neglect, 18*(7), 569-575.

Steward, M. S., Schmitz, M., Steward, D. S., Joye, N. R., & Reinhart, M. (1995). Children's anticipation of and response to coloscopic examination. *Child Abuse and Neglect, 19*(8), 997–1005.

Stoller, R. (1975). *Perversion: The erotic form of hatred.* New York: Pantheon.

Strean, H. S. (1988). Effects of childhood sexual abuse on the psychosocial functioning of adults. *Social Work, 33*(5), 465–467.

Stricker, G. (1967). Stimulus properties of the Blacky to a sample of pedophiles. *The Journal of General Psychology, 77,* 35–39.

Strober, M., Freeman, R., & Morrell, W. (1997). The long-term course of severe anorexia nervosa in adolescents: Survival analysis of recover, relapse, and outcome predictors over 10–15 years in a prospective study. *International Journal of Eating Disorders, 22*(4), 339–360.

Subrahmanyam, K., Kraut, R. E., Greenfield, P. M., Gross, E. F. (2000). The impact of home computer use on children's activities and development. *Future Child, 10*(2): 123–144. [Available on-line PUBMED, www.ncbi.nlm.nih.gov/htbinpost/Wntrez /query, ID No. 11255703]

Summit, R. C. (1983). The child sexual abuse accommodation syndrome. *Child Abuse and Neglect, 7*(2), 177–193.

Swan, H. L. (1984). *Happy bear: Teaching preschool children about sexual abuse.* Kansas City, MO: Kansas Committee for Prevention of Child Abuse.

Tanner, J. M. (1990). Principles of growth standards. *Acta Paideatricia Scandinavia, 79*(10), 963–967. [Available on-line: PUBMED, www.ncbi.nlm.nih.gov/htbinpost/Wntrez /query, ID No. 2264471]

Tarasoff v. Regents of the University of California et al., 13 Cal. 3d 177, 118 Cal. Rptr. 129, 529 P.2d 553, 1974 LEXIS 376 (1974).

Taylor, J., & Daniel, B. (1999). Interagency practice in children with non-organic failure to thrive: Is there a gap between health and social care? *Child Abuse Review, 8*(5), 325–338.

Teall, J. E. (1889). *Slavery and the slave-trade, 1889. Facts and memoranda. Compiled from the slave-trade papers, the statutes at large, and other sources.* London: London, British, and Foreign Antislavery Society.

Tharinger, D., Russian, T., & Robinson, P. (1989). School psychologists' involvement in response to child sex abuse. *School Psychology Review, 18,* 389–399.

Thomas, B. H., & Jamison, E. (1995). Childhood sexually transmitted diseases and child sexual abuse: Results of a Canadian survey of three professional groups. *Child Abuse and Neglect, 19*(9), 1019–1029.

Thomas, K. (2000, April 19). Girlhood interrupted: This teenager's online soulmate was a pedophile. *USA Today (LIFE),* 1D.

Thompson, C. L., & Rudolph, L. B. (1999). *Counseling children.* Palo Alto, CA: Brooks/Cole.

Thompson, N. J., Potter, J. S., Sanderson, C. A., & Maibach, E. W. (1997). The relationship of sexual abuse and HIV risk behaviors among heterosexual adult female STD patients. *Child Abuse and Neglect, 21*(2), 149–156.

Thorndike, E. L. (1904). *An introduction to the theory of mental and social measurements.* New York: The Science Press.

Tierney, K., & Corwin, D. (1983). Exploring intrafamilial child sexual abuse: A systems approach. In D. Finkelhor, R. J. Gelles, G. T. Hotaling, & M. A. Strauss (Eds.), *The dark side of families: Current family violence research.* Beverly Hills, CA: Sage.

Tiffin, S. (1982). *In whose best interests? Child welfare reform in the progressive era.* Westport, CT: Greenwood Press.

Torrey, W., & Drake, R. (1994). Current concepts in the treatment of schizophrenia. *Psychiatry, 57,* 278–285.

Toth, S. L., & Cicchetti, D. (1996). Patterns of relatedness, depressive symptomology, and perceived competence in maltreated children. *Journal of Consulting and Clinical Psychology, 64*(1), 32–41.

Toubia, N. (1994). Female circumcision as a public health issue. *The New England Journal of Medicine, 331,* 712.

Trend, M. G. (1980). Applied social research and the government: Notes on the limits of confidentiality. *Social Problems, 27,* 330–349.

Trepper, T. S., Niedner, D., Mika, L., & Barrett, M. J. (1996). Family characteristics of intact sexually abusing families: An exploratory study. *Journal of Child Sexual Abuse, 5*(4), 1–18.

Uniform Crime Statistics. (1998). *Profile of reported incest crimes.* [On-line]. Available: www.ganet.org/gbi/usrsum.html

United States v. Amaral, 488 F.2d 1148, 1973 U.S. App. LEXIS 6739 (1973).

U.S. Department of Census Bureau. (1926). *U.S. Census Bureau (1923–1926).* Washington, DC: U.S. Government Printing Office.

U.S. Department of Health, Education, and Welfare. (1975). *Child abuse and neglect research. Projects and publications.* (PB 260–800). Washington, DC: Author.

U.S. Department of Health and Human Services, Administration on Children, Youth and Families. (1999). *Child maltreatment 1997: Reports from the states to the National Child Abuse and Neglect Data System.* Washington, DC: U.S. Government Printing Office. [Available on-line: www.acf.dhhs.gov/programs/cb].

U.S. Department of Justice. (1981). *National crime surveys: National sample 1973–1979.* Ann Arbor, MI: Inter-University Consortium for Politicians Social Research.

U.S. Legislative Committee. (1979). *An act to amend title 13 of the United States Code to provide a limited exception to the Bureau of the Census from the provisions of section 322 of the act of June 30, 1932 (Pub. L. No. 96–52).* (Catalogue No. 80021778). Washington, DC: U.S. Government Printing Office.

Varia, R., Abidin, R. R., & Dass, P. (1996). Perceptions of abuse: Effects on adult psychological and social adjustment. *Child Abuse and Neglect, 20*(6), 511–526.

Veach, T. A. (1997a). Cognitive therapy techniques in treating incestuous fathers: Examining cognitive distortions and levels of denial in cognitive therapy techniques. *Journal of Family Psychotherapy, 8*(4), 1–20.

Veach, T. A. (1997b). *Stealing innocence: Measuring child sexual offenders' attitudes toward punishment, sexual contact, and blame.* Paper presented at the Biennial Meeting of

the Society for Research in Child
Development, April 3–6, Washington, DC.

Verduyn, C., & Calam, R. (1999). Cognitive
behavioral interventions with maltreated
children and adolescents. *Child Abuse and
Neglect, 23*(2), 197–207.

Vevier, R., & Tharinger, D. (1986). Child sex
abuse: A review and intervention framework for the school psychologist. *Journal of
School Psychology, 24,* 93–111.

Virkkunen, M. (1974). Incest offenses and
alcoholism. *Medicine, Science and Law, 14,*
124–128.

Walker, L. E. A. (1990). Psychological assessment of sexually abused children for legal
evaluation and expert witness testimony.
*Professional Psychology: Research and Practice,
21,* 344–353.

Walker, L. J. (1989). A longitudinal study of
moral reasoning. *Child Development, 60,*
157–166.

Walker, L. J. (1991). Sex differences in moral
reasoning. In W. M. Kurtines & J. L.
Gewirtz (Eds.), *Handbook of moral behavior
and development.* Hillsdale, NJ: Erlbaum.

Walker, L. J. (2000). *The battered women syndrome* (2nd ed.). New York: Springer.

Walker, N. E. (1999). *Children's rights in the
United States: In search of a national policy.*
Thousand Oaks, CA: Sage.

Waller, D. (1983). Obstacles to the treatment of
Munchausen by proxy syndrome. *Journal of
American Academy Child Adolescent Psychiatry,
22,* 80–85.

Waller, G. (1998). Perceived control in eating
disorders: Relationship with reported sexual
abuse. *International Journal of Eating Disorders,
23,* 213–216.

Wallerstein, J.S., & Bladkeslee, S. (1989). *Second
chances: Men, women, and children a decade
after divorce.* New York: Tichnor & Fields.

Wang, C., & Daro, D. (1998). *Current trends in
child abuse reporting and fatalities: The results of
the 1997 annual fifty state survey* (Working
Paper No. 808). Chicago: National
Committee to Prevent Child Abuse.

Ward, M. J., Brazelton, T. B., & Wust, M.
(1999). Toward understanding the role of
attachment in malnutrition. In D. B. and
D. P. Kessler (Eds.), *Failure to thrive and pediatric undernutrition.* Baltimore: Paul H.
Brookes.

Warner, J. E., & Hansen, D. J. (1994). The
identification and reporting of physical
abuse by physicians. A review and compilation for research. *Child Abuse and Neglect,
18,* 11–25.

Waterman, A. S. (1993). Finding something to
do or someone to be: A eudaemonist perspective on identity formation. In J. Kroger
(Ed.), *Discussions on ego identity.* Hillsdale,
NJ: Erlbaum.

Waterman, J., & Ben-Meir, S. (1993).
Background literature. In J. Waterman, R. J.
Kelly, M. K. Oliveri, & J. McCord (Eds.),
*Behind the playground walls: Sexual abuse in
preschools.* New York: Guilford.

Waterman, J., Kelly, R. J., Oliveri, M. K., &
McCord, J. (1993). *Behind the playground
walls: Sexual abuse in preschools.* New York:
Guilford.

Waterman, J. M., & Lusk, R. (1986). Scope of
the problem. In K. McFarlane & J.
Waterman (Eds.), *Sexual abuse of young children* (pp. 3–12). New York: Guilford.

Waterman, J. M., & Lusk, R. (1993).
Psychological testing in evaluation of child
sexual abuse. *Child Abuse and Neglect, 17,*
145–159.

Waugh, B. (1984). *The children's guardian.* In B.
Waugh (Ed.), *The gaol cradle, who rocks it?*
New York: Garland. (Original work pub-
lished 1873, Crime and Punishment in
England Series. London: Strahan)
[According to Webster's dictionary, a gaol is
an English version of jail.]

Webb, N. (1991). *Play therapy with children in
crisis.* New York: Guilford.

Wechsler, D. (1967). *Wechsler Preschool and
Primary Scale of Intelligence.* New York:
Psychological Corporation.

Wechsler D. (1984). *Wechsler Intelligence Scale for
Children—Revised.* New York: Psychological
Corporation.

Wechsler, D. (1991). *Wechsler Intelligence Scale for
Children* (3rd ed.). San Antonio, TX:
Psychological Corporation.

Weinberg, S. K. (1976). *Incest behavior.* New
York: Citadel Press.

Weiner, N., & Kurpious, S. E. R. (1995).
*Shattered innocence: A practical guide for coun-
seling women survivors of childhood sexual
abuse.* Washington, DC: Taylor Francis.

Weithorn, L. A. (1987). *Psychology and child custody determinations: Knowledge, roles, and
expertise.* Lincoln, NE: University of
Nebraska Press.

Wenet, G. A., Clark, T. R., & Hunner, R. J.
(1981). Perspectives on the juvenile sex
offender. In R. J. Hunner & Y. E. Walker
(Eds.), *Exploring the relationship between child
abuse and delinquency.* Montclair, NJ:
Allanheld, Osmun.

Werner, M. J., Joffe, A., & Graham, A. V.
(1999). Screening, early identification, and
office-based intervention with children and
youth living in substance-abusing families.
Pediatrics, 103(5), 1099–1112.

Wexler, K. (2000, July 18). Father charged in
baby boy's death. *St. Petersburg Times,* P2.

Wexler, S. (1990). Ethical obligations and social
research. In K. L. Kempf (Ed.), *Measurement*

issues in criminology (pp. 78–107). New York: Springer-Verlag.

Whipple, E. E., & Wilson, S. R. (1996). Evaluation of a parent education and support program for families at risk of physical child abuse. *Families in Society, 77*(4), 227–239.

Williams, L. M. (1993). Adult memories of childhood abuse: Preliminary findings from a longitudinal study. *The Advisor, 5*(3), 19–21.

Williams, L. M., & Finkelhor, D. (1995). Paternal caregiving and incest: Test of a biosocial model. *American Journal of Orthopsychiatry, 65*(1), 101–113.

Williams, M. B., & Sommer, J. F., Jr. (Eds.). (1994). *Handbook of post-traumatic therapy.* Westport, CT: Greenwood Press.

Wilsnack, S. C., Vogeltanz, N. D., Klassen, A. D., & Harris, T. R. (1997). Childhood sexual abuse and women's substance abuse: National survey findings. *Journal of Studies of Alcohol, 20*(4), 29–45.

Wind-Weissman, T., & Silvern, L. (1994). Parenting and family stress as mediators of long-term effects of child abuse. *Child Abuse and Neglect, 18*(5), 439–453.

Winn, M. E. (1996). The strategic and systemic management of denial in the cognitive-behavioral treatment of sexual offenders. *Sexual Abuse: A Journal of Research and Treatment, 8*(1), 25–36.

Wolcott, H. F. (1990). *Writing up qualitative research.* Thousand Oaks, CA: Sage.

Wolfe, D. A. (1999). *Child abuse: Implications for child development and psychopathology. Developmental clinical psychology and psychiatry* (2nd ed., Vol. 10). Thousand Oaks, CA: Sage.

Wolfe, V. V. (1996). Measuring post-traumatic stress disorder: The Children's Impact of Traumatic Events Scale—Revised. *APSAC Advisor, 9*(2), 25–26.

Wolfe, V. V., Gentile, C., Michienzi, T., Sas, L., & Wolfe, D. L. (1991). The Children's Impact of Traumatic Events Scale: A measure of PTSD symptoms. *Behavioral Assessment, 13,* 359–383.

World Health Organization. (2001a). *Maternal and prenatal condition.* Switzerland: Author.

World Health Organization. (2001b). *Press releases 1999: United Nations foundation grant to fuel expansion of WHO's children and youth activities.* Switzerland: Author. [Available online: www.Who-int/inf-pr-1998/en/].

Wortman, M. S. (Ed.). (1985). *Women in American law: From colonial times to the new deal.* New York: Holmes & Meier.

Wright, R. C., & Schnieder, S. L. (1999). Motivated self-deception in child molesters. *Journal of Child Sexual Abuse, 8*(1), 89–111.

Wurtele, S. K., Kvaternick, M., & Franklin, C. F. (1992). Sexual abuse prevention for preschoolers: A survey of parents' behaviors, attitudes, and beliefs. *Journal of Child Sexual Abuse, 1*(1), 113–128.

Wyatt, G. E., & Mickey, M. R. (1987). Ameliorating the effects of child sexual abuse: An exploratory study of support by parents and others. *Journal of Interpersonal Violence, 2,* 403–414.

Wyatt, G. E., & Newcomb, M. (1990). Internal and external mediators of women's sexual abuse in childhood. *Journal of Consulting and Clinical Psychology, 58,* 758–767.

Wyatt, G. E., & Powell, G. J. (1988). *The lasting effects of child sexual abuse.* Newbury Park, CA: Sage.

Wyszynski, M. R. (1999). Shaken baby syndrome: Identification, intervention, and prevention. *Clinical Excellence Nurse Practitioners, 3*(5), 262–267.

Yates, A. (1982). Children eroticized by incest. *American Journal of Psychiatry, 139,* 482–485.

Yuille, J. C., Hunter, T., Joffe, R., & Zaparniuk, J. (1993). Interviewing children in sexual abuse cases. In G. S. Goodman & B. I. Bottoms (Eds.), *Child victims, child witnesses: Understanding and improving testimony* (pp. 95–115). New York: Guilford.

Zahn-Waxler, C., Radke-Yarrow, M., Wagner, E., & Chapman, M. (1992). Development of concern for others. *Developmental Psychology, 28*(1), 126–136.

Zaslow, M., & Hayes, C. (1986). Sex differences in children's responses to psychosexual stress: Toward a cross-cultural context analysis. In M. E. Lamb, A. L. Brown, & B. Rogoff (Eds.), *Advances in developmental psychology* (Vol. 4, pp. 285–338). Hillsdale, NJ: Erlbaum.

Zielbauer, P. (2000, October 3). Boy's death prompts inquiry by agency. *New York Times,* B5.

Zimbardo, P. (1973). On the ethics of intervention in human psychological research: With special reference to the Stanford prison study. *Cognition, 22,* 243–246.

Zivney, O. A., Nash, M. R., & Hulsey, T. (1988). Sexual abuse in early versus late childhood: Differing patterns of pathology as revealed on the Rorschach. *Psychotherapy, 25*(1), 99–106.

Zlotnick, C., Ryan, C. E., Miller, I. W., & Keitner, G. I. (1995). Childhood abuse and recovery from major depression. *Child Abuse and Neglect, 19*(12), 1513–1516.

Index

TO THE OWNER OF THIS BOOK:

We hope that you have found *Childhood Sexual Abuse: Developmental Effects Across the Lifespan* useful. So that this book can be improved in a future edition, would you take the time to complete this sheet and return it? Thank you.

School and address:_____

Department:_____

Instructor's name:_____

1. What I like most about this book is:_____

_____

_____

2. What I like least about this book is:_____

_____

_____

3. My general reaction to this book is:_____

_____

4. The name of the course in which I used this book is:_____

_____

5. Were all of the chapters of the book assigned for you to read?_____

   If not, which ones weren't?_____

6. In the space below, or on a separate sheet of paper, please write specific suggestions for improving this book and anything else you'd care to share about your experience in using the book.

_____

_____

_____

_____

_____

Optional:

Your name: _____ Date: _____

May Brooks/Cole quote you, either in promotion for *Childhood Sexual Abuse: Developmental Effects Across the Lifespan,* or in future publishing ventures?

Yes: _____ No: _____

Sincerely,

F. Felicia Ferrara

FOLD HERE

NO POSTAGE
NECESSARY
IF MAILED
IN THE
UNITED STATES

BUSINESS REPLY MAIL

FIRST CLASS   PERMIT NO. 358   PACIFIC GROVE, CA

POSTAGE WILL BE PAID BY ADDRESSEE

ATT: *F. Felicia Ferrara*

Brooks/Cole Publishing Company
511 Forest Lodge Road
Pacific Grove, California 93950-9968

FOLD HERE

Attention Professors:
Brooks/Cole is dedicated to publishing quality publications for education in the social work, counseling, and human services fields. If you are interested in learning more about our publications, please fill in your name and address and request our latest catalogue, using this prepaid mailer. Please choose one of the following:

☐ social work   ☐ counseling   ☐ human services

Name: _____

Street Address: _____

City, State, and Zip: _____

FOLD HERE

NO POSTAGE
NECESSARY
IF MAILED
IN THE
UNITED STATES

BUSINESS REPLY MAIL

FIRST CLASS   PERMIT NO. 358   PACIFIC GROVE, CA

POSTAGE WILL BE PAID BY ADDRESSEE

ATT: *Marketing* _____

The Wadsworth Group
10 Davis Drive
Belmont, CA 94002

FOLD HERE

FOLD HERE